Memoirs from Eldred, New York, 1800–1950

Book 1

The Mill on Halfway Brook

Stories of Families Who Settled Near
Halfway Brook in the Town of Highland, New York
1800–1880

Louise Elizabeth Smith

HALFWAY BROOK

Photo: Gary Smith.

Published by Halfway Brook
Cave Creek, Arizona

Family information online:
http://halfwaybrook.com: Halfway Brook community blog, on-going projects, resources
http://weezy.info: Stories and information about the Crabtree-Higginson, Austin-Leavenworth, Smith-Corbridge, and Fallin-Williams families

Photo and text contributions: Melva Austin Barney, Mary Briggs Austin, Cynthia Leavenworth Bellinger, Gary D. Smith, Daniel B. Smith, Joanna R. Smith
Civil War Letters: Linda Leavenworth Bohs
Cover, interior design, and maps: Gary D. Smith (www.PerformanceDesign.net)
Editing: Gary D. Smith, Cynthia Leavenworth Bellinger, Joanna R. Smith

Copyright © 2010 by Louise E. Smith
Printed in the United States of America
ISBN: 978-0-9826374-0-1

All rights Reserved. Please contact the author for permission to reproduce any part of this book.

Disclaimer: Information and sources were recorded as accurately as possible. Incorrect information is unintentional. Please notify the author regarding errors so they can be corrected in the next edition.

I would like to thank Richard O. Eldred for permission to quote from his book, *The Eldred Family: Elisha Eldred of Minisink, New York, and His Descendants,* Baltimore: Gateway Press, Inc., 1988.

Other books by Louise Elizabeth Smith:
Grandma and Me, and *Aida Austin's 1881 Diary*

Front and back cover photos are in the book with source credits.

Table of Contents

Acknowledgements iv

Dedication v

Map of Northeast United States vi

Map of the Town of Lumberland, 1798 viii

The Mill on Halfway Brook Introduction ix

Ecclesiastes 3 x

Chapter 1: The Town of Lumberland, 1798–1815 1

Chapter 2: The Mill on Halfway Brook, 1815–1825 13

Chapter 3: Life in Lumberland, 1825–1831 21

Chapter 4: Reverend Felix Kyte, 1832–1835 31

Chapter 5: The Mill on Blind Pond Brook, 1836–1849 39

Chapter 6: The Bubbling Spring, 1839–1850 49

Chapter 7: Near Hagan Pond Road, 1851–1860 67

Chapter 8: Letters from a Soldier, 1861–1865 87

Chapter 9: Your Loving Cousin, 1866–1871 133

Chapter 10: Emma Goes to College, 1872–1873 157

Chapter 11: Return to Eldred, 1874–1877 175

Chapter 12: "In Kansas Bright as Fair," 1878 195

Chapter 13: "The Journey's Length," 1879–1880 205

Bibliography 230

Appendix 231

Index 259

About the Author 272

Acknowledgments

I have always admired my grandparents, Mort and Jennie Leavenworth Austin, although I never knew them. Had I known that the few photos and the sparse information that I did have could explode into three books, I doubt I would have started the project.

While writing *Grandma and Me* (about my mother's mother, Amanda Myrtie Crabtree Briggs, who we will meet at some point in this series), I became reacquainted through email with my second cousin (on the Austin side), Cynthia Leavenworth Bellinger.

Cynthia's grandfather, Garfield Leavenworth, was a brother of my grandmother Jennie Austin, and I discovered later he was also a good friend of my grandpa Briggs.

I mentioned to Cynthia that I would like to do a book on my Austin grandparents and asked her if she would write what she remembered of her grandfather Garfield. Cynthia agreed. Neither of us dreamed we could gather enough information to fill even a 50-page booklet about our grandparents.

Then I began to do what I do best—ask questions.

The answers came by phone, in emails, and instant messages. Boxes were sent to me by mail—many boxes, with treasures of letters, diaries, photos, documents, and scrapbooks for me to read, scan, and return.

This book is possible only because relatives have so willingly shared the wealth of family information they have preserved for many years.

Much of the 'treasure' was furnished by my cousin Melva Austin Barney, and my mother, Mary Briggs Austin. The letters and photos they shared, combined with the diaries of Great Aunt Aida and Ella Sergeant Leavenworth (wife of Garfield) reveal the daily lives of family and friends who lived in Eldred.

Linda Leavenworth Bohs contributed her collection of our great-grandfather, Sherman Stiles Leavenworth's Civil War letters, which became a very valuable part of this book.

Another significant addition to the book were the Sherman B. Leavenworth Bible pages shared by Ric Schroedel.

The book would not have happened without the immense help of Cynthia Leavenworth Bellinger. Cynthia enthusiastically helped by researching censuses, driving to Eldred to take photos, reading rough drafts, giving helpful comments and encouragement, sharing photos, transcribing her family diaries, and even indexing—a tedious job. Thank you so much Cynthia.

The following people also contributed in numerous ways, and their help was very much appreciated.

Remains of waterwheel with gear. Photo: Library of Congress, Prints & Photographs Division, HABS, Reproduction number HABS PA,15-CHESP.V,4. See page 48.

Austin Relatives
Carol Austin
Charles Arthur Austin
Mary Briggs Austin
Mary Marie Austin
Melva Austin Barney
Joan Austin Geier
Liz Geier
Margie Austin Maglione
Dawn Lee Austin Segarra
Daniel Smith
Joanna Smith

Leavenworth Relatives
Cynthia Leavenworth Bellinger
Linda Leavenworth Bohs
Madelyn Meyers Busse
Marialyce Kornkven
Gisele Rouillon Leavenworth
Nancy Leavenworth Leo
David Leavenworth
Kelly Leavenworth
Charlee Hirsch Schroedel
Ric Schroedel
Matt Schroedel

Myers Relatives
Christena Stevens Myers
Helen Myers Hulse
Eleanor Myers Rizzuto

Others from the Eldred Area
Howard Barnes
Vernon & Carolyn Hallock Clark
Emily Knecht Hallock
Kevin Marrinan
Eddie Mellan
Chuck Myers
Stuart & Geraldine Mills Russell
Frank V Schwarz
Alice Willis Wojtaszek

Family and Friends
Thank you, too, to my friends and other family members (not mentioned above), who have helped in other ways and been so encouraging about this book project.

Gary Smith
This book would not have been possible without my husband Gary's technical help, design expertise, and editing. He kept the computers working, designed the cover, interior layout, created maps, and retouched photos—all this while doing major, complete renovation of our house and coping with a wife who is always working on this book. Thank you, Gary.

Dedicated To:

My mother, Mary Briggs Austin, and my Austin and Leavenworth relatives
who preserved their Family Histories,
and to the people of Eldred
who have graciously shared their information and photos of the area,
thereby making it possible for this book to be written
to honor the memory of my Austin grandparents,
Charles Mortimer Austin and Jennie Louisa Leavenworth.

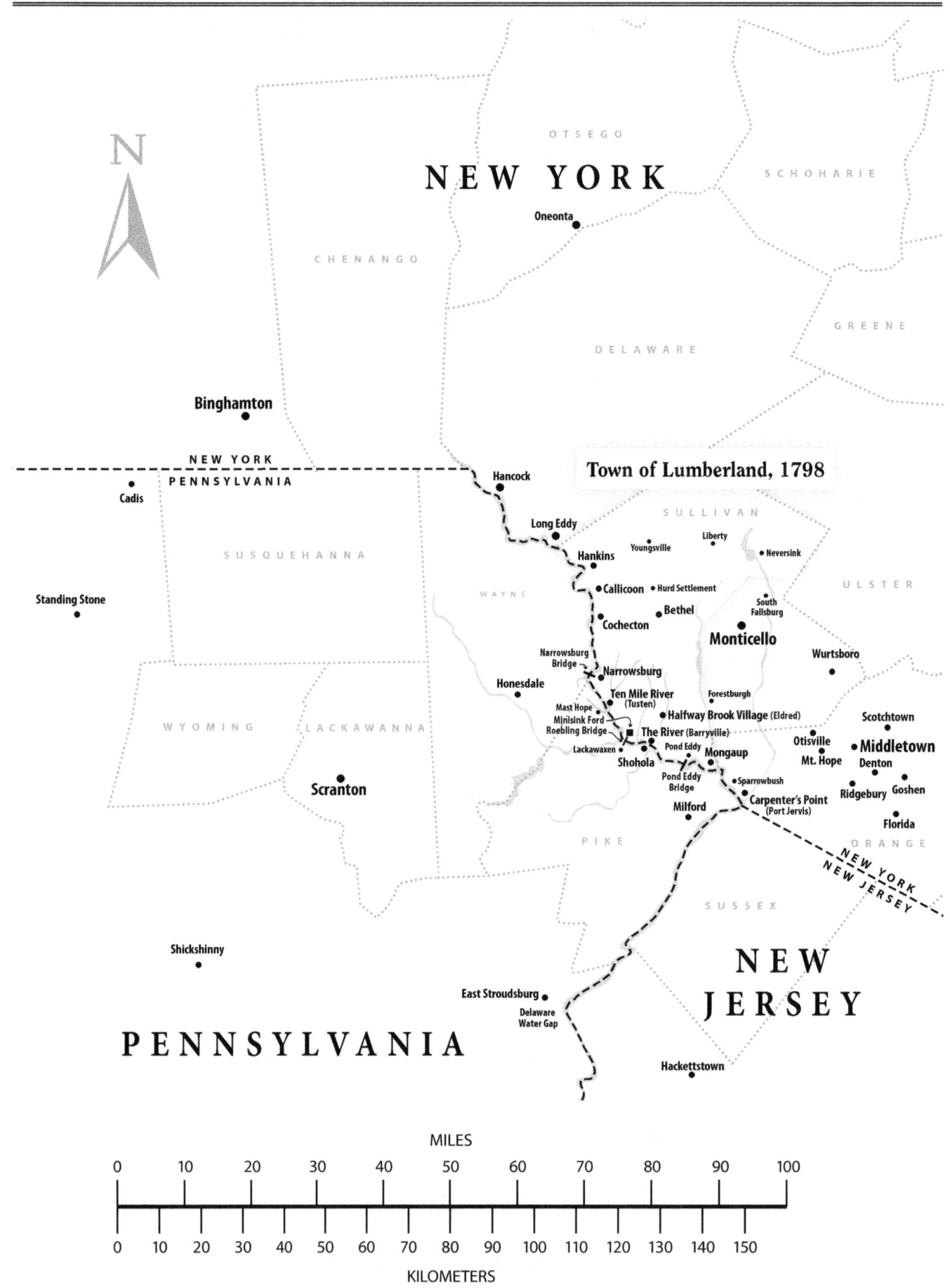

MAP OF NORTHEAST UNITED STATES • VII

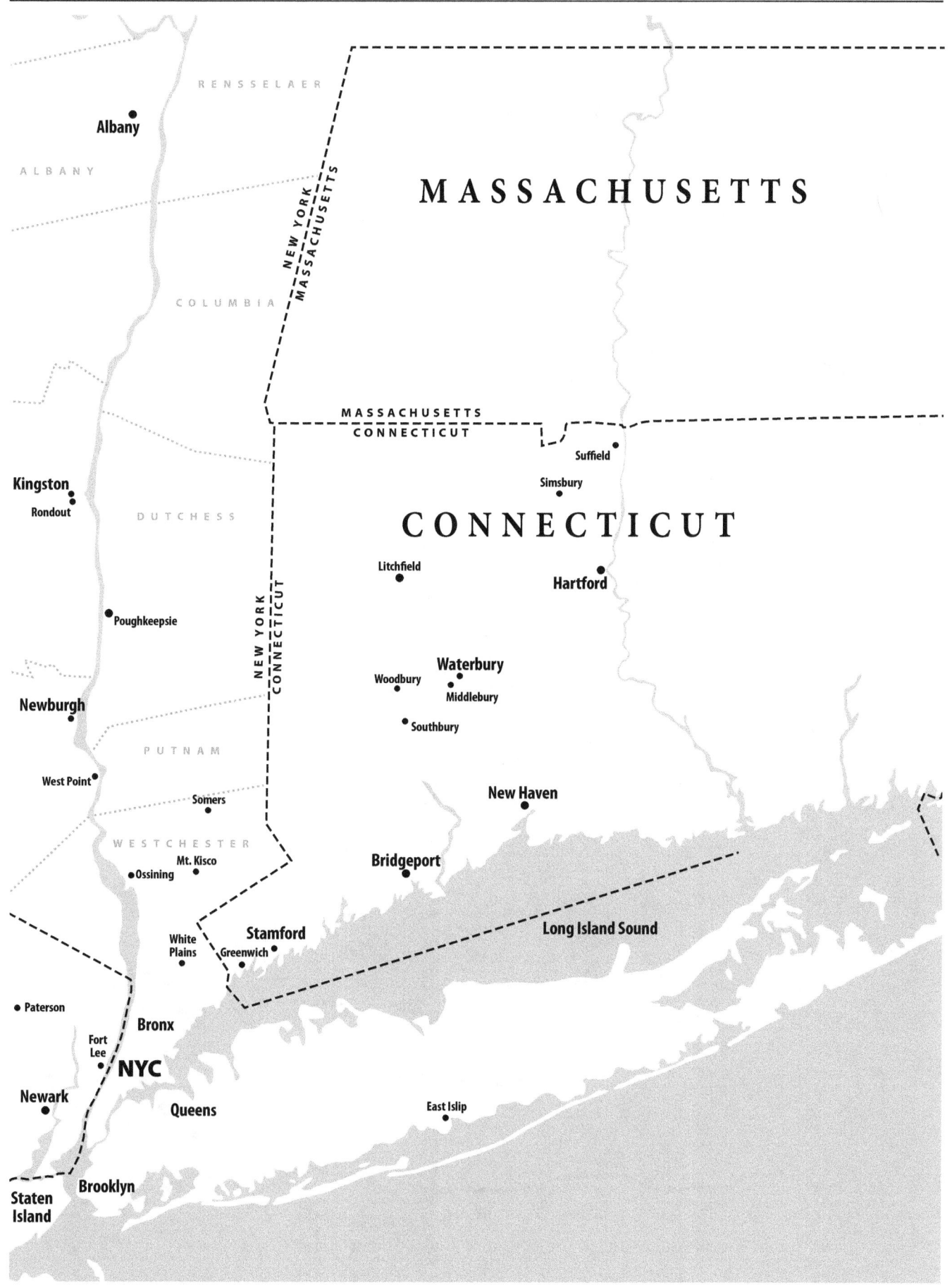

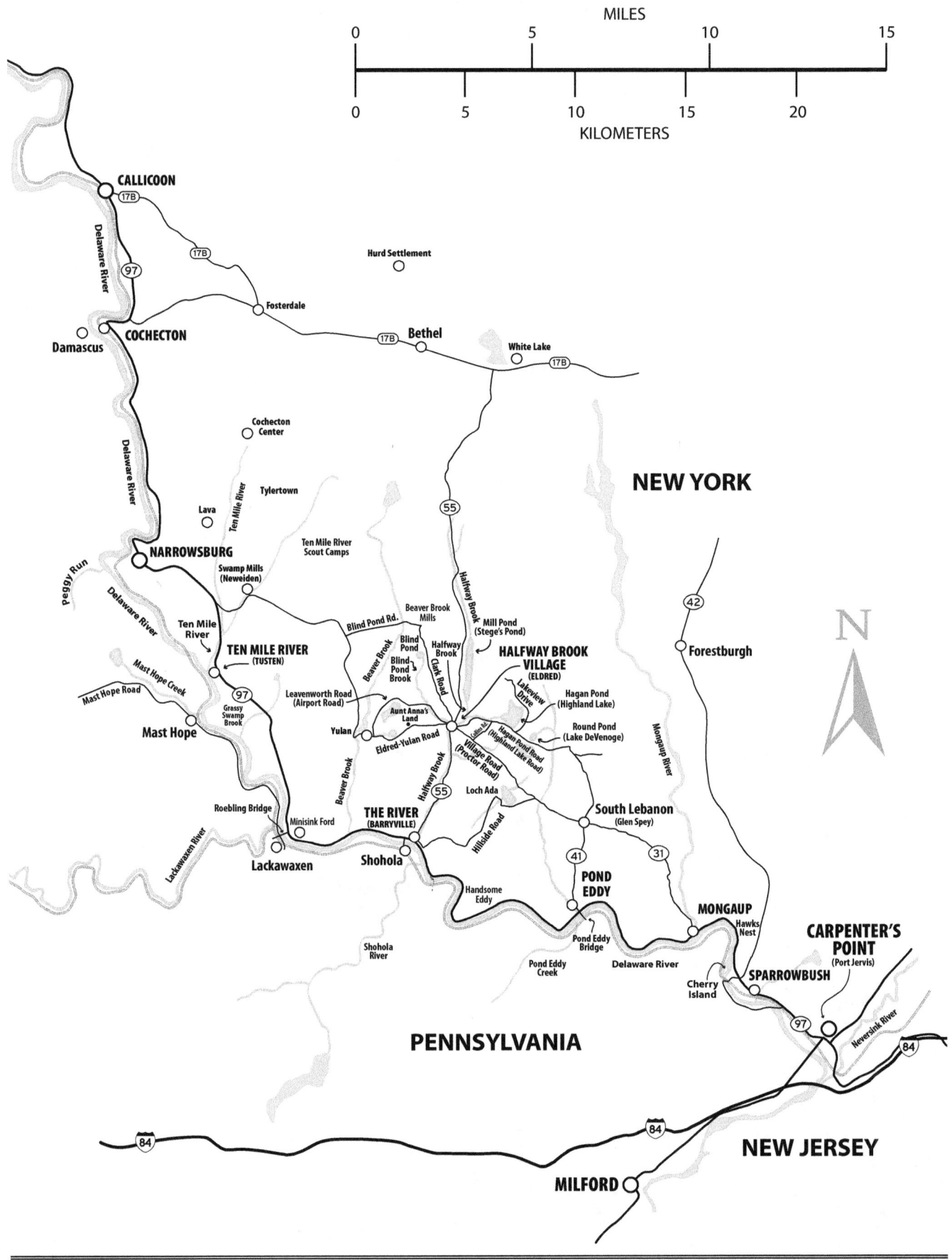

The Mill on Halfway Brook
Introduction for Book 1

The beautiful little hamlet of Eldred is situated in the valley and on the hilltops of the most healthful and charming locality of rugged Sullivan County.

Made beautiful by its magnificent scenery of valleys, hills, mountains, streams, forests and lakes; historic from its location in the Town of Highland, in which the famous battle of Minisink was fought many years ago.

It has pure spring water bubbling merrily out of the hills, and its cool, clear nights make sleeping comfortable and refreshing.
—A Century of Church Life, The Tri-States Union, *August 17, 1899.*

One of the many streams near Eldred, New York. Photo: Mary Briggs Austin.

The lovely and charming town of Eldred, New York, rich in the natural beauty of forests, hills, streams, ponds, and wildlife, was the home of my grandparents, Charles Mortimer Austin and his wife, Jennie Louisa Leavenworth.

First called Halfway Brook Village, Eldred was also the home of Mort and Jennie's parents, grandparents, siblings, aunts, uncles, and cousins, as well as their children, which included my father, Art Austin, their fifth child.

Though I never met them, the few stories I heard pictured my Austin grandparents as loving, caring, gentle people with a unique sense of humor.

Because of my admiration for my father and therefore his parents, I decided to write a book about Mort and Jennie Austin and their ancestors.

The Mill on Halfway Brook tells the story of my relatives as they arrive and settle on land not far from Halfway Brook which would later become Eldred.

Neighbors, friends, and Austin and Leavenworth kinsfolk, as well as three preachers, two churches, local events, and a national war, all play an integral part in my narrative.

I have cousins, siblings, and children that wield a mightier pen than myself, but the honor has fallen to me to compile this history of my family and the village in which they grew up.

Family letters, documents, photos, postcards, and scrapbooks shared with me by Austin and Leavenworth relatives help tell the story of the people who lived in Halfway Brook Village, renamed Eldred in 1873, after my great-great-grandfather, James Eldred.

This story starts in late 1815 with a log house and a sawmill on two acres of land near Halfway Brook, in the Town of Lumberland.

Please join me as my relatives arrive and settle in "the beautiful little hamlet of Eldred."

To Everything There is a Season

To every thing there is a season, and a time to every purpose under the heaven:

A time to be born, and a time to die; a time to plant, and a time to pluck up that which is planted;

A time to kill, and a time to heal; a time to break down, and a time to build up;

A time to weep, and a time to laugh; a time to mourn, and a time to dance;

A time to cast away stones, and a time to gather stones together; a time to embrace, and a time to refrain from embracing;

A time to get, and a time to lose; a time to keep, and a time to cast away;

A time to rend, and a time to sew; a time to keep silence, and a time to speak;

A time to love, and a time to hate; a time of war, and a time of peace.

What profit hath he that worketh in that wherein he laboureth?

I have seen the travail, which God hath given to the sons of men to be exercised in it.

He hath made every thing beautiful in his time: also he hath set the world in their heart, so that no man can find out the work that God maketh from the beginning to the end.

I know that there is no good in them, but for a man to rejoice, and to do good in his life.

And also that every man should eat and drink, and enjoy the good of all his labour, it is the gift of God.

I know that, whatsoever God doeth, it shall be for ever: nothing can be put to it, nor any thing taken from it: and God doeth it, that men should fear before him.—*Ecclesiastes 3:1–14*

Chapter 1
The Town of Lumberland
1798 to 1815

It was the beginning of December 1815. A lone log house and sawmill stood silently on almost two acres of cleared land near the middle of Halfway Brook in the Town of Lumberland, New York. There were no other buildings around for a mile in any direction.

Halfway Brook on its way to the Delaware River. Photo: Cynthia Leavenworth Bellinger.

The lonely house and deserted sawmill were surrounded by thousands of acres of remote, rugged wilderness, rich in natural resources, beauty, and history.

Continuous forests of huge, centuries' old trees—white and yellow pine, oak, chestnut, hemlock, and hickory—carpeted the rolling hills for miles around.

Numerous ponds and lakes of various sizes and lengths dotted the landscape. Nearby Halfway Brook was just one of many streams which flowed into the Delaware River, the southwest boundary of the Town of Lumberland, and the New York/Pennsylvania border.

The waters of the area teemed with eel, shad, trout, bass, pike, pickerel, and sunfish. Countless birds flew overhead, filling the skies and forest with screeching or melodious songs.

Ospreys, bald eagles, bluebirds, cardinals, pileated woodpeckers, wild turkeys, and pheasants flew from tree to tree, swooped down from vast heights or walked on the grounds of their forest home.

In the summer and fall months, bushy-tailed squirrels gathered nuts, as chipmunks scampered about. Rabbits nibbled on the grass and low tree leaves, while raccoons fished in the stream. Beavers built dams on the many streams, and were so plentiful that a brook and town were named after them.

Badgers, opossums, muskrats, woodchucks, porcupines, and skunks lived in the woodlands. Deer were everywhere.

Bears, wolves, foxes, coyotes, panthers, and wild cats hunted in the thickly forested area, and occasionally helped themselves to the settlers' chickens and sheep.

Hunters, trappers, fishermen, and lumbermen were drawn to the area. A number of settlements—Mongaup, Pond Eddy, Shohola (in Pennsylvania), The River, Ten Mile River, Narrowsburgh, Cochecton, and later Callicoon—grew up along the nearby Delaware River.

Mongaup River, the eastern border of the Town of Lumberland, flowed into the Delaware River. At its mouth was the Mongaup settlement. Northwest twenty miles, near the mouth of Ten Mile River also on the Delaware, was the Ten Mile River settlement.

An ancient trail connected the two settlements, and in the middle of the old path, close to

Halfway Brook near where the old log house and sawmill probably stood. Photo: Cynthia Leavenworth Bellinger.

Halfway Brook, sat the log house and sawmill.

From the house and sawmill, Halfway Brook wound a bit southwest for four miles, where it emptied into the meandering Delaware River.

There at the mouth of Halfway Brook was The River settlement, which would later be called Barryville. Opposite The River settlement, and across the Delaware River in Pennsylvania, was Shohola.

The two acres of land by Halfway Brook with the cabin and sawmill, would be settled by James and Polly Eldred at the end of December, 1815. That acreage would eventually be the southeast corner of Halfway Brook Village, often called *the Village*. Much later the Village would be called Eldred.

My Austin and Leavenworth ancestors would settle within two miles to the east and two miles to the northwest of the Eldred cabin near Halfway Brook, in the Town of Lumberland.

The Town of Lumberland, 300,000 acres of heavily wooded rolling hills, was created in 1798, and became a part of Sullivan County in 1809.

Sullivan County abounds in history and stories which can be read in James E. Quinlan's, *History of Sullivan County*. What follows is a brief background history.

The Lenape or Delaware tribe as the Europeans called them, were the original or first inhabitants of what would be the Town of Lumberland. The Lenape fished for shad and trout in the Lenapewihittuk (the Delaware River), and hunted in the surrounding area. Around 1630, Dutch and Swedish trappers and traders arrived in the area. By 1766, most of the Lenape had moved into Pennsylvania.

There was a sawmill at the mouth of the Ten Mile River at least by 1762, when Charles Webb surveyed some 200,000 acres of the 1704 Minisink Patent.

When Mr. Webb surveyed New York's eastern shore of the Delaware River two years later, he found an eddy, which he called, *Big Pond*. Big Pond was later called Pond Eddy.

The only major Revolutionary War battle in the northern Delaware Valley was fought on July 22, 1779. The fighting took place on the plateau above Minisink Ford, six miles south of the mouth of the Ten Mile River.

Joseph Brant, a Mohawk Chieftain and a captain in the British army, led a force of Iroquois and Tories against a colonial militia from the village of Goshen, Orange County, New York. The militia had been hastily put together and was reluctantly led by Lieutenant Colonel Benjamin Tusten, a Goshen physician.

Though help came from the Fourth Orange County Regiment, the colonial militia suffered a devastating defeat. At least 45 militiamen were killed, including Dr. Tusten, for whom the Ten Mile River settlement was renamed.

Around 1790, John Showers ran a tavern near the mouth of the Mongaup River. Native and white hunters traded the furs of animals they had trapped for food, black powder, cloth, or whiskey at John's tavern.

Turkey in Eldred. Photo: Cynthia Leavenworth Bellinger.

Towns on the Upper Delaware River

Cushetunk/Cochecton
In 1754, Connecticut Yankees established Cushetunk and claimed the Delaware River's west bank for the Colony of Connecticut.

Cochecton (*cuh-SHEK-ton*), meaning *low land,* is also called *the flats*. It is rich and fertile, full of fish and game.

Narrowsburg(h)
Narrowsburg (Homan's Eddy), has the narrowest and deepest points on the Upper Delaware River.

Tusten (Ten Mile River)
Tusten at the mouth of the Ten Mile River was first called the Ten Mile River settlement, and grew up around 1751. It was later named for the Revolutionary hero, Dr. Tusten.

Ten Mile River is the site of a large summer camp maintained by the Boy Scouts of America.

Shehola, Shohola
Shehola is Lenape for *slow waters where the geese rest*. The Pennsylvania town Shohola is on the Shohola River directly across from The River or Barryville, New York.

Mongaup
Mongaup is a small, quiet hamlet at the mouth of the Mongaup River, which is still the eastern border of the town of Lumberland.

Sparrowbush
Sparrowbush was named for H.L. Sparrow, a dealer in ship-knee timber. Mr. Sparrow rafted down the Delaware River in the early 1800s.

The land was originally named Sparrow's Bosh. Bosh was a sloping thicket or woods.

Delaware River near Barryville. Photo: Gary Smith.

The Delaware River heads (to the left) towards Carpenter's Point, now called Port Jervis, New York. Photo: Cynthia Leavenworth Bellinger.

In the early 1800s, land cost two dollars an acre; sometimes less. Water power was free and sawmills were cheap to build. Credit was available and creditors would wait to be paid until the timber had been rafted to market and sold.

Men from the nearby states of New Jersey, Pennsylvania, Connecticut, as well as other New York counties, purchased large parcels at the low prices, and built sawmills on various streams, including Halfway Brook.

The property owners did not usually live on the land, but hired the agents who did work locally, and paid them very little money. The lumbermen—choppers, teamsters, and sawyers—who reported to the agents, were poorly paid as well.

The land owners stripped the Town of Lumberland of its valuable timber, turned it into cash for themselves, and gave no thought to the consequences of their short term thinking and careless cutting down of the heavily forested lands.

The Wickham family owned three-fourths of the area around Ten Mile River, where they ran a large lumbering operation in the early 1800s. John Duer had a

Lumber in the Narrowsburg Lumberyard in Eldred. Photo courtesy of Howard Barnes.

Joshua and Mary Austin

Joshua and Mary Austin, were parents of my great-great-grandfather, Ralph Austin.

Joshua's father, Joshua Sr., had a twin named Caleb. It is interesting that Ralph's grandson (my grandfather), Charles Mortimer Austin, was also a twin.

Joshua and Mary Austin had Ralph and Almira, and probably several other children. Joshua Austin lived along the Hudson River at one time.

Perhaps New York was where the family moved to when they lost their lands because they were Loyalists in the Revolutionary War.

There were evidently two Joshuas, father and son. I've gotten the impression that we come from a real nest of Loyalist Austins. Not sure whether this loyalism was not more "philosophic" than active.
—Melva Austin Barney, great-great-granddaughter of Ralph Austin and Fanny Knapp Austin.

The Austins were Torries and had land taken from them by the Rebels.
—Robert Austin, great-grandson of Ralph and Fanny Knapp Austin.

Our family was poor because they took away our lands.—Ralph Austin, son of Joshua and Mary Austin.

Many Loyalists lived in the area of Westchester County, New York. Westchester was where Ralph and Fanny Knapp Austin's nine children were born, though both Ralph Austin and Fanny Knapp were born and married in Connecticut.

Mary Austin died in 1809 and Joshua Austin died in 1828.

Some Relatives in 1798

The following is where relatives in this story were living in 1798—the year the Town of Lumberland was created.

Austin Family
In 1798, Joshua Austin was 50, his wife Mary, 40, son Ralph, 14, and daughter Almira (Elmyra) was 11.

Ralph Austin's future wife, Fanny Knapp was 10. Fanny lived with her parents, Samuel Knapp Jr. and Naomi Palmer, and her 5-year-old sister Clara, in Connecticut.

Eldred Family
James Eldred's parents, Elisha and Mary Hulse Eldred, lived on Elisha's 100-acre farm known as *the Outlet*, (later Minisink, then Wallkill, and now Denton), in Orange County, where Elisha operated a store and inn/tavern. Elisha also had a couple jobs in the local government.

Seven children (ages 1 to 22), lived with Elisha and Mary Eldred. Daughters Amelia, 1 (in Minisink, New York), and Sarah Bowhanan, 19, (in Milford, Pennsylvania), both died in September.

James Eldred, 21, lived in Milford, Pennsylvania, with his brother-in-law. In 1800, James was an auditor of the records of Wayne Co., Pennsylvania.

In 1802, James married Mary (Polly) Mulford, daughter of Abraham Mulford, who had an inn in Milford. The newlyweds moved back to Minisink where their first six children were born (one died). Elisha Eldred died, October 1804.

Leavenworth Family
My Leavenworth ancestors arrived from England by 1680, and settled in Connecticut, where Sherman B. Leavenworth was born August 1, 1808. I have no certain record as to who his parents were.

A Sherman Leavenworth family lived in Waterbury, Connecticut, in 1800, with one son under 10, a father 26 to 44, and a mother 16 to 25.

Ten years later a Sherman B. Leavenworth family lived in Middlebury, Connecticut. There were two sons under 10, a father 26 to 44, and a mother 26 to 44. Could this be Sherman Buckley's family?

Lazerlier Family
Elizabeth Lazerlier, John Van Pelt's future wife, was 9, and lived with her parents, Abraham Lazerlier, a blacksmith, and Mary Webber, in New York City. The Lazerlier family were Huguenot descendants.

Abraham and Mary Webber Lazerlier had five children: Jane Ann, Abraham, Magdalin, Elizabeth, and Mary. Mary Webber's father John Webber, was from Holland.

Van Pelt Family
The Van Pelt family was Dutch. John Van Pelt, 12, would marry Elizabeth Lazerlier. John's parents, Henry Van Pelt and Ann Johnson, probably lived in New York City, as that was where John was born. John had five siblings, the youngest was 1, in 1798.

Myer Family
Martin David Myers, who would marry Jane Ann Van Pelt (the daughter of John and Elizabeth Lazerlier Van Pelt), was not born yet.

Martin's father David Myer was 12, and had 10 siblings. David Myer's parents were Martin Mier and Gerreberg Johannise Ackerman. David's future wife (and Martin's mother), Elizabeth, was 6. If the family was not living in New Jersey, they would be soon.

Briggs Family
The ancestors of Irwin Briggs lived about 250 miles from Lumberland, in Tell, Pennsylvania.

Crabb/Crabtree Family
The ancestors of Myrtie Crabtree Briggs, were Loyalists, and had lived in New Brunswick, Canada, since 1783, when they had abandoned their home in Dutchess County, New York, for their own protection.

---

sizeable lumbering business on Halfway Brook.

There was a small sawmill in Shohola, Pennsylvania, opposite The River settlement.

In 1800, the Town of Lumberland, had a population of 733, most of whom had lumber-related jobs. Sawmills operated on various streams. Halfway Brook was said to have had ten sawmills on its nine miles.

Enormous amounts of lumber were made into rafts and floated down one of the many rivers or brooks in the area that fed into the Delaware River. The Delaware River flowed to Carpenter's Point (Port Jervis) and on south to Philadelphia, Pennsylvania, where the lumber could be sold.

It was around 1764, the year after the French and Indian War ended, when Daniel Skinner made a 15-foot by 80-foot raft from six felled pine trees. Daniel ingeniously lashed these logs together, added a rudder, and floated the raft down the river. The technique was called Timber Rafting.

Leaving Cushetunk/Cochecton where he lived, Daniel, with the help of Josiah Parks, rafted about 200 miles down the Delaware River. They passed the settlements at Narrowsburgh, Ten Mile River, Shohola and The River, Pond Eddy, Mongaup, and Carpenter's Point, and headed southeast to Philadelphia, Pennsylvania, where Mr. Skinner was paid 24 pounds—4 pounds per mast.

The first timber rafts, made of straight pine trees found next to the river bank, were used in the ship building industry. Hemlock trees were also in demand. Their bark was used in the many tanneries in the area.

In his book, *Reminiscences,* John W. Johnston tells about the pine trees in Lumberland in the early years.

The slow growing white pine trees were the most valuable and the main trees lumbered at the beginning. Before 1800, very old, large white pine trees were found in the area. White pine trees, often produced planks 1-1/4 to 2-inches thick, 16-feet long, and 20- to 30-inches wide, with no knots or defects.

Even larger pine trees grew at higher elevations where it was less crowded with more room to grow. A 40-foot canoe with no imperfections was made from one white pine tree. Another pine measured almost five feet in diameter, with a circumference of 15 feet, and had 204 rings. The first limb started almost 70 feet from the ground and had a 32-inch diameter.

The logs that did not go to nearby sawmills were floated individually or on small rafts, known as colts, down the smaller streams to the mouth of the river. There the trees were made into larger rafts and floated to market on the Delaware River.

Winter, when the snow fell, was the best time to draw the logs over the rough log way to the mill or to one of two landings which were about a half-mile apart.

The upper landing cost 12-1/2 cents per thousand boards. The lower landing preferred by the lumbermen cost more—18-3/4 cents—as it was a shorter distance away, and was less work to get to.

Both landings were often so full in the spring, that there was nowhere to put another wagon load of boards.

The lumber community (and hence the whole area) of the Town of Lumberland depended on the spring freshets to get the lumber to market. When the snow and ice melted, and heavy rains came, the water level would raise to the height needed to float the lumber to market.

A spring freshet could last several weeks on large river systems. Sometimes they were accompanied by ice jams and caused flash floods. Too much, too little, too soon, or too late could wreak devastation on the whole lumbering community.

Halfway Brook heads towards the Delaware River. Photo: Cynthia Leavenworth Bellinger.

In the days of plentiful lumber, the surface of the Delaware was literally covered at the time of raging freshets and the consequent catastrophes to the rafts and lumber piles.
—Johnston, p. 253.

Spring was the best time of year for rafting. With the ice gone and the river flowing from a heavy rain or melted snow, the timber rafters could make the trip in three days.

The raftsmen began placing timber into their rafts, and the women folks started preparations for sending their men on their way. The women (baked) a large multitude of bread, pies, cakes, apple turnovers, and other delicacies for the huge dinner-bucket from which the rafting crew would eat its noontime meal while floating down the river.
—Wood, Leslie, Holt! T'Other Way!

From Cochecton, where Daniel Skinner first started timber rafting, it was about 8-1/2 miles to Homan's Eddy, named after Benjamin Homan, a settler in the early 1770s.

Homan's Eddy, later called Narrowsburgh, was the narrowest point of the Delaware River, and overlooked Big Eddy, which was 113-feet-deep—the Delaware's deepest point.

Raftsmen would dock their rafts of logs at Big Eddy, and stay in town overnight, before heading on to the next town on the Delaware River.

For a period of 60 years, millions of feet of the best pine lumber manufactured in any part of the U.S., were piled, rafted and run down the Delaware to the

Did You Know?

Turkeys in Eldred. Photo: Cynthia Leavenworth Bellinger.

Kill/Kille
Kille, meaning *river bed*, is Dutch for creek, as in Wallkill or Beaver Kill.

Callicoon Creek
Dutch hunters named the area *Kalkoenkill* because there were so many *Kalkoen* or wild turkeys.

Delaware
In 1610, Captain Samuel Argall named the Lenape River, and the people living near it, the *Delaware*, in honor of Thomas West, 3rd Baron De La Warr, British nobleman and Virginia's first colonial governor.
—www.lenapedelawarehistory.net

The Largest Raft
A Mr. Barnes took an 85-foot-wide, 215-foot-long raft, loaded with 120,000 feet of lumber down the Delaware River.—www.minisink.org

Town of Lumberland
The Town of Lumberland, created in 1798, was part of both the Hardenburgh and Minisink Patent. It took in what are now the townships (called towns) of Bethel, Callicoon, Cochecton, Delaware, Fremont, Highland, Liberty, and Tusten.

Daniel Bush was nominated and appointed the first Supervisor and Town Clerk of the Town of Lumberland on June 4, 1798. For many years Ten Mile River was considered the central part of Lumberland. Town business and town meetings were transacted there.

The Town (township) of Lumberland today contains the hamlets of Glen Spey, Handsome Eddy, Lebanon Lake, Mongaup, Pond Eddy, Upper Mongaup.

Eldred and Barryville are in the Town (township) of Highland.

Shadow Lake, Liberty, New York. Liberty was at one time part of the Town of Lumberland. Postcard in collection of Mary Briggs Austin.

Looking upriver towards the Pond Eddy bridge. Imagine this as one mass of log rafts. Photo: Cynthia Leavenworth Bellinger.

markets of Trenton, Philadelphia and elsewhere.—Johnston, p. 334.

Travel was very challenging due to the lack of roads in the wild and unsettled land. Transportation between New York and Pennsylvania was also difficult because of the Delaware River, the water boundary between the two states.

In the early 1800s, there were only two roads to the Town of Lumberland—the Sackett Road and the Newburgh-Cochecton Turnpike. Neither of them, perhaps, deserved to be identified as roads.

The Newburgh and Cochecton Turnpike was a 70-mile plank road. It started at Newburgh on the Hudson River, and went west to Cochecton, on the Delaware River. Newburgh became a trade center to get supplies to and from New York City.

So many settlers traveled to the new area that in 1809, Sullivan County was split out of Ulster County (one of the original twelve New York Counties). At the same time, Bethel, which had been part of the Town of Lumberland, became its own Town (township), and included the villages of Cochecton and Delaware.

Later, there were other roads to or through the Town of Lumberland. James Eldred worked on the Mast Hope Turnpike, which started near Middletown, went through Forestburg, and crossed through the Town of Lumberland on its way to Mast Hope, Pennsylvania.

In 1815, work was started on the Mount Hope-Lumberland Turnpike, which went from Orange County to Narrowsburgh, New York, and later to Honesdale, Pennsylvania. George D. Wickham, Benjamin Dodge, John Duer, Benjamin Woodward, Benjamin B. Newkirk, William A. and Abraham Cuddeback were the directors of the Mount Hope-Lumberland Turnpike, segments of which are still in use today.

Wickham, Duer, and Dodge were associated with lumber companies and large amounts of land. Perhaps their interest in the turnpike was related to the lumber industry.

Rope ferries and later cable ferries made it possible to travel across the Delaware River at three places along the New York and Pennsylvania border—Narrowsburgh, Ten Mile River, and Shohola.

Shohola, a small Pennsylvania hamlet located on a twelve to fifteen-mile brook of the same name, had been a major crossing point on the Delaware River for hundreds of years. In 1800, a crude, rope-guided ferry was in operation and was the only way to reach Shohola, directly opposite The River settlement.

Narrowsburgh was about sixteen miles northwest of Shohola. The Narrowsburgh Bridge Company, according to one report, built a 25-foot-wide toll bridge that spanned the narrowest part of the Delaware in 1810. The toll for a one-horse wagon was 37-1/2 cents, 1 dollar for four horses, and 6 cents to walk.

Since a dollar was the going rate for a full day's work, people found other ways to get to the other side of the Delaware River.

The Narrowsburgh bridge became part of a road system which included the Mount Hope-Lumberland Turnpike mentioned earlier. The turnpike consisted of a plank road in many places.

There were some settlers in the Town of Lumberland area before the end of the year in 1815, when James Eldred and his family settled near Halfway Brook.

Narrow Falls, New York, where

Minisink

The name *Minisink* is from the Lenapes of the Minis tribe that lived in the area, and refers to several locations in New York.

Minisink Valley (1650–1783)
The Minisink Valley was a large area which included:
1. On the west: Minisink Ford where the Battle of Minisink took place in the Revolutionary War.
2. On the north: Town of Deerpark, New York.
3. On the east: Port Jervis, New York.
4. On the south: along the Delaware River, past Minisink Island in New Jersey, and down to the Delaware Water Gap in Pennsylvania.

Minisink Patent
In 1704, a land grant of 200,000 acres, known as the Minisink Patent, was granted to 23 people.

The patent included Monticello, Middletown, and Carpenter's Point (Port Jervis). It extended "to the south end of Minisink Island," in New Jersey, and went northwest to Cushetunk/Cochecton. It included much of what would become the Town of Lumberland. Charles Webb surveyed the area from 1762 to 1764.

Minisink Today
The Town of Minisink, settled around 1725 and organized in 1788, was originally much larger than it is today, and shared its northern border with Wallkill Township. Elisha Eldred's family lived in Minisink, and Elisha held a couple positions in the local government.

The old Eldred homestead, located close to or in Wallkill Township, came to be called Denton. Denton is now located in Wawayanda Township, and shares a border with Wallkill Township.

Scotchtown, in Wallkill Township was where Charlotte Ingram, future wife of Sherman Buckley Leavenworth was born.

Postcard entitled "The Highway Mast Hope, PA." Mary Briggs Austin Collection.

the Barnes family settled quite early, was seven miles northwest of The River, and about a mile above Lackawaxen, Pennsylvania. We will meet the Barnes family again when we talk about the Narrows Falls Congregational Church.

In the early 1800s, the Hankins family had a General Store in the Ten Mile River (Tusten) area. Thomas Dunn and his seven sons from New Jersey also lived in the area. The Dunn family settled on land they had bought from the Wickham family, who owned vast acreage on the Ten Mile River.

Sears and Mary Keen Gardner (who we will meet in Chapter Three) were in Pond Eddy on the Delaware River by 1800. The Middaughs also lived there. Levi Middaugh and Solon Cooper were owners of Pond Eddy's first store.

Peter and Hannah Van Auken were in town by the time their daughter Mary Van Auken was born in 1803. Mary would marry Wilmot Clark (who arrived

Halfway Brook by Old Brook Road, after passing under one of the bridges on its way to the Delaware River. Photo: Cynthia Leavenworth Bellinger.

View of Delaware River from Barryville. Photo: Mary Briggs Austin.

Eagle intent on his prey. Photo: Cynthia Leavenworth Bellinger.

in town in 1805). Their son Mahlon Irvin Clark would marry an Austin relative; and their son, George Clark, would have a granddaughter, Ella Phoebe Sergeant, who would marry a Leavenworth relative at the turn of the twentieth century.

North of The River settlement, some 16 miles, was Bethel, where some of its first settlers set up homesteads in 1798. In 1807, around 30 to 40 families, many from Orange County, New York, or Connecticut, arrived in Bethel by way of the Sackett Road or the Newburgh and Cochecton Turnpike.

The Graham and Chauncey Hurd families from Connecticut lived in the nearby Hurd Settlement. These families are of interest because of the Leavenworth story about Sherman Buckley Leavenworth moving from Connecticut with a Hurd family.

The 1810 Census of the Town of Lumberland listed 525 people: 259 were children under 16, and 44 people were 45 or older.

There were fewer people in 1810 than in 1800 because the Town of Bethel had been taken out of the Town of Lumberland in 1809.

Calkins is an old family name in the area. There were several Calkins families in the towns of Lumberland, Bethel, and Thompson, in the 1810 Census.

Descendants of Oliver and Hannah Thomas Calkins are a part of this story. Son Oliver Calkins Jr. had a grandson, Burton Calkins, who would later marry an Austin cousin. Son Elias Calkins had a son Oliver who marries Maria Gardner, a granddaughter of James Eldred.

An Oliver Calkins (there were several) had a family of ten and served as Commissioner of highways in the Town of Lumberland in 1810. Since there was no Town Hall, town meetings were held in the homes of the settlers.

Here are a few of the other families who lived in the Town of Lumberland in 1810:

Alexander Carmichael, a member of the Narrows Falls

Large tree trunk beside Glass Pond on an old photograph. Courtesy Mary Briggs Austin.

Hemlock Trees

The bark of the hemlock tree was used in the many tanneries of the area in the nineteenth century.

Hemlock bark was removed from trees, stacked and dried, and then ground into powder for use in the tanning process.

The tannin found in Hemlock bark preserved the hide by stopping the natural decay process and making the leather flexible and durable.

Animal hides were repeatedly soaked in the bark from the Hemlock tree (or the Chestnut Oak), and mixed with other ingredients. An acidic chemical reaction slowly changed the hide into leather.

Millions of hemlock trees were left to decay, after the bark was removed for the tanneries.—www.minisink.org

When I was a boy, I could walk to town and never touch the ground by hopping from hemlock tree to hemlock tree laying on the ground.—Garfield Leavenworth, born in 1882.

The hemlock trees were cut down for the bark, which was peeled and used in the leather tanning process. There is a marker on route 97 where the tanning mill was in Sparrowbush. —Kevin Marrinan, friend of the Leavenworth family.

Congregational Church, had nine in his family. He was mentioned in land deeds relating to James Eldred and Augustus Austin.

Jeremiah Lilly had eleven in his family, William Middaugh had six, and Barnabus Snow lived alone. The Peter and Hannah Van Auken family had ten members, Joshua Knight's family had nine, Ezekiel Tuthill had eight, Samuel Wells three, and Benjamin Barton's family had two.

In 1811, my great-great-great-grandparents, Asa and Esther Hickok and their children—Reuben, 33, Sylvia, 29, Hannah, 22, Justus, 20, Louisa, 10, and David, 23 (and his wife, Betsy and son)—arrived in the Town of Lumberland. They lived a couple miles north of The River.

About six miles east and a bit south of the Hickok family farm, was South Lebanon (later called Glen Spey), where James Covert and his wife Irene Tompkins had moved after the Revolutionary War.

In November of 1814, James and Irene Covert's son, William Covert, married Anna Ryder in South Lebanon. William and Anna Covert were ancestors of Ella Phoebe Sergeant.

In the fall of 1814, there was a record of a Congregational Church meeting held at the barn of Samuel Watkins on Halfway Brook, and of other meetings that were held at the Hickok Farm.

In 1797, Reverend Isaac Sergeant, a Congregational minister from Ridgebury, New York, started holding religious services among the few settlers scattered in the Delaware River Valley. Reverend Isaac traveled and preached as far north as Cochecton where a church of fifteen people was started, but it continued for only a few years.

Relatives in 1815

In the next chapter, the James Eldred family enters the town of Lumberland a few days before the end of 1815. The 1815 whereabouts and ages of my relatives that are a part of this book were as follows:

Austin Family
In 1815, Ralph Austin and Fanny Knapp had been married for nine years. They lived in Westchester County, New York, with their children: Samuel Knapp, 7, Augustus Alonzo, 5, Clara, 3, and Emma Eliza, born in July.

Fanny's father had died, but her mother Naomi Palmer Knapp was still living. Ralph's father Joshua Austin, 67, was also still living.

Leavenworth Family
Sherman Buckley Leavenworth, 7, still lived in Connecticut, as far as I know.

Sherman's future wife, Charlotte Ingram, 4, lived in Scotchtown, Orange County, New York, where she had been born. Charlotte's father was an Ingram. Her mother was Christine Hayes, daughter of an unknown Hayes and unknown Muller.

Lazerlier family
Abraham Lazerlier, father of Elizabeth Lazerlier, died in 1803. Elizabeth's mother, Mary Webber Lazerlier, then married Robert Taylor, and they had a son, George Washington Taylor.

Elizabeth Lazerlier had married John Van Pelt in September of 1809, in New York City.

Van Pelt Family
John Van Pelt, 29, and Elizabeth, 26, lived in New York City with their children: Peter, 5, and Maria Anthony, 2. Jane Ann, my great-great-grandmother, would be born December 25, 1815.

Myers Family
Martin David Myers, the future husband of Jane Ann Van Pelt, was born November 1815, in New Jersey. His parents were David and Elizabeth Myer. Only two of Martin David's seven siblings had been born.

Briggs Family
In 1815, Benjamin Briggs and Sarah Jeffries (ancestors of Irwin Briggs), had recently married, and lived in Tell, Pennsylvania, some 250 miles from Lumberland. Within 30 years, at least some in the family, including Ben, Sarah, and son James Thompson Briggs, would move to Indiana.

Crabtree Family
Richard Crabtree and Mary Giggey, the ancestors of Myrtie Crabtree (who would be Irwin's wife), still lived in New Brunswick, along with many other Loyalists.

Halfway Brook. Photo: Mary Briggs Austin.

Narrows Falls Church

The following excerpts were taken from the minutes of an old church record:

Saturday, September 10, 1799
On Saturday, September 10, Mr. Sergeant from Ridgebury, Mr. Jones from Chester, and Mr. Crane, from Blooming Grove came and a considerable number of people met. In the afternoon, Mr. Crane preached and Mr. Jones exhorted.

On Sunday, after the communion administered by Mr. Sergeant and Mr. Jones, the ministers, each gave an exhortation to the church and spectators. After the hymn, Mr. Jones immediately rose and preached the third sermon, made the last prayer and dismissed the assembly with the blessing. God blessed us with two fair, sunshiny, pleasant days; and we had a precious comfortable time—a blessed meeting.

Monday, September 23, 1799.
Church meeting held at Jeremiah Barns'; Deaken Carmkel, [Deacon Carmichael] moderator. Voted unanimously that no minister shall be permitted to preach in this church except he first produce credentials or in some other way satisfy the church that he has been regularly and properly introduced into the ministry. A psalm was read and set or raised and we concluded with prayer.—Quinlan, James Eldridge, History of Sullivan County *pp. 322 and 323.*

In late summer 1799, Rev. Isaac helped organize the Narrows Falls Congregational Church. Narrow Falls was where the Jeremiah Barnes Family lived.

In September, fourteen members of the Narrow Falls Congregational Church met at the home of the Barnes family to take the Lord's Supper. Eleven children were baptized.

The original fourteen members of the Congregational Church of Narrows Falls were listed in the Congregational Church's *1899 Centennial* as: John Barnes, Ichabod Carmichael, Asa Crane, Thomas Barnes, Henry Barnes, Jeremiah Barnes, Nathan Barnes, Elizabeth Barnes, Mercy Mason, Phebe Carmichael, Abigail Crane, Rebecca Barnes, Elizabeth Barnes, and Elizabeth Gray.

The Narrows Falls Church that Reverend Isaac helped organize, became the Congregational Church of the Town of Lumberland, and, much later, the Congregational Church of Eldred—its current name.

In 1799, the children of Isaac Sergeant, age 60, and his second wife, Mary Richards, were: Isaac Jr., 18, Abigail, 17, Stephen, 15, and Thomas, 12.

There are a number of people descended from Stephen Sergeant, son of Isaac and Mary Richards Sergeant, who are a part of this story *(See Appendix, p. 235)*.

Rev. Isaac visited the Narrows Falls Church sporadically. But the Congregation continued to meet regularly even though travel by foot, horseback, or in a buckboard was not very comfortable and took a long time.

They kept up their meetings for public worship and social prayer, and monthly Church-meetings, as best they could—meeting sometimes at Narrow Falls, sometimes at Grassy Swamp, or Beaver Brook, or Halfway Brook…—Quinlan, James Eldridge, History of Sullivan County, *p. 322.*

In September 1803, the Church at Narrow Falls held a union-meeting with the Church at Cochecton at Grassy Swamp. At least 400 people attended from the scattered settlements in the area.

Little is known of Rev. Isaac Sergeant after 1805. The Congregational Church continued to have services in log cabins, barns, and sawmills, with an occasional visit from a minister traveling in the area.

In the last week of December, James Eldred, his wife Polly, his mother Mary, and children Amelia, Sarah, Eliza, Abraham Mulford, and Charles Cotesworth Pinckney, left their home near Wallkill and started for the Town of Lumberland.

The road from Carpenter's Point (now Port Jervis) to Lumberland. Photo: Mary Briggs Austin. In 1859, the Hawk's Nest, as this road is called, was a one lane dirt road. It was not paved until 1931. It is possible that James Eldred and/or his family traveled on this road. What this path was like in 1815/1816, I leave to your imagination.

Chapter 2
The Mill on Halfway Brook
The Eldred Family, 1815 to 1825

Sixty years ago in December just closed, Grandfather Eldred came to this neighborhood. At that time it was called Lumberland. Uncle C.C.P. Eldred was a little over seven years old. Came from Orange County, Wallkill Township, to Halfway Brook on the old Cochecton Road.

Here they found a sawmill and log house. No other building of any kind within a mile of this place now called Eldred. They took possession of the house and sawmill. There was about two acres of cleared land.—January 1, 1876, Maria Austin, granddaughter.

Halfway Brook, possibly near where James and Polly Eldred first settled. Photo: Cynthia Leavenworth Bellinger.

At the end of December 1815, the Eldred family of eight arrived at the vacant log house near Halfway Brook, in the Town of Lumberland, New York. They had traveled some 40 miles across rugged territory from the Eldred homestead: James and his wife, Polly; their children, Amelia, 12, Sarah, 10, Eliza, 5, Abraham Mulford, 9, Charles Cotesworth Pinckney (C.C.P.), 7; and James's mother, Mary Hulse Eldred Forgeson.

After making sure his family was safely settled in the house, James put up a temporary stable to shelter the horses, then walked to Monticello to register his claim/deed to the property.

It was important to James Eldred to have a document that he was the official owner, and not a squatter on the land.

Grandfather walked to Monticello. Went to Port Jervis and Wurtsboro and so on to Monticello (48 miles one way). He made the journey in three days. —Aida Austin, granddaughter.

No wonder James made the trip in only three days. Polly, a most remarkable young woman, had traveled over rough terrain in the winter to their new home at the end of her seventh pregnancy.

While James was gone to Monticello, Polly and her mother-in-law most likely kept busy making the house into a home. For a few years (until it was replaced with a frame house in the same location), this home would be full of activity—the busy everyday lives of James and Polly, children running and laughing, weddings, births, church meetings, and deaths.

The new little one arrived January 8, 1816, ten days after the family's arrival in Lumberland. She was given the same name as a 15-month-old sister who had died in December 1814—Phebe Maria.

Phebe Maria would marry Augustus Alonzo Austin, who was almost 6, and lived with his parents, my great-great-grandparents, Ralph and Fanny Knapp Austin, in Westchester County, New York, 100 miles away.

View of the Delaware River that the Eldred Family would have had on the way to the Town of Lumberland if they came from Carpenter's Point (Port Jervis). Photo: Mary Briggs Austin.

Phebe Maria or Mariah, as she was called, would have a half sister, Mary Ann Eldred. And Augustus Alonzo Austin would have a brother, William Henry Austin who would marry Mary Ann Eldred.

The daughters of both Eldred-Austin couples wrote a number of letters that told of their daily lives that have been included in this book.

William Henry and Mary Ann Eldred Austin's son, Charles Mortimer Austin, would be my grandfather. Mort, as he was often called, would marry Jennie Leavenworth, as we shall see.

It would be some years before Augustus Austin or the Leavenworth Family arrived in Halfway Brook, and longer yet before my great-grandfather William Henry Austin (who was not yet born) arrived with his parents, Ralph and Fanny Austin. But I am getting ahead of the story.

Oliver Calkins was Supervisor of the Town of Lumberland in the year 1816, when, according to Mr. John W. Johnston in his book, *Reminiscences*, the Town of Lumberland had four frame houses, nine frame barns, and a gristmill owned by Jeremiah Barnes.

James Eldred owned one of the eight saw mills, and one of only three watches. Since Jacob Manney had the only clock, he furnished the time for the town.

Animals included 19 horses, 34 oxen, and as many cows. There were 10 wagons.

Only 189 acres were improved land and there were $9,200 in debts due. Boards and scantling totaled 182,000; 80,000 were assessed to Alexander Carmichael. Alexander was a deacon in the church and bought land with/near Augustus Austin, son of Ralph and Fanny, sometime around 1834.

In his list of families in the Town of Lumberland in 1816, Mr. Johnston included James Eldred's name along with Alexander Carmichael (mentioned above); Peter Swartwout; R. Hooker; Francis, Abraham and David Quick; James, John, and Joseph Carpenter; John Johnston; Jeremiah and Cornelius Barnes; Reuben Hickok; Jesse and William Wells; and Jacob Manney.

There were records of others that resided in the area by 1816.

Wilmot Clark had lived in the Town of Lumberland for a year. The Schoonovers (from Holland) arrived there by the end of 1816.

The Johnston family were living near Handsome Eddy, Bartow at Barryville, Carpenter and Wells on Beaver Brook. Two miles above Barryville lived a man by the name of Reeves who kept a tavern in a double log house. Two other families on Halfway Brook by the names of Watkins and Carmichael. Hickok, Wiggins, and a black man lived between Beaver Brook and Halfway Brook.—Aida Austin information.

Great-Great-Grandfather James Eldred began lumbering and farming in 1816, though most of the crops were destroyed because it was so cold.

The notorious cold summer of 1816 when not a spear or ear of corn was grown in the land, when rye, potatoes, and onions were the only crops; and when robust men would cradle, rake and bind rye all the day, clad in their deer skin mittens, their heaviest clothing. —Johnston, p. 265.

Halfway Brook leaving the Eldred area. Photo: Cynthia LeavenworthBellinger.

When James Eldred was living in Minisink, he had been the school director and was also involved with the planning of the Goshen and Minisink Turnpike.

After moving to the Town of Lumberland, James continued his involvement with local government, schools, and roads. In March of 1818, James Eldred was an assessor and inspector of schools.

At the end of June 1818, baby Harriet Baldwin Eldred joined her siblings: Amelia, Sarah, Abraham Mulford, Charles (C.C.P. or Cortzi), Eliza, and Phebe Maria.

From 1814 to 1818, the Narrow Falls Congregational Church met at the Denton Farm owned by Asa Hickok, as it was more centrally located. The Denton Farm (not to be confused with Denton, Orange County), was a couple miles north of The River settlement.

Asa Hickok, a Revolutionary War veteran, had married Esther Hinman in Litchfield County, Connecticut, in 1777, when he was 23, and Esther was 15. The family had been in the Town of Lumberland (including my great-great-grandmother-to-be, Hannah Hickok), since 1811.

In 1815 their daughter Sylvia Hickok died at age 34. Sylvia was buried in the old Eldred Cemetery.

In 1818 Asa and Esther's family—Reuben, 40, Hannah, 29, Justus, 27, Louisa, 18, and David, his wife Betsey, and their four children—lived on or near the Hickok Denton Hill farm.

Stephen Sergeant, the son of Reverend Isaac Sergeant, who had helped to organize the church, was 15 when we last talked about him. In September of 1818, Stephen, now 35 and married with a family, held revival

The Eldred Family

Eldred is an Anglo-Saxon word which means wise scholar. *Eld* is one who is wise because of years of experience; *Red* is one who can read.—Eldred, Richard O., *The Eldred Family*, p.6.

Elisha and Mary Hulse Eldred (sometimes spelled Eldredge or Eldridge), the parents of James Eldred, were married around 1775. It is thought that Elisha Eldred's ancestors sailed from England and arrived in Massachusetts around 1640. Elisha Eldred's father is not known.

Mary Hulse Eldred was one of the eleven children of James Hulse and Mary Arnot. The Hulse ancestors were from the Netherlands.

Elisha and Mary Eldred raised eleven children on their 100 acre farm in the old Town of Minisink, New York. Today that property is in Denton, close to Wallkill Township, New York.

In the 1790s, Elisha Eldred held positions in the town of Minisink. Several of Elisha's descendants were also involved with local government.

Two towns were named Eldred after two of Elisha Eldred's sons—Eldred, Pennsylvania, and Eldred, New York.

Elisha Eldred, my great-great-great-grandfather, died at 51 years of age, October 1804, in Minisink, Orange County, New York. Elisha was buried in a small family cemetery on his farm, now at the back of a field behind the Denton Presbyterian Church.

Elisha was survived by his wife Mary Hulse Eldred and eight children, the oldest of whom died a month later.

In October 1806, James Eldred purchased the family homestead from his mother who had married John Forgeson, a 58-year-old widower.

Four years later, James Eldred sold the family homestead, but continued to live in the area until late 1815, when he and his family left for Lumberland. Mary Eldred Forgeson most likely left as well, as her second husband had died, and her other children had moved to towns in Pennsylvania. *Note: See Appendix, pp. 252–255, for more information on the Elisha Eldred Family.*

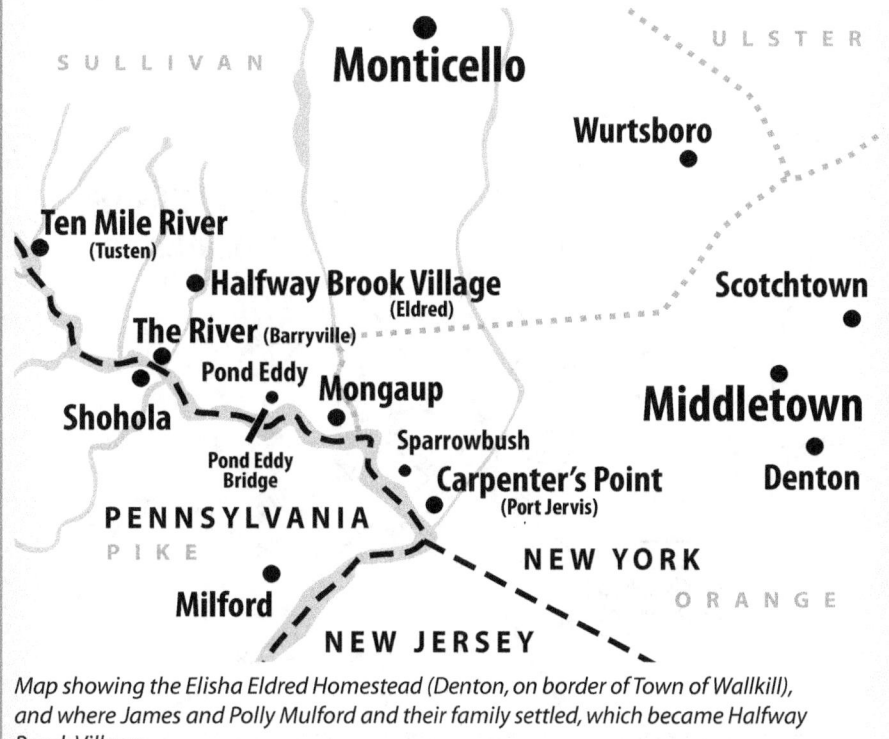

Map showing the Elisha Eldred Homestead (Denton, on border of Town of Wallkill), and where James and Polly Mulford and their family settled, which became Halfway Brook Village.

meetings in Asa Hickok's barn.

As a result of the revival meetings, many new people were added to the church, including the Eldred family: James, Polly, and Amelia; the Hickok family: Asa, Esther, Reuben, Louisa, Hannah, David, Betsy, and Justus; and Mary Wells, future wife of Justus.

On his conversion to God, as you have often heard him say, he searched the Bible diligently to learn the way of truth and path of duty for himself, irrespective of the opinion of others around, or even the church wherein he received his spiritual birth.

In all cases where he deemed there was a departure from true Gospel principle and right, he felt it was duty (however it might effect his popularity or interest) to dissent.—Felix Kyte, Eulogy of James Eldred.

James and Polly were received as members of the church on October 12, 1818, and James was baptized a month later.

The 150 members of the Narrows Falls Congregational Church were scattered over a large region. The people who continued to attend worship services were those close to James and Polly's home, which had become the main place to meet. James Eldred, a careful Bible student, taught the Bible in his home until a church was built.

Young and old gathered at the Eldred home. Years later, Eliza Eldred Gardner (age 84, and living in Barryville), enjoyed telling about the meetings held at the home of her parents, James and Polly Eldred:

If I were 30 years younger, I would walk up to Eldred, even in a storm, if I might see the same spirit of love there now that I saw in those early days.—The Tri-State Union, *1899.*

In November of 1818, Rev. Stephen Sergeant was invited to become the pastor of the Narrows Falls Congregational Church in the Town of Lumberland.

Stephen and Anna Penney Sergeant had five sons, ages 3–12: Ethel B., David Richards, Stephen B., Thomas Lanning, and Isaac Corwin.

There are some handwritten copies of deeds that mention Stephen Sergeant as owner of land that was to the east of Halfway Brook, in the area of Hagan Pond.

Stephen and Anna's son, Ethel B. Sergeant's future wife, Letty Gardner, was 11 years old in 1818. Three sons of Ethel and Letty play a part in this book.

In May of 1819, James Eldred was elected a church deacon, a position he held until he died—nearly 38 years later. James also continued to work in local government. In 1819, he became the Assessor, the Overseer of Highways, and the Commissioner of Schools.

In June of the same year, James and Polly's daughter, Amelia Eldred (almost 16), married Harvey Wheeler, son of Darius and Frances Wheeler.

John Willard Johnston, writer of *Reminiscences*, was born in October of 1819 in Handsome Eddy, near the Delaware River, between The River and Pond Eddy. John W.'s parents, John Johnston and Jane Crawford were early settlers in the area. John, the father, died in 1825. John W., the son, wrote a history of the area and the people that is often caustic and opinionated.

By 1820, George D. Wickham owned 450 acres in Lumberland near to and including The River settlement on the Delaware River, according to Johnston's *Reminiscences*. We read in Chapter One that the Wickham family sold acreage around Ten Mile River to Mr. Dunn and his family of seven sons. Arthur

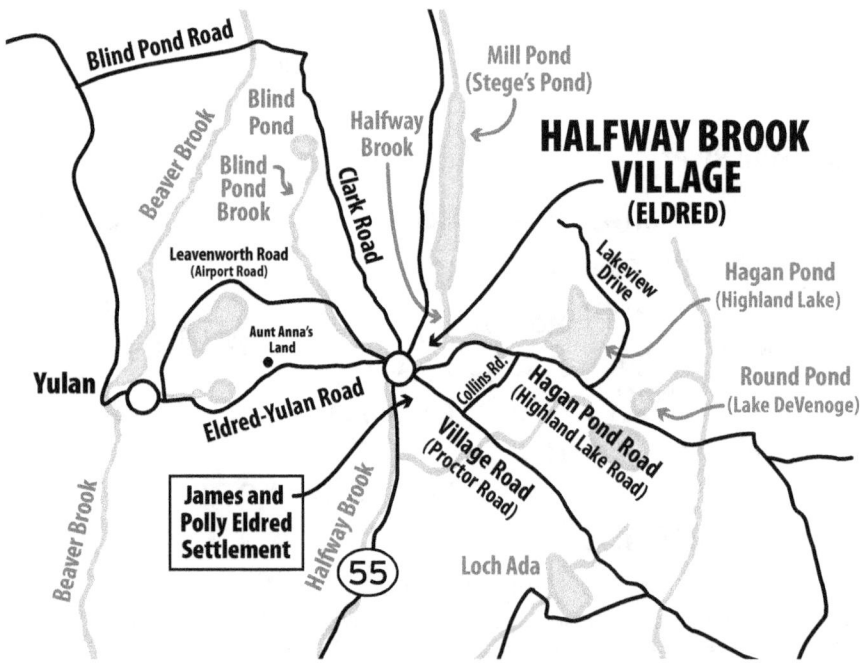

James and Polly Eldred settled in what is now the southeast corner of Eldred, New York.

Hawker, in the *Town of Tusten History*, tells the story of how one of those sons, William Dunn, became a slave owner.

On his way home from New York City, William Dunn stopped at Cuddebackville. While there, a slave mother asked William to buy her 4-year-old son, as she could not provide for him. She also wanted her son close enough that she could visit him occasionally. William purchased the boy and named him James B. Dunn. When James reached adulthood, he was given his freedom.

In 1820, the population of Lumberland, according to the Census, was "569; 566 whites, one slave, two free colored." It is very likely that James B. Dunn was the slave mentioned in the 1820 Census. The censuses called free African Americans "colored" as late as 1870.

There were a number of families who lived in Lumberland in 1820 that are a part of this story. Sears Gardner was the Town of Lumberland's supervisor in 1820. Sears and Mary Gardner's family of nine in Pond Eddy included six children: Joseph, 23, James Keen, 15, Letitia (Letty), 13, Mary, 11, Sears Robert Gardner, 9, Eliza Ann, 1; and possibly a grandfather. James Keen, Letty, Mary, Sears Robert, and Eliza Ann Gardner play a part in this story.

Sears Gardner had married Mary Keen in 1794, the same year that he served as trumpeter of the Volunteer L. Dragons in the "Whiskey Boy Campaign." Sears and Mary Keen Gardner were most likely in Pond Eddy by 1800, when their oldest son Joseph was 3 years old.

Sears Gardner and Elnathan Corey built and operated a sawmill on Pond Eddy Brook, close to the Delaware River, on property they had bought in 1817. There was a later record of a Gardner-Eldred sawmill which was closer to where the James Eldred family lived, and would later become Charles C.P. Eldred's property.

Halfway Brook by Old Brook Road. Photo: Cynthia Leavenworth Bellinger.

According to the 1820 Census, Asa and Esther Hickok had one young child and six adults who lived on their farm.

The census listed twelve people who lived in the home of Oliver Calkins and his wife; seven of the twelve were children.

In 1820, Daniel Van Tuyl and his wife Rebecca Writer, natives of Orange County, New York, and their five children, lived on the 300 acres that Daniel had bought in August of 1816. (In 1818, Daniel had held the office of Overseer of the Poor in the Town of Lumberland.)

The Van Tuyl property was in an area called Handsome Eddy, about 1-1/2 miles south of South

1820 Census— Other Towns

Chauncy, Graham, and Solomon Hurd, Walter Knap, George Pintler, and Moses Calkins were a few of the names listed in the 1820 Census of Bethel, north of Lumberland.

Ralph Austin who lived in North Salem, Westchester County, New York, was possibly my great-great-grandfather.

A letter mentioned in Elias Leavenworth's book *(see p. 41)*, states Sherman Leavenworth and his son William were back to visit their "relatives Ebenezer and Gideon" in Southbury, Connecticut, in 1823. Could this be the father or a relative of Sherman Buckley Leavenworth?

John Van Pelt, husband of Elizabeth Lazerlier, died in May 1820. Peter was 10, Maria 7, and Jane Ann 5. Elizabeth's mother, Mary Webber Lazerlier Taylor was 56.

Martin David Myers was 5. About four of his seven siblings had been born. His parents were David and Elizabeth Myer.

Stephen Sergeant, the preacher, was in the Town of Calhoun, Sullivan County, New York, in 1825. Stephen's family of eight lived next door to his father-in-law, David Penney.

In 1821, Jacob LaBarr and his wife, Sarah Ammerman, lived in Beaver Brook and had a daughter, Mary and a son, Gordon Ransom LaBarr. Gordon was an ancestor of Edey LaBarr Werman who made lists of names on gravestones in several area cemeteries (including Eldred), that have been very helpful.

Postcard of a sawmill owned at one time by W. Wilson, titled, "The Holloway Sawmill, Eldred, New York." The mill was on Route 55 in the curve just south of Eldred, and is no longer there. Postcard courtesy of Larry Stern.

Lebanon (Glen Spey), and along the road to Mongaup. There is currently a Van Tuyl Road in the area.

Effa Caroline Van Tuyl, one of the daughters of Daniel and Rebecca, was 5 in 1820. Effa would marry James and Polly Eldred's son, Charles C.P. Eldred. C.C.P. was 12 in 1820. Effa was known as Aunt Effie in the Eldred-Austin cousin letters we will read later.

James Eldred was School Commissioner in the Town of Lumberland again in 1820. Two of James and Polly's children died that year. In January, Amelia Eldred Wheeler, wife of Harvey Wheeler, died at the age of 16-1/2. Amelia's sister, Harriet Baldwin Eldred, died in October. Harriet was only 2.

In February of the new year (1821), Amelia Ann Eldred was born to James and Polly. This new little one was most likely named for her older sister.

Justus Hickok, (Uncle Justus), married Mary (Polly) Wells in July, 1822. That fall, James and Polly's daughter, Sarah Eldred, 17, married Zophar Carmichael, 23, son of John and Abigail Carmichael (a different family than Alexander Carmichael's at the church).

John and Abigail Carmichael were from the Town of Wallkill, near where the Eldred children had been born. Zophar inherited 65 acres from his father's farm. Did Sarah meet Zophar before they moved to Lumberland at the end of 1815?

Wilmot and Mary Van Auken Clark had been married two years when their son George Clark was born in October, 1822. George would marry Harriet Covert (not yet born), and they would become ancestors of Ella Phoebe Sergeant, future wife of Garfield Leavenworth. Some of Ella's many diary entries, beginning in 1931, are reproduced in Book Two.

In March of 1823, James and Polly's 2-year-old daughter, Amelia Ann Eldred, died. The following year, Harriet Carmichael, the first grandchild of James and Polly, was born to Zophar and Sarah Eldred Carmichael. Perhaps little Harriet brought her grandparents some comfort.

Stephen and Anna Sergeant's son, Ethel B. Sergeant, 18, and Sears and Mary Keen Gardner's daughter, Letty Gardner, 17, were also in town. They would marry in four years.

Letty's brother Joseph Lake Gardner, husband of Sara Purvis, died at age 26, in July, 1824. A sad time for Sears and Mary Keen

Gardner and their family.

Jacob Stage, who later played a part in the Methodist Church, arrived in the area in 1824. His wife-to-be, Martha Carmichael was also in town.

In May of 1824, Thomas W. Clark married 17-year-old Phebe Hazen. (It is not known if Thomas was related to Wilmot Clark.) In a year, Thomas and Phebe would be parents of George Case Clark, born in Mongaup Flats. George Case Clark was an ancestor of Stella Clark, who would marry Clinton Leavenworth, a great-grandson of Sherman B. and Charlotte Ingram Leavenworth.

There were other people in the Town of Lumberland in 1824. Moses Clark, Daniel Case, Ivy Mills, Abraham Ingersoll, John and William Wells, Thomas Wheeler, and James T. and Almira Austin Hooker.

Almira Austin Hooker, Ralph Austin's sister, her husband James T. and children seem to be my first Austin relatives who lived in the Town of Lumberland. By 1824, James, Almira, and their six children lived on 100 acres that they would pay $150 for in July, 1832.

My great-great-grandparents, Ralph and Fanny Knapp Austin, lived in Westchester County, New York, in 1824. Samuel Knapp Austin was 16, Augustus (who would live in the Town of Lumberland in 10 years), was 14, Clara was 12, Emma Eliza was 9, Caroline was 6, James H., 3, and my great-grandfather William Henry was born in March.

In late 1824, Garrett Wilson and three other men purchased Shohola lumber property in Shohola, Pennsylvania, across from The River settlement. Mr. Wilson became the sole manager.

Some New Members of the Congregational Church of Narrow Falls, 1801–1824

1801
Stephen and Alexander Carmichael; James and Elizabeth Reeves.
4 new, 18 total.

1803
James and Lucy Carpenter.
7 new, 25 total.

1818
Reuben, Justus, Betsey, Esther, Louisa, David, Asa and Hannah Hickok; Anna and Daniel Wells; James, Polly V., and Amelia Eldred.
33 new, 58 total.

1819
Elnathan Corey, Francis and Rachel Quick, Harvey Wheeler, Alexander Carmichael, Sally Eldred, Sally Watkins, Anna Sergeant.
5 new, 73 total.

1822
Mary Gardner. 1 new, 77 total.

1823
Mary Wells, Eliza and Harriet Eldred.
5 new, 82 Total.

1824
As a result of the many revival meetings of the Lumberland Congregational Church, there were 83 members by 1824.

In March of 1824, there was a series of revival meetings, and 88 people became members. Some of the new members were Betsey Corey, Thomas Clark, Jacob Stage, Stephen B. Sergeant, Ethel B. Sergeant, Daniel Case, Wilmot Clark, Charles C.P. Eldred, David Sergeant, Ivy Mills, Asa R. Hickok, Abraham Ingersoll, Martha Carmichael (Stage), Letty Gardner (Sergeant), Charity Van Tuyl (Brown), Mary Clark, Moses Clark, James K. Gardner, Martha Clark, Amelia Skinner, Thomas Clark, Phebe Clark (Myers).
88 new, 171 total.

Large logs. Postcard from a souvenir folder entitled "Sunny South" sent to Aida Austin in 1917 from her nephew Mortimer McKinley Austin. From the collection of Mary Briggs Austin.

Eldred Land

After a few years in the house by Halfway Brook, James bought the land and a framed house was built near the mill site for the family.
—Aida Austin, 1939

Around 1825/1826, James Eldred purchased about 684 acres for $500 from John James and Sarah Stewart of the Town of Mamakating. James Eldred seems to have built his framed house on the 84-57/100 acres section shown below. The middle line shown on Aunt Aida's map would seem to be Village/Proctor Road.

1825 John James Stewart of Mamakating to James Eldred
All that certain piece of land situate laying and being in Lumberland Sullivan Co., N.Y., being part of lot 21 in 7th division of Minisink Patent.

Beginning at N.E. corner of 300 acres heretofore sold by said Stewart to Daniel Case in lots 21 and 20, running thence northeasterly along line of lots 21 and 20…to the center of said lot 21 and thence at right angles with said line between lots 20 and 21, across lot 21 to line between lots 21 and 22 thence Southwesterly along line between lots 21 and 22…to land of Daniel Case thence at right angles across lot 21 and 22…to place of beginning. Containing 84 57/100 acres.

Also that certain other part of lot 21 bounded S.W. by 100 heretofore sold to John Barton and N.E. by 300 acres lately sold to Daniel Case, containing about 600 acres more or less.

James Stewart and Sarah Stewart Samuel Smith, Judge of Court of Common Pleas. February 26, 1826. Recorded Nov. 6, 1829.

Map of property sold to James Eldred in June 1825.—from Melva Austin Barney's collection of Aida Austin's papers.

Lumbering was the only business of the section, cutting and drawing logs, sawing and hauling boards, rafting and running lumber down the stream.—Johnston, p. 293.

In 1825, Mr. Wilson with 12 or 15 men, mechanics and laborers, removed the old sawmill, erected a new and larger mill with two saw gates, renewed and raised the dam increasing the water power. Jonathan Rosencrance worked for Mr. Wilson 10 years, constantly engaged in cutting logs, drawing and placing them in the Shohola Brook where they lay until the water of the brook became sufficient to float them to the mill pond.

That was the process by which all the timber of the large tract was made to reach the mill—logs cut and drawn by the teams to the nearest point of the brook and there deposited, either in the water or upon the immediate shore.—Johnston, pp. 305, 307.

At the end of January 1825, Polly, James Eldred's wife, died at the age of 37. Five of James and Polly's nine children were still living. Sarah, 20, was married to Zophar Carmichael, Abraham Mulford was 19, Charles C.P., 17, Eliza, 15, and Phebe Maria was 9. A sad start to a new year for the Eldred family.

I imagine by this time the old log home had seen its fill of life and death, happiness and sorrow, good years and lean. The log home that had provided shelter for James Eldred's family since the end of 1815, was replaced with a new frame house, probably before 1830. The new Eldred home was still near the mill site where the sawmill kept working.

Chapter 3
Life in Lumberland
1825 to 1831

The work of most people in the area was related in some way to lumbering. Each lumbering company had its small community of employees, most of whom lived in make-shift tenements, and some did not have a garden. But all received wages which left no surplus at the end of the year.—John W. Johnston, Reminiscences.

Delaware River View. Photo: Gary Smith.

The sound of sawmills ripping through huge logs to make planks could be heard throughout Lumberland.

Not all of the timber from the area went to local sawmills. A considerable amount of logs sent to the Delaware River by way of the nearest stream were made into rafts and floated to market.

Lumbermen and farmers lived in simple, small homes with no insulation. Barns usually stood across the road from the houses.

Lumbermen also farmed, and their oxen were used for both occupations. Vegetables, rye, corn, buckwheat, and some fruit trees were grown, as well as grain and hay for the stock. Meat and milk came from the cattle, which were free to roam. Chickens provided both meat and eggs.

Fish and eel were plentiful in the Delaware River. The Van Tuyl, Middaugh, Hooker, and other familes kept a barrel of salted eels in the winter. Each child was given a boiled eel and four buckwheat pancakes for dinner. Other families in the area ate rye bread spread with butter or pork grease.

Many wild animals, including bears, roamed the forest in the 1820s. Years later, Jacob Stage's wife, Martha Carmichael, told a story about her grandmother as a young mother. The menfolk had gone some distance to hunt and left Grandmother alone with her children in a recently built house with only a curtain for a door.

When a bear appeared at the door wanting something to eat, Grandmother hid the children under the bed, and beat off the bear with anything she could grab. From then on, Martha's grandmother refused to stay alone when the men were away. Do you blame her?

Getting food and necessities for living was quite challenging in Lumberland's early days. Needed items were purchased from the Village of Newburgh, about sixty miles from Lumberland. The round trip on the Newburgh-Cochecton Turnpike took a week.

Farm produce, cattle, and wood products were transported from Newburgh west on the Turnpike. Items the settlers wanted to sell were sent to Newburgh, and from there transported by boat to New York City, another 67 or so miles away.

A bit later, but still early on, food and dry goods came

The Tri-States—New York, New Jersey, and Pennsylvania—meet at Port Jervis (originally Carpenter's Point), New York. Postcard in Mary Briggs Austin Collection.

from Carpenter's Point (Port Jervis), roughly 20 miles away. At Carpenter's Point, grain could be ground into flour. In the winter, when the Delaware River was frozen, goods were hauled from Carpenter's Point to Lumberland over the ice.

In 1825, a school was started for children who lived near The River settlement in the Town of Lumberland. Sears Gardner was the Town Supervisor, and James Eldred was the Town Clerk, Commissioner of Highways, and Town Marshall.

The community felt they needed a school. As was done in those times, a subscription paper was circulated to see if there was enough interest to start a school. John W. Johnston tells about the school in his *Reminiscences*.

Francis Quick circulated the subscription document on both sides of the Delaware River—from the Van Tuyl property near Handsome Eddy, northwest four miles to the Johnston family's home, near The River.

School would be held for three months of the year at a time, every week day, and on alternate Saturdays. People were to add their signatures and the number of children they were responsible for if they were committed to supporting the school.

Nine parents signed up a total of 28 students. The Francis Quick family and the Van Tuyl family (Daniel and Rebecca), each had five children. The Calvin Crane family had four, as did Jane Johnston, the widowed mother of John W. Johnston. The Levi Middaugh family had three. So did James and Almira Hooker. Daniel Pool had two children. The Nicholas Morris family and David Quick's family each had one. It was agreed that there was enough support for a school.

The school house was built southwest of Hugh Quick's home on a level piece of land surrounded by trees and a nearby spring of water.

With the help of their axes and oxen teams, the men and boys built a 16-foot square log schoolhouse in eight days. The walls were 7-feet high. Three walls each had a window. The fourth wall had a huge chimney and fireplace. The door had a wooden latch and string. There was even a place to hang hats and bonnets.

The teacher had a chair, and students sat on wooden slabs with legs made from saplings.

School opened on the first day of August, 1825. Miss Fannie Hooker, 51, was the teacher. Aunt Fannie, as she was called, taught for $10 a month, and boarded at homes of the her students. She was the sister of James T. Hooker, husband of Almira Austin.

Miss Hooker was quite tall

Eel Weir

Eel weir near Pond Eddy, New York. Photo: Cynthia Leavenworth Bellinger.

Eels are born in saltwater, but migrate to fresh water where they live before returning to the sea to spawn.

To the left is an eel weir/trap (two stone walls that form a "V") in the Delaware River near Pond Eddy. The eels run the Delaware River from the end of September though October.

Eels are funneled into the V-shape and then drop down into a wire cage under the water (where you see the wooden contraption.) After being scooped up and put into burlap bags, the eels are cleaned and then smoked.—David Leavenworth, September 2009.

Lord & Taylor Department Store

Lord & Taylor, based in New York City, New York, is the oldest upscale, luxury department store chain in the United States.

Lord & Taylor began in New York in 1826 as a small dry goods store owned by cousins Samuel Lord and George Washington Taylor, immigrants to New York. They located their store near the North River waterfront in New York's Greenwich Village.

The store later moved to a place uptown on the Ladies' Mile, which catered to the wealthier clientele of the "carriage trade."

Lord & Taylor became a major fashion retailer, and the first major store on Fifth Avenue, New York City.

Note: George Washington Taylor was the step-brother of Elizabeth Lazerlier Van Pelt, my great-great-great-grandmother.

Ice gorge in the Delaware River at Hancock, N.Y., 50 miles northwest of Eldred, N.Y. Postcard is in the collection of Mary Briggs Austin.

with large black eyes and a strong loud voice. She wrote poorly, but was a fluent reader and a good speller. She mainly used *Noah Webster's Spelling Book*, and the *New Testament* as a reader, as they were available to most of the students.

In winter, the fathers cut the trees and took the logs to the schoolhouse. The larger boys cut and prepared the wood for the fireplace, and the stronger girls helped to carry it in. The older girls scrubbed the school house on alternate Friday evenings when there was no school the following day. The younger children often stayed and played while the older girls worked.

The children walked to school in summer heat, spring rains, and wintry blasts, often with the same clothing. One little fellow, who traveled two miles to school, wore a muslin shirt with collar, coat, vest and pants, stockings and cowhide shoes, a hat, and a little mantle made of a single piece of cloth for his shoulders. His two sisters were similarly dressed.

The summer of 1826, Aunt Fannie left. Dick Manning taught that fall. Apparently Mr. Manning's teaching was not up to expectation. The school session was postponed until winter, when an older man, Mr. Furman taught for two weeks, then left for an offer he thought was better.

After a few years, the building was no longer used as a school, as it was difficult to get to and too far away. In mild weather, however, the building was used for religious meetings where David Hickok preached and Levi Middaugh and Francis Quick exhorted and prayed. Eventually, the old schoolhouse rotted and fell down.

By 1826, the area where the Eldred family had settled was known as Halfway Brook Village, but was usually called *the Village*. Letters to the area were addressed to "Lumberland."

In February, a year after his wife Polly had died, James Eldred, 48, married Hannah Hickok, 37. Hannah, daughter of Asa and Hester Hinman Hickok, was my great-great-grandmother.

Delaware River. Photo by Aida Austin in the collection of Mary Briggs Austin.

The Delaware River at Barryville, New York. Postcard courtesy of Mary Briggs Austin.

Great-Great-Grandfather James Eldred probably met Hannah and her parents at the Congregational Church which had been held in his home.

Hannah was most likely well acquainted with the Eldred children: Sarah Carmichael, 21, and married with children; Abraham Mulford, 20; Charles Cotesworth, 18; Eliza, 15; and Maria, 10. (Grandmother in the Eldred-Austin cousin letters refers to Hannah Hickok Eldred.)

The Congregational Church of Narrow Falls now met in the schoolhouse in the Village.

Rev. Stephen Sergeant had left for a Presbyterian Church (and also seems to have sold his land). The Congregational Church had no pastor for six years. Deacons James Eldred and Alexander Carmichael helped direct the congregation during this difficult time. James Eldred described the church situation in this letter:

About twenty of its members have been excommunicated. Sixteen of which were for intemperance.

Our Pastor Rev'd Stephen Sergeant has approached the church and told us we were not established under the government of God's Word, and has gone to the Presbyterians.

Some who we looked to as Fathers in Israel and Mothers, also, have had no regard to their obligations and teach others to regard it not, (and united themselves to the Methodist people).

Others have sickened and gone as we hope from the evils to come, others have moved out of the country, others have taken letters of dismission and joined to other churches in Christian order.—James Eldred letter.

In September 1827, James Eldred's daughter, Eliza Eldred, almost 17, married James Keen

Eliza Eldred, daughter of James Eldred and wife of James K. Gardner. Melva Austin Barney Collection.

D&H Canal

The Delaware and Hudson Canal opened in October 1828. It had taken 2,500 men and 200 teams of horses three years to dig and blast through 108 miles of wilderness to connect the Delaware and the Hudson River.

The canal began at Rondout Creek near Kingston and went through several areas, including the Neversink River Valley on its way to Port Jervis on the Delaware River.

The canal then ran northwest on the New York side of the Delaware River, crossing into Pennsylvania at Lackawaxen and on to Honesdale.

The canal was divided into three sections for operational purposes: the Lackawaxen: from Honesdale to the Delaware; the Delaware: along the river from there to Port Jervis; and the Neversink: from Port Jervis to Kingston.

To get the anthracite from the Wurts brothers' mine in the Moosic Mountains near Carbondale to the canal at Honesdale, the canal company built a gravity railroad. The state of Pennsylvania authorized its construction on April 8, 1826.

On August 8, 1829, the D&H's first locomotive, the Stourbridge Lion, made history as the first locomotive to run on rails in the United States.
—www.en.wikipedia.org.

Child leading mules near Rosendale, New York, on the Hudson part of the Delaware and Hudson Canal. The mules are eating from woven baskets.

The barge has just left Lock No. 9, north of New Paltz, New York, on the Delaware and Hudson Canal.

After leaving Lock No. 8, the barge loaded with firewood continues northeast towards Rosendale, New York. The man on the left is steering the barge. The mules towing the barge are in the distance on the towpath. The above photos taken by William or John Crabtree in the late 1800s are courtesy of The Century House Historical Society.

Railroad cars transfer their loads of anthracite (hard) coal to D&H Canal boats in Honesdale, Pennsylvania. Source: Delaware and Hudson Railroad and Canal, by Wayne County Historical Society. Reproduction number HAER PA,64-HOND, 3-1.

Gardner, 22, son of Sears and Mary K. Gardner. The year before, James K. Gardner had started manufacturing wheelbarrows.

In 1827, James Eldred was Inspector of Schools and Town Clerk (until 1832) for Lumberland.

In December of 1827, my great-grandmother, Mary Ann Eldred, the future wife of William Henry Austin, was born to James and Hannah Hickok Eldred in Halfway Brook Village, Town of Lumberland, Sullivan County, New York.

The Town of Lumberland, especially The River settlement on the Delaware River, was a very busy place from 1826 to 1828.

The Delaware and Hudson Canal, which would play a vital part in the growth of the communities along or near the Delaware River, was being built, and new job opportunities were opening up. The area would no longer be supported solely by the lumber industry. Places for lodging and food would be needed for the workers and the travelers on the canal.

The 108-mile long Delaware and Hudson Canal went from Honesdale, Pennsylvania, near the Delaware River, to Kingston, New York, near the Hudson River.

The first canal boats loaded with coal arrived at the Hudson River in November 1828. From then until 1899, barges carried anthracite coal from the Moosic Mountains of Northeastern Pennsylvania mines to the coal markets of New York City, by way of the Delaware and Hudson Rivers.

Mr. Johnston recalled watching the first canal boat:

Barryville, the old Gristmill. Postcard is in the collection of Mary Briggs Austin.

On a pleasant October evening of 1828, when a child of about five years of age, I stood beside the towpath held by my mother's hand, and looked upon the first boat that passed up the canal on its journey to Honesdale for a load of coal.

After the lapse of more than seventy years, I can picture to my fancy the marks and features of the horse that towed the pioneer boat—a light sorrel of medium size, compact in form, having a narrow white strip in the face and white forward feet.
—Johnston, pp. 125–6.

In the Town of Lumberland, the canal went some 17 miles—from the Mongaup River to a point close to the junction of the Delaware and Lackawaxen Rivers. Originally there were eleven locks, but it was increased to fourteen.

By means of aqueducts it crossed four principal streams—the Mongaup, the Pond Eddy Brook, the Halfway Brook, and the Beaver Brook…To each and every lock, a dwelling house was erected for the use of the lock-tender, and located beside the towpath and central part of the lock, if the ground permitted.
—Johnston, p. 19.

The person (often a boy aged 12 to 16) who led the mules pulling barges along the towpath, was paid three dollars a month. This included walking 15-20 miles a day, pumping out the barges, and tending the animals.

At first, it took a week to go the entire length of the canal. The canal was closed on Sunday, and in the winter when the water froze up or was likely to.

A number of new towns sprang up. The Town (township) of Cochecton was formed from the Town (township) of Bethel on March 25, 1828. Cochecton (the Town) included the villages of Cochecton, Cochecton Center, and Tylertown.

Carpenter's Point, renamed Port Jervis in 1827, became a main port on the D&H Canal. John B. Jervis, for whom Port Jervis was named, was a Delaware and Hudson Canal engineer.

A blacksmith shop, a gristmill, and a broom handle factory were established at The River settlement shortly after 1828.

Pond behind the Barryville Gristmill. Postcard is in the collection of Mary Briggs Austin.

Later a glass factory opened which made molded glass.

Mr. Johnston tells about the store that Mr. Forgerson kept at what would soon be called Barryville:

Forgerson kept the only store in the region, cleared land, ground a little feed, and sawed a little lumber for customers. In 1830, he built a dwelling house still continuing his mercantile business in the old store.

Gardner Forgerson had been an agent in George D. Wickham's Ten Mile River lumbering operation. In 1828, Forgerson bought Wickham's property at The River settlement (Barryville), and built a home for his family there two years later.

James K. Gardner and his wife Eliza would have a son Stephen St. John Gardner, who would live on Forgerson's property and whose house would have part of Mr. Forgerson's original structure.

Lumberland still bustled with activity after the D&H Canal was completed. The River settlement at the mouth of Halfway Brook resonated with the sounds of a thriving community at work. You might call the cacophony—*The Work Symphony*.

Axes chopped, saws buzzed, trees fell, saw blades whirred, logs floated in rafts down the river, and canal workers walked along the river path shouting to the mules pulling the canal boats as people passed by.

Cart wheels thudded along the rough paths, horse hooves clopped, and merchants sold their wares in a sing-song voice.

Oxen plowed gardens with an occasional shout from the farmer as various barnyard animals clucked, neighed, or oinked.

Glass Factory Pond. Postcard is in the collection of Mary Briggs Austin.

Sherman B. Leavenworth

I always heard from Dad (Clinton Leavenworth) that Sherman B. came from Connecticut into Eldred through Monticello with the Hurd family in covered wagons. They came with the Hardenburgh Lumber Company from Connecticut.
—Linda Leavenworth Bohs.

From several sources I have pieced together a possible scenario from several sources of the early years of my great-great-grandfather, Sherman Buckley Leavenworth.

About 1828, Sherman B., age 20, moved from Connecticut to Sullivan County in New York, with the Hurd family in a covered wagon. The men worked for a Connecticut Lumber Company that would be lumbering in the New York area.

There are records of a Hurd family marrying into the Leavenworth family, so perhaps the Leavenworths moved with the Hurd family who were relatives.

Elias Leavenworth (not a direct relative) wrote, *A Genealogy of the Leavenworth Family in the United States*. Towards the end of the book, a Sherman Leavenworth is mentioned as living near Monticello.

Ten miles west of Monticello is the town of Bethel, New York, where several Hurd families had settled by 1810. The town, *Hurd Settlement*, four miles north of Bethel, is on modern maps.

Is it possible that Sherman Leavenworth, mentioned in the *Leavenworth Book*, lived near Bethel or the Hurd Settlement, and "Monticello" was referring to Monticello and the nearby area?

In the 1830 census of Bethel, a Truman S. Leavenworth was listed as living in Bethel, 12 miles north of what was then Halfway Brook Village. Truman's household consisted of one female and two males, all between the ages of 20 and 30.

Our Sherman B. would be 22 in 1830. Could Truman be his brother, and Sherman lived with him?

By 1840, Sherman Buckley Leavenworth was in Halfway Brook Village as he was listed in the 1840 census of Lumberland.

Not all the sounds were raucous or loud. Children laughed as they played hide and seek. Women baked, gardened, sewed, made bread, knitted, washed clothes, sang lullabies to their babies, and made huge meals to feed hardworking husbands and growing children, who were hopefully helping out by getting water from the well or firewood for cooking and keeping warm.

There were conflicts on the waterways. Timber from the area being rafted down the Delaware River to Philadelphia for the ship building industry interfered at times with the progress of the canal boats. Soon aqueducts would alleviate the problem.

The D&H Canal would play an important part in shipping the bluestone that was accidentally discovered some twelve miles north of Port Jervis, around 1835, by "Uncle Steve" Griffin, who was rattlesnake hunting. That was the story told in the March 1889 issue of the *New York Times*.

Though plentiful in the area, it would be another 30 years before the bluestone on either side of the Delaware River became curbs and sidewalks for New York City.

About 1828, Sears and Mary K. Gardner left Pond Eddy and moved to the east side of Halfway Brook Village, to property they owned north of Village Road near Halfway Brook. Sears Gardner may have owned the property with Abraham Mulford Eldred at first. It would later be owned by C.C.P. Eldred.

Sears and Mary K. Gardner's daughter, Letitia (Letty) Gardner, married Ethel B. Sergeant, son of Stephen and Anna Sergeant, in October of 1828.

In the late 1820s, there was still not a good way to travel on land. Whether you walked or rode a horse, the roads were rough and through the wilderness.

Whether by foot, horseback, canal or all three, Doctor Perkins left Poughkeepsie, New York, in 1829, and managed to arrive in Lumberland, where he would be the only physician for over 300 square miles.

Fortunately, the people were usually healthy, according to Mr. Johnston in his *Reminiscences*, where he describes the good Doctor Perkins.

Doc Perkins used five or six prescriptions to treat disease. He did not like the home remedies or superstitious notions that prevailed at the time.

Doc Perkins first boarded at Robert Land's house at Beaver Brook, four miles back from the river and canal. The fun loving, agreeable doctor always wore a suit of heavy winter clothes, and traveled on horseback without a padded saddle or coated stirrups.

Mr. Johnston described the travels of Doctor Perkins:

Thus for 24 years, he traveled many thousands of miles over the rough highways, the narrow timber roads, the cow paths; over hills and through valleys, through dark, dense wildernesses and groves of lofty timber, during night and day, amid sunshine and storm, cold and heat.

Eldred-Gardner Sawmill

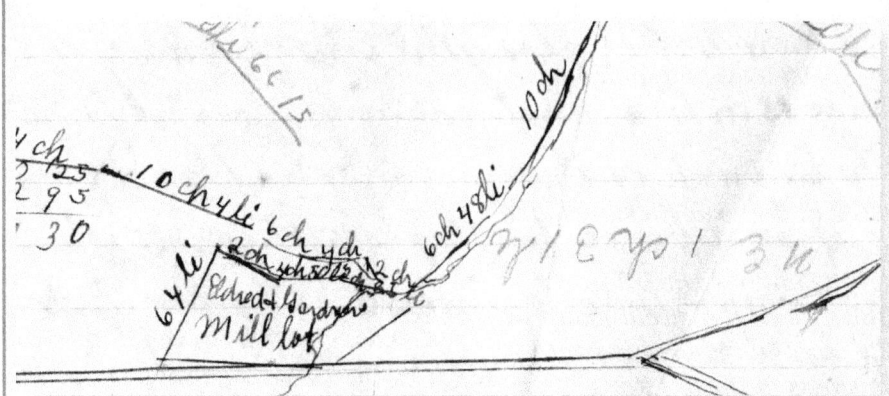

Map on copy of June 1828 land deed from John Wells to Sears Gardner. Melva Austin Barney Collection.

The above map on a copy of the June 1828 land deed from John Wells to Sears Gardner, shows an Eldred-Gardner Mill lot where Sears and Mary K. Gardner lived at one time. Abraham Mulford Eldred may have been co-owner at first.

The property was near Halfway Brook, north of what is now Proctor Road, just before the "Y" in the road to Highland Lake, and was later owned by C.C.P. Eldred. In 1851, the Post Office was in the home of C.C.P., which was on this property.

Commencing on west line of lot 21 in 7th div. of Minisink Patent, S. 47 degrees E., 4 chains to sandstones E. side of main road leading up the Halfway Brook. Containing 49 acres.
—excerpt from John Wells deed to Sears Gardner, 1829.

Rod, chain, links, and furlongs

A rod equals 16.5 feet or 25 links. One chain equals 4 rods.

The rod, a measurement of medieval times, was still used in the mid-1800s.

An acre in medieval times was one chain or four rods (ox goads) long, by one furlong (in the UK, ten chains).

A furlong was "one plough's furrow long" or the length of a furrow that could be a plowed by a plough team without resting.

The length of the furlong and the acre vary regionally, due to different soil types. In England the acre was 4,840 square yards, but in Scotland it was 6,150 square yards, and in Ireland, 7,840 square yards.

Where They Lived in 1830

Town of Lumberland

According to the 1830 Census, there were 926 people in the Town of Lumberland. This included 427 children under age 14, six people in their 70s, three in their 80s, but no one in their 90s.

Sears and Mary K. Gardner had five in their home, ages 9 to 29. Their daughter Mary Gardner married Benjamin C. Austin, (from the other Austin family in town), in 1830, sometime after the census was taken.

Uncle Justus and Polly Hickok had three children under 10.

James T. and Almira Austin Hooker had six children under 19, one person under 20, one under 50, and one under 80 years old.

Laurence Ingraham had three under 15, and possibly his mother or mother-in-law, age 60 or over.

The Daniel Van Tuyl and Daniel Owens families were also listed.

Alexander Carmichael and his wife had four children under 15.

Elnathan Corey had a full house of nine. Robert Land and his wife had five children under 15.

Gardner Forgerson and his wife had four children under 10, and six others from 16 to 39. In the next chapter, Gardner Forgerson helps out the new Congregational Church pastor, Felix Kyte.

The LaBarr family still lived in Beaver Brook and included Gordon Ransom LaBarr who was around 10.

Jacob Stage was not yet 30.

Stephen and Anna Sergeant had three sons at home—Stephen, 20, Thomas L., 17, and Isaac C., 15.

Their son Ethel Sergeant and his wife Letty Gardner lived next door with their 1-year-old. Ethel and Letty's son Alvah Sergeant was born in Beaver Brook, in June 1831. Alvah Sergeant would have a son who would marry a daughter of Harriet Covert born in September 1831, to William and Anna Covert in South Lebanon.

Harriet Covert would marry George Clark, son of Wilmot and Mary Van Auken Clark. George Clark's brother Mahlon Irvin Clark, 3, would marry Laura Austin.

John Bishop and his wife Julia had a son under 5. John's father Stephen and possibly some brothers lived in Lumberland. John plays an unexpected part in our story.

Thomas W. Clark, husband of Phebe Hazen, and father of George Case Clark, died in Mongaup, in 1829. Phebe married Moses Myers. They would be the parents of Abel Sprague Myers, a grandfather or great-grandfather to some of the people we will meet in this book.

Other families included Solomon Hurd, Robert Many, Daniel, Samuel and William Wells, and John Wheeler.

Not in Lumberland
Leavenworth Family

Truman S. Leavenworth and three Hurd families were listed in the 1830 Census of Bethel, New York.

Three people were listed as living with Truman Leavenworth—one female and two males between the ages of 20 and 30. Was Sherman B. Leavenworth, 22, one of the men listed in Truman's household?

A Gideon Leavenworth lived in Middlebury, New Haven, Connecticut.

Austin Family

The Austin family lived in Somers, Westchester County, New York. Ralph (Rolf in this census), 46, and Fanny Knapp Austin, 42, William Henry, 6, Ann Mary, 3, James H., 9, Caroline, 13, Emma Eliza, 15 (Emma died in October), Augustus A., 20, and Samuel Knapp, 22. The census shows another young man in his twenties.

Ralph and Almira's father, Joshua Austin had died July 1828.

Hickok Family

Asa and Esther Hickok, and son David H. and his wife and family were in Warren Township, Bradford County, Pennsylvania, in the 1830 Census.

Myers Family

Martin David Myers, 15, lived in New Jersey with his parents David and Elizabeth Myer, and seven siblings.

Van Pelt Family

Elizabeth Lazerlier Van Pelt, and children, Peter, 20, Maria, 17, and Jane Ann, 15, lived in New York City. Elizabeth's mother, Mary Webber Lazerlier Taylor, was 66.

Delaware River near Barryville. Photo: Mary Briggs Austin.

Doc Perkins charged 25 cents for a visit to the village or the area nearby, with the option to pay or not. A visit to Ten Mile River from Barryville (11 miles through the woods), was 75 cents. One family of five children and a mother, he contracted for $5 a year. Some families never paid the doctor, though he had called on them for 18 years.—*Johnston, pp. 340, 342–3.*

You may remember that in the early 1800s, Solon Cooper and Levi Middaugh ran the first store in Pond Eddy. Mr. Cooper mysteriously disappeared in 1830. Thus ended the Middaugh and Cooper store.

The Congregational Church was still struggling without a preacher in 1830 when circuit riding preachers from the Methodist Episcopal Church, began teaching in villages on both sides of the Delaware River in the tri-state area of New York, Pennsylvania, and New Jersey.

Mr. Grace and Mr. Street preached every two weeks in the Town of Lumberland. Visits were made during the day, and services were held at night.

It is quite possible that Sherman Buckley Leavenworth, my great-great-grandfather, lived in the town of Bethel some 11-1/2 miles away from Halfway Brook, by 1830. By 1835 *(see Chapter Five)*, Sherman B. and his wife Charlotte Ingram, from Scotchtown, New York, lived in Halfway Brook Village.

James Eldred and his family lived south of Village/Proctor Road. One source said that James built a store around 1830. By 1830, James had built the Eldred Homestead which replaced the original log cabin.

The Eldred Homestead, (no longer in existence), was built by James Eldred and operated by him. It was used as a tavern at one time, and known as Temperance Tavern.

It was still there when I lived in Eldred—a few hundred feet back from what is now the main road, and as far as I know was the first permanent building in Eldred. (An old sign was found in the attic referring to such.)
—Melva Austin Barney.

There were many temperance groups in New York in the 1830s, so it would not be a surprise to have an inn in town that did not serve alcoholic beverages.

One room of the Eldred Homestead/tavern was used for the Lumberland Post Office when James became Postmaster on October 5, 1831.

By 1831, The River settlement had its own Post Office named after William T. Barry, the Post Master General. The town was then called Barryville, although it continued to be referred to as The River.

In 1832, the good doctor Perkins married Comelia Dabron, and they moved into the old Hickok farmhouse, two miles from Barryville.

By 1832, James Eldred and Hannah Hickok had been married six years, and their daughter, Mary Ann Eldred, was 5 years old.

Zophar and Sarah Eldred Carmichael, 27, had at least three children. The youngest was Lewis Carmichael born in 1831. The family eventually lived in Wallkill on the Carmichael family farm.

Abraham Mulford Eldred, 26, had purchased several large tracts of land, and was lumbering and farming. Uncle Mulford, as he was called, was also active in government. He had been elected constable of Lumberland in 1830, and was also the collector of taxes, and inspector of schools in 1830, 1832, 1834. He was single until about 1838.

In 1832, Charles (C.C.P.) Eldred, 24, a farmer and lumber dealer, was not yet married.

Eliza Eldred Gardner was 22, and had been married five years to James Keen Gardner. Eliza and James K. had Charles, 2, and baby Chauncey, who died in August. The family would soon move to Beaver Brook where James K. would be a supervisor for a lumbering company.

In two years Phebe Maria Eldred, 16, would marry Augustus Alonzo Austin, whose whereabouts in 1832 are unknown. Perhaps only Phebe Maria, 16, and Mary Ann, 4, lived at home with James and Hannah Eldred in 1832.

Delaware River at Barryville, fall 2008. Photo: Mary Briggs Austin.

Chapter 4
Reverend Felix Kyte
The Congregational Church, 1832 to 1835

You ask the probable amount we would raise per Sabbath. I think we could raise $5 dollars per Sabbath for a season amongst ourselves.

At the place in which we live there is a school house in which we hold our meetings on every Sabbath on Halfway Brook, four miles from the Delaware and Hudson Canal. Several miles west, there is a meeting house, but few of our members are there and no meeting kept up."—August 7, 1832.

Felix Kyte in later years. Courtesy of Chuck Myers.

So wrote James Eldred in a second letter to Felix Kyte of New York City, to answer Mr. Kyte's questions.

In 1832, the Congregational Church had been without a pastor for six years—since Rev. Stephen Sergeant had left and gone to the Presbyterian Church. The congregation was meeting in a small school house at Halfway Brook Village, and the membership had dropped to 50.

The deacons, including James Eldred and Sears Gardner, had taken over the pastor's responsibilities, and thought the church needed a full time pastor. Sears Gardner, had seen Felix Kyte's advertisement for a position as minister of a Congregational Church in the *New York Observer*, and encouraged James Eldred to respond to the ad.

Felix Kyte, a schoolteacher from Lydd, England, was living with his wife and two sons in New York City, where there had been many deaths due to the cholera epidemic. Left with fewer students to teach, Felix was considering leaving. Felix was also a clerk for the New York Congregational Association (N.Y.C.A.), which promoted pure Congregationalism (many churches were becoming Presbyterian, apparently), in New York City and elsewhere. The N.Y.C.A. had encouraged Felix to advertise in the *New York Observer* to see if any Congregational Churches wanted a minister.

James Eldred's first letter invited Felix Kyte to visit the Village in Lumberland, at least ninety miles away. Felix wrote back, and asked some questions, which James answered in his second letter—they would pay traveling expenses, they could afford $5 per Sabbath. James also explained where they met and why the church was down to 50 people.

The N.Y.C.A. agreed that Felix Kyte should go and see if the church at the Village was the right situation for him. Felix Kyte left New York City in August 1832, and sailed north 64 miles to Newburgh on the Hudson River.

Felix took the stage from Newburgh to Monticello, another 40 miles. Then, another 20 miles

The Delaware River flowing by trees near Barryville, fall 2008. Photo: Mary Briggs Austin.

answer as soon as possible.
Remain yours respectfully,
James Eldred, for the committee.

The decision was to accept the call, and Felix was ordained by the association September 30, 1832, at Providence Chapel, Thompson St. in the city of New York.

And so it was that Felix Kyte and his family moved to Lumberland, where he would be the pastor of a church of 50 people who met every Sabbath in a school house in Halfway Brook Village, in a "private conveyance" (his words), to the Village, by way of Forestburg, to the Eldred home.

Felix described his trip in his 1875 biography.

This way, through Newburgh and Monticello, was at that time, the only way of reaching Lumberland by public conveyance from New York, except that by steamboat up the North River to Rondout, and thence by slow travel of the canal to Barryville, taking nearly a week to reach there by that route from New York.

I found it a new country to me. All things in the way of lumbering were strange to me, but now being on the spot, Mr. Eldred or others accompanied me to such neighborhood as they deemed it advisable in which to hold services.

I spent four Sabbaths among them and held also some week day appointments in different places of the town and after the expiration of this time, I returned to the city and recommenced my school, leaving it with the church to decide in reference to any call. Thus the matter rested until the following letter was received.

*Lumberland, Sept. 18, 1832
Sir:
This will inform you that we have had a vote in church for to ask your services with us and wish to have them as soon as circumstances will anyway permit.*

We have circulated our subscription in our neighborhood and have so much subscribed as to give us some encouragement, but at Ten Mile River, the people almost to a man subscribed, but they are poor and their subscriptions are small, yet they seem very anxious to have you come.

We as a committee to wit, Alexander Carmichael, Daniel Wells, Sears Gardner, Justus Hickok, and myself have finally concluded to say we will ensure you two hundred dollars and find you a room for your family for your pastoral duties and sixteen dollars a month for teaching our school five days in a week.

We are ignorant of what would have been expected from us by you. All we could consistently do, as we have thought, is done and if the propositions are such as can not meet your mind, we hope that no offense will be given by our offer, and would wish to have an

Cholera

Partially because of the cholera epidemic in New York City in 1832, Felix Kyte and his family sought a new location and by the end of the year lived in Lumberland.

Cholera must also have spread to Lumberland as Almira Austin Hooker and her son died from Cholera in August of 1832.

Cholera, also called Asiatic Cholera, is caused by a bacteria. It is an infectious gastroenteritis transmitted to humans through contaminated food or water.

Cholera originally found in India, was spread by both land and sea trade routes to Russia, then Western Europe, and on to North America.

John Snow (1813–1858), a physician and self-trained scientist, found the link between cholera and contaminated drinking water in 1854.—http://en.wikipedia.org.

1832 Preventatives of Cholera!
Be Temperate in eating and drinking. Avoid Raw Vegetables and Unripe Fruit! Abstain from COLD WATER, when heated, and above all from Ardent Spirits, and if habit have rendered them indispensable, take much less than usual.—*1832 hand bill from the New York City Board of Health.*

Chapter 4: Reverend Felix Kyte, 1832–1835 • 33

four miles from the Delaware River.

Felix, his wife, Eliza Creiger Kyte, young sons Felix and Thomas, and adopted niece, Amanda Osborn, left New York City on October 6, 1832, and headed in a steamboat on the Hudson River for Rondout, about 90 miles away.

The family then traveled the Delaware and Hudson Canal on a canal boat. As the boat sailed the D&H, little Thomas Kyte called out the warning, "'B'idge ahead."

The family arrived at Barryville on October 11, and were met by Gardner Forgerson who kindly received them at his house.

The next day, Mr. Forgerson took the Kyte family in his wagon to the Village. Felix then went back to Barryville to get their furniture.

Eliza Kyte and her children stayed near the Eldred home in Halfway Brook. Eliza was left on her own because Hannah Eldred, was so busy she could not entertain.

Perhaps Hannah Eldred and her daughters, Maria, 16, and Mary Ann, 4, were preparing rooms where the Kyte family

Near where Mrs. Kyte "had a cry," Halfway Brook heads for Barryville after it flows from under a bridge on Old Brook Road. Photo: Cynthia Leavenworth Bellinger.

would stay. Hannah may also have been watching little Charles, 2, son of her stepdaughter Eliza Eldred Gardner, whose son Chauncey had died in August at 7 months.

Eliza Kyte, quite tired from all the travel, may have wondered what she had gotten herself into with the city so far away and a rugged wilderness all about her. But brave Mrs. Kyte, in hopes of meeting her husband bringing the furniture, started walking in that direction with her sons, calling for her husband.

Felix, some four miles away, did not hear his wife calling, of course. When her husband did not answer, Eliza Kyte did the most reasonable and stress reducing thing she could do. Eliza "sat down by the road and had a cry."

(The road was actually at that time a timbered swamp. Later it became Henry Lilly's field.)

Felix soon arrived with the furniture, and by the time Mr. and Mrs. Kyte arrived at the Eldred home, their rooms had been prepared in the upper part of the house, and Mrs. Kyte felt better. The Kyte family lived at the Eldred home until April 1833.

Felix Kyte taught at the district school at Halfway Brook Village during the week. He preached every other Sabbath at Ten Mile River, and walked 10 miles each way. He preached at Ten Mile River in the morning, at Beaver Brook in the afternoon, and at Halfway Brook where he lived, in the evening.

The homes in the area were quite scattered and there were no organized churches within 20 miles in either direction. So Felix

Highway scene near Kingston, New York. Rondout ("ron-doubt") mentioned by Felix Kyte, was a port on the Hudson River about a mile away from Kingston. "Rondout" comes from "Reduyt," the Dutch word for the English word, "Redoubt," which means fort.

The Flood in May, 1832

Halfway Brook as it leaves Eldred and heads towards the Delaware River. Photo: Cynthia Leavenworth Bellinger.

During the winter, large quantities of lumber from the Halfway Brook mills were drawn to Barryville, made into rafts, then taken to Handsome Eddy, two or three miles further down the river. There they waited for the spring freshets.

At Handsome Eddy, considered a safe place for rafts no matter what the water level, the rafts were combined into larger rafts—a double raft made of two single rafts lashed together, which was the usual, or a six-handed raft made of three rafts. The completed rafts were anchored and lashed together before they were launched into the Delaware River.

In early spring 1832, at least 2,000,000 board feet, and 20 to 25 double rafts of sawn lumber sat at Handsome Eddy, ready to float to market. The water level of the river remained low through the first week of May, which was unusual. Owners were anxious to get their rafts to market; the raftmen were uneasy about doing so in such low water. What to do?

Starting May 8, 1832, it rained violently day and night for three days and nights. The Delaware River, a raging flood, was covered with the valuable lumber and rafts which had been anchored in Handsome Eddy. Only David Quick's raft was saved because it was in a favorable position.

The "May flood," was the highest known until the flood of 1869 and one in 1895, which was 16 inches higher.—*from Johnston's Reminiscences, p. 276.*

was often called upon for funerals in the region. Since it disrupted his teaching, it became necessary to quit his school responsibilities.

Felix walked everywhere. After a year of walking to three churches, the people insisted that he should also travel to The River or Barryville and preach. Finally, a horse was donated to Felix.

A good brother, then a resident at Hagan Pond tendered me a horse that had become unfit, through age, for this business of lumbering. (For lumbering at that time was the sole business of the country, there being scarcely a farm, worthy of the name anywhere around.)

The donor of this horse remarked that he would take it out in preaching. Another friend supplemented the generous donation of the horse, by donating an ancient half-worn out wagon.

A four day meeting was planned for the area. The schoolhouse was too small, so the barn of Deacon Sears Gardner was temporarily used. A stand was made for a pulpit, and boards for seats.

Rev. Mr. Howell, of Wantage, pastor of the Minisink Church, and Rev. Cornelius Elting, were invited to attend and to assist Felix, which they did.

In later years, Felix's son, Joseph Kyte, told how well the people treated the minister's family. He remembered going to Mr. Covert's at South Lebanon (Glen Spey) where they feasted on what they supposed to be roast beef, but found it was bear meat.

In the spring of 1833, it was suggested that the Kyte family go down the Delaware River on a raft ride towards Trenton to reach New York City—free except for over night expenses.

No other means of travel existed for getting to the City from this place but by private conveyance to Monticello, 20 miles thence to Newburgh by stage and from there by steamboat to New York.—Felix Kyte.

The Kyte family left the Village on Monday. That evening it started to rain and a flood took out the bridges on Halfway Brook Road. Since the family could neither return home, nor start their raft venture with the river so high, they stayed at the home of Oliver Skinner at the mouth of Halfway Brook for a week.

Immense quantities of broken rafts and loose lumber was carried down the stream to the loss of lumbermen generally, but the height of water abating, we at last got started on a raft.

During our stay in the city, we learned that the canal (the Delaware and Hudson Canal, our intended way home) had received much damage by the flood and that we could not return by the same until the damages were repaired. Thus we were detained in the City much longer than it was our intention to be from home. At length, however, we got back.—Felix Kyte.

In Lumberland, James Eldred continued on as a church deacon, and was also Lumberland's Town Clerk from 1833 to 1837.

Stephen St. John, Benjamin Dodge, and Mr. Hartwell, wanted to start a lumbering establishment on land they had bought, and intended to ship logs on the D&H Canal.

The company needed a manager and superintendent at their Beaver Brook location, and hired James Eldred's son-in-law, James K. Gardner. James K. was experienced with lumbering, as well as the running, repairing, and managing sawmills, which he had probably learned from his father, Sears.

Around 1833, James K. Gardner sold his home (the first one as you entered the Village going north from Barryville), to his wife Eliza's brother, Charles C.P. Eldred. Then James K., his wife Eliza, and their children, Charles, 3, and baby Maria, moved to Beaver Brook.

Charles C.P. Eldred was a farmer and a lumber dealer. In his lifetime, like his father James, C.C.P. held several positions in local government, such as inspector of schools, overseer of highways, and town clerk.

Since C.C.P. was single, the Kyte family moved into his home (the former James K. Gardner home). Charles C.C.P. then boarded with the Kyte family in his own home.

In December, Francis Kyte was born. Mary Ann Cregier, Eliza Kyte's niece, came from the city to help her aunt (a rather important event for one Sears R. Gardner—Mary Ann's visit, that is).

In October of 1834, C.C.P. Eldred married Effa Caroline Van Tuyl, 19, daughter of Daniel and Rebecca Van Tuyl, at Handsome Eddy. The new couple needed C.C.P.'s whole home to live in, so the Kyte family moved again.

This time Felix and his family moved to a little house owned by Sears Gardner.

In early November 1834, Sears R. Gardner, son of Sears and Mary Keen Gardner, married Mary Ann Cregier, 17, Mrs. Kyte's niece.

At first, the Gardner newlyweds lived with Mr. Sears Gardner senior, and his wife Mary K., but there came a time when the younger Gardner couple, wanted the house the Kytes were in. Once more the Kyte family moved.

The 'new' house, owned by H. Lilly, was located at the southwestern edge of the village. The Kyte family lived there about a year and a half, including the year of the deep snow in 1836, when their son Joseph was born.

When the property changed hands in 1836, Felix purchased land from James Eldred that was in a different location. Eventually Felix received a deed for the land—*finally* a Kyte Family Homestead.

The congregation appreciated Felix's hard work and the decision

The Kyte family would have passed this section of Halfway Brook on their way to the Delaware River to take a raft ride to New York City. Photo: Cynthia Leavenworth Bellinger.

was made to build two church edifices.

So it was finally decided to build one church at the Village to belong wholly to the Congregational Church and that at Barryville to be held in partnership with the Episcopal Methodists.

They were both built by the same architect or rather mechanic for there was very little architecture about them. On being finished they were duly dedicated by appropriate services.—Felix Kyte, 1835.

Both the Barryville and Lumberland Congregational congregations had new buildings to meet in before the end of 1835.

The Barryville Congregational Church was completed first and had its dedication on September 17, 1835.

November 12, 1835, thirty-six years after its organization as the Narrow Falls Church, the Congregational Church at Halfway Brook was dedicated and called the First Congregational Church of Lumberland. Daniel Wells, Henry L. West, Richard West, Sears Gardner, Charles C.P. Eldred, Samuel C. Maney and James Eldred were the first trustees.

In March 1836, Felix Kyte was voted as their regular minister. In April, Daniel O. Skinner, age 90 (not the river rafter), was chosen Clerk of the church, and Justus Hickok was chosen Deacon.

How exciting to know that the Lumberland Church built in 1835—now the Congregational Church of Eldred—still stands.

James Eldred continued as trustee at the church, served as an assemblyman in the New York State Legislature from 1835 to 1836, and at some point, was Justice of the Peace.

You may remember, from a letter James Eldred wrote, that Rev. Stephen Sergeant left the Congregational Church in 1826 to go to a Presbyterian Church. Rev. Stephen, his wife Anna, and his family were in Lumberland in 1830, but seem to be in Pennsylvania in 1834 and 1835.

In 1834, Stephen and Anna's son Ethel Sergeant and his wife Letty Gardner had been married four years and lived in Yulan. Three of Ethel and Letty's sons, Alvah, 3, Isaac, a newborn, and James Gardner Sergeant, not yet born, play a part in this story.

Isaac would be the grandfather of Chuck Myers. James G. Sergeant would be mentioned in the Civil War letters. Three of the children of Alvah Sergeant and his wife Phebe Owen (age 1 in 1834), also play a part in this story.

Remember Phebe Hazen, the widow of Thomas W. Clark, and

The Kyte Family's Home

The Kyte family lived in several places before they finally owned their own home, shown in the upper left hand corner below.

The H. Lilly home is shown in the lower left hand corner.

Opposite the Congregational Church is the home where C.C.P. Eldred lived in 1867. That property at one time was owned by Sears and Mary K. Gardner.

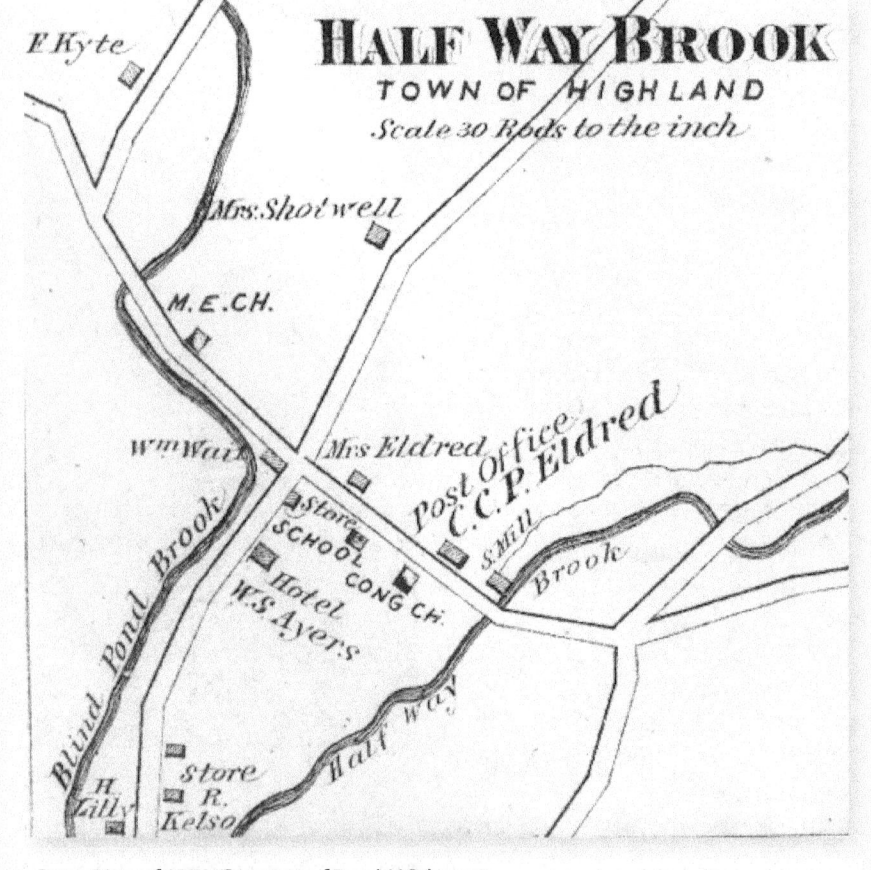

Beers Map of 1870. Courtesy of Frank V Schwarz.

Post card of the Congregational Church. The belfry was added in 1879. Courtesy of Mary Briggs Austin.

Church News

1832 Congregational Church New Members
Effie Van Tuyl.
5 new, 180 total.

1833 Congregational Church New Members
Daniel C. and Salome Skinner, Asa Middaugh.
4 new, 184 total.

1834 Congregational Church New Members
Mary Ann Creiger (Gardner), Augustus Alonzo Austin, Tjerck Ingram, Eliza Owen, Mary West, Mary A. Eldred (Austin).
17 new, 201 total.

Congregational Churches
The Congregational Church of Narrows Falls became the First Congregational Church of Lumberland in 1835, and they had a new building to meet in. The First Congregational Church of Barryville, also had a new place to meet.

The Congregational Church of Lumberland, which is still standing, cost $1,200 to build and seated 200 people. The Barryville Church, that Felix Kyte also pastored, cost $1,800 to build, and seated 150 people.

Methodist Episcopal Church
In 1835, the Methodists had a permanent minister in Barryville. Preacher Badgely had been a circuit rider on both sides of the Delaware River for two years, going as far as Port Jervis. Minister Badgely preached in Lumberland until 1846. Most of the preachers who followed him preached for one year. It would be 1859 before the Methodists had a church building of their own.

---

mother of George Case Clark? Phebe has been married to Moses Myers about four years. In two more years they would have a son Abel Sprague Myers, an ancestor of Chuck Myers just mentioned, as well as Gladys Myers Austin, mother of my Austin cousins.

A future resident of the area, Oliver Blizzard Hallock, the ninth child of Thomas and Julia Van Tuyl Hallock, was born in May, 1834, in Orange County, New York. Oliver Blizzard (isn't that a great name?) was an ancestor of Stella Clark, wife of Clinton Leavenworth, who would be a son of Garfield and Ella Sergeant Leavenworth.

Oliver B. Hallock was also an ancestor of Douglas Hallock (husband of Emily Knecht Hallock) and Carolyn Hallock Clark. Both Emily and Carolyn have helped with information and photos for this book.

The first clue regarding a main Austin family member in Lumberland comes from a Congregational Church record stating that Augustus Alonzo Austin (son of my great-great-grandparents, Ralph and Fanny Knapp Austin), joined the Congregational Church of Lumberland July 1834, and was baptized August 24, 1834.

When and why did Augustus move to Lumberland? Was it to visit his Uncle James Hooker, widower of Almira Austin Hooker, his aunt? Was it related to the lumber industry and the papermill his father Ralph Austin owned? In November of 1834, Felix Kyte commented that Augustus was a merchant.

Augustus Austin bought large tracts of timberland, in Sullivan County and was beloved by his woodsmen, according to Alonzo Eugene Austin, the grandson of Augustus Austin.

On November 13, 1834, Augustus Alonzo Austin, son of Ralph and Fanny Knapp Austin, married Phebe Maria Eldred, the daughter of James Eldred. Augustus was 24, and Maria was 18. Rev. Felix Kyte performed the wedding ceremony at the Eldred home. Justus Hickok and Sears Gardner of Lumberland were the witnesses.

Augustus's brother and my great-grandfather, William Henry

Austin, 10, lived in Westchester County. Maria's half sister, Mary Ann Eldred, my great-grandmother, was 7.

Mary Ann Eldred's half sister Sarah (Sally) Eldred may have lived with her children in Halfway Brook. Sarah's husband Zophar seems to have gotten into debt due to some bad land investment in Sullivan County.

Zophar worked for $30 dollars a day in Ohio in 1836. In a letter to Sarah's brother C.C.P., Zophar tried to persuade Sarah to move to Ohio with their children, Harrriet, 12, Lewis, 11, John Mulford, 7, Elimina, 4, Charles, 2, and baby Polly Maria Carmichael.

Apparently Sarah said no, as Zophar, Sarah, and children were in Orange County, in 1840.—*Eldred, Richard,* The Eldred Family, *pp. 31–33.*

In a later chapter we will read a letter that Mary Ann Eldred wrote to her parents, James and Hannah, when she visited her sister Sarah's family in Orange County, New York.

Mary Ann and Sarah's sister Eliza and her husband, James K. Gardner, lived in Beaver Brook with Charles, 6, Maria, 2, and baby Stephen St. John Gardner in the fall of 1835. Did James K. and Eliza name their new son after Stephen St. John, one of the partners in the Lumber Company where James K. was supervisor?

James K. Gardner's name is on two land deeds of Sherman B. Leavenworth. The 1864 deed said the land belonged to St. John and Dodge in 1841.

In the next chapter we meet Sherman B. Leavenworth, my great-great-grandfather, and his wife Charlotte Ingram, my great-great-grandmother. Sherman Buckley had been in Sullivan County since at least 1828, and was in Halfway Brook Village by 1834, according to the 1855 census and Sherman's obituary.

In 1835, Sherman B. and Charlotte Ingram Leavenworth had been married three years. Baby Harriet arrived in June.

Note: The Felix Kyte information came from two main sources: "The Kyte Narrative of 1875," *republished in 2000, by The Shohola RR and Historical Society (courtesy of Churck Myers); and my great Aunt Aida Austin's handwritten copy of Felix Kyte's biography (courtesy of Melva Austin Barney).*

Families Not in Lumberland in 1835

Martin David Myers
Martin D. Myers married Sarah Griffith in July 1836.

Van Pelt Family
Elizabeth Lazerlier Van Pelt 46, lived in New York City, and had been widowed 15 years. Her daughter Maria Anthony died in March, at the age of 22.

Elizabeth's son, Peter Van Pelt, was married to Sarah Looker. Their children were John Henry, 2, and baby Maria.

In October, Elizabeth's daughter Jane Ann, and her husband, Henry Cripps Webb, welcomed baby Charles Cripps Webb.

Elizabeth's mother Mary Webber Lazerlier Taylor was 71.

Austin Family
Ralph and Fanny Knapp Austin were in Westchester, with six children ages 1 to 23: Clara, Caroline, James H., William Henry, Ann Mary, and little Laura Austin. Laura would marry Mahlon Irvin Clark.

Samuel Knapp Austin married Susan Teed, daughter of Isaac and Phebe Golding Teed, in September.

Briggs & Crabtree Families
The Briggs family was still in Tell, Pennsylvania, and the Crabb Family still lived in New Brunswick.

Congregational Church of Eldred, July 2007. Photo: Gary Smith.

Chapter 5

The Mill on Blind Pond Brook
The Leavenworth Family, 1836 to 1849

Sherman B. Leavenworth was a small man but could handle a team of oxen like nobody could.—Garfield Leavenworth, grandson.

Lumber at Narrowsburg Lumber Co., a mile or so away from the original Leavenworth Homestead. Photo courtesy of Howard Barnes.

Five miles northwest of Halfway Brook Village was Beaver Brook (sometimes called Beaver Brook Mills), where James K. Gardner supervised a lumbering operation for St. John and Dodge. James K., his wife Eliza Eldred, and their three children lived in the area in 1836.

Between Beaver Brook Mills and Halfway Brook Village, was Blind Pond, which had a brook of the same name. A mile or so southeast of Blind Pond was a sawmill powered by Blind Pond Brook.

Visible from the sawmill was a bunkhouse built by a lumber company (perhaps the nearby St. John-Dodge operation), as living quarters for the lumberjacks that worked for them.

Sherman B., or Buckley, as Sherman Buckley Leavenworth was called, was one of those lumberjacks. Sherman B. had probably moved from Connecticut to Bethel, New York, with his Hurd relatives when he was about 20. Buckley and his wife Charlotte Ingram were in Halfway Brook Village at least by 1835.

Charlotte, according to the family story, was the cook for the lumberjacks who lived in the bunkhouse. That may indeed be the case, considering that several of Charlotte's granddaughters, including my grandmother Jennie Leavenworth Austin, were excellent cooks that could easily prepare large meals.

Charlotte Ingram, of Scottish ancestry, from Scotchtown, New York, was in Sullivan County by 1831. Where Charlotte and Buckley met are unknown, but they were married February 29, 1832.

In 1836, Buckley and Charlotte had a 1-year-old daughter, Harriet. Their first child born in January 1833, had died at two days old. I imagine that Harriet was good company for Charlotte while the men were out lumbering.

By 1840, Harriet Leavenworth, 5, had two new sisters. Sarah Jane was 3, and Amelia Ann was born in September. Possibly Charlotte's mother, grandmother Christine Hayes Ingram, lived with the family. The 1840 census indicated the family had an older woman living with them.

I remember hearing that Charlotte's sister lived with them for a while, so maybe it was her mother.—Linda Leavenworth Bohs.

The Lumbermen

No matter what job a lumberman had—woodchopper, sawyer, or teamster—lumbering was very demanding and often dangerous work.

In the early 1800s crosscut saws were scarce, expensive, and had to be imported from England. So trees were chopped down with axes. Men were so skilled at felling trees that they could drive a stake into the ground with the tree as it fell.

Pitsawing or whipsawing was used to make planks before the sawmill was available. It involved two men, a long saw with cross handles at each end, and a pit.

The most skilled man was the top sawyer who guided the saw along a chalk line. A second sawyer, called the pit man, held the other end of the saw in the pit below. *Pitman* was the name given to the wooden beam attached to the crank on the sawmill wheel. The sawmill did not entirely replace pit-sawing at first.

A May 11, 1872 article in The New York Times had this to say about the daily lives of the lumbermen:

The wood-chopper, with his axe on his shoulder and a piece of raw pork and dry bread in his pocket starts for the woods before daylight on Winter mornings, whether the day promises to be fair or foul. All day long he swings his ax in the forest, knee-deep, perhaps, in snow, and returns to his cabin at night to play the inevitable game of euchre with some companion, and then stretch himself on the floor before the fire-place, and take his night's rest.

The teamster is always en route for the woods before daylight, and has probably "snaked" into the mill a dozen noble logs, before a respectable breakfast time in town. The sawyer has his mill ripping and tearing away as soon as he can see…after a breakfast of bacon and buckwheat cakes.

Sources:
- Defenbaugh, James Elliott, *History of the Lumber Industry of America*, 1907.
- Fox, William Freeman, *A History of the Lumber Industry in the State of New York*, Sixth annual report of the New York Forest, Fish, and Game Commission, 1901.
- *The New York Times, The Lumber Trade: History of the business in New York and Pennsylvania*; Narrowsburg, N.Y., May 11, 1872.

The Bishop and the Bunce families listed in the 1840 Census of Lumberland, would play a part in the lives of Buckley and Charlotte, and their children.

The Hezekiah Bunce family from Connecticut settled north of the Leavenworths—east and a bit north of Blind Pond. Hezekiah Bunce, 59, and his sons Thomas, 29, Hezekiah Bunce Jr., 17, and George, 14, were the only ones listed in the 1840 census.

Perhaps Hezekiah Bunce and his older sons were building a home for the rest of the family—Julia (wife of Hezekiah), and children (ages 7 to 28), Lucy, Elizabeth, Julia, Mary Ellen, and William. The entire Bunce family seems to be in the area by 1841.

Mary Ellen Bunce, 12, would have a connection with the Eldred family, as we will read in the next chapter.

John Bishop and his family were last mentioned in 1830. John's wife Julia died in 1836, and he was left with the care of their sons, Oliver, 1, and Ichabod, 6.

It appears that John Bishop then married Sarah Ingram, Charlotte's sister. John and Sarah's son Stephen Bishop was born in 1840. Oliver was 5, and Ichabod was 10. There was also a young man under 20, living in the home as well as John's mother Anna Bishop, who was about 79.

This is Sherman Buckley about 1890. From Cynthia Leavenworth Bellinger.

Possibly Charlotte Ingram Leavenworth. Photo courtesy of Gisele Rouillon Leavenworth.

Leavenworth Family Information

Thomas Leavenworth, the common ancestor of all the Leavenworths in the United States, migrated from England and settled in Woodbury, Connecticut, between 1664 and 1680.

There was a record of a Thomas Leavenworth, quite possibly the same person as the one who immigrated to the U.S., that paid a hearth tax in the parish of St. Clare, Southwark, London, in 1664.

Elias Leavenworth wrote about Thomas Leavenworth in *A Genealogy of the Leavenworth Family in the United States*:

The commonly received opinion that the said Thomas came over soon after the restoration of Charles the second, a period when many dissenters and republicans found it both convenient and safe to leave their country to escape the dangers and persecution of those unhappy times.

It is quite probable, therefore, that the first Thomas brought with him from England the means of establishing himself comfortably here, on his arrival.

The surnames *Leuenot* and *Leouenot*, predecessors of the Leavenworth name, were written in the *Doomsday book*—a survey of all English landholders and their possessions implemented by William I of England, and recorded in 1086.

In 1627, there was the mention of the family name, *Levenoth*. By 1629, the current spelling of *Leavenworth* was found in London, England, and it was said that the spelling has not changed since then.

The meaning of Leavenworth

The Leavenworth family may have lived on the leven (flat area) by the Worth River, or in an area between the Leven and Worth Rivers.

Llyvngwert (local Welch) meant smooth, level farm, castle or court on the Worth or place on the river Leven.—Arthur, *Etymological Dictionary of Family and Christian Names*.

Worth (*Weorthing* in Anglo Saxon) is a place warded or protected, and also a name of a river in England.

The Leavenworths came from the area of the Leven and Worth Rivers.—Charlee Hirsch Schroedel, Leavenworth descendant.

Who were Sherman Buckley's parents?

There is no way to know for sure who Sherman B. Leavenworth's parents were, but Elias Leavenworth's, *A Genealogy of the Leavenworth Family in the United States,* p. 326, lists "disconnected" Leavenworth families that are of interest.

A John Leavenworth was mentioned as having a son named Sherman, a son-in-law named Truman Stiles, and grandchildren, Sherman Stiles and Harriet L. Stiles.

My ancestor, Sherman Buckley Leavenworth, had children named Harriet, Sherman Stiles, and John Leavenworth. Sherman B. also had a grandson named Truman. Perhaps this was the family of my great-great-grandfather Sherman B. Leavenworth.

John Leavenworth, was a miller, who lived at White Oak in the town of Southbury, Connecticut. John was also a near relative of Gideon and Ebenezer Leavenworth. During the American Revolution, John Leavenworth supplied the French troops with wheat, corn, butter, and pork as they passed through.

John Leavenworth had four daughters and a son, Sherman Leavenworth, who married an Esther Gunn.

There was a record of a Charlotte Gunn, born in 1781, who married a Sherman Leavenworth. Perhaps her name was Esther Charlotte Gunn.

There is a record that my cousin Cynthia obtained from the town of Middlebury in July, 2002. It was a copy of a December 1814 deed signed by a Sherman B. and Charlotte Leavenworth selling land in Middlebury, Connecticut, to Ransom Gunn for $20.

This Sherman B. Leavenworth could not be my great-great-grandfather, Sherman B. who also married a Charlotte. He was only 6 years old at the time. It would be interesting to know if Sherman B. and Charlotte Leavenworth of Middlebury, were my great-great-grandfather Sherman Buckley's parents, and therefore my great-great-great-grandparents.

According to the Elias Leavenworth Book, *Sherman or his son, William, or both, removed to Monticello, New York, and were back at Southbury in 1823, on a visit.*

I wrote in an earlier chapter that Monticello was near Bethel, New York, and the possibility of that being where my ancestor Sherman B. Leavenworth lived at one time.

The information on John Leavenworth and his descendants was from a Mrs. Loch who lived in Watertown, Connecticut, in 1871. Mrs. Loch was a daughter of Truman Stiles and his wife Lemira Leavenworth, daughter of John Leavenworth.

Elias Leavenworth (1803–1887), author of *The Leavenworth Family*, set up scholarships at Hamilton College in New York, and Yale, for male descendants with the Leavenworth name, in his 1887 will, which are still in place.

The Bunk House

Old photo of the Leavenworth home in the collection of Linda Leavenworth Bohs.

The early bunkhouses for lumbermen were small with dirt floors. Their later living quarters were usually in a larger building.

The ground floor contained a room for the cook (who could be a woman, as in the case of my great-great-grandmother Charlotte Ingram Leavenworth), and a dining room. Meals were served on long board tables, and the crew were only allowed in the room at meal time. A "men's room" was at the end of the room where the crew could relax, read, grind their axes, or tell stories in the evening.

A ladder went to the attic where there were tiers of bunks for sleeping. A one story log building was used as a barn for the horses and a storehouse for hay and oats.

In the above old photo of the Leavenworth home, the larger building on the right (which is no longer there) and the small one story building in front, seem to match the description of the loggers' living quarters mentioned in this sidebar.

When it was in use, the first floor of the larger building (on the right) was the family's summer kitchen and the upstairs was the servant quarters.—*Louise Austin Smith*.

Source: Fox, William Freeman, *A History of the Lumber Industry in the State of New York*, published in the *Sixth Annual Report* of the New York Forest, Fish, and Game Commission, 1901.

Blind Pond, source of Blind Pond Brook, 2009. Photo: Kelly Leavenworth.

The fall of 1842 was a very sad time for Buckley, Charlotte, and Harriet. Sarah Jane, 5, and Amelia Ann, 2, died eleven days a part.

Four months later, in February, to the relief of Buckley and Charlotte, a healthy baby boy was born—Sherman Stiles Leavenworth, my great-grandfather. Sherman's "big" sister Harriet was almost 8.

Almost two years later, in December of 1844, Atwell Bishop Leavenworth was born. His middle name was the same as his Uncle John's last name.

In January 1848, Hezekiah Bunce Leavenworth was born. He seems to have been named after their neighbor, Hezekiah Bunce.

Sometime before 1850, the Bishop family moved to Standing Stone, Pennsylvania, 110 miles northwest of Eldred. Uncle John, and cousins Stephen and Oliver, play a part in this story in about 23 years.

Sherman B. and Charlotte had yet another bouncing baby boy, John Ellis, born February 1851. And finally a little sister for Harriet. Julia Ann, was born March of 1855. Harriet was 20.

There is a story (told here by Linda Leavenworth Bohs and Cynthia Leavenworth Bellinger) in the Leavenworth family as to how Sherman B. Leavenworth acquired some of his land:

After working for some period of time, the Lumber Company lumbered all they could and then found that they weren't allowed, for some reason, to cross the Delaware River to cut more trees—possibly because across the Delaware was Pennsylvania—so they left.

The Lumber Company owed Sherman B. about six months of back wages and offered him a

Chapter 5: The Mill on Blind Pond Brook, 1836–1839

View of Echo Hill Farmhouse from Blind Pond Brook, spring 2009. Photo: Cynthia Leavenworth Bellinger.

Mill on Blind Pond Brook

Stone walls where the mill used to be.

Detail of stone walls.

The posts that at one time were vertical. Photos: Cynthia Leavenworth Bellinger.

The top two photos show where the old mill used to stand. The two stone walls were built to channel the water to the mill.

A sluice was created utilizing the large vertical posts placed vertically in the brook. Horizontal boards would be raised or lowered against the posts. In this way the flow of water to the waterwheel could be regulated.

choice—the land with the Echo Hill bunk house and mill or land on the flats in Sparrowbush along the Delaware River (on the way to Port Jervis)—later the Erie Railroad Station in Port Jervis.

Since he was going to farm, Sherman B. chose the land in Eldred, as he was afraid the Delaware River would flood the land in Sparrowbush.

He would have been a very rich man if he had chosen the Sparrowbush land and then sold it to the railroad later on.

Sherman B. had 265 acres according to the 1875 New York Census. His known original land deeds (which we will discuss in a few paragraphs) account for 206 acres. Was Sherman B. given 59 acres? In 1864, Sherman B. paid

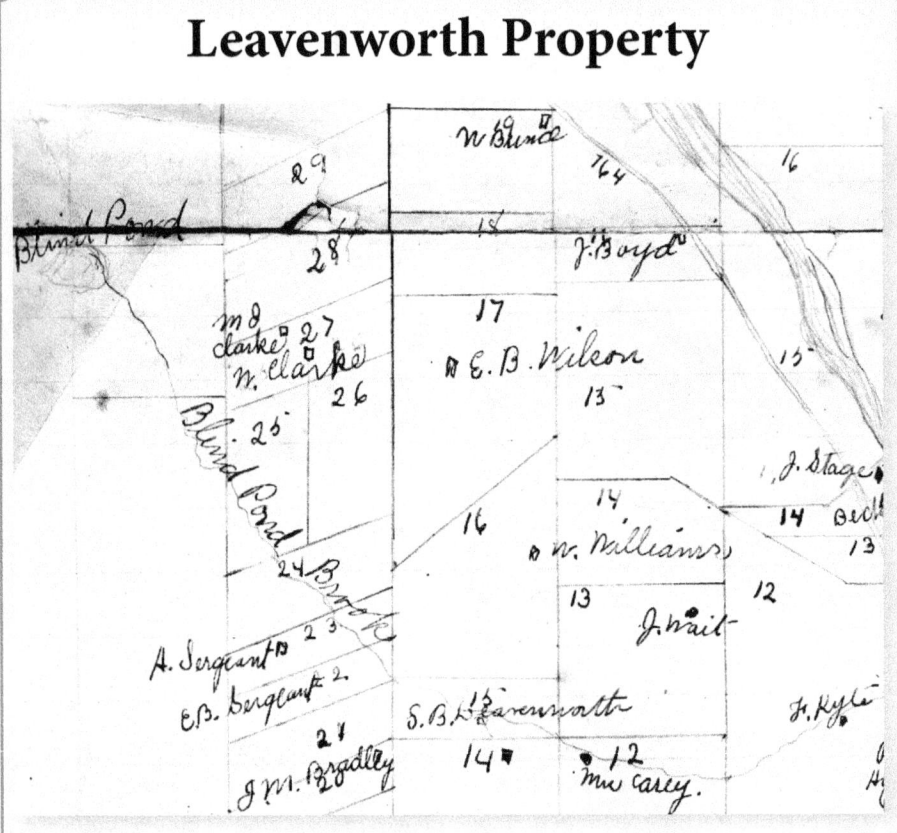

Leavenworth Property

Blind Pond: upper left. Notice where the Bunce, Clark, Sergeant, and Bradley families live. Felix Kyte's residence is also shown. This seems to be a copy of the Beers 1870 map that Aida Austin drew. Courtesy of Melva Austin Barney.

$150 for six acres with a mill. In 1841 the mill had been owned by James K. Gardner, Benjamin Dodge, and Stephen St. John. Perhaps St. John was the "etc." of the Dodge, Hartwell that Johnston mentioned in his *Reminiscences*.

It is a part of the 50 acres… sold by her [Johnston's mother] to Dodge, Hartwell etc. then manufacturing lumber on Halfway Brook, and designing to transport a part of their product by canal, bought this as a lumber dock. Soon after they abandoned the project and sold the property to the Canal Company.
—Johnston, p. 323.

Did the Dodge, (St. John), Hartwell Company also have land in the area of Sparrowbush/Port Jervis which it sold to the Canal Company who in turn sold the property to the railroad?

Buckley had quit lumbering and was farming, by the early 1850s. At some point Sherman B. had over 250 acres of land—what is now the entire Airport Road, to Aunt Anna's property. What is known today as Airport Road was called Leavenworth Road back then. As each new offspring grew up, they got a piece of the land.
—Linda Leavenworth Bohs.

Upon coming to Eldred (then known as Halfway Brook), he purchased a tract of land in the clearing of which he immediately engaged. He developed one of the most productive farms in that whole district which consists of about 150 acres.—Sherman B. Leavenworth's obituary, 1895.

Sherman B. Leavenworth's original land deeds were referred to in the 1893 land document of Sherman Stiles Leavenworth. The June 1851 deed, for 100 acres (4-1/2 miles from the berm of the Delaware and Hudson Canal) was conveyed from James K. and Eliza Gardner (and signed by them) to Sherman B. for $1,300. It mentioned *privileges for a sawmill*—six acres that still belonged to James K. and Eliza Gardner.

The six acres mentioned in the 1851 land deed were conveyed to Sherman B. in 1864, by John Conkling and others for $150. The 1875 deed conveyed 100 acres from Robert and Amanda Kelso for $500.

By the 1970s–80s, 75 of Sherman Buckley's 265 acres remained in the Leavenworth family.

The property the bunk house was on came to be called Echo Hill Farm, and the bunk house, Echo Hill Farm House. They will be featured in Book Two.

If you were to visit the old Leavenworth homestead today, you could see the remains of the sawmill on Blind Pond Brook where Sherman Buckley Leavenworth worked. An 1856 map shows the sawmill's location as right behind the Echo Hill house. The home is still visible from where the mill once stood.

It was in this house that Buckley and Charlotte's children, some grandchildren and some great-grandchildren were born. My grandmother, Jennie Leavenworth Austin, was born in the Leavenworth Homestead, as was her first child.

The Echo Hill Farm House still stands today. In 2007, thanks to Alice Willis, the owner at the time, my cousin Cynthia (our tour guide who grew up in Eldred), myself, and my husband Gary had the opportunity to go inside. We noticed that the floor boards that were visible were of varying widths, a characteristic of utilizing an entire tree as they often did in the early years.

When Kevin Marrinan, a friend of the Jim Leavenworth family, did some remodeling work at the Echo Hill Farm House, he discovered that the home was constructed with vertical planks 2-inches thick and as wide as 18-inches. This confirmed the record in the New York Census of 1855 stating that Sherman B. Leavenworth had a plank house. *Note: Special thanks to Cynthia Leavenworth Bellinger, Linda Leavenworth Bohs, and Kevin Marrinan, for much of the information here.*

We will hear more about the Leavenworth family in letters that Great-Grandpa Sherman S. wrote home during the Civil War. Sherman's two brothers, Atwell and Hezekiah, and cousins Oliver and Stephen Bishop also fought in the war.

After the Civil War, Sherman S. Leavenworth would marry Maria Louisa Myers (whose family had not yet arrived in town). Felix Kyte, who we read about in the last chapter, would perform the wedding ceremony of Sherman and Maria.

The newlyweds would live at Echo Hill Farm House (Book Two), and raise seven children, including my grandmother, Jennie Louisa Leavenworth. Jennie later would marry Charles Mortimer "Mort" Austin, son of William Henry and Mary Ann Eldred

Lumber Companies and Land Deeds of Sherman B. Leavenworth

Blind Pond Brook. Photo: Cynthia Leavenworth Bellinger.

Hardenburgh or Connecticut Valley Lumber Company?

Both the Hardenburgh Lumber Company and the Connecticut Valley Lumber Company are mentioned in family stories as the company Sherman Buckley Leavenworth worked for. Perhaps when Sherman B. came from Connecticut, it was with a Connecticut Lumber Company to work on Hardenburgh Patent land.

In the fall and winter of 1807–08, John De Witt, a large owner of Hardenburgh Patent lands, contracted with two men, one of them named Curtis Hurd, "to chop and clear one hundred acres on the flat a little south of Youngsville, for which he paid them 163 pounds, 19s. His death in April 1808 frustrated this plan."—*Child, Hamilton,* Gazeteer and Business Directory of Sullivan Co., N.Y., *1872–1873, p. 122.*

Curtis Hurd lumbered on Hardenburgh Patent lands in Youngsville, which was seven miles away from the Hurd Settlement. It may match up with the story that Sherman Buckley came with the Hurd family from Connecticut.

Leavenworth Deed Excerpts

Sherman B. Leavenworth's land deeds of 1851, 1864, and 1875 total 206 acres. Here are excerpts from the deeds of 1851 and 1864.

1851: Lot Number 18 in the 7th division of the Minisink Patent...20 links northeast of the brook below the sawmill now or formerly standing of the aforesaid lands of Stacy Beaks formerly owned by him—containing 100 acres of land as surveyed by Phineas Terry in November 1829—excepting and reserving therefrom a certain location made by David Hulse surveyor containing privileges for a sawmill and conveyed to James K. Garder November 2, 1841.

1864: Also, one other tract or parcel of land (containing six acres) situate in said Town of Highland—conveyed to said Sherman B. Leavenworth by John Conkling and others by deed dated the 29th day of February, 1864...it being the same land which Abraham Ingersoll and wife conveyed by deed bearing date the second day of December, 1841, to James K. Gardner, Benjamin Dodge and Stephen St. John recorded in Sullivan County, 25th May, 1842.

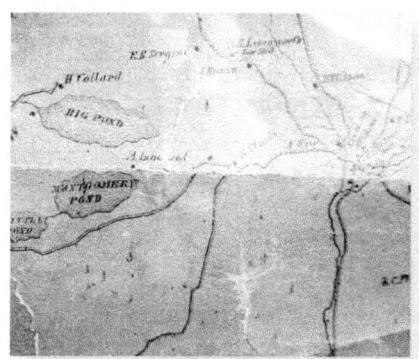

1856 Map showing mill on Leavenworth property. Courtesy of Kevin Marrinan.

Austin. But again, I am getting ahead of myself.

We will leave the Leavenworth family in 1855, with their six children, Harriet, 20, Sherman Stiles, 12, Atwell Bishop, 11, Hezekiah Bunce, 7, John Ellis, 4, and newborn Julia Ann (Annie), and go back to Halfway Brook Village, where in the year 1839, William Henry Austin, 15, and his parents Ralph and Fanny Knapp Austin, had recently arrived.

Ralph and Fanny's son Augustus Alonzo Austin, and his wife Phebe Maria Eldred had lived in the Village for five years and had a son Alonzo Eugene Austin, 2. Mortimer Bruce, second of their twelve children, would be born in December.

William Henry Austin's future wife, Mary Ann Eldred, was 12 years old, and lived with her parents James and Hannah Eldred.

Mary Ann's Grandfather Asa Hickok (Hannah's father) had died in 1836, and was buried in Cadis Cemetery, Cadis, Pennsylvania—over 100 miles northwest of the Village.

Mary Ann's Grandmother, Mary Hulse Eldred Forgeson (James Eldred's mother) had died in 1837. Grandmother Mary had probably lived with her son James, since he and his family arrived in Lumberland, late 1815.

In 1838, Mary Ann Eldred's brother-in-law, James K. Gardner was the Supervisor for Lumberland and her father, James Eldred, was the School Commissioner.

In 1838, Mary Ann's stepbrother, Abraham Mulford married Elizabeth Wheeler, who had moved to Lumberland with her parents when she was young.

Mulford lumbered and farmed his large tracts of land, and was also active in government as Constable, tax collector, and Overseer of Highways, District 8, in the Town of Lumberland from 1845–1846.

The Austin family settled on over 200 acres on the east side of the Village of Halfway Brook, next to Mary Ann Eldred's brother, C.C.P. and his wife, Effa Eldred.

Martin D. and Jane Ann Myers arrived in the early 1850s, and lived east of the Austin land.

The Leavenworth Bible

FAMILY RECORD.

BIRTHS.

S. B. Leavenworth Augᵗ 1, 1808.

Charlotte Ingram Janʸ 12, 1811.

First child Janʸ 26 1833.

Harriet Elizabeth June 17, 1835.

Sarah Jane Oct 10 1837.

Amelia Ann Sepᵗ 30, 1840.

Sherman Stiles Febʸ 14, 1843.

BIRTHS.

Atwell Bishop Dec 25ᵗʰ 1844

Hezekiah Bunce Jan 14ᵗʰ 1848

John Ellis Feb 23ʳᵈ 1851

Julia Ann March 22ⁿᵈ 1855

This is a page from the Sherman B. and Charlotte Leavenworth Bible. See Appendix, page 256, for more scans from the Leavenworth Bible. Special thanks to Ric Schroedel for sharing the Leavenworth Bible pages.

People of Lumberland 1836 to 1839

A number of new arrivals (some being babies) joined the residents of the Town of Lumberland from 1836 to 1839.

C.C.P. and Effa Eldred's first child, George Washington Eldred, was born at the beginning of the year. George W. would be a best friend of Sherman S. Leavenworth, who mentioned George Eldred in his Civil War letters.

George W. Eldred's cousin, Polly Maria Carmichael *(see p. 236)*, daughter of Zophar and Sarah Eldred Carmichael, was also born in 1836.

In March, 5-1/2-year-old Charles Gardner, son of James K. and Eliza Gardner, died in Beaver Brook. (Charles Gardner was also a cousin of George W. Eldred.)

The LaBarr family still lived in Beaver Brook. Gordon Ransom LaBarr was 15.

Job Rider, a foreman for the D&H Canal, arrived in Pond Eddy around 1836. Job lived in the lockhouse below the tow path, opposite Lock number 67.

Job Rider and his wife, Susan A. Van Tuyl (daughter of Daniel and Rebecca Van Tuyl), had four children, including Mary Alice who married Daniel Hallock, and Rebecca Jane who married James E. Gardner.

James E. Gardner, son of James K. and Eliza, was born in Beaver Brook, the year after Job Rider settled in Pond Eddy. When James E. grew up, he kept a store at Shohola, Pennsylvania.

Abel Sprague Myers son of Moses and Phebe Hazen Clark Myers, was also born in 1836. Phebe had married Moses Myers after her first husband Thomas W. Clark died, and had a son George Case Clark who plays a part in this story.

Little Abel S. Myers would have a grandson Chuck Myers, a friend of my parents. Abel's granddaughter Gladys Myers Austin, would be the mother of my Austin cousins, Melva, Joan, Margie, and Dawn Lee.

Three new Eldred cousins—two Gardner and one Austin—were born in 1837.

Cousin William H. Gardner was born to Sears R. and Maria Creiger Gardner, but died when he was 24 days old. James Gardner Sergeant, son of Ethel and Letty Gardner Sergeant, was born in July. Cousin Alonzo Eugene Austin was born to Uncle Augustus and Aunt Maria Eldred Austin, in August.

In August of 1838, a most unfortunate event happened to Rebecca Van Tuyl, wife of Daniel Van Tuyl, and mother of Effa Eldred and Susan Rider.

Aunt Becca, as she was called, rode out alone on horseback at eight in the morning, to be with her daughter, Susan Rider, whose baby was due soon.

Aunt Becca followed the towpath of the Delaware River canal east from Handsome Eddy to Pond Eddy where Job and Susan Rider lived—a six mile trip. Where the path curved to the left, away from the river, Mrs. V. had an unfortunate fall from the horse and died that afternoon. The Van Tuyls had been married almost 28 years and had eight children.
—*Johnston, pp. 197–8.*

By 1839, James K. and Eliza Gardner had five children, including the two youngest—Sarah Elizabeth and Caroline—born in Beaver Brook.

James K.'s youngest sister, Eliza Ann Gardner had married Isaac Young in 1835. In 1839, the Youngs seem to have two young children. Isaac and Eliza Ann would have a son, Coe Young, an ancestor of Louis Maudsley, also a friend of my parents.

Three more Eldred cousins were born in 1839. Cousin Polly Vanorsdol Eldred, daughter of C.C.P. and Effa Van Tuyl Eldred was born in May.

Cousin Mortimer Bruce Austin, son of Augustus and Maria Eldred Austin, joined his brother Alonzo Eugene.

Cousin Amelia Eldred, first child of Abraham and Elizabeth Eldred, was also born in 1939.

In 1839, my Myers ancestor, Martin D. Myers, lived in New Jersey, and was married to his first wife Sarah Griffith. Martin and Sarah's son, Benjamin, would be born in 1840. (My Austin cousins are related to two different Myers families.)

In New York City, Jane Ann Van Pelt Webb, and her first husband, Henry C. Webb, had two sons, Charles Cripps, 4, and John Henry, almost 2.

Jane Ann's mother, Elizabeth Lazerlier Van Pelt, was 50. Jane Ann's Grandmother, Mary Webber Lazerlier Taylor, was 75.

Jane Ann's brother Peter Van Pelt and his wife Sarah Looker had two children, John Henry and Maria.

Halfway Brook on its way to meet Blind Pond Brook south of Eldred. Photo: Cynthia Leavenworth Bellinger.

Early 19th Century Up and Down Sawmill

This unusual survivor of a water powered vertical saw with few changes was located in Chester County, Pennsylvania, and photographed in 1961. It is typical of the sawmills that were in Lumberland.

It is a water-powered vertical saw with a single blade and wooden log carriage set in a heavy wooden frame. The saw operated at 100–130 strokes per minute and the log advanced approximately two feet per minute. The saw was contained in a framed superstructure on a stone foundation built over a millrace. A wooden undershot waterwheel was housed in a shed on the side. Water was supplied by an adjacent stone dam.

The sawmill was dismantled and moved to the National Museum of History and Technology, Smithsonian Institution, Washington, D.C.

Overall view of sawmill.

Vertical saw can be seen above the wooden log carriage set.

Waterwheel with gear.

Interior view of sawmill.

Remains of concrete sluice.

Remains of water channelling walls. Photos: Library of Congress, Prints & Photographs Division, HABS, Reproduction number HABS PA,15-CHESP.V,1-6.

Chapter 6
The Bubbling Spring
The Austin Family, 1839–1850

Half a mile to the east of a small village, in one of the valleys, a road leading from the village, cuts through the middle of an old farm and midway across the farm, a few rods back from the road toward the north stands a one and a half story frame dwelling.

A little west of this, where the land begins to slope toward the southwest, a large spring sends forth a clear stream of water that ripples down through the meadows with the same sweet murmur of the long ago.—Aida Austin, granddaughter of Ralph and Fanny Austin.

What was once Austin property that faced Village Road. Photo: Cynthia Leavenworth Bellinger.

North of Halfway Brook Village, and a tad east, was a long, narrow 1-1/2 mile inkblot of a lake called Mill Pond. Thick forest clothed the shoreline and surrounding area of Mill Pond which was later named Stege's Pond.

Southeast of Mill Pond was Hagan Pond, a lake shaped like a hand missing two fingers. A streamlet spilled out of Hagan Pond's thumb, sputtered through low lying land and a tiny pond, then meandered west to meet Halfway Brook which rippled from the south end of Mill Pond.

The stream and brook went southwest past Sears Gardner's property and sawmill which would one day belong to C.C.P. Eldred. They went under the Village Road, waved hello as they passed James Eldred's original homestead, then hurried on to meet Blind Pond Brook.

Slightly east of where Halfway Brook flowed by Sears Gardner's property, the Village Road split. Hagan Pond Road on the left, went northeast to Hagan Pond. To the right, Village Road (now called Proctor), continued south through the town of Lumberland, then through South Lebanon (Glen Spey), and, depending on the road choice, went to Pond Eddy or Mongaup.

That split, or "Y" in the road, just east of the Village, formed two sides of the triangular-shaped Austin property, which eventually contained about 260 acres.

The delightful spring of water mentioned at the start of this chapter was on the Austin property and still active in the 1940s.

The old spring house had a little bubbling spring with shelter and stones to set things on. It was cool in warm weather, and there was always running water.
—*Joan Austin Geier.*

Augustus Austin, son of my great-great-grandparents Ralph and Fanny Knapp Austin, was in Lumberland at least by 1834. Most likely Augustus moved to Lumberland for lumber related work.

In July of 1834, Augustus

Corner of Highland Lake (Hagan Pond) Rd. (left) and Proctor (Village) Rd. (right)—the start of the triangle of what was once Austin property. Photo: Cynthia Leavenworth Bellinger.

Stege's Pond/Sidwell Lake; Hagan Pond/Highland Lake; former Austin property.

joined the Congregational Church. And in November, Augustus Austin married Phebe Maria Eldred—the baby who had been born to James and Polly Eldred in January 1816.

When William Henry Austin was fifteen, he moved with his parents, Ralph and Fanny Knapp Austin, to Halfway Brook Village from Westchester, New York. —Robert Austin, grandson of Henry Austin.

Great-Grandfather William Henry was fifteen in 1839. Ralph and Fanny Knapp Austin lived in Lumberland, probably on the property with the spring. Six of their children were in the area by 1840.

The families of the two older sons, Samuel Knapp and Augustus, were listed in the 1840 Census. Samuel K. Austin, the oldest, and his wife, Susan Teed, had two young sons. Augustus and Phebe Maria Austin also had two young sons, Alonzo Eugene and Mortimer (Mort) Bruce.

Ann Mary, 13, and Laura, 6, the youngest daughters of Ralph and Fanny, were listed as living with Fanny in the 1840 Census.

Ralph Austin, 56, and sons, James H., 19, and William Henry, 16, were not listed with Fanny and her daughters, but match up agewise to those listed in the household of Augustus Austin.

Ralph and Fanny's daughters Clara, 28, and Caroline, 22, were not in the 1840 Lumberland Census. Both girls may have been married—Clara to Edward Teed and Caroline to Mr. Newman—and stayed in Westchester.

At some point, there were two houses built on the Austin land. Perhaps Ralph and/or his older sons, Samuel Knapp and Augustus had first bought land, cleared it, and put up a home. Ralph, Fanny, and the younger children may have lived in that home when they arrived from Westchester. A second home could have been built later.

William Henry Austin's family, including my grandfather Charles Mortimer, would live in one of the homes.

Ralph and Fanny Austin seem to have moved permanently to Halfway Brook by 1840, but

Stege's Pond or Sidwell Lake, was first called Mill Pond. Mary Briggs Austin Collection.

there were Westchester County documents with both their names on as late as 1844.

In 1844, James Eldred, his wife Hannah, and daughter Mary Ann, 17, probably still lived on the land James had originally settled in 1815. The Eldred land was south and a bit west of the Austin property. By 1844, James Eldred owned extensive acreage, and at one time his pasture land was south of the Austin property.

Daniel Van Tuyl, who we read about earlier, died of typhoid fever in 1844. Daniel was the father of Effa Eldred, wife of C.C.P., and Susan Rider, wife of Job.

Daniel Van Tuyl's sister Julia Hallock, and her family, husband Thomas W. Hallock, and their children, including Oliver Blizzard, had been living in Lumberland for three years.

Oliver Blizzard (age 11 in 1845), was an ancestor of Stella Clark who would marry a great-grandson of Buckley Leavenworth. Oliver Blizzard's brother Daniel V. Hallock would marry Job Rider's daughter, Mary Alice.

Job Rider, who worked on the D&H Canal, died in March 1845, and left his wife Susan Van Tuyl Rider, with four children—Rebecca (who would marry James E. Gardner), Mary Alice (just mentioned), Augusta, and Fernando.

James E. Gardner, 8, lived with his parents, James K. and Eliza Gardner, and siblings—Maria, 12, Stephen St. John, 10, Sarah Elizabeth, 6, Ann Eliza, 1, and baby Horace (who died the next year). Twins Edward and Edwin and little Caroline had died young.

James K. Gardner's parents, Sears and Mary Keen Gardner, were in their early 70s, and lived in the Village.

In 1845, Lumberland was home to hunters, tanners, lumberjacks, timber rafters, canal related workers, as well as shoemakers, blacksmiths, wagonmakers, carpenters, and any other job necessary in a town. The D&H Canal had brought more people to the area, and by 1845,

Austin Ancestors

The name *Austin* comes from the Latin word *Augustinus,* and means great, venerable, royal, or renowned. Austin was a very common name during the Middle Ages in Western Europe.

It is believed that our family goes back to Richard Austin, a tailor of Bishopstocke, Hampshire County, England.

In May of 1638, the tailor Richard Austin, his wife Elizabeth, and their sons Richard, 6, and Anthony, 3, sailed from South Hampton, England, to the New World on the ship *Bevis*. Richard's sister, Annis Austin Littlefield, and her six children sailed with them.

Richard Austin and his family first settled in Charlestown, Massachusetts. Two months later at the age of 40, Richard died and left Elizabeth a widow with two young sons in a new land.

When my ancestor, little Anthony Austin was older, he married Esther Huggins. Anthony and Esther moved first to Rowley, Massachusetts. In 1674, the couple moved to Suffield, Connecticut. Anthony was Suffield's first Town Clerk, and served the town for 27 years. Anthony was also schoolmaster from 1696 to 1707.

Very soon after the settlement of the plantation, the school master was sent for, in the person of Anthony Austin. He was a very satisfactory teacher, and town clerk for many years.—Suffield, A Sketch, Connecticut Quarterly, *Vol.1, No. 1, Jan., Feb., and March, 1895.*

In the 1690s, there was a Massachusetts/Connecticut border dispute in the area where Anthony Sr. lived. Anthony was Town Clerk at the time. Two of his letters appealing for reason and right to try and resolve the disagreement are in the Appendix *(p. 240)*.

In 1708, Anthony Sr. died at age 72. Anthony Sr. and Esther Austin had seven children. I am related to Anthony Sr. through his son Anthony Austin Jr.

Anthony Austin Jr. married Abigail Holcomb. They had twelve children including twins Caleb and Joshua Austin Sr. *(See sidebar, p. 52, The Austins of Shickshinny Lose Their Land, for more information about Caleb and Joshua Sr.)*

Joshua Austin Sr. married Tryphena Hathaway (isn't that a great name?) and they had seven children: Joshua (my relative, born 1748), Tryphena, Ralph, Ruth, Elijah, Deborah and Shadrack.

Joshua Austin Jr. born 1748, was the father of my great-great-grandfather Ralph Austin.

The Anthony Austin line can be traced back to Tichfield, Hampshire, England, when Richard (Asten) Austin (Father of the Richard who sailed to America) was born in 1547–48.

It is of great interest to me that Jane Austen, a favorite authoress of mine, lived in Hampshire, as had my Austin ancestors.

Jane Austen, lived from 1775–1817, some years after the Richard Austin family left Hampshire, England for the New World.

summer boarders and sportsmen started to arrive.

Moses Myers, 35, and his wife Phebe Hazen Clark had been married 15 years, and possibly lived in Bethel, with their five children, including son Abel Sprague Myers, 9. Able Sprague's

The Austins of Shickshinny Lose Their Land

A story is told about several Austin men from Suffield, Connecticut, who settled in Shickshinny, Luzerne County, Pennsylvania, some ninety miles from Halfway Brook Village. Though not a story told in my family, these Austin men seem to be relatives of my ancestor Ralph Austin.

Joshua Austin (Sr.) was the grandfather of my Ralph Austin. Uncle Ralph Austin was the son of Joshua (Sr.), a brother of Joshua Austin (Jr.), and therefore an uncle to "my" Ralph Austin.

Joshua Austin (Jr.), the father of Ralph Austin, was not mentioned in the settling of Shickshinny. He seems to have stayed in Connecticut where his son, Ralph Austin, my great-great-grandfather was born in 1784.

In 1774, Joshua Austin (Sr.), his son Elijah Austin, and twin brother Caleb Austin, settled on land along the Susquehanna River in what became Shickshinny, Luzerne County, Pennsylvania. Uncle Ralph may have already been farming in the area. He also operated an inn there.

In 1769, an off-and-on bitter land ownership dispute (Pennamite-Yankee Wars) between the colonies of Pennsylvania and Connecticut began.

Each colony had a double claim to the same land. King Charles II of England had made overlapping land grants, first to Connecticut in 1662, and then to William Penn in 1681. Both the Susquehanna Land Company of Connecticut and William Penn's sons from Pennsylvania had purchased the same region from native tribes in the area.

The land dispute was not fully resolved until 1800, and would affect the Austin families.

It was January, 1774, when the Connecticut General Assembly created a new town in Litchfield County, Connecticut. The town—from the Delaware River to a line fifteen miles west of the Susquehanna River—was under the law and protection of the colony of Connecticut. That the town was in Pennsylvania's Susquehanna River Valley, two hundred miles west of Litchfield County, did not seem to be a problem.

Joshua Austin (Sr.), and his brother Caleb obtained half of the original right of the Susquehanna Land Company claim of Shickshinny. Joshua Austin (Sr.) surveyed the land within the years 1774 and 1775.

Joshua (Sr.) is said to have returned to Suffield, Connecticut, during the Revolutionary War, and in 1779, moved back to Shickshinny with his wife Tryphena Hatheway Austin, and their son, Shadrach, 9.

At the end of 1782, the Pennsylvania-Connecticut boundary dispute was settled in favor of Pennsylvania. But disagreements as to the land rights of the Connecticut settlers continued.

Joshua Austin (Sr.) was listed in the 1790 Census of Luzerne County, Pennsylvania, with two males, age 16 years and up—most likely Joshua and his son Shradack, 20.

There are records that Joshua Austin (Sr.) conveyed some 300 acres "at a place called Shickshinny, on the west bank of the Susquehanna River" to "my beloved son Elijah Austin," in 1790; and that Caleb Austin also conveyed land to his son, Gustavus. Caleb Austin died in 1792.

Many Connecticut settlers, including the Austins, ended up loosing their lands to Pennsylvanians. Uncle Ralph Austin's land went to a Matthew Hollenback. Uncle Ralph moved first to Ohio and eventually to Illinois, as did Elijah Austin.

Around 1800, Joshua Austin (Sr.) and his son Shadrach Austin petitioned the Commonwealth of Pennsylvania to retain the land they had lived on for twenty-six years. The petition was refused.

Instead, the land was granted to the Pennsylvanian, Jeremiah Thatcher, who had been granted the title in April 1784.

Mr. Thatcher, who died in 1802, willed that his land be sold to Shadrach Austin. Shadrach bought the property from the executors for $600. The land remained in Shadrach's family until 1924, when Sarah Elizabeth, his great-granddaughter sold the land.

Joshua Austin (Sr.), died in 1802, at the age of 82, and was buried in Shickshinny, Pennsylvania. His wife Trypehena died in Massachusetts in 1802, at a daughter's home.

Uncle Ralph lived in Shoal Creek, Illinois in 1825. Elijah Austin died in Paris, Illinois, in 1829. Shadrach Austin died in Muhlenburg, Pennsylvania, 6 miles from Shickshinny, in 1850.

Sources:
- Austin, Robert K., compiler, *Austins in Shickshinny, Luzerne County, Pennsylvania*, www.afaoa.org/search/Spring_2002_NewsletterA.pdf, p. 4.
- Bradsby, Henry C., ed., *History of Luzerne County, Pennsylvania, Vol. 1*, 1893.
- McGhan, Judith, *Genealogies of Connecticut Families*, 1988, pp. 62–64.
- *http://www.luzernecounty.org/living/history_of_luzerne_county.*

The Susquehanna and old canal at Shickshinny, Pennsylvania, c.1890. Photo: Library of Congress Prints and Photographs Division Washington, D.C., I.D.: det 4a07811, http://hdl.loc.gov/loc.pnp/det.4a07811.

future wife, Hannah Maria Van Schoick, 7, was the daughter of William Van Schoick and Huldah Bross who lived at Ten Mile River.

Phebe Hazen's son by her first marriage, George Case Clark, 20, was a sawmill lumberman. George Case Clark married 25-year-old Mercy Harding Brown, widow of Silas Brown.

Mercy's 3-year-old daughter, Joanna Brown, would marry Isaac Bradley. Joanna and Isaac Bradley would live close to the Leavenworth family and have seven children who play a part in this story.

The Leavenworths, Buckley and Charlotte, had three children: Harriet, 10, Sherman Stiles, 2, and Atwell Bishop, 1. (Little Sarah Jane and Amelia Ann, had died in 1842.)

Abraham Mulford Eldred and his wife Elizabeth had four children, Amelia, 5, Benjamin Franklin, 4, Josephine, 3, and Augusta Maria, 1. Uncle Mulford was Overseer of Highways for District 8 in 1845. Mulford seems to have been the co-owner of the Eldred/Gardner mill. Mulford sold his half of the mill lot, "The equal undivided half of a certain lot and sawmill and house, etc.," to his brother C.C.P.

Uncle Mulford had made a number of land transactions which would cause a problem when he died. There are copied records of land deeds and transactions between Abraham Mulford Eldred and Augustus Austin, on land west of the property where Buckley and Charlotte Leavenworth lived. Perhaps Mulford's family lived there.

Straight north of Buckley and Charlotte Leavenworth was the Bunce family—Hezekiah and Julia, and their children Thomas, Lucy, Elizabeth, Julia, Hezekiah Jr., George, Mary Ellen, and William. Thomas, George and Mary Ellen play a part in this book.

The two homes on the Austin property, probably taken in the early 1900s. The oldest home is on the left. The people are unknown. Photo: Mary Briggs Austin Collection.

It is not known if Charlotte Leavenworth's sister Sarah Ingram and her husband John Bishop still lived in the Village in 1845. By 1850, they lived in Pennsylvania.

Northwest of Buckley and Charlotte Leavenworth, lived Wilmot and Mary Van Auken Clark and their eight children. George Clark would marry Harriet Covert. Mahlon Irvin Clark would marry Laura Austin.

The Sergeant family lived west of the Leavenworths. Ethel Sergeant (son of Stephen and Anna Sergeant) and his wife, Letty Gardner (daughter of Sears and Mary Keen Gardner), had been married 17 years in 1845. Three of their sons, Alvah, 14, Isaac, 11, and James Gardner Sergeant, 8, play a part in this story.

Abraham and Sally Ingersoll had at least three maybe four daughters, and probably lived near the Leavenworths.

Alexander Carmichael had been a member of the Congregational Church since 1801. He and his wife Elizabeth, had six children, and lived north of the Austin land, on the north side of Hagan Pond Road. Augustus Austin made at least one joint land purchase with Alexander.

Felix Kyte, the Congregational minister, and his wife had at least eight children, mostly sons, in their household.

C.C.P. and Effa Eldred had four children: George Washington, Polly V., Rebecca (called Bec or Becca in the cousin letters) and baby Jane Eliza Eldred. Their son Lamont died in 1843, at 3 months.

At the Ralph and Fanny Austin household were their children:

Fanny Knapp

Knapp is the English word for *Cnoep*, a Saxon word which means a summit (knob) or hill top.

Great-Great-Grandmother Fanny Knapp was born in 1788, in Stamford, Connecticut, the same city her ancestors from England settled in 1641. Her parents were most likey Samuel and Naomi Palmer Knapp.

Fanny Knapp married Ralph Austin, December 31, 1806, in Greenwich, Connecticut. Their nine children were born in Westchester County, New York.

Fanny Knapp Austin was a tailoress. Two of Great-Great-Grandmother Austin's letters from Halfeway Brook are in Chapter 7.

Side view of the home of Ralph and Fanny Austin. Photo courtesy of Mary Briggs Austin.

Great-Great-Grandfather Ralph Austin. Photo: Mary Briggs Austin Collection.

William Henry, 21, Ann Mary, 18 (who married Perry Schoonover in June 1846), and Laura, 11. It is not known where their son James H. Austin lived.

Uncle Justus Hickok (Hannah Eldred's brother), and his wife, Aunt Polly, had David H., 22, William, 18, Ann Eliza, 15, Robert, 11, Mary, 10, Benjamin Merwin, 7, Galen, 3, and Charles, 1. Several of the Hickok children play a part in this story, including Ann Eliza's marriage mention in a letter in this chapter.

Hannah Eldred's and Justus Hickok's mother, Esther, died in Cadis, Pennsylvania, in April 1844, at the age of 84. Esther Hinman Hickok was buried in the cemetery in Cadis, beside her husband, Asa Hickok, who had died in 1836.

There are several letters from the 1840s in my mother Mary Briggs Austin's letter collection included in this chapter.

In 1845, James and Hannah Eldred's daughter Mary Ann was 18. The next two letters *(see the originals in Appendix, pp. 241–2)* indicate that Mary Ann sometimes stayed with her half sister Sarah Carmichel and her family, in Middletown, New York.

Sarah, her husband Zophar Carmichael, and eight of their children lived on a farm in Middletown, Orange County, New York. Mulford was 16, Lewis, 14, Elimina, 13, Charles, 11, Maria, 9, Emeline, 4, Sarah, 2, and Decatur was a baby. Harriet, the oldest daughter, was married to David Young.

This first letter was from Mary Ann Eldred, to her parents, James and Hannah Eldred.

Middletown, June 19, 1845
Mr. James Eldred, Lumberland
Dear Parents,
 Yours, dated June 13, came to hand June 15. I perused its contents with pleasure and I was happy indeed to hear from you both. I attend school every day regular when I am well.
 I have lost eight days on account of my being sick with the hives. I caught a bad cold and then was sick to my stomach. I purchased me a box of McAlister All-Healing Salve and think it has helped me.
 I am quite well at present and hope these few imperfect lines will find you enjoying the same blessings.

Ossining, New York

Ralph had a paper factory, possibly in Ossining, New York. Ralph didn't get along with anyone. He was stingy with money, and complained that all his dad's land was taken away.—Robert Austin, Ralph's great-grandson.

Robert Austin (my uncle Bob), recalled in a phone conversation with me that his great-grandfather Ralph Austin had lived in Ossining, New York—possibly where Ralph had a paper mill.

There was a bit of a laugh in Uncle Bob's voice when he mentioned that the town was originally called Sing Sing, but that the infamous prison of the same name gave the town a bad name. So the citizens changed the name to Ossining, in 1901.

The name Sing Sing came from the Sint Sincks of the Mohegan tribe. Sint Sinck means "stone upon stone" and referred to the extensive beds of limestone found in the southern part of the village.

In 1685, Frederick Philipse purchased land from the Sint Sincks. The Philipses were Loyalists during the Revolutionary War, so New York State imprisoned the head of the Manor and confiscated their lands in 1779. Many of the former tenants of the land bought their farms back from the state.

In the 1800s, Sing Sing was a busy port on the Hudson River. Farmers from across the northern part of the country brought their produce and livestock to Sing Sing to be shipped to New York City by sloop or steamboat.

Austin/Eldred Lands

C.C.P. Eldred's house where he had the post office in one room starting in 1851. The bridge over Halfway Brook is in the lower left. The Austin Land was to the right. Photo in collection of Mary Briggs Austin.

Halfway Brook between what was C.C.P. Eldred's property and what was the Austin property. Photo: Cynthia Leavenworth Bellinger.

In Chapter Two was an 1825/1826 map of James Eldred's 684+ acres of land. In cousin Melva's collection of Great Aunt Aida Austin's documents are a number of other copied land deeds.

Most of the conveyances showed a number of acres owned by James Eldred, his sons C.C.P. and Abraham Mulford Eldred, and son-in-law, Augustus Austin. Also mentioned were Alexander Carmichael, Sears Gardner, and Stephen Sergeant.

It would be interesting to know who first owned the large triangle of Austin land (eventually 260 acres) formed by Village, Hagan Pond, and Collins Roads.

It would seem that Augustus Austin who arrived in town in 1834, first owned Austin land there. A line on one page said, "A.A. Austin 1834," but there was no other information. Another entry read that Augustus bought 126 acres in 1844, of C.C.P. Eldred and/or Mulford in Lot 22.

Augustus Austin and his family moved to New York City after 1850.

In 1850, James Eldred sold 16 acres to his son-in-law, Henry Austin, brother of Augustus, also a son-in-law of James Eldred. In 1854, C.C.P. Eldred conveyed seven acres to his half sister and Henry's wife, Mary Ann Austin.

There is no record of when Henry Austin became owner of the Austin acreage, but the Beers 1870 and 1875 maps show W.H. Austin as owner of that triangle-shaped property, containing around 260 acres.

Henry and Mary Ann Austin lived on that Austin property and raised their children there. Henry, as we shall read, suffered a financial setback and could not keep his property. A grandson of Augustus bought the land, at least by 1900.

One map (the roads aren't quite right), of Aida Austin showed A.A. Austin as owner of the same land the 1870 map showed to be Henry's land.

Charles C.P. Eldred, had property west of the Austin Family, and west of Halfway Brook, but east and close to the Village.

James Eldred's original land seems to be south of his son, C.C.P. Eldred. In 1939, Aida commented on the original location of James Eldred's house:

George Crandall owns the place now and he and his wife live there. The post office erected on the east side of the house and connected with it by a doorway leading into the sitting room was torn down when the Crandalls remodeled the house some years ago.—Aida Austin, daughter of William Henry and Mary Ann Eldred Austin.

Aida's map showing the Crandall home, originally the James Eldred homestead. Courtesy of Melva Austin Barney.

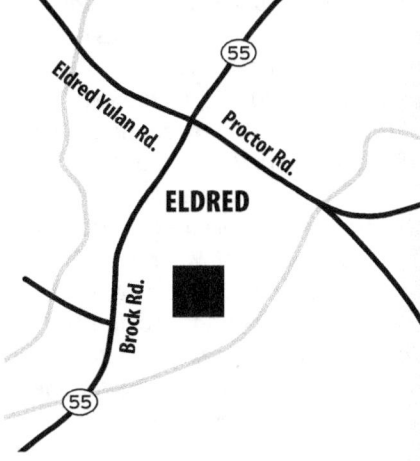

Current map with the approximate location of the James Eldred Homestead.

Letter addressed to James Eldred from daughter Mary Ann. Courtesy of Mary Briggs Austin.

1845 Land Mortgage Sale

In late 1845, James Eldred received a copy of a newspaper notice stating that his son Abraham Mulford Eldred and his wife Elizabeth had defaulted on their mortgage for several land parcels. What follows is an excerpt from that newspaper article.

Whereas Abraham M. Eldred of the town of Lumberland, and Elizabeth his wife, did by indenture of mortage on the 27th of May, in the year 1842, mortgage to Daniel Hilferty, of the town of Deerpark, recorded in Sullivan County Record of mortgages in book No. 8 on p. 240, 241, 242, 243, and 244, on the 11th day of July AD 1842, the sum of eleven hundred and two dollars and forty-six cents, principal and interest:

Notice is hereby given that default having been made in the payment of the monies, the said lots, pieces and parcels of land and premises will be sold at public auction on the sixth day of March 1846 at 11 o'clock at the hotel of Stephen Hamilton, in Monticello.

One of the lots was described as: *Comprehends or includes a certain Saw Mill and privilege of water on Half Way Brook, heretofore occupied by James Eldred, and a lot or parcel of land on which said Mill stands, etc., bounded southerly by a road adjoining the line of the land of James K. Gardner, across said brook up the same to a waste way or water course, from the head race of said mill along the same on the east, round and down on the west, so as to contain and include the privilege of the water for said mill, with the log-way and the roads to and from said mill, and adjoining the place of beginning, containing one acre of land, more or less.*

Another lot description: *One hundred acres lying on the north east end of five hundred and twelve acres of land purchased by the said William Anderson of George D. Wickham and John Duer, being in lot number 19, in the 7th division of the Minisink patent;*

And another lot description: *All that certain lot piece or parcel of land beginning at a corner in lot No. 22, twenty rods southeasterly at right angles of the north-east corner of a lot of land in lot No. 19, sold to William Anderson for James Eldred, and thence to the said corner, thence southwesterly to the corner of Stephen Sergeant's lot, thence at right angles across said lot to the line of 21, thence to the place of beginning, containing 475 acres, more or less, excepting and reserving out of this last described lot, a half an acre of land in No. 20 where the meeting house stands, and excepting and reserving about thirty acres, and also about two acres sold and conveyed to Dodge and St. John, according to their respective deeds of conveyance.*
Dated December 8, 1845
Daniel Hilferty, Mortgagee
Wm. B. Wright Attorney

Last Sunday I attended a meeting and heard a first rate sermon from first John 1:9. I enjoyed myself very well. I find the promises of God are true—whosoever calleth upon me in the name of the Father, him will I in no wise cast off.

There is a good library in this district. It consists mostly of religious books and books of science. I have two books on hand. One is a religious book and the other is the history of geology of New York. It is larger than your large Bible. It is a very instructive book indeed.

Sarah is quite well and all the rest of the family. Zophar has had to stop work a day or two for work got blockaded. Most all the hands had to stop work. Mulford is doing first rate.

Mother, if you have not made your dress you had better not make it until I come home. If Sarah comes home when there's vacation, I shall come home with her. I have got me a new bonnet. I sold Sarah my old one.

If I had me a school, I should like it much better, but however I will try and get along the best I can.

Give my love to all inquiring friends and especially to Mary Bunce and Eliza. If you see Ann Eliza, tell her to write to me and I will answer it.

Dear Parents, remember me in all your prayers and I will try to pray for myself. Not forgetting to thank you, I got my grammar before I borrowed many of Laura's. I could not wait any longer.

In June 1845, there was a ruinous fire in the woods near Ten Mile River. Large quantities of valuable timber were consumed as well as several saw mills. The principle sufferers were Hankin &

Chapter 6: The Bubbling Spring, 1839–1850 • 57

Bennett, Charles S. Woodward, Roberts & Barnes, and Dodge & St. John.—Quinlan, J.E., *History of Sullivan County*, p. 652.

This next letter *(see original in Appendix, p. 242)* was from Phebe Maria Eldred Austin in Lumberland. You may remember that Phebe Maria was the baby born in January 1816.

Uncle Augustus and Aunt Maria Austin had been married 12 years, and had five children— Alonzo Eugene Sr., 9, Mortimer Bruce, 7, Antoinette (Net), 6, Adelaide (Addie), 5, and little Miranda (Rand), 1.

Aunt Maria (Phebe Maria Austin) wrote this next letter to her half sister Mary Ann Eldred visiting their sister, Sarah Eldred Carmichael, in Middletown.

Lumberland, July 13, 1846
Dear Sister,

I have delayed writing longer than I intended, but these lines will inform that we are well at present and I hope they will find you the same.

There's been a freshet in the Halfway Brook. It has done much damage. There is not a bridge or dam left between here and Barryville. It has damaged us more than fifty dollars.

The Mongaup was very high. There was a young man drowned in that stream. It was James White and old Mrs. Skinner was buried last Thursday. Miss Margette West has been married.

Since you left, Perry [Schoonover] and Ann [newly married to Perry] are thinking of going to Mount Hope and Middletown in four weeks.

Miranda has been ill sometime with the canker and is very troublesome. I can hardly get time to write this miserable scribble.

Ann sends all the love I can get in this letter, but I must draw to close. You must give love to Sarah, Elimina, and all the children. Tell Sarah she must come and see us without fail.

You must write again soon and let me know if she has done up some cherry for me.

Father, Mother, and Charles are well. You must be a good girl and come home soon as you can. I want to see you very much. The children are all sleepy and make such a noise, I must say good night. From your affectionate sister,

P.M. Austin

Phebe Maria Eldred Austin, mentioned the death of Mary Skinner in her letter. Four months later, Mary's husband, Daniel Skinner who had been a Revolutionary soldier, and a clerk for the Congregational Church at age 90, died in November 1846, at the age of 100.

Abraham Mulford Eldred, husband of Elizabeth Wheeler, died in September 1847. He was not yet 41 and left behind five children. The oldest was 7.

In October, Jane Eliza Eldred almost 3, daughter of C.C.P. and Effa Eldred, died.

James and Eliza Gardner moved from Beaver Brook to Barryville in 1848, where James opened a general store and later operated a mill.

James K.'s parents, Sears and Mary Keen Gardner, then moved to Barryville and lived with James K. and Eliza and their family.

They were from Connecticut, good men and good mechanics… The structure is now quite large. This was the home of James K. Gardner and family from his

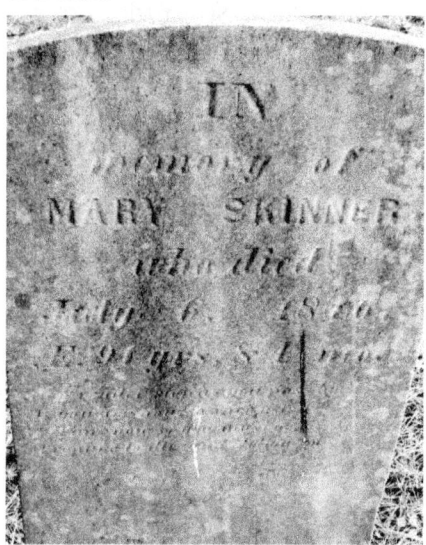

1845 newspaper advertisement for McAlister's all-healing Ointment that Mary Ann Eldred commented on in her 1845 letter.

Gravestone of "old Mrs. Skinner" who died on July 6, 1846 at age of 91 years, 4 months. Photo: Cynthia Leavenworth Bellinger.

entry as a resident of Barryville.
—Johnston, p. 335.

Zophar and Sarah Carmichael had a new daughter, Eliza, in July, 1848; and Uncle Augustus and Aunt Maria had a new daughter, Justina.

The stone reads, "In memory of Daniel Skinner who died at the age of 100 in 1846." Photo: Cynthia Leavenworth Bellinger.

Narrowsburgh, the narrowest, deepest part of the Delaware River, was called Homan's Eddy or Big Eddy, until 1840. On September 9, 1840, the Post Office in Big Eddy, Pennsylvania, closed, moved to Narrowsburgh, New York, across the river, and reopened.

The author of the first letter from Narrows Burgh may have been Lydia Wheeler. I have no other information about her.

Narrows Burgh, March, 1848
Miss Mary A. Eldred, Lumberland
My dear friend,

I thought I would spend a few moments this day noon in writing to my long cherished friend.

The scholars are playing outdoors and I am left alone in the schoolhouse. So my thoughts naturally run on home to home friends.

This is a beautiful day, and this is a very pleasant place. The school house is pleasantly situated a short distance from the river on a hill.

How I wish you and Hezekiah would come up here; it would just be a pleasant ride for you when it is good going. But the traveling is very bad at present.

I should like to go home and make a visit, but am afraid if I go now, I shall miss seeing the river break up. They say it is quite a curiosity to see the ice go through the eddy.

I like it here very much so far, and I like the people. I meet with some once-in-a-while that inquire all about Mr. Eldred and his family and some that used to be acquainted with my father.

I have just returned from a walk. It is another damp dark day. The lady that was with me gave an account of the Big Eddy bridge going off last spring and of a number of accidents that have happened.

Near the bank of the river where we were walking is a large hill which they roll their lumber down and has caused many accidents. It is called Peggy's Runway. It derived its name from an old woman who lived at the foot of the hill many years ago, when it was thick swamp. To go upon this hill and take a view you can see a great distance off, is delightful.

How I wish you were here. I think of going home on a raft as far as Barryville. There will be a number of rafts going from here and I wish you would come up to go down with me.

The lady with whom I am now boarding says if you come, I must certainly bring you here, for she would like to see you. She says she has nursed you when you were a babe. She used to be acquainted with Maria. Her name then was Betsy Johnson. It is now Mrs. Case.

I hope you will write me soon and tell me all the news you can think of, and don't you go to getting married before I see you, or without giving me an invitation to the wedding.

Let me know how you are getting along, and when you think of going to the City.

Where is Felix Kyte [Rev. Felix Kyte's son] now? I have not heard from him since I have been here. He did not know whether he should continue at Beaver Brook or not when I saw him last. I told him he had better take the school at the mouth of the Lackawax if he did not stay there.

P.S. Please direct your letter to Narrows Burgh, Sullivan Co., N.Y. The post office is across the river. We have to travel over a large new bridge to get there and people have to pay three cents for walking over, but I can go free—good says I.

Tell Mother I wish she would send me 5 dollars if she can. I forgot to tell her when I wrote her by Mr. Wiggins. Give my special love to her and your Mother.

Narrows Burgh, May 3, 1848
Miss Mary A. Eldred, Lumberland
My dear friend,

I have seated myself to inform you, of my success in gaining a school for you.

I saw Mr. John Dexter soon after I came up, and he asked me if I had found a teacher for them yet. I told him that I knew of two that were wishing to get a school. Having heard of a district about a mile or two from here destitute of a teacher, I inquired of him if they did not wish to get one there.

Mr. Dexter said he supposed they did and would speak to them about it. Having heard that a family by the name of Gale were acquainted with your father, I told Mr. Dexter they could get you there, thinking it would be pleasanter for you to go among your father's acquaintances even if they were strangers to you, supposing of course, I could get the other school for Eliza.

The Narrowsburg (contemporary spelling) Bridge completed in 1953. Photo: Cynthia Leavenworth Bellinger.

1845 and 1848 Letters

In my mother's wonderful eclectic collection of family treasures were letters from 1845 and 1848. The letters were folded into an envelope, and then addressed.—*Louise Austin Smith.*

You can not imagine how tickled I felt with anticipation of having my two old companions so near me that I might see them once in a while. The one I expected to get for Eliza is about two miles from here, and the other is between three and four miles.

I did not see Mr. Dexter again until yesterday and he requested me to write Miss Eldred to come as soon as you could conveniently for they were very busy at present and did not know how to spare time to go after you, and said he would rather pay your fare in the stage or your expenses any other way as they were so busy with their lumbering.

And he said that respecting the other school, they had concluded not to have a school there at present on account of some money matters.

I was very much disappointed for I was almost sure of that school for Eliza. I spoke to her you know about the school first before you had said anything to me about it.

Mr. Dexter desired me to tell you that you might come as far as Mr. Ross' the first night. He is one of the employers about half a mile up the river from Murry's, the tavern. It is on this side where he lives, but the tavern is on the other side. If you will write me as soon as you can conveniently and let me know what day you will come, I will meet you to Mr. Murry's.

There is to be a circus or show in Honesdale the 18th of this month. The greatest I suppose that ever was known there. How I should like to go, but I don't expect to. Do not let anyone see this. I must bid you good night.

LAW [Lydia A. Wheeler]

The next two letters mention the July 1848 wedding of Eliza Hickok, daughter of Uncle Justus, to Lewis Bolton.

Uncle Justus Hickok and Aunt Polly's children were ages 4 to 25 in 1848: David Hinman, Reeves W., Ann Eliza, Robert Land, Mary, Benjamin Merwin, and Charles.

Narrows Burgh, July 1, 1848
*Miss Mary A. Eldred, Lumberland
Ever Dear Mary,*

I was so in hopes you would get some way to come down today for I want to see you very much. Your mother talks of coming to see you the fourth and she wants me to go along. Perhaps I will. I was down to Eliza's a week today and staid all night. We went to the river to meeting on Sunday, but we went over to see Elmira on Saturday afternoon. It was quite dark when we crossed the river to go home, but Elmira and Mr. Fish went part of the way.

I suppose you have heard by this time that Eliza and Lewis were to have been married today. George has had an invitation ever since the first of April, but Eliza has backed out.

She told me the whole particular from the beginning

to the end. I hope she will never repent.

You wanted to know whether I had heard from Hez? I had a letter from him and Eliza last Saturday. He is coming home the 20th or the 25th to stay four days on a week at the longest. Then I am to go back with him and stay a spell.

I want to see you very much before I go for I may never see you again and I want to have a long talk with you. You know of course by this time that I am not married yet. I can't tell when I shall be. Hez sent his love to all inquiring friends.

It is supper time and I must bid you good by. My love to Lydia and all inquiring friends.

Write soon. From your affectionate friend, Mary Bunce

Photo labeled Mary Bunce. Melva Austin Barney Collection.

Narrows Burgh (possibly) August 8, 1848

Miss Mary A. Eldred, Lumberland
My dear friend,

I will now begin with or about Eliza's wedding which came off the Saturday following your exit from Lumberland or according to record, July 22, 1848.

It was getting late when I got there and she had not dressed yet. Eliza had been almost crying and said she was afraid I was not coming and believed she should not have been ready that night if I had not come.

Aunt Polly was in very good spirits, but Uncle Justus's face was half a yard long.

Eliza was up a few minutes and I went home with her and stayed all night. Lewis came up that night. I knew he was coming and I wanted to see him and get an introduction to him beforehand. I like him good, what acquaintance I have with him.

But I must tell you, when we were getting ready to go, Aunt Polly says to Lewis, nobody asks you to go to bed, I should think somebody might ask you to go to bed. Nobody says anything to you about going to bed at all. So much sport or laughter I have not enjoyed since.

There were not many to the wedding, but there were many wishes for you. Mary Bunce did not get there till after the knot was tied, but I suppose she has told you all about that, for probably she has written you.

I have not seen either Lewis or Eliza since the great event except when they went buzzing by in a carriage up to Mr. Bunce's to set up with Hezekiah who was taken sick soon after his arrival which was the same Saturday of the wedding.

Hezekiah was to have gone back last Fryday, to see about some trunks that had been taken back in the cars to the City, but his sickness prevented him. Mary was going with him, but as he was not able to go, he sent Mary on in the stage Friday and wrote to Foster to meet her.

You can not imagine how I want to see you. I have so much to tell you. But I must add another story here. Mrs. Kyte had a niece by the name of Emily Osborn who came up with Lucy.

Felix gave me an invitation to take a boat ride with them on the Hagan Pond which I accepted and on our return, he gave me a paper to read which William had sent him. It had a piece in it about a picnic party in New Hope which William had marked for him to read. There is one sentence in it that had the word auburn which he marked as being the color of his girl's (Miss Murray's) hair, Felix said. The sentence is this, "While pendant hung, the auburn curl from the lady's brow."

But I must not forget to tell you about the newcomer [Justina Maria] to Mrs. Maria Austin's that came to town one day last week Wednesday or Thursday. You must send us a name of the feminine gender and a pretty one too, for it is the prettiest you ever saw. Little Josephine Eldred [daughter of Mulford and Elizabeth Eldred], is very sick, do not expect her to live.

How is Mrs. Johnson up to the Eddy? I heard she was taken very low again. I hope you call and see her often as you can. Give my especial love to her.

I wish Mary, you would wear my cotton flannel skirt home with you when you come. Do not forget it. It is at Dexter's.

I am boarding to Nancy Austins. Old Mrs. Austin was

there. She found out I was writing a letter at the school house. She said if I was writing to Mary Ann, I must tell her that Old Mrs. Austin said she must take good care of Henry for he has gone up there somewhere to work. She believes that will be a match yet.

My respects to Louisa. Remember me, your ever affectionate friend,
Lydia Wheeler

There was happiness and double sadness for Ralph and Fanny Knapp Austin in 1849.

On January 9, 1849, my Austin great-grandparents were married. William Henry Austin, son of Ralph and Fanny Austin, married Mary Ann Eldred, the only child of James and Hannah Hickok Eldred. Rev. Felix Kyte performed the ceremony.

In June, Ralph and Fanny's daughter Caroline Austin Newman died before the age of 31. And in August, another daughter, Clara Austin Teed, died at the age of 37.

In March 1849, Sears Gardner, 75, died at the home of his son James K., where he had been living. J.W. Johnston remembers Sears Gardner in *Reminiscences*:

Sears was a good citizen, a kind generous neighbor and a decently honest man, whose fatality it seemed to be to live and die poor.—Johnston, p. 178.

Do you remember Mr. Forgerson who helped Felix Kyte and his family out in 1832? Mr. Forgerson sold all his land and interests in Barryville for $14,700 to Chauncey Thomas, James K. Gardner, and Elias Calkin, then moved to Goshen, New York. Chauncey sold his interest, leaving James K. Gardner and Calkin as the owners.

Erie Railroad

Erie Depot, Port Jervis, New York. Postcard from 1907, to Jennie Austin. Collection of Mary Briggs Austin.

The New York & Erie Railroad was first chartered in April of 1832. It was to be of a broad six-foot gauge and to run from Piermont, New York, through Port Jervis, and on to the shores of Lake Erie.

Work began on the Erie Railroad in 1838 and ten years later it reached Port Jervis.

The Railway was completed in 1851. The first passenger train passed through Port Jervis on May 14, 1851. President Millard Fillmore and Senator Daniel Webster were on board.

Daniel Webster sat in a rocking chair fastened to a flat car so as not to miss the scenery. The last spike ceremony was held near Cuba, New York.

In 1859, the railway name was changed to the Erie Railway.

Port Jervis, which was also a port on the Delaware and Hudson Canal, became the main engine terminal facility and the headquarters for the Delaware Division of the Erie Railroad. —*www.minisink.org.*

James K. ran the mercantile trade and Calkin managed the farm…The grist mill, sawmill, wharfage, etc…was done in joint interest. When they died, their sons, Stephen St. J. Gardner and Oliver Calkin became the owners.—Johnston, pp. 321–322.

Both Narrowsburg and Tusten prospered and grew from the 1850s to late 1800s. Tusten's economy was tied heavily to the lumbering and later stone quarrying businesses. At its fullest development, Tusten had a sawmill, a grist mill, two stores owned by the Crawford and Hankins families, a tavern, a school, and a Baptist church.

A cable ferry and stone docks delivered goods across the river and back from the railroad. Tusten even had its own Post Office located in the Hankins Store on Crawford Road [which] also served as a stopping place for raftsmen up until the 1880s.
—Hawker, Arthur J., Town of Tusten History.

In 1850, the population of the town of Lumberland was 2,635. The few census records reviewed

Hotel Arlington in Narrowsburg. Postcard courtesy of Mary Briggs Austin.

Beginning at S.E. corner of Benjamin C. Austin's shop lot on East side of Halfway Brook...to line between 21 and 22...across said lot 21 to the W. bank of Halfway Brook, thence down the same to the N.E. corner of said... Austin's shop lot thence along his line to the place of beginning. Containing 16 acres.

The boundaries given in surveyorese looks to me as though Henry's property was near or in the actual village center, starting at the shop of Benjamin C. Austin.—Melva Austin Barney.

for this book show the people in the area as lumbermen, teamsters, farmers, carpenters, milliners, and tailors/tailoresses.

The Lilly family had sixteen people ranging in age from 11-month-old Melissa to 96-year-old Margaret, living in two houses. Their occupations included a farmer, two teamsters, and a lumberman.

Benjamin C. Austin was a wagonmaker, mechanic, and blacksmith, with property worth $1,200. (It's unknown if he was related to my Austin family.) Records state that in 1840, Mary Gardner, Benjamin's first wife, died. In 1850, Ben C. married Sarah Tone. Ben's children were Martin Van Buren Austin, Mary Austin, Ira McBride Austin, Sarah Austin, and Harriet Austin.

Henry Palmer, a blacksmith, from Orange County, boarded with Benjamin C. and Sarah Austin. Quite likely, Henry was apprenticing with Ben C. Henry Palmer plays a part in this story.

George Clark, son of Wilmot and Mary Clark, married Harriet Covert, the daughter of William Covert and Anna Ryder, in 1850.

Mary Henrietta Austin, the first child of Henry and Mary Ann Eldred Austin, was born in February of 1850, according to the 1850 Census taken in July.

Great-Grandpa Henry Austin and his brother Augustus were farmers. Henry had at least 16 acres. He bought the land in the spring of 1850 from his father-in-law, James Eldred, for $200. The land was next to Ben C. Austin's blacksmith and wagon shop. J.W. Johnston, Justice, signed the deed September 16, 1850.

Sears Gardner marker. Photo: Cynthia Leavenworth Bellinger.

Augustus Austin had been buying land for some time and by 1850 seemed to have had quite a bit of acreage which was worth $3,000.

Elizabeth Carmichael, wife of Alexander Carmichael, died July 4, 1850, at the age of 67. Alexander Carmichael had been a deacon in the Congregational Church.

By 1850, James Eldred, 72, had about 35 grandchildren. James, also a deacon in the Congregational Church, was listed as a farmer in the census, which said that granddaughter Harriet Eldred lived in his home.

Harriet Eldred, 4, was also listed as living with her siblings, Amelia, 11, Benjamin Franklin, 10, Josephine, 8, Augusta Maria, 6, Mary Eliza, 3, and her mother Elizabeth Wheeler Eldred, widow of Uncle Abraham Mulford Eldred.

Uncle Mulford had died in 1847 without a will. Since his personal property was not enough to pay his $973.96 debt, a sale was held in December 1849. James Eldred, Mulford's father, bid $95 and received a deed for the 123 acres in February 1850.

James Eldred's property in

Roebling Aqueduct: Build the Canal Above the River

Roebling Aqueduct showing the piers and suspension cables.

Roebling Aqueduct shown in use for canal traffic. The house on the far end is in New York. Photos: Library of Congress, Prints & Photographs Division, HABS, Reproduction number HAER PA,52-LACK,1-20, 24, 37.

Roebling's Delaware Aqueduct is the oldest existing wire suspension bridge in the United States. It runs 535 feet from Minisink Ford, New York, to Lackawaxen, Pennsylvania. It is also known as the Delaware Aqueduct, or Roebling Bridge. Begun in 1847 as one of four suspension aqueducts on the Delaware and Hudson Canal (D&H), it was designed by and built under the supervision of John A. Roebling, who would design the Brooklyn Bridge twenty years later.

The Delaware and Hudson Canal and Gravity Railroad was a system of transportation between coal fields of northeastern Pennsylvania and markets on the Hudson River that operated from 1828 until 1898, with enlargements after the 1840s.

Two important local industries with conflicting needs brought about construction of Roebling's Delaware and Lackawaxen Aqueducts: canal traffic and timber rafting. Since the mid-1700s, timber from the Delaware valley had been floated down the Delaware to shipyards and industries in Trenton and Philadelphia.

The D&H Canal operated a rope ferry crossing of the Delaware at Lackawaxen but it created a major bottleneck before the aqueduct was built, as there were numerous collisions with timber rafts headed downstream. In 1847, to alleviate both problems, the D&H Canal Company approved Russel F. Lord's plan to substitute two new aqueducts in place of the rope ferry.

After evaluating several options, Lord recommended designs submitted by John A. Roebling who had already built a wire suspension aqueduct at Pittsburgh in 1845. Roebling's suspension designs allowed adequate space for the passage of ice floes and river traffic. An immediate success, the $41,750 Delaware Aqueduct and the $18,650 Lackawaxen Aqueduct (only the abutments remain) reduced canal travel time by one full day, saving thousands of dollars annually.

Almost all of the Delaware Aqueduct's existing ironwork—cables, saddles, and suspenders—are the same materials installed when the structure was built. The two suspension cables are made of wrought iron strands, spun on site under the direction of John Roebling in 1847. Each 8-1/2-inch diameter suspension cable carries 2,150 wires bunched into seven strands.

Sources: http://en.wikipedia.org/wiki/Roebling's_Delaware_Aqueduct, http://www.nps.gov/upde/historyculture/roeblingbridge.htm, and www.upperdelawarescenicbyway.org.

Austin crazy quilt pillow coverlet. Louise Austin Smith Collection.

1850 was valued at $1,500 and C.C.P. Eldred's property was valued at $2,000.

C.C.P. Eldred and Effa's son James Daniel Eldred (whose 1870s letters we read later), was almost 1 year old. Big brother George W., who we hear more about later, was 14, and sisters Polly, Becca, and Maria Adeline, were 11, 8, and 3. Peter Schoonover, 60, the father of Perry Schoonover who had married Ann Mary Austin in 1846, also lived with C.C.P. Eldred and Effa Eldred.

In September of 1851, Charles C.P. Eldred was appointed to be postmaster. The Lumberland Post Office was switched from one room in the James Eldred home, to one room in the home of C.C.P. Eldred, James's son. James Eldred had been Postmaster for almost 20 years.

C.C.P. Eldred's home was across from the Congregational Church, west of Halfway Brook.

Around 1851, Mary Ann Austin's friend Mary Bunce (now married to Lewis Carmichael), wrote her a letter that was in my mother's collection of old letters.

Lewis Carmichael was the son of Zophar and Sarah Eldred Carmichael. Since Sarah was Mary Ann Austin's half sister, Lewis was Mary Ann's nephew.

Lewis Carmichael had begun railroading on the Delaware and Hudson Canal Railroad when he was 15, and had risen to the position of Assistant Superintendent. Lewis Carmichael married Mary Bunce in 1848. In 1850, Lewis and Mary Bunce Carmichael lived with his parents, Zophar and Sarah, in Orange County, New York.

Lewis and Mary Carmichael's daughter, Mary Ella was born in 1851, the same year they moved to Indiana. By 1854, the Lewis Carmichael family had moved to Iowa, as did some other Bunce and Carmichael families.

Lewis Carmichael built a large portion of the Michigan Southern Railroad. We read a bit more about Lewis and Mary in a later chapter.—*Courtesy of Marnette Hart Click, descendant of Lewis and Mary Bunce Carmichael.*

West Point, New York, July 10, early 1850s
*Mrs. Mary A. Austin, Lumberland
Ever Dear Mary,*

It is with pleasure I once more seat myself to answer your letter. Lewis tells me sometimes that he shant let me go home in three years. I never want to see another railroad much less live on another.

The weather is so warm it seems sometimes as though I must die. It is very sickly here. I have got one sick man to take care of. He has been sick one week tomorrow. The doctor has been here today to see him, but he is feeling better. He boards with us. His name is Matthew More, cousin to Lewis.

And yesterday, my girl was sick abed. I was afraid that we were all going to be sick together.

Oh how I do want to see you Mary. I shall have to come about the time you know when that is.

I wonder how all the folks are in Lumberland. The next time you write to me, you will please write a longer letter and tell me all the news there is agoing.

How I do wish that Polly Maria [Lewis Carmichael's sister] would come and stay with us as long as we stay here. And now I will close. Give my love to all inquiring friends and write soon.

From your sincere and affectionate friend,
Mary E. Carmichael

Sometime after 1850, Uncle Augustus, Aunt Maria, and their children (ages 2–13): Alonzo Eugene, Mortimer Bruce, Net, Addie, Rand, Edward, and Justina, (baby Joshua was not in the 1850 Census), moved to New York City.

Martin D. Myers & Jane Ann Van Pelt

The year 1840 was a very sad time for Jane Ann Van Pelt Webb, who would one day be the mother of Maria Louisa Myers, future wife of Sherman S. Leavenworth, son of Sherman B. Leavenworth.

Jane Ann and her husband Henry Cripps Webb had visited England where Henry had been born. But Jane Ann, very homesick, had sailed back to the States early. There she awaited her husband's arrival. But Henry never sailed back as he died in England on March 3, 1840, at age 32.

Four months and two days later, in July of 1840, Jane Ann and Henry Webb's 2-1/2-year-old son, John Henry Webb died. That left Jane with her 5-year-old, Charles Cripps Webb.

The year 1841 was a difficult one for Martin David Myers, son of David and Elizabeth Myer of Bergen County, New Jersey. Both Sarah Griffith, Martin's wife of 4-1/2 years, and their young daughter Elizabeth died in 1841. Martin was left with Benjamin, his son that was not yet 2 years old.

In September of 1843, Jane Ann's grandmother, Mary Webber Lazerlier Taylor died. You may remember that Grandmother Mary's son, George Washington Taylor, was a half brother to Jane Ann's mother, Elizabeth Lazerlier Van Pelt.

In April of 1845, five years after Henry Webb's death, and four years after Sarah Myers's death, Jane Ann Van Pelt Webb and Martin David Myers, both 29, were married at the Brooklyn Madison Dutch Reformed Church on Franklin Street, in Brooklyn.

The following February, their son, George Washington Taylor Myers, was born there in New York City. It would seem that baby George was named for Jane Ann's Uncle George Washington Taylor.

George W. T. Myers's brother, David William Myers, was born the end of July 1848. But David died March 21, 1850 at age 1-1/2. ❧

In August 1854, seven acres of land were transferred to Mary Ann Austin from her brother, C.C.P. The acreage in Lot 21, seems to be south of town near where Blind Pond Brook and Halfway Brook joined. The transaction was signed by James K. Gardner, Mary Ann's brother-in-law.

Beginning at a stake standing at the SE side of a small brook (Blind Pond Brook) in what is called the middle of said lot 21 running thence etc...to the corner at the end of an old dam across said brook (Halfway Brook) thence...to a large white pine stump on west of Halfway Brook and on the side of an old road...

I suspect that by 1855, Uncle Augustus had a truck carting business in New York City with James H. Austin, his brother.

The 1858 letter of James H. Austin in the next chapter, indicates that he and Augustus taught their brother Henry 'the ropes' of carting.

In the 1860s we will start reading the Eldred-Austin cousin letters that the girls wrote back and forth. The Austin families often traveled between New York City and Halfway Brook Village. The city cousins spent summers in Halfway Brook Village for many years. And it seems, the country cousins often spent the winters in New York City.

Gravestone for Elizabeth Carmichael. Photo: Cynthia Leavenworth Bellinger.

Church News

New Members of Lumberland Congregational Church

1838
Felix and Eliza Kyte.
16 new, 221 total.

1839
Harriet H. Carmichael Young.
5 new, 226 total.

1840
Mary Myers, James Austin, Moses Myers, William and Mary Mapes, Julia Bunce, Garrett Hazen.
14 new, 240 total.

1841
Mary A. Eldred, 4 new, 244 total.

1842
Alexander Boyd, Catharine Dodge.
8 new, 252 total.

1843
Ethel B., Letty Sergeant.

1844
Elizabeth Eldred.
7 new, 264 total.

1850
George W. Eldred, Edward Wilson.
5 new, 280 total.

Deacons in the Congregational church
1849 to 1860 Sears R. Gardner
1849 to 1890 Charles C.P. Eldred
Charles C.P. Eldred was very active in the work of the church and served as a deacon from 1849 until his death in 1890.

Methodist Episcopal Church
About 1850, S. B. Leavenworth converted to the Methodist Episcopal Church.

But for now, we will go back to 1851. Henry Austin farmed and lived in Halfway Brook Village with his wife Mary Ann, daughter Henrietta, and new baby, Edith Emogene, who plays a major role in the rest of this book.

There was talk in the town of splitting Lumberland. There were strong feelings on both sides.

Martin D. and Jane Ann Van Pelt Myers (my great-great-grandparents), and their children, would arrive soon in the Town of Lumberland. The Myers family from New York City, settled near the intersection of Collins Road and Hagan Pond Road. They would be country neighbors to Henry and Mary Ann Austin and their daughters.

Silver platter with inset detail of the initials "MA," for Mary Austin, Henry Austin's wife. Courtesy of Mary Briggs Austin.

Chapter 7
Near Hagan Pond
Myers, Van Pelts, and Lazerliers, 1851 to 1860

The Webbers came to America for freedom of government and the Lazerliers for freedom of religion. They were among the Huguenots. The Van Pelts came through a sense of roving.—Jane Ann Van Pelt Myers Family History.

The home of Martin D. and Jane Ann Van Pelt Webb Myers near Hagan Pond. Photo courtesy of Mary Briggs Austin.

It was 1852 when Martin David Myers, his wife Jane Ann Van Pelt Webb and their three sons arrived in the Town of Lumberland.

The Martin D. Myers family settled east of the Austin property, underneath Hagan Pond's thumb, but on the south side of Hagan Pond Road, close to Collins Road.

Martin D. and Jane Ann each had a child from their first marriages. Jane Ann's son, Charles Cripps Webb, was 17, and Martin's son, Benjamin Myers, was 13. Martin and Jane Ann's son, George Washington Taylor Myers, was 6.

In New York City, Martin D. had been a carpenter and Charles a clerk. Now Martin would farm, though it's quite possible he would continue with his carpentry. Their home, built in the early 1850s, would become one of the boarding houses in the area.

Jane Ann's mother, Elizabeth Lazerlier Van Pelt, moved with the Myers family either at this time, or six years later when her son Peter died.

Martin and Jane Ann's country neighbors, Henry and Mary Ann Austin, had two little girls: Mary Henrietta, who we know almost nothing about, and Edith Emogene, whose poems and letters add so much to this story.

In May of 1853, Henry and Mary Ann Austin welcomed a new daughter to their family, Maria Adelaide Austin. There are a few of Maria's letters in this book. Maria seems to be the quiet, reserved, shy one in Henry and Mary Ann's family.

Henry's parents, Ralph and Fanny Austin, and sister Laura, 19, also lived on the Austin property.

When the New York City Austins—Uncle Augustus, Aunt Maria, Alonzo Eugene, Mortimer Bruce, Net, Addie, Rand, Edward, Tina, and little Christina—visit their Austin country cousins in the summer, they would meet Martin D. and Jane Ann Myers and their family.

Dr. Perkins and his wife, who we met in Chapter Three, moved to Rondout, New York, in 1853. The good doctor lived there quite some years, and died at age 89.

On December 16, 1853, my great-grandmother Maria (pronounced Mariah) Louisa Myers was born at Martin D. and Jane Ann's home near Hagan Pond.

Early photo of the home of Martin and Jane Ann Myers. Courtesy of Stuart and Geraldine Mills Russell.

A question had been festering in regards to dividing the Town of Lumberland. The roads were very rough and dangerous, and the traveling distance too great for many people to gather for town meetings.

There was much dissension. One group, which included James Hankins, Duncan Boyd, and Sears R. Gardner, petitioned for another town to be split out of Lumberland. This was agreeable to the prominent citizens, but not the majority of the townspeople.

Twenty-two people, including Justus Hickok and Benjamin C. Austin, made a counter proposal to create two new towns. This was agreed on, and December 17, 1853, the towns (townships) of Highland and Tusten were created.

So Maria Louisa Myers, my great-grandmother, was born in the Town of Lumberland, and the next day, Maria, without changing locations, lived in the Town of Highland, still in Sullivan County, New York.

The New York State Census taken in 1855 listed Sullivan County's population as under 30,000. People had moved from different counties in New York, and different countries including England, Ireland, Scotland, and France. Occupations itemized on the census sheets for Highland included carpenters, tailors, farmers, and lumberers.

Maria Louisa's parents were entered on the census sheets as Martin D. Myers, a farmer, and Jane A. Myers, both 39 years old. Maria's brother, George W.T. Myers was 9, and her half brothers Benjamin Myers and Charles Cripps Webb were 16 and 20.

Charles Cripps Webb's future wife, Sarah Shotwell was 14, and lived with her parents, Caleb and Sarah Shotwell. Caleb was a farmer.

Sherman Stiles Leavenworth, Maria's future husband, 12, lived on the west side of town with his parents, Buckley and Charlotte, and siblings: Atwell, Hezekiah, John, Harriet (Hattie), and baby Julia Ann.

Buckley, 46, a farmer, had been in town 28 years, and had a plank house. Charlotte, 43, had been in town 24 years.

It's not known when Hattie started teaching, but she lived in Sparrowbush and was a teacher, at some point. In the last chapter we met Hattie's future husband, Henry W. Palmer, 26. Henry had been in the area four years. In 1855, he boarded with the David Ayres family.

Charlotte Leavenworth's sister Sarah Ingram and her husband John Bishop lived in Standing Stone, Bradford County, Pennsylvania. Their sons were Ichabod, 25, Oliver, 20, and Stephen T., 15.

Ethel B. Sergeant's family lived west of the Leavenworths. Ethel, a farmer, owned farmland, and had been in town 13 years. Ethel, 48, his wife Letty Gardner, 47, and their children, Isaac, 21, James 17, Mary, 15, Caroline, 12, and Jane, 9, lived in a frame house.

Alvah and his wife Phebe Owen had been married four years and lived next to his parents, Ethel and Letty Sergeant.

To the north of the Sergeants lived Wilmot Clark, 58, his wife Mary, 52, and children, Mahlon Irvin, 27, Charles, 22, Mary, 20, Clarrissa, 18, and Martha, 7. In five years, Irvin, a farmer, would marry Laura Austin who lived on the other side of town.

Wilmot Clark had been in town 40 years. His wife Mary Van Auken was born in the Town of Lumberland in 1803. In 1850, Mary's elderly parents, Peter and Hannah Van Auken lived with them. Hannah died in 1852, and Peter died a few years later.

Wilmot and Mary Clark's son, George, had been married to Harriet Covert for five years, and they had three children.

Mercy Harding Brown and her second husband George Case Clark had been married for ten years and lived in Bethel. They had four children, but it would be another 12 years before the birth of John Henry Clark, ancestor of

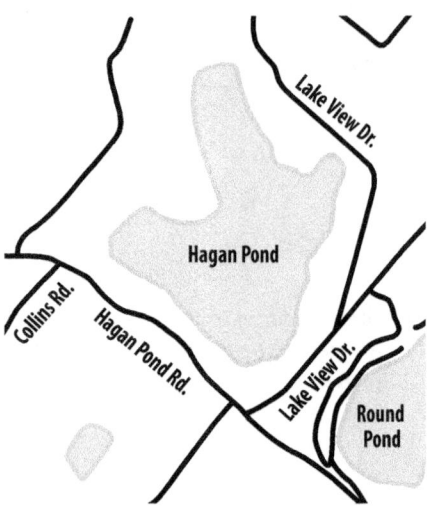
The Myers lived south of the thumb, on the south side of Hagan Pond Road.

Hagan Pond, now called Highland Lake. Photo: Cynthia Leavenworth Bellinger.

Stella Clark, who would marry a Leavenworth descendant.

Alexander Boyd, 62, a farmer, was one of several families from Scotland. Alexander and his wife Elizabeth, 43, lived in a frame house, and had been in the area for thirteen years. Their sons, Comfort, 12, and James, 6, play a part in our story.

The 1855 Census Marshall was Charles C.P. Eldred, 46, a farmer. His household included wife Effa, and their children (ages 3–19): George W., Polly V., Becca, Maria Adeline, James D., and Sarah J. The family had a boarder, Charles Smith, 26, a wheelwright.

C.C.P. Eldred's sister Eliza was married to James K. Gardner, a merchant. In 1851, James K. had been an elected representative for Sullivan County, as had his father-in-law, James Eldred, sixteen years earlier.

James K. and Eliza Gardner had a busy household: James E., 17, Sarah Elizabeth, 15, Ann E., 10, Grandma Mary K. Gardner, 80, and a married daughter, Maria Calkins, 21.

James K. and Eliza's son Stephen St. John Gardner, 19, attended the University of North East Pennsylvania in Bethany. While at the university, Stephen received a letter from his cousin, George W. Eldred:

A friend and I went to Hagan whortleberrying yesterday. Got half a bushel, and no mistake. We got nicely [out] of the marsh, when it began to rain right along. We had the misfortune to spill about a peck of our berries and did not get more than half of them.

I know of nothing else to write only Oliver Calkins was here today and Oh! what a nice shower we had. He stopped and bunked in with us till most 6, when he gave out, and put for home, thinking it never would quit raining.

Grandfather [James Eldred] is well as common today, so are all the rest, except Palmer who had an attack of cholera morbus last even, but is coming up again.
—Eldred, Richard O., p. 73.

Sears R. Gardner (brother of James K.), was a lumberman. Four of Sears R. and his wife Mary Ann Creiger's children died at a young age. But in 1855, they had seven children (from 1 month to 14 years old): Elizabeth, Felix K., Sears E., Albert, Mary E., Anna, and Maria (who died at 4 months).

Henry and Mary Ann Austin were very busy. William Henry, 31, was farming. Mary Ann cared for their children, Mary Henrietta, Edith Emogene, and Maria (ages 5, 4, 2). Grandfather James, 77, and Grandmother Hannah, 65, lived with Henry and Mary Ann.

In October, Henry and Mary Ann's first son, James Eldred Austin, named for his grandfather, James Eldred, was born.

Henry Austin's mother, Fanny

View of Highland Lake, north of Highland Lake Rd. Photo: Cynthia Leavenworth Bellinger.

Elizabeth Laserlier Van Pelt

Back of photo (probably written by Charlotte Leavenworth), reads: Great-Grandmother Van Pelt, Holland Dutch. From the collection of Cynthia Leavenworth Bellinger.

Elizabeth was the daughter of Abraham (1755 to 1803), and Mary Webber Lazerlier. The Lazerlier family were Huguenots.

Since *Lazerlier* has many spellings, I have chosen to use the spelling Elizabeth used in her Bible records.

John Van Pelt, son of Henry and Anne Van Pelt, and Elizabeth Lazerlier were married in September 1809, in New York City.

John and Elizabeth Van Pelt had three children: Peter, Maria Anthony, and Jane Ann Van Pelt.

Years later, when the Van Pelt family estate was settled, my grandmother Jennie Leavenworth Austin received $9—enough to get some glasses, I was told.

The above photo may be of a missing painting of Elizabeth.

Elizabeth's long, thin fingers seem to have been inherited by a number of her descendants, including my father, Art Austin.
—*Louise Austin Smith.*

Austin, was 67, and a tailoress. His sister, Laura L. Austin was 21. Ralph Austin was not listed in the 1855 census. Perhaps Ralph and his sons James and Augustus were working in New York City.

In New York City, Uncle Augustus and Aunt Maria had a new little one, Clementina Austin. They would have two more girls, Grace Emma, and Ida Belle.

Oliver Perry Schoonover, 35, a waterman, and Ann Mary Austin, 28 (sister of Henry and Augustus), had been married for nine years. Perry had lived near the Village for 19 years.

Hannah Eldred's brother, Uncle Justus Hickok, 63, and his wife Aunt Polly, 55, had children, Robert, 22, Mary, 20, Merwin, 17, Charles, 11, and a grandchild, George W. Hickok, 7 months old, living with them.

Justus and Polly's son David Hickok, a farmer, his wife Mary, and a boarder from France, Philip Wandling, 21, also lived with the Senior Hickoks. David and Mary's son Olin would be a good friend of my Grandpa Mort Austin, though neither were born until the mid-1860s.

William Hickcok, 27, also a son of Justus and Mary, was a boat builder. William and his wife of six years, Almeda, 23, had two children, Justice, 2, and Emma, 5 months.

Thomas and Julia Van Tuyl Hallock and their family had lived in Lumberland for 14 years. Their son Oliver Blizzard was 21.

The Bunce brothers, George 29, and William 21, lived on the Bunce property. It is unknown if their parents, Hezekiah and Julia Bunce were still living.

Moses Myers (a sawyer), and his wife, Phebe Hazen Clark, had been married 25 years. Their son Abel Sprague Myers was 19.

Elizabeth Van Pelt's Bible

Elizabeth Van Pelt printed on Bible Cover.

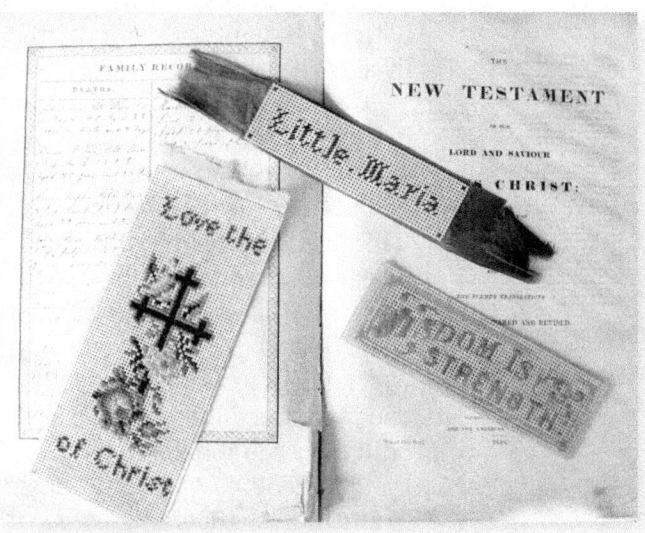

Needlework bookmarks in Elizabeth Van Pelt's Bible, probably sewn by young Maria Myers Leavenworth.

BIRTHS.

John Van Pelt was born June 14th 1786

Elizabeth Lazerlier was born July 16th 1789

Children

Peter L Van Pelt was Born June 8th 1810

Maria Anthony Van Pelt was born Febuary 28th 1813

Jane Ann Van Pelt was born December 25 1815

Henry Cripps Webb was born December 3 1807

Grand Children

Charles Cripps Webb was born October 10 1835

Page from Elizabeth Van Pelt's Bible. More Van Pelt Bible page records in the Appendix, p. 257. Photos: Gary Smith.

Dear Daughter

Elizabeth Laserlier Van Pelt's husband, John Van Pelt, died at age 33, when her children Peter, Maria Anthony and Jane Ann were ages 10, 7, and 4-1/2. Elizabeth's daughter Maria Anthony Van Pelt, died when she was 22.

When daughter Jane Ann Van Pelt Webb's husband, Henry Cripps Webb, died in 1840, and their son, John Henry Webb died four months later, Elizabeth must have had much empathy for Jane Ann.

In the front of Elizabeth's 1830 Van Pelt Bible, in exquisite handwriting, Elizabeth wrote a touching note to her daughter, Jane Ann, and gave her the Bible.

Letter to Jane Ann from her mother. Photo: Gary Smith.

Dear Daughter,
In presenting you with this Holy book, permit me to say, that my heart's desire and prayer to God, is that you may read and understand it; that its sacred contents may cause you to walk close with God, and that with David you may be able to say, my soul panteth after thee even as the Hart panteth after the water brook; remembering that those who lean on him will never be confounded nor dismayed; but shall go from strength to strength in this nether world, and hereafter, appear in the [clouds] above, to join the innumerable company around the throne in songs of ceaseless praise.
   From your affectionate Mother,
Elizabeth Van Pelt
   To Jane Ann Webb

Jane Van Pelt Webb Myers on the left. Photo: Courtesy of Cynthia Leavenworth Bellinger.

Their daughters were: Sarah, 15, Emeline, 10, and Eliza Jane, 7. (The Moses Myers family was related to Gladys Myers Austin, but not the Martin D. Myers family.)

Hannah Maria Van Schoick, future wife of Abel Sprague Myers, was 18, and lived in Ten Mile River with her parents William Van Schoick, 52, a farmer, and his wife Huldah, 44.

Maria Hankins was 1 year old. She would be the second wife of Abel S. Myers, and grandmother of Chuck Myers.

Alexander Carmichael, a farmer, was 76, and a widower. We met Mr. Carmichael near the start of our story as a deacon in the Congregational Church. He had been in town fifty years.

Felix Kyte, 55, and his wife Eliza, 45, had four sons and a daughter (ages 4 to 19) still at home.

Robert Owen, 24, a farmer, and his wife, Elizabeth Tether, 25, were both in town. In 1851, Elizabeth had arrived in the U.S. from England with her parents, Edward and Elizabeth Tether.

Robert's parents, Morgan Owen and Elizabeth Barnes, were both 55. Daughter Ethalinda, 18, lived with them.

George Mills, 54, a farmer, and his wife Margaret Clark Mills, 56, were both born in Scotland, and had been in town for three years. George and Margaret Mills had a 5-year-old granddaughter, Martha Mills. Martha would marry George W.T. Myers.

Martha's parents, Alexander and Margaret Gillies Mills, had built a boarding house on Hagan Pond in 1850.

In June of 1856, Augustus "Gus" Waterman Myers was born to Martin D. and Jane Ann Myers. Great-Grandma Maria Louisa was

2-1/2 and her big brother George Washington Taylor was 10. One year later, in June of 1857, Jane Ann's son, Charles Cripps Webb, married Sarah Shotwell.

In January of 1857, my great-great-grandmother Fanny Knapp Austin wrote to her children from Halfeway Brook. Perhaps the letter was written to the children who lived and/or worked in New York City. Great-Great-Grandpa Ralph Austin may also have been there. *Special thanks to Melva Austin Barney for sharing this letter. (See pp. 242–245.)*

Moscow, Pennsylvania, was mentioned in the letter and was approximately 50 miles away. Bilious fever also mentioned in the letter, consisted of a high temperature combined with what sounds like the stomach flu.

Halfeway Brook, January 11, 1857
Dear Children,

You must excuse my not writing sooner. I have been waiting for something pleasant to write but sicknefs and glome overspreads our Neighborhood.

Our house had escaped until yesterday, Henry was brought from Moscow very sick. The Doctor pronounced it the Billous feavor, but he is better this morning. I feel in hopes it is a lite case. It is the prevailing epidemic and the scarlet fevor. The Doctor says he has 40 patients down with them and many that will not recover.

My health is about as it was. My cough is better. My appetite is good if I do not work too hard. A little work goes a good way with me. I have not been able to go any more except when they come after me.

Mr. Stage took me up to his house. I was there over a week and

Webber, Laserlier, Van Pelt, Myers

The following hand-written notes were found in the Van Pelt family Bible. Titled, "Grandmother Myers' Family History." It was possibly copied by a daughter of Sherman S. and Maria Myers Leavenworth.

The family of Webbers were very wealthy and came from Holland after they loaned the Dutch government a vast amount of money.

One of these Webbers, whose name I do not know, had a son, whose name we think was John. He had a child whose name I also do not know, and she married a Lazalier. They had a daughter named Elizabeth. Mr. Lazalier died. His widow married a Taylor. Mr. and Mrs. Taylor had a son George Washington Taylor. The daughter of Mrs. Taylor by her former husband (Mr. Lazalier) married Peter Van Pelt [should be John], and they had a daughter Jane Ann who was your mother and my grandmother. Thus the strain of our ancestry from the Webbers as father told it to us.

The Simonsons attempted to trace the family and I think it was Wm. Simonson who tried to raise the money $20,000 to go to Holland. But it was necessary to have the family tree.

They hunted all over and father was the only one who had seen it.

Grandmother Taylor, nee Webber, had shown it to him when he was a boy. He remembered she often told him about the ancestry and wealth that was behind us. She kept the tree in a drawer of an old fashioned table he said. But after she died, the furniture was all sold and the tree must have gone with it.

It is through the Webber family that we are in line of heirs for the Trinity and Annika Jinks property. But they said that will never be settled so I guess we will never see it. Father always said that to get the money back from Holland that was loaned, the government at that time, would probably cause a war between the two countries, as it was so complicated.

The above named George W. Taylor founded the firm of Lord and Taylor, N.Y. City.

Note: The Trinity and Annika Jinks (Jans) property is a rather complicated story regarding lawsuits between Trinity Church and the descendants of Anneke Jans over land ownership that goes back to the early days when the Dutch were in New York City.

would have stayed longer, but Mrs. Stage would wait on me so much I thought that I would come home, but it has been so cold.

I was sorry but Old Mrs. Eldred [Hannah was a year younger than Fanny], makes my fire in the morning and washes for me and I knit and work for her.

I have not been up to Mr. C.P. Eldreds. They have been down for me several times. Last nite, Mr. Eldred was here. He said he would send for me. I promised to go and stay all the week. They have some gloves they want manufactured. I will turn over a new leaf. My hand shakes so bad I can not write much.

I had a very plesent New Year to Mr. Stages. We had good vituals and good company. George [Stage, 24] was home and Albert [Stage, 22] inquired after you and Lucy. George said I must give his compliments and best respects to you both. Albert said he would rather fetch them himselfe. Mrs. Stage said you promised to write to her.

George and Albert was up to

Others in 1855

Henry Wilson, 65, a farmer, had been in town 12 years. Henry and his wife Margaret, 49, had four children, ages 4 to 15.

Edward Wilson, 35, was also a farmer. Ed and his wife Phoebe, 28, had been in town five years and had four children.

James, 36, and Mary Carpenter, 22, had been in town since they were born. James was a farmer.

Joseph Carpenter, 66, a farmer, had been in town 63 years—since 1792. His wife Dorcas, 62, had been in the area since she was 4.

William Wells, a farmer, had been there since 1790, when he was 3. His property in 1850 was valued at $5,000. William's wife Elizabeth was there in 1817. William and Elizabeth had boarders—the Hendrickson family of three and James Quick.

Jonathan Lilly, 61, a farmer, lived in a log house and had been there nine years. His wife was 51.

Jesse and Lucy Barker from England had been in town three years. He was a tailor.

Daniel and Elizabeth Cornwell, in town since 1838, had nine children. The older three, Martha, Robert, and Mary, were teachers.

M. Wallace, 26, from Scotland, was a Milliner.

Coe Finch Young, son of Isaac and Eliza Ann Gardner Young, was 9. Coe Finch Young was an ancestor of Louis Maudsley.

Elizabeth Wheeler Eldred, widow of Uncle Mulford, married Gilbert Travis. In 1855, the couple lived in Tompkins, New York, with their 1-year-old son Milton Travis, and Elizabeth's children, Amelia, Benjamin, Augusta, Harriet L., and Mary Eliza Eldred (ages 8 to 16).

In 1855, Sarah Labarr, 59, was listed with sons William, Increase, and Jacob LaBarr.

Sarah's son Gordon R. LaBarr and his second wife Susanna Fetter had been married a year. In December of 1856, their son Calvin, the first of nine children, would be born.

In 1855, James Thompson Briggs, his bride of one year, Catherine Thrush, and his parents, Benjamin and Sarah Jeffries Briggs, lived in Wabash, Indiana.

Arnold and Rachel Crabtree lived in Kane County, Illinois, in 1855. Their son, John George Lewis Crabtree was born in July. John Lewis would be the father of Myrtie Crabtree. Myrtie would be the future wife of Preacher Irwin Briggs. Their family would arrive in Barryville around 1934.

Mr. Clarks [Wilmot and Mary Clark] on New Year's Day. He said Mary was grieving about you going away, but Clarry was in good spirits and found it was his birthday and when he started for home she gave him such a snowbawling it was a caution. They heard I was there and would have come, but it was so slippery they gave it up.

You would like to know of Mr. Kyte's donation. Well they must have had a very agreeable time at evening. All the Gentleman except their sons was Mr. Squire Clark and Mr. George Eldred. He went over to Mr. Mannys and got Catharine and sister Polly and fetch them up to Stages after George, but was disapointed and had to wait on them both.

Isaac Bradley was here last evening. He has been driving team for Mr. Gohara. They tried to get him to take Liza Mariah. They offered him the team and would pay her way. He tolde them when he wanted to go, he was able to pay his own fare. He is sick of the whole of them. He talks of coming to New York in a few weeks. Mr. Waterman has made him a good offer.

Wednesday morning: I waited to see how Henry got along. He is better. Mr. C.C.P. Eldred is a calculating to come to New York next week and I want you to be shure and come with him. If he does not come soon, you must come the first opportunity. The sooner the better. Perry and Ann [Austin Schoonover] was up here and said he would earn $1 (?) a week.

Ann is poorly. She thinks she cannot live until spring. Give my love to all.

Tell Mortimer [her grandson Mortimer Bruce Austin] to write and I will tell him all about the

View of Delaware River above Shohola. Photo possibly taken by Aida Austin.

weddings. Oliver Dunlap and Caty Devenport was married on New Years. There is 3 or 4 more such a coming soon. Tell Adelina I will answer her soon.

No more at present. I remain your mother with affection,
Fanny Austin

Dear Son [James],
If you will assist Laura something to get back with, I think she will pay you when she can earn it. I was not pleased with her coming. If she had laid out her money for clothing, it would have been better, but I thought she would not be contented untill she tried it.

I found she was working too hard, but Mr. C.C.P. Eldred is coming soon. He expects next week and she must be ready to come with him. Without fail, we all miss her much.

No more at present. I remain your loving Mother,
Fanny Austin

James Eldred, my great-great-grandfather had arrived in Lumberland the end of 1815. He had been a deacon in the Congregational Church from 1819–1857, a Postmaster from 1831–1851, a member of the State Assembly in 1835, and Judge of Common Pleas for several years.

James Eldred had not been well in his later years. The 1855 Census indicated that James and his wife Hannah had been living with their daughter Mary Ann and her husband Henry Austin.

In April of 1857, James Eldred, died at 79 years of age. James Eldred was survived by his wife Hannah, five children—Sarah Carmichael, Charles C.P. Eldred, Eliza Gardner, Maria Austin, Mary Ann Austin—and around forty grandchildren.

It was said that James Eldred was a careful Bible student and that he loved to sing beloved church hymns. As he was dying, James asked his loved ones and friends to gather around his bed to sing, *In Songs of Sublime Adoration and Praise*. They were unable to sing the hymn, so James tried to sing the hymn himself.

Verse 1:
In songs of sublime adoration and praise,
Ye saints, who the gospel embrace,
Break forth and extol the great Ancient of Days,
His rich and distinguishing Grace:
His love, from eternity fixed upon you,
Discovered its heavenly flame,
When each with the cords of his kindness He drew,
And brought you to love his great name.

O! had He not pitied the state you were in,
Your bosom his love had ne'er felt;
You all would have lived, would have died too in sin,
And sunk with the load of your guilt.

Verse 2
There was nothing in you that could merit esteem,
Or give the Creator delight:
But "even so, Father!" you ever must sing,
"Because it seemed good in Thy sight."

Then give all the glory to his glorious name;
To Him all the wisdom belongs;
Be yours the high joy still, to acknowledge his fame,

Felix Kyte: Donation

The word *donation* is mentioned several times in letters in this book. What follows is an explanation of the word by Rev. Felix Kyte in his biography of 1875.

I have received many and continued favors from your hands especially at the commencement of each succeeding year. New Year's Day having for many years been appointed for a donation visit. I will here describe them as they used to be.

On those occasions it was the custom to come to my house, some with teams and others that had none, to chop and draw me firewood of the branches of the trees where trees have been cut down in the woods for timber. And thus a pile would be collected; sometimes enough to last for most of the year instead of allowing it to rot on the ground and always by the consent of those who claimed to own it.

While female friends and sisters of the church would, from what was brought, provide a suitable meal for those who were in attendance whether they labored themselves or sent their workmen. All were made heartily welcome and all served alike.

The idea then was if a minister is called to labor—let him be paid his salary, the moment the good people have a mind to give him over and above, then in plain and appropriate language call it a donation. The labor was all voluntary neither asked nor imposed. It was a sociable gathering for the whole day and as pleasant to the donors as to the donee. And what was bestowed in money or otherwise was in strict reality a donation. Such were the old times in reference to that subject.—Felix Kyte, 1875.

James Eldred's Will

In the name of God amen. I James Eldred of the Town of Highland in the County of Sullivan and State of New York of the age of Seventy nine years on the 7th day of October AD 1856, and being of sound mind and memory, do make publish and declare this my last will and testament, in manner following, that is to say,

First I give and bequeath to my wife Hannah Eldred all my house hold goods and furniture of every description and all my Landed property. Except one tenth part of the estate of Robert E. Manny deceased, the said tenth part of the above estate of Robert E. Manny deceased I give to James K. Gardner and Charles C.P. Eldred to be equally divided between them.

I release all my claims against the estate of Zophar Carmichael. I also release all my claims against Augustus A. Austin and give him fifty dollars out of a note I hold against Samuel Dewitt.

The demands I hold against Chauncey Thomas, also the balance of the notes I hold against Samuel Dewitt after paying Augustus A. Austin the fifty dollars before mentioned, I give to my wife Hannah Eldred for her support during her natural life and if any of the above property be left after her decease, the same is to be applied to the benefit of William H. Austin family.

All the notes and accounts between myself and Charles C.P. Eldred after paying funeral expenses and Physicians bills etc, the balance to be paid to my wife Hannah Eldred. In witnefs whereof I have here unto set my hand and seal this 27th day of March in the year of our Lord, 1857. James Eldred.

(Ell), 2. Lon was my great uncle and plays a major part in this story. I will often refer to him as Uncle Lon.

Remember James K. and Eliza Gardner? Their daughter Sarah died in 1857, at age 18. The next year, their son, Stephen St. John Gardner, was Supervisor for the Town of Highland—probably not a surprise. Stephen's father, James K., both grandfathers, Sears Gardner and James Eldred, and Great-Grandfather Elisha Eldred, had taken part in local government.

In Cousin Melva Austin Barney's treasury of letters, was a letter to Fanny Knapp Austin, from her son James Austin. The letter was dated February 1858, and was probably written from New York City. *(See Appendix, pp. 247–8.)*

New York, February 23, 1858

Dear Mother,

I received your letter of the 19th yesterday and was glad to hear that you was better, but was sorry to hear that you had not received my letter of the 16th for I wrote by first maile after receiving yours by Felix Kyte. I have thought it was mislaid in the Post Office as is often the case. And sometimes it happens that letters do not arrive at their destination for sometime after they are mailed.

I again risk Two Dollars by Maile. I do not like to send this way, but you are in want of the money and so I risk it. I should send you a larger sum if I was shure you would get it. I think before long, some person of our acquaintance will be en-route for Lumberland and then I will remit to you.

In the meantime, get of your

And crown him in loftiest songs.

Rev. Felix Kyte, who had first met James in 1832, had this to say: *Where is the cabin he has not entered going from house to house, as it were preaching Christ!*

The May 1, 1857, *Sullivan County Democrat Republican* commented about James: *As his life was one of great usefulness, his end was both peaceful and happy.*

In September, five months after his grandfather Eldred's death, Albert Alonzo Austin was born to Henry and Mary Ann Austin. Lon, as he was called, was welcomed by his four siblings: Mary Henrietta, 8, Edith Emogene, 6, Maria Adelaide, 4, and big brother James Eldred

Winter 1857

The winter of 1857 was particularly disastrous to the Erie Railroad on the Delaware Division. There were extraordinarily deep snows and heavy ice in the Delaware River.

On February second the ice went out with a big flood, and carried away the railroad bridge east of Narrowsburg, New York.

The river froze up again and another flood came February 18th. The railroad bridge that the previous flood had demolished was well along toward restoration, but most of the new one was carried away by the second flood.

J. Hardenbergh, bridge foreman, was working next to the Pennsylvania bank when the flood came, and the timber broke up and crashed away behind him as he ran for the shore, his feet being scarcely lifted from one timber before that timber would fall before the flood. His escape was miraculous.

Pending the replacing of the railroad bridge below Narrowsburg, through traffic over the Erie was virtually suspended. Local passengers were ferried across the Delaware.

Livestock was a great item of traffic on the Erie in those days. While the bridge was gone, cattle, sheep and hogs were unloaded at Narrowsburg and driven through Wayne County, Pennsylvania, to the junction of the Honesdale and Mast Hope turnpike, sixteen miles, and thence back over the turnpike to Mast Hope, a total distance of thirty-five miles, where they were reloaded on cars in waiting at that place for them.—Mott, Edward H., Between the Ocean and the Lakes: The Story of Erie, 1899, p. 441.

---

friends what things you want to make you comfortable and do not pinch yourselves for food or fuel and I will pay the bill. You may rely on it. I trust you will not run up a large bill extravagantly, but get all you want to make you comfortable.

Keep Laura home with you. Do not think of trying to live alone. It is my particular wish and request that she remain home with you. Tell her that I will try and do something for her next summer in the way of dresses etc.

Tell Henry that probably there may be a chance for him to bring Cart this spring at Peckslip with Alonzo. Alonzo thinks of trying to make the arrangement so as to drive the two horse trucks and let Henry have his place with the Cart.

If business starts when the Hartford Steamboat begins to run, which will be in the course of two or three weeks, that is if the spring is not too backward, I think there will be a chance for him. Tell Henry not to rely too much on coming to the city. To warrant him a situation this spring, I do not.

Church in the distance. Mary Briggs Austin Collection.

Winter along a brook in Highland Township. Photo courtesy of Mary Briggs Austin.

Highland and Tusten

The Town (or township) of Highland was split from the Town of Lumberland in 1853. It included Barryville, Halfway Brook Village, Hagan Pond, Minisink Ford, and Yulan.

Yulan townsfolk first requested the name Laurel, but the Post Office rejected their request because there were already too many towns named Laurel. *Yulan,* Japanese for laurel, was the compromise.

The Town (or township) of Tusten, also created in 1853, from the Town of Lumberland, included Beaverbrook, Lava, Narrowsburg, and Swamp Mills.

Swamp Mills folk wanted *Laurel Glen.* Again the Post Office said no. The names of two local families, Newman and Weiden were combined for Neweiden.

My grandmother, Mabel Owen, was born in Yulan. The Owen family had been in the area since the 1700s. Her father, Robert Owen, lived in Yulan for most of his life and was engaged in several business enterprises in the general area. He was the son of Morgan Owen and Elizabeth Barnes. They were buried in Eldred Cemetery, so at least in later life made their home there also.

Mabel Owen's mother was Elizabeth Tether who was born in Sleaford, England and from her scrapbook, came here in 1851. One of her brothers who had preceded her to the U.S.A., had first gone to Hawley, Pennsylvania. I remember that one of Grandma's Tether cousins was a dentist there. So that might have been her first step toward Eldred.

My grandfather Edwin Van Schoick Myers was born in Swamp Mills and from stories he told, he was there at least until he was 8, when his father remarried. His mother died when he was 5 and he was cared for by his maternal grandmother (Van Schoick) who lived next door in a house with a porch where she would sit and smoke a pipe. He was born in a log cabin.
—Melva Austin Barney.

On my mother's side, my great-grandfather came to this country to Tusten in 1853, and settled in the Lava area up here. His name was Nicholas Scheidel and Tusten was already formed when he settled.
—Emily Knecht Hallock.

Note: The Myers family mentioned here are related to Gladys Myers who married Charles Raymond Austin, son of Mort and Jennie Austin.

If Alonzo or myself can get him a situation this spring. I will do it. I would like to have Henry this spring, even if he did not stay. He'd have the summer—for by coming here and learning the city and how to do business would be a great advantage to him and he could take right hold of my work this fall.

The maine thing is to learn the different Steam Boats and Rail Roads. He may get along with business and Peck—Just the place to learn. So I think that he should come and drive a few months.

But should he have a good chance for business at Lumberland, he had not better let it slip. But I think he may rely on having a good situation.

In one year's time Alonzo will soon ascertain what prospect there will be for him and will write. In the meantime, tell him not to be discouraged, for I think the prospect is good ahead.

Augustus' folks [family] are all well. Harriet Teed leaves there next Saturday for home. Her Father is not so well again. We are all well and doing well. More soon.

Your affectionate son,
James H. Austin

In May of 1858, Jane Ann Myers's brother, Peter Van Pelt, died at the age of 47. He had lived 14 years longer than his father, who had died at the age of 33. If Jane Ann's mother Elizabeth Van Pelt hadn't moved to Halfway Brook Village with the Myers in 1852, she most likely moved after Peter's death, to be with Jane Ann, her only living child.

Six weeks after her brother Peter Van Pelt's death, Jane Ann and Martin D. Myers had their last child, Charlotte Elizabeth (Lottie)

Corner of Collins and Highland Lake Rd. Photo: Cynthia Leavenworth Bellinger.

Myers. Lottie's brother George W.T. was 12, her sister Maria was 4-1/2, and her brother Gus was almost 2.

Remember little Joanna Brown? Joanna was a young lady of 16 in 1858. In August, Isaac A. Bradley and Joanna Brown were married. Isaac and Joanna's seven children play a part in the story in Book Two. Isaac Bradley built a home for his family not far from the Leavenworth homestead.

Elizabeth Persbacher, daughter of Jacob Persbacher and Catherine Kreiter from Germany, was born October 1858, in Shohola, Pennsylvania. Elizabeth would marry Isaac Sergeant (who was 24 in 1858), a great-grandson of Rev. Isaac Sergeant. Isaac and Elizabeth's daughter Minnie would marry Archibald A. Myers, father of Charles Henry Myers. Chuck Myers, a friend of my parents, has contributed information on Felix Kyte and answered questions for this book.

At the end of September, 1858, Abel Sprague Myers (future grandfather of Chuck Myers) married Hannah Maria Van Schoick. Abel and Maria would be great-grandparents of my Austin cousins, Melva, Joan, Margie and Dawn Lee. It was exciting to receive a copy of the wedding photo of Abel S. and Maria Van Schoick Myers that is included in this chapter.

There was yet another marriage in 1858. Amelia Eldred, daughter of Uncle Mulford and Elizabeth Wheeler Eldred, married John Hancy, who was born in Switzerland and had immigrated to America in 1857. We'll hear more about John Hancy during the Civil War.

After Uncle Mulford's death, his son, Benjamin Franklin (Frank) Eldred, lived in Tompkins, New York, with his mother Elizabeth and his stepfather, Gilbert Travis.

About 1859, Frank Eldred went to work for John Barnes in West Damascus, Pennsylvania. There he met Almira Barnes, daughter of John and Elizabeth Holbert Barnes, who he seems to have married within a year.

Harriet Leavenworth, Buckley and Charlotte Leavenworth's daughter married Henry Palmer in Port Jervis, in 1859. Henry and Hattie Palmer lived in Port Jervis, where Henry was a blacksmith and Hattie was a teacher.

Over in Yorkshire, England, in April 1859, Albert Ewart was born to William and Pamela Tipling Ewart. Albert would be the husband of Henry and Hattie Palmer's daughter, Edith Palmer, who would be born in 1861.

Almost a year after little Lottie Myers was born, Elizabeth Lazerlier Van Pelt died—June 12, 1859. Elizabeth (my great-great-great grandmother) was the mother of Jane Ann Myers.

Elizabeth Lazerlier Van Pelt. Cynthia Leavenworth Bellinger Collection.

Abel Myers and Hannah Maria Van Schoick

Wedding photo of Abel Sprague Myers and Hannah Maria Van Schoick. Photo courtesy of Joan Austin Geier.

Great-Grandparent's Wedding Portrait

Her unaccustomed gown is grand and prim,
Billowing taffeta in a bold plaid,
High lace collar, dark braid trim.
Her little face is pinched.
In her lap, her hand extends to show the ring.
Someone must have said, "Place it so..."
and, so, she did.
Great-Grandfather holds her other hand.
Her fist is clenched.
I feel he loves her.
I know he loves her.
He sits there, tense,
With my cheekbones and my son's puzzled eyes.

I want to tell him he will not fail her.
I want to take her in my arms and kiss away her fear.
—Joan Austin Geier.

Maria was 5-1/2 years old when her grandmother Van Pelt died. Several needlepoint bookmarkers sewn by Maria were in her grandmother, Elizabeth Van Pelt's Bible *(see p. 71).*

In September of 1859, Clarissa Clark, daughter of George Clark and Harriet Covert, was born. Clarissa Clark would marry Frank Roberts Sergeant (not yet born), and their daughter Ella Phoebe would marry Garfield Leavenworth.

Frank Roberts Sergeant would be born in 1861, to Alvah Sergeant and Phebe Owen. Phebe Owen's parents were Morgan and Elizabeth Barns Owen. Elizabeth Barns Owen, 58, died in December, 1859.

Morgan and Elizabeth's son Robert Owen, 30, was married to Elizabeth Tether. They would be the future grandparents of my aunt Gladys Myers Austin.

In 1860, Mary Ann Eldred Austin received a letter from an Emma Teed. The letter indicated that Henry and Mary Ann Austin were taking care of Henry's niece, Clara Teed, daughter of Edward Nelson. Clara Austin Teed, Edward's wife, and Henry Austin's sister, had died in 1849.

Aida Austin had this to say about the Teed family, and the following letter:

The only Teeds I remember of hearing mentioned were Susie Teed and Clara Teed, a young girl who lived with us a few months when my sisters were children. I often heard them speak of her, and I always thought Susie Teed was the mother of that Clara Teed until I found among some old letters the following one.

From this letter it is evident that Emma's mother was an Austin and it seems to me that the Clara she was writing about must have been her younger sister, and that their mother was Clara Austin a daughter of Ralph Austin.

New York, February 19, 1860
Dear Aunt Mary,

I received your kind letter and was much pleased to hear from you. If everything is true that I hear, I have not many out there but you and Uncle Henry. Well, how do you and Clara get along?

Uncle Augustus and Aunt Maria and all are well. Little Emma has been quite sick with the measles, but she is better now. She is a dear little lamb.

I want you to make out your bill for Clara's board since she has been with you and send it to me and I will send the money to you. You must not hesitate to do it. I wish you to for I don't want any one to keep her for nothing. She is not dependent on anyone for her living.

Gravestone for Elizabeth Owen
Photo: Cynthia Leavenworth Bellinger.

I suppose that my dear Aunt Ann [Ann Austin Schoonover] thinks that I wanted her to take Clara and take care of her.

I want Clara to come the first opportunity for Uncle Nelson wants her here. He is going to sell our house and lot. He can't administrate it until she comes in.

Write and let me know when she is coming and send her alone and I will meet her at Jersey City. She must come without fail this week.

Send her trunk all for she will stay here when she comes. Give my very best love to Uncle Henry and Clara and the children and reserve a good share for yourself.

Please do send your bill with Clara and oblige me. I enclose three dollars for Clara to come home with. Send her as soon as you can. No more at present.

Your affectionate Niece,
Emma Teed

In 1860, Laura Austin, the youngest of Ralph and Fanny Austin's children, married Mahlon Irvin Clark, 31. My mother's letter collection included the certificate of Mahlon and Laura's wedding, and a letter to Laura from her mother. *(See Appendix, pp. 248–49.)*

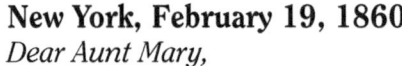

Gravestone of Elizabeth Van Pelt in the old Eldred Cemetery. Photo: Gary Smith.

Highland, June 10, 1860

Mr. and Mrs. Mahlon I. Clark,
Half Way Brook Village

I do hereby certify that on the tenth day June instant at the house of Wm. H. Austin in said town of Highland, Mahlon I. Clark of said town of Highland and Laura L. Austin also of said town of Highland were, with their mutual consent, lawfully joined together in holy matrimony, which was solemnized by me in the presence of James H. Austin, Mrs. Hannah Eldred, Mary Ann Austin, Ralph Austin and Fanny Austin,

All of said town of Highland attesting witness.

And I do further certify that the said Mahlon I. Clark and Laura L. Austin are known to me to be the persons described in this certificate; and that I ascertained previous to the solemnization of the said marriage that the parties were of sufficient age to contract the same, and that there appeared no lawful impediment to such marriage.

Given under my hand, this the fifteenth day of June A.D., 1860.
George T.B. Stage,
Justice of Peace

Around 1860

Laura,

I sent Irvin's socks. I had no measure to go by. Mrs. Clarke brought yarn and said there was enough for 2 pair. I should have made them longer, but I thought I would do as she said, but it lacks one knot of being enough and when I get that you shall have the other pair.

I thought I would send these for he mite want them. You must come when you can.

I had a letter from James. He appears to be in good spirits. His horse is alright. He lives with the same family he did. His business is good and a prospect of its being better than ever it was.

Augustus's folks [family] are all well. I creape along about as well as ever. Mrs. Dunlap washed for me yesterday. My neighbour calls often to see if I want helpe. I have got wormwood and am going to use it for I think it is dropsy that makes me weak for my appetite is poor. I have everything I wish for, but do not eat much. James told me to get whatever I want and I do. My love to your both.

Adieu, Fanny Austin

The national news in 1860 was not good. South Carolina seceded

---

Roebling-Chauncey Bridge

Postcard of Barryville Shohola Bridge and Lookout Mountain. Courtesy of Mary Briggs Austin.

Until 1856 there had only been a crude rope guided ferry that connected Shohola, Pennsylvania, to Barryville, New York. There became a need for a bridge with the building of the Erie Railroad Depot at Shohola, Pennsylvania.

A suspension bridge, designed by John Roebling, was built about 1855, by the Barryville and Shohola Bridge Co. The bridge originally cost $9,000, and was completed by 1856.

Chauncey Thomas was in charge of building the bridge, and Johnston believed him to be incompetent.

The two towers were each 12 feet square at the base and 40 feet in height, and placed on an abutment of stones, one at Barryville, and one at Shohola.

The towers stood 495 feet apart and supported two wire cables 10 feet apart 2-1/2 inches in the diameter and suspended from tower to tower, with braces and guys...

In time of high wind it would oscillate up and down to the extent of three feet rendering it impossible for a team or a person to cross.

On the evening of the 2nd of July 1859, an unusual gust of wind from the North struck the bridge, over came the guys, turned the structure upon the edge and demolished it.

The bridge was reconstructed at a cost of $4,000.

The bridge was originally constructed with one main span. There is more about the bridge in the next chapter.—*Information from: Johnston, Reminiscences, p. 321, 349, and www.bridgemeister.com/.*

View of the Delaware River. Mary Briggs Austin Collection.

from the Union. Soon there would be a horrid war, and many of the Town of Highland's young men would fight in it, and some would not return.

In 1860, the population of Highland was 958; Lumberland was 970. The Pony Express had ten-day mail service from Missouri to California. It's hard to believe that was thought of as fast.

Before starting the chapter on the Civil War, here is a synopsis of the people in town, or relatives not in town in 1860.

Uncle Justus, 68, and Aunt Polly, 57, had four children living with them: Robert, 25, Benjamin Merwin, 21 (a dry goods clerk), Mary, 19 (a dress maker), and Charles, 17 (a farm laborer).

Merwin was also listed in Shohola with the Chauncy Thomas family. It may be that Chauncy owned the store Merwin worked at, and Merwin was at the store when the census was taken.

William Hickok, 31, a carpenter, and his wife Almeda had four children at home.

Three Hickok brothers, Benjamin Merwin, Charles, and William, would soon be going off to war, as would Comfort Boyd.

Comfort Boyd, 16, and his brother James, 12, were sons of Alexander Boyd, 67, and his wife Elizabeth, 50. Alexander was a farmer with property valued at $2,000.

William and George Bunce, bachelor farmers, seem to be the only ones left of the Bunce family in the area.

George Washington Eldred was a teacher in 1860. His cousin Stephen St. John Gardner, 25, was married to Louisa McElroy and lived in Barryville. Stephen's brother James E. was married to Rebecca Rider, Job Rider's daughter, and they had two sons.

James K. Gardner, father of Stephen and James E. Gardner, and husband of Eliza Eldred Gardner, died in Barryville, June 30, 1860.

James K. and Eliza were very active in the Congregational Church at Barryville, and James K. served as a deacon of the church for several years. In 1852, James K. was elected to be a representative to the New York State Legislature. He held several local offices such as justice of the peace.—Eldred, Richard O., p. 39.

After her husband's death, Eliza lived with her son Stephen St. John Gardner, in Barryville. The Austin cousin letters indicate that Eliza also visited and stayed with her sister Maria Eldred Austin in New York City.

The Leavenworth family lived north of Barryville, on the west side of Halfway Brook Village. The home that Sherman B. Leavenworth, 52, his wife, Charlotte, 49, and their children: Sherman Stiles, 17, Atwell (written as Etwell in the census), 15, Hezekiah, 12, John, 9, and Julia Ann Leavenworth, 5, lived in, would one day be called Echo Hill Farm House. Buckley was a farmer with property valued at $2,500.

Harriet (Hattie) Leavenworth, 26, and her husband, Henry

The Hawk's Nest, the route from Port Jervis to Eldred, is a popular background for car advertisements. In 1859, the Hawk's nest became a one lane dirt road. Photo courtesy of Mary Briggs Austin.

Palmer, 31, lived in Wallkill, Orange County, New York, where Henry was a blacksmith. Son Sherman V. Palmer, named after his grandfather, no doubt, was 2 months old. Little Sherman must have died young. Later the Palmers would adopt two sons. One of the sons, Harry C. Palmer, was born 1860, in Port Jervis, New York.

West of the Leavenworth farm were the Sergeants, descendants of Rev. Isaac Sergeant and his son Stephen Sergeant who we first met in 1799.

Alvah Sergeant, 29, was a farm laborer with property valued at $200. His wife Phebe, 26, was busy running a household with four children—Jane, 8, Esther, 6, Edgar, 5, and Alice Amelia, 2. Alice Sergeant would marry an Englishman, Thomas Alvin Hill, who was 9, in 1860.

It would be almost 1900 when Thomas and Alice Sergeant Hill's daughter Bertha would be born. Bertha would marry a descendant of George W. Eldred. John Thomas Hill, another son of Amelia and Thomas, would have a son, Alfred Hill, a friend of my parents (who I vaguely remember); and a daughter Gladys Hill who would marry Raymond Myers, brother of my aunt Gladys Myers Austin.

Alvah's parents, Ethel and Letty Sergeant had a daughter Caroline, 18, at home. Ethel, a farmer, had property valued at $1,200.

North of the Sergeants, not far from Blind Pond, was the Wilmot Clark family. Wilmot Clark, 62, was a farmer with real estate valued at $2,000. His wife Mary was 57. Daughters Clarissa, 22, and Martha, 10, were at home. Son Mahlon Irvin, a farmer, and his new bride Laura Austin, lived there also.

Round Pond or Lake DeVenoge

Lake DeVenoge (Round Pond). Photo: Cynthia Leavenworth Bellinger.

Southeast of Hagan Pond, where the Martin David Myers family settled, was Round Pond, a lake fed entirely by underground springs, and 60 to 80 feet deep at the center.

Today Round Pond is called Lake DeVenoge. The DeVenoge family from France was listed in the 1855 census. And Aunt Aida Austin wrote about going to see Dr. Leon DeVenoge in her 1881 diary.

The DeVenoge Family apparently had plans for a vineyard in the area, but the climate did not cooperate. Dr. Leon, encouraged people that the area would be helpful for those with tuberculosis, and ended up owning quite a bit of property. Sometime after 1916, a golf course was created on what had been Dr. DeVenoge's land. That golf course would play a part in World War II.

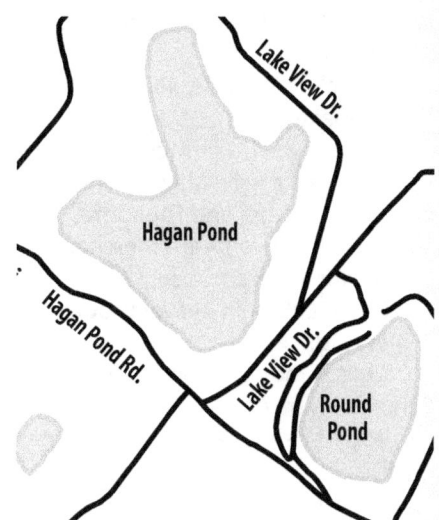

Map showing Hagan Pond (Highland Lake) and Round Pond (Lake DeVenoge). Halfway Brook Village (Eldred) was to the west.

Wilmot and Mary Clark's son George lived in the area. George Clark, 30, was a farmer with real estate valued at $2,000. George's wife of ten years, Harriet Covert was 28. Their family was: Mary Jane, 9, Martin, 7, Ella, 3, Clarissa (Ella Phoebe Sergeant Leavenworth's mother), 9 months, and Samuel Clark, 78, who was blind.

Abraham Ingersoll, 52, was a farmer with real estate valued at $5,000. His wife Sarah or Sally, was 44. Abraham and Sally had six daughters and two sons: Matilda, a milliner, Susan, a dressmaker, Eliza, Jane, Henry, Norma, Sarah, and Stephen. It's possible that Abraham and Sally, their six daughters and two sons lived near the Leavenworths.

Others in 1860

Jonathan Lilly, a laborer, and his wife Lana, had property valued at $400. Henry Lilly, a farmer, and his wife Lydia, had property valued at $2,000.

B.J. Sprague, was a blacksmith, and had three children, Agath, Josephine and Eliza—15, 11, 4.

Jacob Stage, a farmer, had property valued at $2,500. He and wife Martha had five children living with them—George, a school teacher, Albert, Chauncey, Charles, and Elizabeth.

Edward Tether, 64, a farmer, and his wife Elizabeth had property valued at $1,000. Their children: Jane, 19, and Joseph, 17.

Cornelius McBride, 46, was a basket maker.

Samuel West, a farmer from Vermont had a wife, May, and two children, Marietta and Theodore.

Caleb Shotwell, 44, a merchant had a wife, Jane, and a son, Azuba.

Calvin LaBarr in Beaver Brook was 4 years old.

Able Sprague and Maria Van Schoick Myers had a son, James.

Robert Kelso was 29, and a farmer from Ireland. His children were Emma, 4, Edward, 2, and Robert, 1.

David Young, 41, was a farmer with real estate valued at $3,000. His wife Harriet Carmichael was a granddaughter of James Eldred. There is a photo of their daughter Libby in the Appendix, p. 236.

Lewis Carmichael, and his wife, Mary Bunce, and their children, lived in Iowa. (Lewis was Harriet's brother.)

Clinton Briggs, 3, was the son of James Thompson and Catherine Thrush Briggs who lived in Wabash, Indiana. Clinton would be the father of Irwin Briggs, future preacher in the Methodist Churches of Highland. Clinton's grandparents, Benjamin and Sarah Jeffries Briggs, died in Wabash, Indiana, in the early 1860s.

John G.L. Crabtree, 5, his parents, Arnold and Rachel Crabtree, and both sets of Crabtree Grandparents—Richard and Mary, and Elijah and Priscilla—lived near Chicago, Illinois.

Richard and Mary Crabtree lived near Edward and Mary Donaldson Higginson (from Ireland) and their children. Edward Higginson would fight in the Civil War.

Possibly Alonzo Eugene Austin, son of Uncle Augustus. Cynthia Leavenworth Bellinger Collection.

Benjamin Parker, 42, and his wife Emaline, 37, had eight children. Their daughter Letitia Parker had married Samuel C. Myers in 1859, and Felix Kyte had performed the ceremony.

Samuel C. Myers does not seem to be in the direct line of either of the Myers families in this story, but Samuel would be one of the men that fought in the Civil War.

The Henry Austin household was still pretty full and busy in 1860. Henry, Mary Ann, children, Mary Henrietta, 10, Edith, 8, Maria, 6, James Eldred, 4, and Albert Alonzo, 2, as well as Grandmother Hannah Eldred, 71, and the Austin Grandparents, Ralph Austin, 76, and Fanny Austin, 72, were listed as living together in the census. From the Emma Teed letter, it seems that Clara Teed had joined the group for a few months. Perhaps they lived in two homes on the Austin property. Henry Austin was a farm laborer with real estate valued at $800.

Around 1860, the Eldred-Austin cousin, Alonzo Eugene Austin, married Isabelle Johnson Camp. Isabelle, or Belle as she was called, was born about 1840 in New York City.

Alonzo Eugene Austin, son of Uncle Augustus and Aunt Maria, had grown up in Halfway Brook, lived his teen years in New York City, and seems to have studied to become a Presbyterian minister.

The Collins family from Ireland lived to the east of Henry Austin's land and would play a part in the lives of my Austin great-grandparents and grandparents.

In 1860, James Collins, 58, was a farmer with real estate property valued at $2,000. James's family included wife, Isabella, 56, Mary Jane, 25, Robert B., 20, a farmer, Maria, 28, a school teacher, Emma, 8, and William, 5. Son Thomas Collins was not mentioned in the census.

The Collins family lived between my Austin great-grandparents and my Myers great-great-grandparents. Martin D. Myers was a farmer with property valued at $1,500. Martin and Jane Ann, both 44, had George W., 19, Maria, 6, Augustus, 4, and Charlotte, 2. Catharine Van Pelt, 18, was domestic help. Was Catharine Van Pelt a relative?

Jane Ann's son, Charles Cripps Webb, had been married to Sarah Shotwell for three years.

Not too far from the

Church News 1850 to 1860

Congregational Church of Lumberland on 1904 postcard.

Congregational Church Members

1850
George W. Eldred, Edward Wilson.
5 new, 280 total.

1854
Sarah Ingersol, Mary E. Sergeant.
6 new, 303 Total.

1855
David Hickok, Phebe Wilson.
2 new, 305 Total.

1856
Phebe, Alvah, and Caroline Sergeant, Wm. Kyte.
6 new, 311 total.

1857
Eliza J. Gardner, Susannah Ingersol, Catharine Van Pelt.
3 new, 314 total.

1858
Rebecca C. Eldred, Felix J.S. Kyte, Mary Austin.
29 new, 343 total.

1859
Harriet E. Newcome, Isaac and James G. Sergeant, Marietta West (Eldred/Hoatson), Esther and Eliza Ingorsol.
16 new, 359 total.

1860 to 1884
Ethel B. Sergeant deacon in Congregational Church.

Methodist Church

In the 1850s, and perhaps before, the Methodist Episcopal Church met in a building across the brook and across the road from the current Church property.

Jacob Stage, a supporter and friend of the several preachers, recommended the purchase of the present church site.

On November 22, 1858, Daniel Kilferty and his Wife, deeded the present 1/2 acre of Church Property, for $10 to Jacob Stage and the other Trustees: John Whilly, James Collins, Samuel Wells, Samuel Lefarge, Sarah E. Tuthilll, Sherman B. Leavenworth, John Badger, and Hugh Ross.

The Halfway Brook Village Methodist Episcopal Church was built very near the site of the old church building. Rev. Joseph Miller was the preacher at the time.

The church was dedicated July 4, 1859, by the Rev. J.O. Wisner. The members owned both the property and building.

Shortly after the church was built, a wagon shed was added for the use of the members who drove some distance to church. A belfry was added sometime later.

Baptist Church

The Baptist church in Barryville, was built by March 1860, and was known as the Barryville and Shohola Baptist Church.

Postcard of Methodist Church in Eldred. Mary Briggs Austin Collection.

Martin Myers family was the DeVenoge family who lived on Round Pond—later called Lake DeVenoge. Leon DeVenoge, 32, a farmer from Eberney, France, had property valued at $4,000. His wife Catharine, 25, was born in Ireland, and daughter Mary, 3, was born in New York. Great Aunt Aida Austin wrote about going to see Dr. DeVenoge in her 1881 diary, which we will read in Book Two.

John Bishop, his wife Sarah Ingram, and son Stephen Bishop, 20, lived in Standing Stone, Pennsylvania. The whereabouts of John's son Oliver was unknown.

Alexander Carmichael, who we first met as a deacon in the Congregational Church with James Eldred, died in 1860. Alexander was 82.

On April 12, 1861, at 4:30 a.m., Confederate batteries opened fire on Fort Sumter, firing for 34 straight hours.

The Civil War had started and affected the Village of Halfway Brook, including some of my relatives.

In this next chapter on the Civil War years, I have interspersed excerpts of some Eldred-Austin cousin letters with excerpts from the main set of letters—those of Sherman Stiles Leavenworth. Sherman's letters home during the Civil War years give glimpses into the war as well as life back home in Halfway Brook Village.

Note: I want to thank Linda Leavenworth Bohs for permission to print the Civil War letters of our great-grandfather Sherman Stiles Leavenworth, which add much to the understanding of the area and to the times. Sherman's letters have been somewhat edited for easier reading.

Eldred Methodist Church with wagon shed and belfry. Photo: Mary Briggs Austin.

Chapter 8
Letters from a Soldier
1861–1865

We are about 15 miles from the rebels, so close that their cannons can be heard when there is any battles fought. We were cheered all the way through New York, but when we came through Baltimore, we did not get many cheers.

We are going to stay here about two weeks and then we are going to start for Arlington Heights, about four miles the other side of the Potomac River. We are going to get 80 rounds of cartridges a piece today. There is canon a firing across the river now. There was a man took out his watch and the cannons were firing at the rate of 15 a minute.

This is a good deal nicer country than Sullivan County. I have not much time to write now. Tomorrow I will write another letter. You must write all the news that is going on home and you must write whether you are all well or not and how you are all getting along.
—Sherman S. Leavenworth

Envelope addressed to Sherman Buckley Leavenworth in Lumberland. Courtesy of Linda Leavenworth Bohs.

So wrote dark haired, 18-year-old Sherman Stiles Leavenworth to his family in Lumberland. Sherman, a farmer, was five feet, ten inches tall with hazel-colored eyes. He had enlisted as a private in Company B, 56th Regiment, New York Volunteer Infantry, at Newburgh, New York, on August 17, 1861, to serve three years. Company B, 56th Regiment was stationed in Washington D.C. with the 10th Legion, 56th Regiment which defended the capital until March of 1862.

The letter was eagerly read at home by Sherman's father Buckley, mother Charlotte, brothers, Atwell Bishop, 17, Hezekiah Bunce, 15, John Ellis, 10, and 6-year-old sister Julia Ann (Anna or Annie in Sherman's letters).

Sherman's sister Harriet and her husband Henry Palmer lived near Middleton, New York, about 45 miles away. It is not known if their son, Sherman Palmer was still living in 1861.

Two of the Leavenworth neighbors had babies in 1861. And both babies would eventually be connected to the Leavenworth family.

Frank Roberts Sergeant born to Alvah and Phebe Owen Sergeant, would marry Clarissa Clark (who was 1-1/2 years old), and their daughter, Ella Phoebe, would marry a son of Sherman Stiles Leavenworth.

Isaac and Joanna Brown Bradley's newborn, a spunky little girl named Amelia, would be the wife of John Leavenworth, and live a rather long and adventurous life.

Maria Myers, 8, future wife of

Sherman S. Leavenworth. Courtesy of Cynthia Leavenworth Bellinger.

Edna Gardner, granddaughter of Stephen St. John and Louisa Gardner, played the organ at my parents' wedding and gave my mother this 4-inch tall bisque doll. It is now one of my treasures.

Sherman S., lived on the east side of Eldred with her parents, Martin D. and Jane Ann Van Pelt Webb Myers, and siblings: George W.T. Myers, 15, Gus, 5, and Lottie, 3.

In February, Maria's mother, Jane Ann, became a Grandmother when her son Charles C. Webb (from her first marriage), and his wife Sarah Shotwell had a daughter, Clara Webb.

South of Eldred, in Barryville, James K. Gardner, son of Stephen St. John and Louisa Gardner, was born in June. James K. Gardner, named after his grandfather, would marry Ella Breen. They would have a daughter Edna Gardner who would play the organ at my parents' wedding and give my mother a 4-inch tall bisque doll dressed in old fashioned clothes—one of my treasures.

The month before Sherman S. enlisted, his good friend George W. Eldred, a school teacher (who we met earlier), enlisted at Newburgh, to serve three years. George W. was 25, had blue eyes and dark hair, and was five inches shorter than Sherman.

George W. Eldred's parents were Charles C.P. and Effa Van Tuyl Eldred. George was a cousin to the Eldred-Austin cousins, including my Grandfather Mort Austin, who was not born yet.

In his letters of 1861 to 1865, Sherman Stiles often mentioned a neighbor, James Gardner Sergeant. James Gardner, son of Ethel and Letty Gardner Sergeant, enlisted in the 87th N.Y. Regiment in October 1861.

Sherman S. received a letter from home in October and wrote back with his typical greeting and ending.

October 11, 1861

Dear friends,

I thought I would write you a few lines to let you know how I am getting along. I am as well as common at present and you must write as soon as you get this and let me know how you are all getting along, whether you are all well or not. I got your letter today and was very glad to hear from home.

Doctor Vanetten was down here yesterday and vaccinated all the soldiers. All the soldiers had to have it done whether it was done before or not for they say it runs about every seven years. I had it in my arm. I saw Mr. Eldred

> "The following is a list of the men from the Town of Highland, who enlisted in the Civil War.
>
> "Ira M. Austin, Jacob Beck, DeWitt Brown, Geo. Bunce, Gareth T. Clark, Theo. Cotton, Geo. N. Courtright, Geo. Davenport, John Davis, John J. Drake, Johnstone Dunlap, Milo Dunlap, Geo. W. Eldred, Chas. Hickok, Merwin Hickok, Wm Hickok, Chas. Jennings, Addison La Forge, Andrew J. Lawrence, Atwell B. Leavenworth, Hezekiah B. Leavenworth, Sherman S. Leavenworth, Wm Leibla, Dennis S. Middaugh, Adelbert Myers, Charles Myers, Moses Myers, Samuel Myers, Wm Myers, Gilbert Nelson, Manning S. Nelson, Newton B. Nelson, Geo. W. Parker, Martin Quick, Wm Schofield, Isaac Sergeant, James G. Sergeant, Henry Shaw, Wm Smalling, William Smith, Harlan P. West, Theo. West, Edw. B. Wilson, Horton Wilson, Jas. C. Young, L. Coe Young and Samuel M. Young.
>
> "These names were taken from a record in the possession of Rev. John R. Ralph, pastor of the Barryville M.E. Church who will be glad to receive any names which may have been omitted from this report."

A roster of the men from the Town of Highland that enlisted to fight in the Civil War. Copied from scrapbook of Mrs. Mae H. Parker. From the note book of Aida Austin. Courtesy of Melva Austin Barney.

today and Mrs. Eldred. I was very glad to get the things that you sent. You must write who sent the cranberries and chestnuts.

I have got a testament that the captain gave me. All the soldiers have one. They were presented to the soldiers by the Newburg Bible Society.

You must write everything that is going on up home and how you all get along. You must write how much corn and potatoes and buckwheat you have.

It is thought that we will leave here between now and the twentieth.

The lieutenant colonel's name is Ellis. He had a brother killed at the battle of Bull Run. The officers of our company are the best officers on the ground. Their names are Captain Thayers, Lieutenant Vanderburg, Lieutenant Lommis. I will get my likeness taken soon as I can get out on a pass.

I have no more to write at present except that you must write without fail as soon as you get this and let me know how you are getting along.

S.S. Leavenworth

On October 21, 1861, Sherman B. and Charlotte Leavenworth had a new granddaughter—Edith May Palmer, daughter of Henry and Harriet Leavenworth Palmer. Four days after Edith May's birth, Uncle Sherman wrote home again.

October 25, 1861
Dear friends,
Atwell must write me a good long letter as soon as you get this.
I got my gun as soon as I got here. It is a minimusket. It will shoot 900 yards and kill a man. It has the 3-cornered bayonet, but they are the best ones I ever saw.
We are to start Tuesday for Washington. You can tell Horton that we have got guns that will make a fall at 3/4 of a mile. We are to get our canteens and knapsacks before we go away.
James Sergeant is not down here. Only the right and left flanks have the rifle musket.
S.S. Leavenworth

Our Mother, Fanny Austin born April 29, 1788, died June 6, 1861. Wife of Ralph Austin. Photo: Gary Smith.

In June 1861, two months before Sherman enlisted in the Civil War, my great-great-grandmother, Fanny Knapp Austin, died. Fanny Knapp, the wife of Ralph Austin, and mother of nine children, including my great-grandfather, William Henry Austin, had outlived at least three of her children and was buried in the old Eldred Cemetery. After Fanny died, Great-Great-Grandfather Ralph went back to Westchester, New York.

Both Eldred-Austin families had a new addition to their family in November. Great Aunt Aida or Ida (spelled both ways) Austin, the sixth child of William and Mary Ann Austin, joined her siblings, Mary Henrietta, 12, Edith Emogene, 10, Maria Adelaide, 8, James Eldred (Ell), 6, and Albert Alonzo (Lon), 4.

We will be hearing much more about my great aunt Aida Austin, and her brother, my great uncle Lon through letters, diaries, photos, and numerous other items which were shared by my cousin Melva Austin Barney and Mary Briggs Austin, my mother.

Uncle Augustus and Aunt Maria Austin in New York City had a granddaughter, Olinda Ann Austin, the first child of Alonzo Eugene Sr. and Isabelle (Belle) Camp Austin.

Uncle Augustus and Aunt Maria had children who were still at home: Mortimer Bruce, Net, Addie, Miranda (Rand), Edward, Justina, Christina, Clementina, Grace Emma, and little Ida Belle Austin.

Back at Halfway Brook Village, Charles Myers, son of Samuel C. Myers and Letitia Parker, was 4 months old when his father Samuel was made a Corporal in Company F, Excelsior Brigade, 70th N.Y. Volunteers.

Libby Kyte's Teachers

My teachers were Miss Ellen Beakey, George and Albert Stage, George Dubois of Bethel, Harriet Leavenworth, George Egbert Mapes and Theodore Mapes. I attended school here until I was 9 years old. I went to New York City to live with brother Francis to go to school, but stayed only three months when I was taken with the measles.

I went to school at home until 1861, then for two or three years I attended at Shohola and Barryville. I boarded with Mrs. C.P. Fuller. In the fall of 1865, I went to see brother Joseph who then lived at Waterford, Maine.—*Elizabeth (Libby) Kyte, daughter of Rev. Felix Kyte.*

November 19, 1861
Dear friends,
The last news I have heard of our army is that there has been two forts taken lately. It doesn't seem as if we are as close to the enemy as we are. I guess if any regiment is sent on, this regiment will be one.
If anyone had all the grain that comes to Washington in a week, they would have enough to stand them as long as they lived. I never seen so much grain before. There comes in train loads and trains are not short ones neither.
S.S.L.

November 21, 1861
Dear friends,
I am as well as common at present. I seen a possum today. It is the first one I ever saw. One of the men out of the Middletown company killed it. It was about as big as a woodchuck and about the same color.

We had a brigade drill today under brigadier General Davis. It is the first one we have had, but I expect we will have to have one every day now. We are to go, so I heard today, in a brigade of New York troops over the Potomac.

Thare is a great many kinds of punishments in the army. Thare is a man in this regiment that had a barrel with a hole cut through the head of it put over him and stood up on another barrel.

I have got one letter since I have been here and that was one that had been wrote while I was at Newburg. I have bought me a pair of buckskin gloves for a dollar and aim to pay for them payday.
S.S.L.

December 6, 1861
Dear Brother,
I got the dinner yesterday that you sent me. The chicken was first rate and so was the cake.

We went down to Washington yesterday. We was in the reception room of Uncle Abe's house. I never thought thare could be as nice a room as that was. We were in the Smithsonian Institute. I seen more sights in thare than I ever seen before.

The fellows that I tent with is Samuel Bardsley, James Lewis, John McCabe, John Lavermire. Samuel Bardsley is my next best friend to George Eldred. He is an Englishman, but he is honest and he don't brag any like most all others of his country.

I weigh 151 pounds with all my clothes on without my equipment on. It has not snowed any here yet. It is a nice warm day here today.

I will send you a breast pin with the picture of McClelland on it.
S.S. Leavenworth

Washington, December 20, 1861
Dear friends,
I have found out where James Sergeant is. He is in the 87th Regiment Co. C. He came down to our camp yesterday. I did not expect to see him. He has been sick, so I understand him to say, for about two weeks in the hospital, but he is better now. His regiment is going in the same brigade that ours is.

Thare is strong talk in the papers here that England is going to pitch into the north. If she does, I think she will get enough of it. Thare has been talk so I have heard of enlisting more men so if the British interfere, we will have men enough to send to Canada to fight them there.

If Atwell gets a chance to enlist, he better not, for they can swear volunteers in as regulars for 5 years if they are a mind to. Thare has been talk of this regiment being regulars. If George goes in as one, I think I shall, but I think it is a great chance if they do. I expect it is a great consolation to the Tories if there is any prospects of the British helping the south.

Aunt Sal's folks and old Mr. Wilson are tickled half to death about it I suppose.

Write what Isaac Bradley is about and whether he has got his house built yet or not.

I got your first letter since I commenced this one.

James is camped about a quarter of a mile from here. I am going to write him a letter tomorrow.

Thare is a regiment of Lancers that drill about on 1/2 of a mile from here. Their weapons are lanced about 15 foot long.

Our captain told us this morning that we was going down to Pensacola in about two weeks. We have to go through with skirmish drills now days—that is learn to fight in squads of four or more laying down to fire, turning over on our backs to load. It is darned hard work. You have to go double quick so much but I can stand it well anough.

You said you would like to be down to Washington to see some of the nice sights. You had better keep out of the army to see them.

If you was down here, you would not have any fresh pork or any other good things. I have got so used to camp life that I like it first rate.
Sherman S. Leavenworth

1862
Edward Higginson, my maternal great-great-grandfather, joined the 23rd Illinois Infantry Volunteers as a private with Company A, on January 6, 1862, at Chicago, Illinois, to serve three years.

Edward Higginson and Mary Donaldson had immigrated from Ireland in the 1850s, and seem to have been fairly poor. Their fourth child would be born in March. Perhaps the enlistment bonus, equal to several months wages, was a factor in Edward enlisting.

My maternal Crabtree ancestors were neighbors and very good friends with the Higginson family. The family story was that Arnold Crabtree said he would help Edward's wife, Mary Higginson, with chores like getting wood while Edward was gone to war.

During the war, Mary Higginson and her children lived on the second floor of the Crabtree family's house.—Myrtie Crabtree Briggs.

By 1862, Narrowsburg had three hotels, two churches, five

Enlistments in the Civil War

56th Regiment, July 16, 1861
George Eldred, 25, enlisted at Newburgh, to serve three years; mustered in as a sergeant, Co. B; discharged for disability, November 2, 1863, at Beaufort, S.C., 56th Regiment Infantry.

July 16, 1861
Ira Austin, 20, enlisted, at Newburgh to serve three years; mustered in as private, Co. B, August 17, 1861; re-enlisted as a veteran, February 29, 1864; mustered out with company, October 17, 1865, at Charleston, S.C., 56th Regiment Infantry.

August 3, 1861
Sherman Leavenworth, 18, enlisted at Newburgh, to serve three years; mustered in as private, Co. B, August 17, 1861; re-enlisted as a veteran, February 29, 1864; promoted to corporal, July 13, 1864; mustered out with company, October 17, 1865 at Charleston, S.C., 56th Regiment Infantry.

March 30, 1864
Hezekiah Leavenworth, 18, enlisted at Deerpark, to serve three years; mustered in as private, Co. B, March 30, 1864; died of chronic diarrhea, April 25, 1865, at Sparrowbush, N.Y., 56th Regiment Infantry.

87th Regiment and 40th Regiment, October 16, 1861
James Gardner Sergeant, 24, enlisted at Mount Hope, to serve three years; mustered in as a private, 87th Regiment Infantry Co. C, Oct. 17, 1861; transferred to Co. C, 40th Regiment, September 6, 1862.
    Promoted to corporal, October 1, 1863; re-enlisted as a veteran, December 29, 1863; letter of company changed to D, July 7, 1864; promoted to sergeant, March 1, 1865; first sergeant, April 17, 1865; mustered out with company, July 27, 1865, near Washington, D.C., 40th Regiment Infantry.

168th Regiment and 40th Regiment, October 11, 1862
Isaac Sergeant, 28, enlisted at Mount Hope to serve nine months with the 168th Regiment Infantry; mustered in as private, Co. A, January 23, 1863; absent, sick at Chattanooga, since October 16, 1863, and mustered out of company.
    Isaac Sergeant, now 30, enlisted at Goshen, to serve one year with the 40th Regiment Infantry. Mustered in as private, unassigned, September 5, 1864; discharged, May 7, 1865, at Hart's Island, New York Harbor.

143 Regiment, New York Volunteers
Dennis Middaugh, Private, Co. A.

10th Regiment, Ohio Volunteers
William Leibla, three years, Co. G.

54th Regiment, November 18, 1863
George C. Bunce, 36, enlisted at Goshen, to serve 3 years, and mustered in as a private, Co. G, November 18, 1863; discharged for disability, March 7, 1864, at Folly Island, S.C., 54th Regiment Infantry.

November 20, 1863
Atwell B. Leavenworth, 19, enlisted at Goshen, to serve three years, and mustered in as a Private, Co. E, November 20, 1863; died, November 14, 1864, at Folly Island, S.C., 54th Regiment Infantry.

August 30, 1864
Comfort A Boyd, 20, enlisted at Goshen, to serve one year, and mustered in as private, Co. L, August 30, 1864; mustered out, July 5, 1865, at Charleston, S.C., 56th Regiment Infantry.

---

stores, three blacksmith shops, a carpenter shop, a harness shop, an undertaker, a half mile trotting course, and several places to eat.
—*www.tusten-narrowsburg.org.*

Felix Kyte, the pastor of the Congregational Church, and his family lived not far from the Leavenworths. Perhaps you remember that Felix and his family first arrived in Halfway Brook Village in 1832. Felix spoke about those first 30 years:

I have preached alternately in the churches with few omissions for over 30 years or ever since they were erected as well at outer stations at different points during the same time. In the mean time, a new generation has arisen and many beloved ones have either gone to the tomb or moved away. Many are now around me whom I married, having families, whom I knew either as children or as having remembrance of their birth, also have my own family grown up, some being married and having children.

Northwest of the Kyte and the Leavenworth families, lived Irvin and Laura Austin Clark whose first child, Ellsworth, was born in 1862. Ellsworth was a cousin to my grandfather Mort Austin. A 1906 letter written by Ellsworth to his brother was found in a collection of Leavenworth papers.

Washington, January 16, 1862
Dear friends,
    I don't know what they can want better than we eat. We get rice and molasses twice a week, beefsteak twice a week, pork and beans and corned beef the rest of the week. One loaf of bread a day, coffee twice a day, pea soup once in a while, sometimes ham,

potatoes once or twice a week.

The smallpox was in this regiment a while ago, but it is all gone now. I thought I would not write about it at the time for fear you would think I would catch it.

You wanted to know how I got my washing done. We pay a sixpence a piece for a shirt and the same for a pair of drawers. It is cheaper than to wash them ourselves.

I got your letter yesterday and one from Harriet. Harriet's letter stated that they were all well.

I don't know what is the reason you have not got any letters sooner. I write one every two or three days. We have not got our pay yet, but expect to get it now everyday.

Me sending my money home must interfere with Aunt Sal's business a great deal that she should get so mad about it.

You can tell the folks that we have plenty to eat, plenty to wear and every one is contented that is not too shiftless to be contented with anything.

It is thought that this war will be soon over when McClelland pitches into the secessionist.

Our guns got the name of being the best guns that has been seen yet. One of the other regiments are going to be armed with the same kind of guns. If you should hear one of them shot, you would think they kill by the way the bullets whistles. It goes as far ahead of the common cut rifle as you can think.

Sherman S. Leavenworth

Washington, January 18, 1862
Dear Friends,

It is nasty and muddy under foot and we don't have to drill when it is muddy. It is reckoned that thare will be some savage fighting going on in a month or two.

We are going to be presented with the nicest flag in the United States. Uncle Abe is going to be here when it is presented.

I want you to write if you have got that money from Mr. Eldred yet that I sent home.

S.S. Leavenworth

Washington, February 1, 1862
Dear Friends,

Thare was a skirmish across the river the other day. Our troops killed thirty of them which was all but one. They was Texan Rangers, but they was not a match for northerners. Van Wyck says we will go to Fort Monroe.

I am sorry to hear that Hezzy has got such a bad sore throat. I wish you would write and tell me who directed your letter dated the 27, about the Dewitt desertion. It is not so. He is here and likely he will be here, for he can not get away very well.

They are trying to pass a bill against franking the letters, but I can pay the postage on my letters. You will see twenty dollars along there before long. I guess I am waiting for George to get a pass so I can send it by express.

You must write all the news that is going on up home. George is well. James was up here the other day. He was well.

S.S. Leavenworth

Washington, March 1, 1862
Dear Friends,

One thing you wrote that you had about made up your mind to enlist. You had better take my advice and not come. You would likely have a nice ride coming here, but you would get nothing

1907 Postcard to McKinley Austin born in 1899. McKinley was a grandson of Sherman S. Leavenworth. "McKinley, I suppose you read about this great man in school." —Miss Shaw. Courtesy Mary Briggs Austin.

but a hardboard to sleep on and we do not have a good living as we got up to Newburgh. If you will mind what I write, you will be better off. Besides, it is purty certain we will move after payday which is in a few days.

We was mustered in for pay yesterday. I intend to send 40 dollars home. Vanwyck has left his seat in Congress for to take charge of his regiment.

I received that paper you sent to me and was very glad to get it. That box has not got here yet. We can get cake and such things, but it is better what comes from home.

You must not enlist for anything. You will be sorry if you do. You could get in this

company. If you did, you would go in the company that you enlisted in. You had better let it alone.
S.S. Leavenworth

April 26, 1862,
Dear Brother,
Thare is not much news around here now, only that it is likely that there will be a great battle before long.

We are about two miles from the enemies lines. We have been routed out a number of times to be ready to fight the enemy nights. By hearing the report of musketry, their lines of batteries is two miles from here. I was up within 800 yards of it and seen our batteries through shells in it. It was fun alive to see the burst in their works. They have sharp shooters to keep them room working their guns while our gunners throw the shells in them all sorts.

I seen James yesterday. His regiment lays about four miles from here in another direction from Warwick Court house, rather more advanced on the enemy works than we are.

You need not come down here for father need not let you come. As soon as you are not of age that is not of the right age. You are under eighteen. If they come after you give them the clothes and don't go. You must not come for if you got sick to Middletown, you would not live to see home.
S.S. Leavenworth

On May 20, 1862, President Abraham Lincoln signed into law The Homestead Act, which gave freehold title to 160 acres of undeveloped land in the American West. The person to whom the title was granted had to be at least 21 years of age, and to have built on the section, and lived in a house (at least 12 by 14 feet), for five years.

The Briggs, Crabtree, and Higginson families would take advantage of the Homestead Act in Nebraska in the 1880s.

July 8, 1862
Dear friends,
Thare is not much news around here. Now we lay about a mile from the James River. Our troops are preparing to make a stand here. We lay under cover of the gunboats.

The guns on the boats are the largest kind of gun. Some of the guns carry balls and shells weighing 2 pounds. If you should hear the shell go screaching through the air as they go flying back in the country 3 or 5 miles, you would not wonder the rebels dread them. They will shoot 5 miles.

I wish you would send me a county paper once in a while. I will send you the money to pay postage on them if you will. Send the "Republican" if you can.

You must write to me if you got the check cashed. I guess I can send home twenty dollars this time if we get paid. Write if Anna has grown any since I seen her. Write what the neighbors are at.

Father and the boys must not work hard enough to hurt themselves. If the work is too hard, they must hire some one to help them. I will send 20 dollars every time I get paid. Tell Johney he must be good to Mother. I think likely I will send him a little money on payday. Well, no more at present,
S.S. Leavenworth

July 26, 1862
Dear Brother,
I expect you are in the haying heavy now. I am glad to hear that the corn looks well. I suppose you will have plenty of rye bread next winter. I wish I had some now. We get a good deal of bacon. It is the worst meat I ever ate.

56th Regiment

The 56th Regiment, New York Infantry was organized at Newburgh, N.Y., and mustered in October 28, 1861. They left for Washington, D.C., November 7, 1861, where they were attached to 1st Brigade, Casey's Division, Army of the Potomac, until March 1862.

Colonel Ellis, was proud of his officers and regiment as he had instructed and drilled the men and officers, and thoroughly taught them the duties of soldiers, all the routine of military business, and brought the regiment to a high state of discipline and efficiency. Colonel Ellis very much wanted to command it as its colonel, and used all his best endeavors and influence to that end.

But Col. Van Wyck would not consent and his influence, coupled with the fact that he had recruited the regiment, enabled Van Wyck to retain the command of the boys he so much loved and assured them that he would not desert them, and would look after them during their term of service according to his promise to their parents, families, and friends.

Col. Ellis, much to his regret, was obliged to sever his connection with the regiment.

The 56th Regiment lost one Officer and 63 Enlisted men, killed and mortally wounded; and three Officers and 213 Enlisted men by disease. Total: 280.—*www.itd.nps.gov/cwss/regiments.cfm.*

I got a letter yesterday from Harriet stating that they was going home a visiting. I would like to see Anna. I would like to see you all. Tell Anna she must learn to read and write as quick as she can. You must write whether she can read and write along in the book that she has.

I would like to see the steers. They must have grown very fast. Write whether you have worked them alone yet. Write how Mr. Bradley's oxen looks. I am glad you have got such a nice looking bull. I think it must be the worst punishment that Aunt Sal can be afflicted with—to be so she cannot get any huckleberries. She must be raving about it.

I don't think the Monitor would stand any chance at all with its big 200-pounder, if she should come down here and have an engagement with it.

Write if there has been anything heard about James Sergeant yet. I have not heard anything about him. Write what our folks think, whether I had better write Isaac Bradley a letter once in a while.

I am well and hearty now, but took to blue hill for a kind of dysentery that the soldiers have a good deal. It does not hurt anyone very bad if they don't let it go too long. I am not bad off with it.

Write how Mr. Sergeant's folks seem about James. Harriet wrote to me all about the picnic. They had purty smart speakers. I guess George and Joe and Miller are all well. Tell their folks. I would like to have some good Republican write me.

S.S. Leavenworth

July 30, 1862

Dear Brother,

I am as well as common at present, only I have got the

U.S.S. Onondaga, a double-turreted monitor, on the James River, Va., 1864. Photo: National Archives photo no. 111-B-368.

scurvy very bad. It is the worst disease I ever had. I have got it so bad that I can only get two or three hours sleep along towards morning.

Thare is quite a good many got it here. One man in another regiment has got it so bad that he has got a solid scab all over his breast and stomach as thick as your hand. They say it will surely kill him.

The doctors say that if we don't stop eating so much greasy and salty meat, it will surely kill us. They say that we must live on vegetables. If we can not get that, we must go out in the woods and browse. Vegetables cost a tremendous price.

I will send you all my wages I possibly can, but I must save enough to keep me from eating so much salt and greasy meat which I have to. If I don't have some money, the surgeon says I must stop eating it if I want ever to get well, and it keeps getting worse. I would like to send you all my wages if I possibly could. Besides the scurvy, I have got boils all over my arms like I had on my body one winter.

The papers can say what they are a mind to or any person. I know this is a very unhealthy place. I guess the generals and government know it too, but don't like to own it.

The rebels congratulate themselves in having us in unhealthiest parts of Virginia.

Colonel Van Wyck made us soldiers a speech last night at dress parade about home traitors. I bet it was as smart as any he ever made in Congress, only a little more harsh, but not too much so. I wish you could have been here to hear him. He put them down as mean, sneaking, miserable wretches, meaner than the adders that crawl in the dust that stay at home and hiss out their serpent stings at the ones that lay in the swamps along the James and Chicohomany Rivers.

I got a letter from Comfort Boyd giving me a good deal of advice. I am glad that James Sergeant is safe. I heard that he was a prisoner in North Carolina.

We have just been turning in our old cartridges and drawn new ones. The kind we have we only have to ram them once, then we are ready to cap the gun. It saves a good deal of time. We have the Springfield rifle musket with the minie ball.

You must write how you are getting along with the work. Let me know what most of the people think about the war. I suppose you and Isaac Bradley go a fishing quite often.

"Rosin ready for export." From "Sunny South" Postcard folder sent to Aida Austin in 1917. Mary Briggs Austin Collection.

Antietam

Antietam Bridge, Maryland, September, 1862. Soldiers and wagons crossing the bridge. Photo: National Archives photo no. 165-SB-19.

The Battle of Antietam/Sharpsburg was fought September 17, 1862, near Sharpsburg, Maryland, and Antietam Creek.

It was the first major battle in the American Civil War to take place on Northern soil, and the bloodiest single-day battle in American history: Union, 2,108 killed, 9,549 wounded; Confederacy, 2,700 killed, 9,029 wounded.

President Lincoln used this costly Union victory to issue a preliminary Emancipation Proclamation on September 22, 1862, freeing slaves in Confederate-held states. It went into effect on January 1, 1863.

Johnny must write me a good long letter. Write as soon as you get this. Write all the news.
S.S. Leavenworth

August 19, 1862
Dear Brother,
I am as well as common, but nearly covered with boils, but as they are good for me other ways, I get along without complaining although, they hurt purty hard. I have had two lanced on my arm. If it was not for them, I believe I would have the fever now.

I expect the drafting business makes a greate excitement amonge the tories up there. You must write what George Clark says about it, and what Aunt Sal says.

Two of our gunboats shelled the woods right acrost the river from here yesterday. They say some rebels came down there and fired at one of our boats. If they were there, I guess they got out quicker than they came in. We expect to go away from here now. All the time two or three divisions are under marching orders, but none of the officers can tell where we are going.

Write what Isaac Bradley says about the draft.
S.S. Leavenworth

Yorktown, August 30, 1862
Dear Brother,
I received your letter today and was glad to hear from you that you were done haying and harvesting. I am glad to hear that the boys seem to be so willing to enlist. You may go to Goshen and see them drill if you are a mind to, but don't enlist for anything. You better take this advice.

I am very glad to get the papers that the boys sent me. Also the head of rye. It looks nicer for rye than the wheat down here.

I am glad to hear you have so many apples.

Payday is near at hand. I have made up my mind that every payday that I see after this, that I will send 20 dollars home.

I guess it is so that the Arkansas has went in. Then Isaac Bradley does not like to leave home situated as he is at present.

If you get a letter from Uncle John's folks, write to Stephen and tell him to write me a letter.

Tell Mrs. Sergeant that we can learn nothing further about James than he was taken prisoner. We cannot see his regiment for it is with (Pope) and we are at Yorktown. I am going out now to get something to send in this letter.

We can get clams here anytime we are a mind to go in the river and get them. We have clam stews all we want of them, but we will not have it so nice all the time.

These strings what I send in this letter, one is the circumference and the other is the diameter of a ten-inch gun.

S.S. Leavenworth

Where was James Gardner Sergeant? In October 1861, James had mustered in with the 87th Infantry. December 2, 1861, under the leadership of Col. Stephen A. Dodge, the 87th Infantry left New York for Washington, and served with the Army of the Potomac, until September 6, 1862.

The 87th suffered its first losses at Fair Oaks/Battle of Seven Pines, Virginia, where 76 men were killed, wounded, missing, or captured.

The 87th also participated during the Seven Days' Battles from June 25 to July 1, 1862, where 38 were wounded or killed.

The 87th then joined in Gen.

Four Trees

Trees on the Leavenworth Homestead. Photo: Gary Smith.

Sherman B. and Charlotte Leavenworth had four sons. Sherman S., Hezzie B., and Atwell B., were in the Civil War. Son John E. was too young to fight in the Civil War, but fought out West with Custer.

When I visited Eldred in July 2007, Alice Willis, owner of the Leavenworth Homestead, told the story of how a tree was planted for each of the Leavenworth sons that went to war. The tree would be cut down if the son did not come back from the war.

In the photo above, the trees on the right are said to be where the original four trees were planted. —Louise Austin Smith.

Typical Iron clad Union gunboat. Photo: USS St. Louis, James Ead's first 'City Class' Ironclad Gunboat, renamed Baron de Kralb, in October, 1862. Photo: Naval Photographer, unknown. Source: http://steamboattimes.com/civil_war_ironclads.html.

Pope's Virginia campaign, August 26 to September 2, where it suffered a loss of 68—3 died, 6 were wounded, and 57, including 7 officers, were missing.

The 87th Regiment was consolidated with the 40th Regiment, N.Y. Infantry, and its members completed their term of service.—*The Union Army: A History of Military Affairs in the Loyal States, 1861-65, Vol. 2,* 1908.

James G. Sergeant was one of the men transferred to the 40th Regiment, in September 1862, and

A 200-pound (8-inch) Parrott rifle in Fort Gregg on Morris Island, S.C., 1865. Sherman Leavenworth mentioned a 10-inch (300-pound) gun in his letters. Photo: National Archives photo no. 165-S-128.

was safe as you will soon read.

In Richard Eldred's, *The Eldred Family*, pp. 73–4, there is a letter from Sherman's friend George W. Eldred to his mother, Effa Van Tuyl Eldred. George mentioned calomel in his letter. Calomel, also called mercuric chloride, is a white powder used as a purgative and a fungicide.

October 3, 1862
Dear Mother (Effa Eldred),

A week ago last Friday, I had a toothache in the whole of the teeth on the right side of my face. I went to the steward to get some medicine for it and he gave me an overdose of Morphine which soon stopped the aching, but it made me very dumpish and took away my appetite.

I lay in my bed until Saturday evening without getting any better when I sent Rider up for Doctor Van Etten. He came and gave me some medicine and told me I was a candidate for the Fever. Monday he gave me an emetic.

For four days I was tied to my bunk with alternate fever and slight chills. What you might call intermittent fever as it was not the regular ague.

I had no appetite and did not eat anything but a piece of toast about two inches square. I also drank very little as I supposed that would make my fever worse and I had calomel or something similar for medicine with orders to take it in molasses.

Since then, I have been taking quinine and Jamaican ginger until today when I quit taking medicine, and am going to let nature do the rest.

George Washington Eldred

Yorktown, October 16, 1862
Dear Brother,

Thare does not seem to be much fighting going on now. We are drilling skirmish drill and bayonet exercises. Nowadays, the skirmish drill is to deploy to the right and left five paces apart in a line, then advance loading and

Minie Ball

The use of rifles in battle was impractical and largely limited to corps of elite marksmen. Expensive, tight fitting projectiles had to be jammed into the grooves of the rifle's muzzle, a time-consuming process.

Round balls did not fit so tightly into the barrel, and therefore did not suffer from the slow loading problem common to rifles. Black powder also quickly obscured the battlefield, which led military leaders to conclude that the greater range of rifles was of little value on the battlefield. Therefore they preferred the faster loading smooth bore weapons over the more accurate rifles. The invention of the Minie ball solved the slow loading problem.

The Minie Ball got its name from its inventor, Captain Claude Minie of the French Army. It was conical in shape and made of soft lead, with two or three grease grooves around its body. Upon firing, the hot gases expanded into the hollow base of the ball, forcing the soft lead into the rifling grooves inside the barrel. These grooves, which spiraled as they traveled the length of the barrel, imparted a spin to the ball, increasing the effective range to 300 yards, or more; up to 600 yards to hit either the man or the horse he was riding. By comparison, the obsolete .69 caliber smoothbore had a maximum effective range of 100 yards or less.

Against a defensive line using musket fire, a frontal infantry charge was likely to be successful only if the assaulting force moved quickly enough. The widespread use of the Minie bullet shifted the balance greatly to the defense's favor. Nevertheless, Civil War generals continued ordering such attacks, learning only after hard and bloody battlefield experience that their strategy would have to be altered. *Sources: http://www.civilwarhome.com/weapons.htm, http://en.wikipedia.org/wiki/Rifles_in_the_American_Civil_War.*

The Goose Lot and Stone Walls

Stonewalls on what was Leavenworth Property.

Stonewalls in 2009.

Inside the Gooselot.

Photographs courtesy of Cynthia Leavenworth Bellinger.

John Leavenworth mentioned the stone walls on their property in a letter to his brother Sherman. Here are some photos of the walls, and the goose lot.

The goose lot was a large area surrounded by stone walls with a space that was left for a gate.

The geese had one wing clipped so they couldn't fly over the stone walls.

The Leavenworths raised geese for their meat and eggs. Their feathers were used for stuffing pillows and comforters.

The walls were probably built in the Civil War era.

Dad mentioned that Atwell was working on stone walls before he went to war and probably the goose lot was part of that too.—Cynthia Leavenworth Bellinger.

One of the stories said that because the men were fighting in the war, it left the ladies at home to finish making the rock walls. The ladies carried the rocks in their aprons to the place they needed to be, or so the story goes. Some of those rocks were pretty heavy.—Louise Austin Smith.

firing. It is to find out the strength of an enemy that lays in a wood or any worse, out of sight.

Always before an attack, the attacking forces throw their skirmishers out ahead and deploy them. The skirmishers then advance driving the pickets off the enemy, till they come on the enemy so strong that they can not drive them or they find out his position, and what strength he appears in. They then commence to retreat, keeping in line, firing. If they see anything to fire at, they retreat back to the rear. They are then sent to their respective regiments, then the attack is commenced, if the officers in command think it is best.

The bayonet exercise is learning the thrusts, parries and volts. The thrusts is thrust lung and lung out, thrusting at different parts of the body is this at the right shoulder or breast.

In quarter, thrust at the left leg. In second, thrust at the center of the body. I don't know whether you will understand this or not. There are some French words in it as it is a French drill mostly. If I can ever get a drill book, I will send it to you and then you can see for yourself.

They practice shooting with the big cannons now. They fire from the fort down past our camp. The 100-pound rifle shot makes a screech that you can hear 2 miles or over. They go away down towards the bay 2, 3, and 4 miles.

Thare is parrot guns at the fort that will shoot 6 miles, so said. They are the best guns in the service, dahlgren guns and columbaids. The columbaids are the biggest. There is one large mortar, also brass howitzers.

I have seen the big guns throw shell grape and solid shot. The grape for the big guns weigh about a pound, bound up in canvas bags. Thare is also what is called shrapnel shot. It is 9 shots which weigh 6 pounds each.

A round flat piece of cast iron that will fit the bore of the cannon is laid down with three little indentures in the side of it. Then three shots are laid on a ring made out of iron about as big as a nail rod which leaves a place for three more shots than another ring, and three more shots then a piece of iron like the one on the bottom.

Then thare is a bolt run through both pieces and drawn down tight on the shot by a bar on top. When this is fired, it flies all to pieces and it does quarter the pieces of iron and ring does as much execution as the shots.

I am glad to hear that James is safe. Mr. Sergeant's folks must feel more contended about it. I heard that Alfred Crawford was home. It seems that George Parker is going to try which regiment he likes best. I heard old Seymour was going to nominate him.

I have been in what you might call one battle, White Oak Swamp. Thare was no musketry, but the heaviest cannonading any time during the war. I have been in four or five reconnoiters. When we were fired on, I never had a shot at the enemy, but it was not because my will was not good enough. It was because I had no chance.

Never mind if Aunt Sal's folks and Bradleys are getting very thick. It is natural for Aunt Sal to be very thick with anyone before she blows out about them.

I would like to see your new fallow, also the old one. Write if you have sown the old fallow again. I am glad the corn is good. I am glad the potatoes are of a good quality, what thare is of them. It is very few sweet potatoes we get here. They are easier got up north than here. I am sorry the pumpkins are no better. I wish I could get home as to get some of those squashes and some fresh pork.

Stickels is in the company now. Us boys from up around home get along very well.

Write whether Mr. Skank has put any fallow yet. The rye will be apt to get ahead far enough so the frost will not kill it on the flat meadow. The rye seems to turn out first rate, six bushels to the hundred sheaves.

I guess you got the gun middling cheap. Was Leamandos Consons (?) company raised in Tusten, Highlands, and

Confederate money in the collection of Mary Briggs Austin.

Lumberland? How does buckwheat turn out?
S.S. Leavenworth

Yorktown, November 3, 1862
Dear Brother Atwell,
I was glad to hear you was all well.
It seems that Isaac and Perkens are going to try soldiering a while. Don't you enlist. If you could not stand it to Middletown, you could not stand it here in camp where you would have to stand out in rainstorms often. Now I will answer your questions.
I have as comfortable clothes as anyone could wish. I come out $3 in debt to Uncle Sam for the clothes this year. It is not as much as I thought I owed him. I will have $40 to send home this time if I am paid all that is due me.
We can get papers to go anywheres. Inside of the pickets we get clams once in awhile. Now a fellow by the name of John Crosby went with me yesterday and we got a good mess. Yorktown is not as big as Barryville.
Thare is not many gunboats here now, only two. I believe the old Alabama may get fetched up one of these days.
You wanted to know if I had more than one blanket. I have got two. The weather is not very cold here yet. We get very good rations now. Jim Mulligan is not in this company. I don't know where he is.
I was very glad to get those flowers that Anna sent me. Write if Anna grows much.
Write what you shot his bull for. Your musket kicked like a cannon. I am glad you have rye.
I would write you all the particulars about me being in the guard house, only Harriet said in her letter she was going home and

The 13-inch mortar "Dictator" mounted on a railroad flatcar before Petersburg, Virginia., October 1864. Photo: National Archives photo no. 165-SB-75.

Columbiad guns of the Confederate water battery at Warrington, Florida (entrance to Pensacola Bay), February 1861. Photo: National Archives photo no. 77-HL-99-1.

Gun crew of a Dahlgren gun at drill aboard the U.S. gunboat Mendota, 1864. Photo: National Archives photo no. 111-B-374.

Ralph Austin, my great-great-grandfather. Photo courtesy of Mary Briggs Austin.

she can tell you all about it.

We shoot at targets now days. We shoot Tuesdays and Fridays. I come second closest to the bull's eye, Tuesday. A fellow by the name of Litts came closest to it next. We received by General Keys today an inspection.

I will send Johnny a Confederate bill. It was struck in Philadelphia but it is just like one that was taken out of a dead rebel Captain's pocket at Williamsburg.

S.S. Leavenworth

Yorktown, December 1, 1862
Dear Brother Atwell,

I was glad to hear that you are all well. It is a rainstorm here now. I just came off of guard this morning and just missed the storm. We have got a middling good tent.

Now how do you think we built the house that we live in? Now we got sticks 5 foot long. We then dug a trench around the space that we wanted the tent to cover, then we stood the sticks close together as they could be stood, the trench being 2-foot deep. We then plastered the cracks up with mud and stretch our tent on top of them. It makes a very good tent.

We have not got our pay yet, but I guess we will get it before long. I have not got any mittens, but if we ever get paid, I can get a pair. I am glad that you and Hezzy weigh as much as you did. I will weigh myself the first

Mortimer Bruce Austin wrote a letter to his grandfather Ralph Austin in January 1863. Photo courtesy of Melva Austin Barney.

chance I get. I am glad you got the fallow so near cut. I lost your letter yesterday and can not find it.

S.S. Leavenworth

Yorktown, December 11, 1862
Dear Brother,

On the 11th, early in the morning we fell in line and was marched off with packed knapsacks. We were marched to Gloster County and when we were there, marched 15 miles to Gloster Court House where we camped.

We went there with the calculations of fighting rebels, but they had run. I went on picket the same night. It was cold as the deuce and the officer that was officer of the guard put us under cover of a fence as much as he could so we would not be so apt to get fired at. We laid close and kept a sharp look out. There was a picket shot and killed on post. The next morning we came off of picket.

The general gave orders for a detail to be made out of each regiment to go and forage. They went out in the country taking every horse, pig, sheep, ox, they could find. Also searched the houses taking all the guns powder and lead, whiskey, cider and so forth.

They did not get orders to take fowls, but they did not wait for the orders and I guess the general did not care much. When we went there you could hear the roosters crow in every direction, but when we came away you could not hear one. We had all the fowls we could carry in the forenoon of the twelfth while the first foraging party was out. We seen fellows coming in with lots of hens, turkeys and geese.

They told us that they did not

see how we dare come so far out with out arms as there was rebels in the swamps right below the farm, so we began to make our way to camp, for if they should get us, they would cut our throats in a minute.

We got to camp about noon. Then we went out on a foraging party. We went to the same house and got three horses, a team of mules. They made a great cry, but we showed them as much mercy as the rebs commonly show us.

We got paid yesterday. I sent $35 in an express envelope to father last night. I wish he would let mother have $10 of it.

Write as soon as you get this and let me know if you got the money and if you are all well or not. Write all the news. Write a good long answer. Excuse poor spelling, bad writing, as this is wrote with a rebel pen. No more at present.

S.S. Leavenworth

1863

The following letter from the collection of Melva Austin Barney, was to Ralph Austin from his grandson Mortimer Bruce Austin, son of Uncle Augustus and Aunt Maria Austin.

The letter mentioned Uncle Samuel had been discharged from the army. Most likely Samuel was Ralph's son, Samuel Knapp Austin.

There is a record of a Samuel K. Austin fighting in Pennsylvania's 28th Regiment. In October 1862, the surplus men of Pennsylvania's 28th Regiment were organized into companies in Pennsylvania's 147th Regiment, where a Samuel K. Austin is again mentioned.

Cousins William and Charles Austin, and their mother, were also talked about in the letter.

Stereographs

Stereographs from the collection of Mary Briggs Austin.

A stereograph is a double-image of the same subject that, when viewed through a stereoscope, looks three-dimensional.

After 1856, double pictures were taken with twin-lens cameras which looked like three dimensions when viewed through a stereoscope.

Stereography, first described in 1832, by the English physicist Charles Wheatstone, works only with photography, as no artist can draw two scenes in exact perspective from viewpoints separated only 2-1/2 inches—the normal distance between human eyes.

Wheatstone's mirror stereoscope was not practical for use with photographs. But in 1851, the Scottish scientist, Sir David Brewster, exhibited his simplified viewing instrument at the Great Exhibition in the Crystal Palace, London. Queen Victoria was entranced by the stereo daguerreotypes. Three-dimensional photography soon became a popular craze.

The London Stereoscopic Company was formed in 1854. Between 1860 and about 1920 a stereo viewer was commonplace in British and American homes, where a simplified and cheap hand viewer was introduced by Oliver Wendell Holmes.

Millions of stereographs were circulated in the years before newspaper reproduction of photographs.—*Source: www.stereoscopy.com/faq/whatis.html.*

"Siege of Vicksburg: Assault on Fort Hill" by Thure de Thulstrup, 1883. This image displays the intense fighting between Union and Confederate forces on June 25th, 1863, at Fort Hill. John C. Pemberton's Army of Vicksburg were able to stop the assault of Union Forces which lasted 26 hours. Source: http://www.army.mil/-images/2007/07/01/5978.

William and Charles may be sons of Samuel Knapp Austin, and his wife Susan Teed Austin. William as we will find out later, also fought in the Civil War.

New York, January 6, 1863
Dear Grandfather [Ralph Austin],
Your letter of December 18th came to hand in due time and I was very glad to hear from you, but sorry to hear that your health continues so poorly and hope this may find you enjoying better health. I have sent you a paper today by mail containing some very important news which I know you will read with a good deal of pleasure.

General Rosencrans has gained a great victory over the Rebels at Murfreesboro, Tenn. After fighting five days, the Rebels retreated in great disorder and our army is in pursuit of the fleeing enemy. The loss is said to be very heavy on both sides.

There has also been a great battle at Vicksburg and we have gained another glorious victory and the Stars and Stripes are now waving over Vicksburg, and Mississippi is cleared of the Rebels. But there is no need of my saying anything about the battles, as you can read it in the papers. We have not as yet received any particulars, but as we do I will send you another paper.

We are having very fine weather here at present, and so far we have had an exceedingly mild winter.

Business is quite dull at this time, but has been very fair until within a few weeks past. Uncle James is working in the store that he used to cart for and is as well as usual. Father's business has been pretty good until lately.

Uncle Samuel was at our house Christmas and stayed two or three days. He has got his discharge from the army. He looks much better than he did when he was here before.

I received a letter from cousin William Austin last month stating that he was at Nashville and enjoying good health. Said that he had been to Memphis and seen his mother and brother Charles. I don't think of anything more of importance to write about. All the folks are enjoying good health except mother who has been sick since Christmas but is getting better.

Give my love to all inquiring friends and reserve a share for yourself. I remain as ever your affectionate grandson,
M.B. Austin

Ralph Austin's great-grandson, Charles Raymond Austin, would be born in 1900. Raymond would fight in another war and write letters home to his parents, Mort and Jennie Leavenworth Austin. One of Raymond's letters would mention that two cousins of his father, Mort Austin, had died in the Civil War.

Charles Raymond Austin would marry Gladys Myers, whose father, Edwin Van Schoick Myers, was born to Abel Sprague and Maria Van Schoick Myers in March 1863. Edwin would be a good friend to Mort Austin, Raymond's father, and my grandfather.

Port Royal, South Carolina, March 13, 1863
Dear Brother Atwell,
In answer to yours of Feb. 22. I am glad to hear that you are all enjoying good health.

We have just come in from drill. It is a new drill to us. It is to embark in surf boats off of the transports and land anywhere along the seashore, whether under the fire of the enemy or not. We did it good for ones that are calculated to be green hands at the business.

The surf boats will hold from 30 to 50 men. We started at 11 o'clock a.m. and got back to camp at 5 o'clock p.m. We expect to have to drill it more before we leave here before long.

You say there was a surprise party at our house. What kind of a party is a surprise party? Write who all was there.

I seen one of the Monitors today. I do not care much how soon we leave here. I will soon have two years of my time in.

We hear here that there has been certain propositions about drafting being made up north. If so, I suppose it stirs up the minds of the cowboys to the highest pitch of excitement.

Write how Isaac Bradley gets along. Write if you hear how James Sergeant likes soldiering.

We expect to hear of some fighting up towards Richmond soon. We heard that we were to go back to Virginia from another report. We heard that we were to wait here till spring time set in, then attack Charleston or Savannah.

Write if Annie can read very good or not. Write who all was to that surprise party. Coe and Miller is well. It is purty warm here. The sun, when it rises and sets, looks just as it does in Indian summer. We are to get fresh bread today. We have not had it only once or twice since we left Newberg. The sand drifts like snow down here.

We hear the reports of heavy artillery off towards Savannah once in a while.

S.S. Leavenworth

Harriet and Henry Palmer adopted a son Harry who was a year older than their daughter Edith. Harry was mentioned in the 1865 Census, but it is not known when he was adopted. The baby in the following letter could be either Edith, 1-1/2 or Harry, 2-1/2.

Seabrook Island, South Carolina, April 23, 1863
Dear Brother,

I am glad you improve in your studies so fast as you say you can write as good as I can. Now you must study and learn all you can. If they take photographs in Port, I wish you would all get yours taken and send me. I will send two dollars in this letter to pay for them. If it is more than pays for them, get a few postage stamps. We can not get any here.

We got paid the other day. I am going to send home $30. I would like to send more, but I want to keep a little more than I did the other payday, as I got out of money and did not have any writing paper nor any money to get it with.

I am glad that the baby is such a nice one. That was a nice lock of hair. I am glad you sent it. Write how old the baby is.

You write that you would like to enlist. You will have the chance to yet. I never seen anyone improve as fast as you do both in writing and composing. You must continue to study and I warrant you will have a good education by the time you are 20 years old.

I would like to have you send me a county paper once in a while if you can as well as not.

S.S. Leavenworth

Seabrook Island, South Carolina, May 1863
Dear Brother Atwell,

General Ferry has moved his headquarters on this island. I guess we will stay here this summer. It is very warm here at present. It is a great deal easier soldiering down here than it is in Virginia.

The news here is that Hooker has achieved some brilliant victories around Richmond. I suppose that James Sergeant has been in some of those battles. You must write whether James has been in any battles or not.

We have a very nice place to go in bathing. It is sea water. I go in every day.

We went on picket last Thursday and stayed a week. Our company and company E was on reserve. Some of the boys of our company shot an alligator and let Col. Van Wyck have it. He is going to have it skinned and send the skin home stuffed.

We are going to move camp tomorrow. We are not going to move far. It is a very nice shady camp. I guess we will move before long as the Arago has arrived at Port Royal.

There is ovens being put up here for the purpose of baking bread for the army here. For a days ration of bread, a soldier is allowed 12 ounces. Therefore we get a loaf of bread of 12 ounces. It is all a person wants with his other rations.

The officers and privates of this regiment are going to make Colonel Van Wyck a present. The officers are going to present him with a horse. The privates with a sword and sash.

When you write, you must write if James has been in any battles yet. That is lately. There is not any prospects of us doing fighting here right away. There is 6 Monitors in the harbor at present.

6 o'clock p.m.: We had preaching by a stranger at 3 o'clock p.m. He goes around to all the regiments a preaching. He was a very smart speaker. I have not heard his name yet.

The 3 soldiers that went on furlow out of our company went today. I do not know whether I will get a furlow or not. If I do not, if nothing happens, I will get a discharge in just a year.

We expect the mail from the Arago everyday now. I never seen so many snakes and so many different species. One of the boys caught a rattlesnake today. The captain has got him alive. There are rattlesnakes, king snakes, moccasins, black snakes, garter snakes and ever so many other kinds that I do not know the name of yet.

One of the boys in Co. G caught a young fawn the other day. It was the handsomest animal I ever saw. There are black squirrels, also gray squirrels. We see them running through the live oak trees, not white oak trees, and I never have climbed after them yet.

May 25, 9 o'clock p.m.: I just received your letter of the 15th. I am glad to hear that you are all well. The furlow men were all sent. The reason is I believe that we are to go in to active service. I have not heard where it is yet.

I have a notion to write a letter to James. The war in Virginia seems to be carried on with more vigor than it has anytime before. I will try to see what I can do about sending you a drill book. Write soon.

S.S. Leavenworth

Ralph Austin 1784–1863

My great-great-grandfather Ralph Austin, born in Connecticut, son of Joshua and Mary Austin, died, June 4, 1863, in Westchester, New York, at the age of 79. He was buried in Westchester, New York.

Ralph Austin went back to his old home and died there and was buried there. But Grandmother Austin is buried in the Eldred Cemetery by her daughter Ann Mary Schoonover.—Ralph's granddaughter Aida Austin.

Seabrook Island, South Carolina, June 18, 1863

Dear Brother,

We have been on picket for a week. We did not see much of the rebels while we were on picket. They came near our picket line Tuesday. They hollered at us and we at them. There were eight cavalry of them on Tuesday.

We heard a very heavy cannon balling in the direction of Folley Island. We have since heard a report that it was the rebels shelling our troops on the island. The lieutenant of a company of engineers here, a regular officer, is appointed chief of artillery. He is going to Folley Island and is going to bombard the rebel earthworks on the island opposite of it.

June 21: On the 17th when we came off of picket we were relieved by the 10th company. They tried to establish a new picket line. Farther out, two companies marched out of a sugar mill when thare was a regiment of rebel cavalry in the rear of them. They marched back as quick as they could and if they had been ten minutes later, they would have been taken prisoners, if they could not have fought their way out.

After they had got back to the old picket line, the rebels came down to a house, about 900 yards distance from the picket reserve. Thare was about 800 calvary of them. When they got to the house, the cavalry wheeled out of the way and the rebs opened fire on our picket reserve, with two field pieces which they had fetched with them, masked among the cavalry. They did not do much damage.

They wounded one man and shelled a man through two horses. We had two guns that returned their fire and after awhile silenced one of their guns, but they played around the house till the gunboats threw some shells over when they began to run and get out of the way as quick as possible. Our artillery threw some solid shot at them from the picket line. The reason that they did not give them a few shells, they had fired all they had there and did not have any at the time.

We get fresh bread every other day here. We do not have much fatigueing to do now. I was on yesterday. We went up along the picket line and worked on a fort. It is nearly done I guess.

S.S. Leavenworth

Seabrook Island, South Carolina, June 26, 1863

Dear Brother Atwell,

I am glad to hear that you are all well. We heard last night that the rebels are in Pennsylvania. I do not see what the generals in command of our troops in Virginia can be about to let them get in that state to do much damage. No doubt the fellows in Captain Mallers company was very glad to get home.

I suppose that James has seen

Ralph Austin, May 16, 1784–June 4, 1863.

more fighting at Chancelorsville than any time before that.

If the drought is so hard, it will be apt to injure the crops considerable. You must write how Aunt Sal's folks gets along with their farming. Write how many of her girls is to home. Write which ones you drove out of your boat.

Write how Isaac Bradley gets along on his place. Write if Mr. Bradley works up to his place.

I have not seen a place in the south that I like as well as Orange or Sullivan County. I think it looks gloomy around a plantation when it is deserted by its owner. There is lots of fat rattlesnakes and other kinds of snakes.

S.S. Leavenworth

July 1–3, 1863, Battle of Gettysburg, Pennsylvania

Samuel C. Myers, 28, fought at the Battle of Gettysburg, and was severely wounded on July second. Samuel died at the end of July, and left a young wife Letitia, and a son, Charles Myers, 2.

Near the old Leavenworth plot in the old Eldred Cemetery is a gravestone marker in honor of Samuel C. Myers which says:

Fallen in defense of his country to his honor this monument is erected by his citizens and friends: the Battle of Yorktown, Williamsburg, Chancellorsville, and Gettysburg witness his courage and fidelity.

The following poem sent to Mrs. Laura Clark was written out by Carrie Newman. Carrie may have been a daughter of Caroline Austin Newman (1818–1849), sister to Laura Austin Clark. Perhaps Carrie sent the poem in sympathy to her Aunt Laura when an Austin relative died in the Civil War. The poem has some similarities to the ballad, *Anne Lisle*, written in 1857.

July 1863

For Mrs. Laura Clark
*Down where the waving willow
Neath the sunbeams smile*

Samuel C. Myers grave marker. Photo: Cynthia Leavenworth Bellinger.

*Lay a soldier weak and wounded
In delirium wild.
Through his veins the raging fever
Wild and swift did roam
And the soldier's brain was wandring
Mid the scenes of home.*

*Fond Mother Dear Father
To the soldier come*

Dedication ceremonies at the Soldiers' National Cemetery, Gettysburg, Pennsylvania, November 19, 1863. Source: Library of Congress Prints and Photograps Division, Washington, D.C. 20540, reproduction number LC-DIG-cwpb-00651 DLC.

> Four score and seven years ago our fathers brought forth on this Continent, a new nation, conceived in Liberty, and dedicated to the proposition that all men are created equal.
>
> Now we are engaged in a great civil war, testing whether that nation, or any nation so conceived and so dedicated, can long endure. We are met on a great battle field of that war. We have come to dedicate a portion of that field, as a final resting place for those who here gave their lives, that that nation might live. It is altogether fitting and proper that we should do this.
>
> But, in a larger sense, we can not dedicate— we can not consecrate— we can not hallow— this ground. The brave men, living and dead, who struggled here, have consecrated it, far above our poor power to add or detract. The world will little note, nor long remember what we say here, but it can never forget what they did here. It is for us the living, rather, to be dedicated here to the unfinished work which they who fought here have thus far so nobly advanced. It is rather for us to be here dedicated to the great task remaining before us— that from these honored dead we take increased devotion to that cause for which they gave the last full measure of devotion— that we here highly resolve that these dead shall not have died in vain— that this nation, under God, shall have a new birth of freedom— and that government of the people, by the people, for the people, shall not perish from the earth.
>
> Abraham Lincoln
> November 19. 1863.

For his brain was wildly wandring
Of the scenes of home.

On his ear there fell the chiming
The old church bell
Come his mother tones so holy
That he loved so well.
Hears the murmur of the brooklet
In the quiet dell
Scenes of life and joyous childhood
O'er him cast their spell.

Fond Sister Dear Brother
Greet the soldier now
As he feels his mother's kisses
On his aching brow.

Farewell mother I am going
To my home above
Place my head upon your bosom
Kiss your darling boy
Lay my form beneath the churchyard
Where I loved to stray
Near the old church
Where in childhood
First I learned to pray.

Fond Mother Dear Father
To the soldier come
For his brain was wildly wandring
Of the scenes of home.

But my Mary cease her weeping
When forever I am gone
Bid her o'er my grave murmur
Sadly and forlorn.
Slow the soldier's eyes were closing
Faintly came his breath
With a murmur twas but Mary
Slept the sleep of death.

Weep comrades for the soldier
Who has left your band
Make his grave beneath the willow
In the Southern Land.

Gettysburg address in Lincoln"s handwriting on an envelope. Source: Library of Congress, Rare Book and Special Collections Division, Washington, D.C. Photo ID: http://hdl.loc.gov/loc.rbc/lprbscsm.scsm0717.

Folly Island, South Carolina, July 24, 1863

Dear Brother,
I just got over a purty severe fit of the fever and ague. I do not know but what I will have it some yet.

We lay about three miles from Fort Sumter. I would like to have you hear the cannons thunder as they do now. I tell you it is a sight to look right over in Charleston Harbor and see the shell burst.

Saturday, we had quite a heavy fight on James Island. We were waken up early in the morning by heavy, heavy firing. The Rebs had fetched a battery in the night and planted it within 2 or 300 yards of the gunboat Pawnee and stationed sharp shooters along the banks of the river closest by and as soon as it was daylight, opened with 16 field pieces on the gun boat.

Soon as they went to move the guns aboard the boat, the sharp shooters picked them off. They had to slip their cable and drop down stream as quick as they could. While this was going on, the Rebs came down on us in front with two pieces of cannon and 9000 infantry.

We had just got out of camp and formed the left of the third line of battle when both sides opened with their cannons. The firing had just commenced when our regiment had to go and form on the second line of battle. When we had got formed on the left of the second line, our company was sent down an old road towards the river to watch if we see any cavalry trying to flank us, as there was such reports.

We had just got where the road ended on a large marsh when the Rebs from the other side of the marsh, where they had a battery, let us have 5 or 6 shells. They burst just right. If they had come 20 yards closer, they would have killed most of the company.

We then went into the edge of the woods when there came another shell and cut two pine nearly off. The gunboats soon gave them an invitation in the shape of two 100-pound rifle shells, to leave, which they did in a hurry.

The same night we retreated across to Coal Island. We stayed there a day, then we went by steam boat to Folly Island where we are now. We can see Fort Sumter from here. We are about 7 miles from Fort Sumter. We can see all the shells thrown by either side from here. Our gun boats have been shelling Fort Wagner on Cummins Point, but it has not surrendered yet. It has been charged twice by our troops, so we hear, with heavy loss, but without success.

July 26: I am well today. We hear that our troops are going to make an attact tomorrow by land and water on the rebel fortifications—that is with heavy artillery as we have got some of the land batteries finished. Our side is mounting heavy siege guns every day and night.

Thier were six 200-pound guns came in on the barge. One of the fellows out of our company that is on detached duty up in front, said that they tried two of the snorters that we have just got mounted. The first two shots fired from them burst on Fort Johnson, right under the muzzle of the guns. Then they heaved one clear over Fort Sumter into Charleston.

Fort Sumter, S.C., April 4, 1861, under the Confederate flag. Photo: National Archives photo no. 121-BA-914A.

Aunt Sal?

When reading Sherman's letters home, it doesn't take long to wonder, "Who was Aunt Sal?"

It is not known if Aunt Sal was an actual relative, or a neighbor who was called Aunt Sal. Who would have so many daughters? I hope I haven't falsely accused Mrs. Ingersoll of being Aunt Sal, but she does have six daughters in the 1860 census. What do you think?

Ingersoll Family, 1860
Abraham Ingersoll, 52
Sarah or Sally, 44
Matilda, 24
Susan, 22
Eliza, 18
Jane, 17
Henry, 11
Norma, 9
Sarah, 6
Stephen, 3

"Sugar Cane." Postcard from a souvenir folder entitled "Sunny South" sent to Aida Austin in 1917 from her nephew Mortimer McKinley Austin. From the collection of Mary Briggs Austin.

54th Regiment

The 54th Regiment was all German men at its start. The 54th was organized at Hudson, N.Y., and mustered in September to mid-October 1861.

They left for Washington, D.C., October 29, 1861, and were attached to Provisional Brigade, Casey's Division, Army of the Potomac, until December 1861.

The 54th was ordered to cross the Potomac and then assigned to Steinwehr's Brigade, Blenker's Division, all composed of Germans at Hunter's Chapel, Virginia.

George Bunce and Atwell Leavenworth enlisted in November 1863, four months after the Battle of Gettysburg where the 54th had lost a total of 102 men.

After Gettysburg, the 54th was reassigned to the south. They arrived at Folly Island (where Atwell Leavenworth died in November 1864), near Charleston, South Carolina, in August 1863.

The 54th Regiment lost 3 officers and 144 enlisted men, a total of 147; 26 of the enlisted men died in the hands of the enemy.—www.dmna.state.ny.us/historic/reghist/civil/infantry/54thInf/.

I guess the Rebs thought it was purty, all shooting. The Rebs have planted a new battery. Every once in a while they throw a shell in to our camps. That is the ones in front. They have killed and wounded 12 since yesterday morning. The Lieut. Col. of the 10 company had his leg taken nearly off by a shell right in camp. His leg had to be amputated. The doctors do not think he will live.

We get very miserable rations at present. All we get is wormy crackers and salt junk beef. I guess we will get more presently. Do not say anything for anyone that hears that I wrote such a thing would think I was getting tired of it here, but I ain't. I would be ashamed to whine about it like some I have known after they got tired of the job. I have never found it so hard yet.

The reason we do not get better rations is because we are moving so much. You wanted to know if I had milk here anytime. I don't believe that I have had two quarts of milk in two years. We can get butter down here, but it is so thin it can be nearly poured. We don't get potatoes now, but I guess we will get them before long. Last night thare was a boat sent to Fort Wagner by the rebels loaded with ammunition.
S.S. Leavenworth

Beaufort, South Carolina, August 25, 1863

Dear Brother John,
Since I wrote last, we have moved from Folly Island on account of the regiment not being fit for duty on account of sickness.

After we got all the work done and just the day before they opened with the heavy guns on the enemies' works, they sent us off up here. The nicest place that I have been since I have been down south. It has got the most and nicest shade trees in of any place that I ever saw.

I guess I have only been sent here to recruit up a little. We expect some drafted men in our regiment soon as we had some officers go after them quite a good while ago. It beat all to see the darkeys down here. Thare is many quantities of them here.

I am over the fever and ague. There is the best water here that I have seen since we have been down here. It is a watering place where the planters used to come to in the summer time so they say here.

I have to go out on picket once in a while. We hear that Fort Sumter looks purty ragged and I do not doubt it a bit, if it has the benefit of enemy shots out of the line and 300-pounder parrot guns that are mounted on its rear. The walls are 8 foot thick in the rear and we have heard that since they have opened on it with the heavy guns that they have filled through it. The rebels fill the holes up with sand bags.

The shells that is fired out of the parrot guns at a wall is made with a percussion cap with a short fuse between it and the powder. When the shell is fired against a wall it goes in about 3 or 4 and soon as it gets in it bursts throwing out of the wall, cartloads of brick and cement. They are a great thing to tear down a wall.

We do not hear much news down here from the army of the Potomac. I guess they are not on the move. You must write who all is drafted around home.

The next time you write, you must write what Horton is at and what he says and thinks about the war. Write how Isaac Bradley gets along. Write all the news you can. Write what old Aunt Sal says about the draft.

You must be a good boy and one that behaves the best from now till I get home. If I ever do I have got a present worth having and the one that is the best boy and helps the most gets it. You must help mother all you can.

S.S. Leavenworth

Do you remember Mary Keen Gardner, the wife of Sears Gardner, from the beginning of our story? Sears and Mary Keen Gardner and their son Joseph had first settled in Pond Eddy around 1800. Sears and Mary Keen were living with their son James K. Gardner, in Barryville when Sears died in 1849. Son James K. Gardner died in 1860, so it is unclear where Mary Gardner was living when she died late summer 1863, at the age of 88.

Mary Keen Gardner's children Letty Gardner Sergeant and Sears Robert Gardner were still living, as was daughter-in-law, Eliza Eldred Gardner.

Mary Keen Gardner also had a number of grandchildren; some have been a part of this story: Stephen St. John Gardner; Maria Gardner Calkins; Alvah, Isaac, and James G. Sergeant; Coe Young; and several children of Mary Gardner (who died in 1840) and her husband, Benjamin C. Austin.

Beauford, South Carolina, September 26, 1863

Dear Brother Atwell,

I am glad that the north is whipping the southerners. So like the deuce they are going to enlist regular cavalry here. They are going to give 400 dollars bounty and 30 days furlough.

The bounty is to be paid 50 dollars for every pay day besides the regular pay, till it is paid. If it proves true, Coe and myself is going to enlist. Do not say anything to Coe's folks about it as he may want to inform them about it himself.

The reason that I think about reenlisting again is because I like it better than anything else, not as it is any easier than any other employment, for where it is easier in some things, it is harder in others. Besides 400 dollars is not picked up every five years, besides the regular wages that we can get.

You must write where the regiment is that Isaac Sergeant belongs to. I had my likeness taken and sent to you. I do not know what is the reason that you have not received it yet.

If that is so about Aunt Sal having one of her girls married, she feels rather more pacified than she used to about three years ago.

You must write how you and Isaac Bradley agrees nowadays. You must write how the draft gets along up there.

S.S. Leavenworth

Sherman has mentioned James Gardner Sergeant, son of Ethel and Letty Sergeant, several times in his letters. James G. was in the 40th Regiment Infantry and promoted to corporal on October 1, 1863. He reenlisted as a veteran at the end of December.

James Sergeant had a brother Isaac (mentioned in Sherman's last letter) who enlisted as a private with the 168th Regiment Infantry, in January 1863. Isaac became sick at Chattanooga, and mustered out October 16, 1863.

At the end of October 1863, C.C.P. and Effa Eldred's daughter, Polly Vanorsdol Eldred, married George Egbert Mapes.

C.C.P. and Effa Eldred's son George W. Eldred was discharged from the 56th Regiment Infantry, November 2, 1863, at Beaufort, South Carolina. While on duty in the Peninsula War in Virginia, George W. Eldred had been disabled by malaria fever and chronic diarrhea.

Overseas in Charsonville, France, Jean Charles Rouillon, son

Atwell Leavenworth's enlistment record, November 21, 1863. Source: National Archives and Records Administration.

Wall across Blind Pond Brook by the Leavenworth Homestead. Photo: Cynthia Leavenworth Bellinger.

of Lubin Rouillon and Florentine Louis, was born on October 30, 1863. Jean Charles would marry Blanche Olga Malinge, who was also born in 1863.

Jean Charles and Blanche would be the grandparents of Gisele Rouillon who would marry Jim Leavenworth, a future grandson of Sherman Stiles Leavenworth. Jim and Gisele would meet during another terrible time of War.

In November of 1863, Net Austin, daughter of Uncle Augustus and Aunt Maria, wrote to her Aunt Mary Ann Austin.

Net mentioned an Isaac Teed, who was probably related by marriage to two of Ralph and Fanny Austin's children. Son Samuel Knapp Austin had married Susan Teed; and daughter Clara Austin had married Edward Nelson Teed.

Perhaps Will, mentioned as dying from war wounds in the next letter, was Cousin William mentioned in Mortimer Bruce Austin's January 1863 letter to his grandfather Ralph.

November 15, 1863
Dear Aunt Mary,

Isaac Teed was here Thursday. We went to a party in the evening and had a right nice time.

He had a letter from cousin Eddie about a week ago. He said that poor Will was dead. He lived eight days after being shot and was insensible all the time.

Net Austin

Beaufort, South Carolina, November 17, 1863
Dear Father (Sherman Buckley),

Enclosed you will find 15 dollars which is all I have to send this pay. I wish I had more to send. I think I will have every pay day after this.

It is reported that our regiment is to go to Florida, and march towards the interior to get contraband.

We got our conscripts week before last. They are drilling every day now, but they have not got their guns yet. I wish the next time you write from home that whoever writes, will write where Atwell is and I would like to have him write to me and let me know where he is and how he likes soldiering. Our time will be out next summer.

If I get out of this regiment all right, I think I will enlist again in the cavalry.

I can not think of anything more to write at present except I would like to hear if you are all well.

S.S. Leavenworth

Less than a week after the previous letter was written, Sherman's brother, dark haired, blue-eyed Atwell Bishop Leavenworth, a farmer, enlisted in Goshen, as a substitute. Atwell, almost 19, was five feet, eleven inches tall and mustered in as a private for three years in Company E, 54th Regiment Infantry, New York Volunteers, with Captain Blon.

George Bunce, who lived north of the Leavenworths, had enlisted at Goshen, a couple days before Atwell, as a private to serve three years in the 54th Regiment Infantry.

In December, Ann Mary Austin Schoonover wrote her sister Laura Austin Clark.

Barryville, December 23, 1863
Dear Sister Laura,

I received yours of the 22 and now I am on my bed with the stand by it, with a pillow for me to rest on while I write. Four weeks yesterday, I was taken sick with the bilious fever, very sick. The day before I was very smart, so Perry went down the River and was gone a week. I was down all the time, but nights I kept getting worse. On Saturday, they thought I would not live for a while.

I don't think I ever was so sick before, but through the mercy of God, I am getting better. Oh how thankful we ought to be for such a Friend when we feel all other Sources failing us, that we take a Saviour to look to, knowing he never will leave nor forsake us, but will be our guide even unto death.

I feel to exclaim with the Psalmist, Bless the Lord oh my Soul, and all that's within me Bless his holy name for all mercys to me.

I will not be able to come either Christmas or New Years. We intend to come when I get able.

I would like some of your pot cheese, first rate. I've been wanting it since I began to eat. I do not have much appetite. I have a very good girl. We pay her ten shillings a week. I expect I shall have to keep her sometime yet.

Perry saw James when he was in New York. He was boarded at Augustus's, and had a situation in the Bibb House. Henry was here this week. He had received a letter from New York that Spencer's Lawyer had written for $100 more for Pappy's board. I would like to have you come and see me if you can without hindering Irv's work. We can write to each other. Kiss tiger for me. You did not say whether you had heard what has happened.

Martha Clark has got a babe a week old. I must close for I am very tired. I remain yours,
A.M. Schoonover

1864

In January of 1864, John Hancy, husband of Amelia Eldred (Uncle Mulford's daughter), enlisted as a private in Company G, 5th Regiment New York, Heavy Artillery.

In the following letter, we learn that Henry and Mary Ann Austin's daughter, Emma, 13, was living with her Austin cousins in New York City, and attended school there.

Emma's sister, Aida Austin, later commented that Susie Teed in this 1864 letter *could not have been Susan Teed who married Samuel Austin, or Nettie would have called her Aunt Susie.*

Sunday, January 31, 1864

Dear Aunt Mary [Austin],

I received your very welcome letter last week and will now try and answer it.

For a great wonder, we are all well. Mortie [Net's brother], has been quite sick with a bad cold. He was so sick that he could not go to the store for a week.

Susie Teed has been down every day since New Year's Day. She is coming over next week to spend the week with us.

Uncle James went up to Mount Kisco Saturday after Aunt Julia. She has been up there three weeks. He is going to bring her down Monday. Hope we will see a change in him. He has looked like an enraged rat ever since she went away.

Mother got your carpet Thursday. I think you will like it first rate. It will look very nice when you get it down. How I wish I could come up and help you with it. Mother says you must sew the breadths together and tack it around the sides. It will last so much longer if you do. I hope you can get it down before the Lady of the Lake gives you another call. It will be a rich surprise for her. Worse than a blue pill. It's her own fault however, not ours.

We were to a large surprise party up town Tuesday evening. We had a very nice time. Got home at 5 o'clock in the morning.

Emma is very well, though in rather a bad fix today. Her trunk has got a spring lock. Well she got the key inside and accidentally put down the lid. And as a matter

Sherman S. Leavenworth reenlistment record, February 28, 1864. Source: National Archives and Records Administration.

of fact of course, we had not a key that would unlock it, but will get one tomorrow. It's fun to hear her talk about it. She says if she ever has a trunk of her own, she won't have an old stuck lock on it.

She gets along first rate at school. She is at the head of her class.

Has Uncle Henry given up coming to Brooklyn? How I wish he would come. How is little Lonie and Eldred? How I do want to see them and all the rest. Give

Hezekiah Bunce Leavenworth enlistment record, March, 1864. Source: National Archives and Records Administration.

A circa-1860s advertising note for Drake's Plantation Bitters. From the collection of Mary Briggs Austin.

my love to Grandmother [Hannah Eldred].

With much love to you all. Write soon and oblige. Nettie

In February of 1864, Sherman S. Leavenworth reenlisted as a veteran. At the end of March, Sherman's 16-year-old brother, Hezekiah Bunce Leavenworth, enlisted at Deerpark for 3 years.

Hezekiah B. Leavenworth was five feet, nine inches tall with blue eyes and brown hair. Hezekiah, a farmer, mustered in as a private in Company B, 56th Regiment, New York Volunteers, with Captain Melville Sears.

Back home in Halfway Brook Village, in 1864, Buckley Leavenworth added the six acres with the mill to his property. The acreage in the Town of Highland was conveyed to Sherman by John Conkling and others on February 29, 1864.

It was the same land which Abraham Ingersoll and his wife conveyed by deed in December 1841 to James K. Gardner, Benjamin Dodge, and Stephen St. John. The property had been surveyed by David Hulse October 12th, 1840, as follows: *Beginning at a stake and stones on the west bank of a Saw Mill Pond...*

In March 1864, George Bunce was discharged for disability at Folly Island, South Carolina.

April 27, 1864
Dear Brother Sherman,

We are all well at present. We have got our new barn a going up at last. We are doing the foundation now and we have put the last stones in that you pried up in the ten acres fallow, the last after mine that you worked here.

Harriet is well. The report around here is that George is going to have his discharge and come home and you must write how he is and if it is so.

If I had a dollar I might get lots of nice things. I am back home again. The last we heard from you, you were on Saybrook Island. They don't draft any around here, but strong talk we would see greys heels up in the air.

Steamer Arago. Source: Missouri Republican, *August 30, 1860; reprinted in* Early Tales and Sketches, *Vol. 1.*

Me and father saws down to the mill.

You must write about Mr. Young's boys. Mother wishes you back to Yorktown again as she could send you something. Mother says you must write her a good long letter from Atwell. Write soon,
John E. Leavenworth

U.S. Transport Arago, May 16, 1864
Dear friends:

We are on the Arago off Cape Hatteras. We are southward bound for Beaufort. We came through to N.Y. the same day that we left home. We took up our lodgings in the care that we came down in for the good reason that we could get no better.

Saturday morning we were ferried across the river to the pier at the foot of Chamber Street. We were then marched immediately to pier 37 at the foot of Beach Street and embarked on board of the Arago. We have had fair weather so far and enjoy ourselves very well taking all things in consideration.

The weather is rather perferibel to what it was off the cape nearly two years ago. The wind has a decidedly different pitch now from what it had then and the waves then and now differ immensely in size. Happily, the difference is better for us at present. I can see a ship laying off to the westward. Nothing but her sails are discernible against the sky.

I have not seen Hez since I left but I guess he will be along. All the recruits have been sent where he is, so I hear.

I guess that with a little imagination we could easily come to the conclusion that we hear mosquitoes hum and rattlesnakes rattle, and smell musk and orange blossoms, as I think that mosquitoes and rattlesnakes begin to the former to fly, the latter to crawl, and the orange trees and the alligators must omit musk now that it is warm weather down in that portion of secessiondom called South Carolina's sultry clime.

I suppose that we will soon be going through the usual routine of soldiers life in camp in the sunny south weather. It will be more agreeable than a 35 days furlow attended to a certain period suitable to the mind of a certain representative of the 56th Regiment remains to be seen.

I do not know when we will land, but I presume that it will be tomorrow.

We did not get our bounty at New York, but we are to receive it down here. We will come out all OK with that. Then I will send the money to get the house filled and enough to pay for the part of the furniture that I agreed to.

If you get Hezey's money first, use that and square him and me by paying him all that he paid over his part towards it, paying out of the money that I send home.

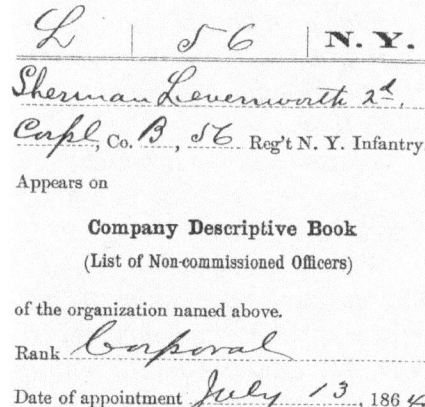

Corporal Sherman Leavenworth, July 13, 1864, listed in Company B, 56th Regiment, N.Y. Infantry. Source: National Archives and Records Administration.

"A southern barbecue." Postcard from a souvenir folder entitled "Sunny South" sent to Aida Austin in 1917 from her nephew Mortimer McKinley Austin. From the collection of Mary Briggs Austin.

Fill the house as good as you possibly can for the money that we send for the purpose, and if what we calculated was not enough, let us know and we will send enough. I will put some postage stamps in the letter for you to send my count book which I forgot.

John must write how he gets along with the work and if he got the money I sent him. He must work good for as soon as I can get the money, I am going to send him enough to get him that fiddle. He must get someone to get it that understands how to select a good one for the price he pays. You can get them at Port.

Try and improve in writing letters—that is in writing and composing.

If you get that instrument, you must not spend too much time with it, but must only use it when you have time. Then put your attention to that and nothing else. Always learn plenty of tunes and get them good.

There is $18 of ration money coming to us at least. I do not know whether we will get it. Have you got those slippers yet?

S.S. Leavenworth

On board the U.S. Transport Arago, May 17, 1864
Dear Friends,

It is still very pleasant weather. The sun shines out very warm. I guess by night, if nothing happens to put us back or delay us, we will in 24 hours be in the land of orange trees and palmettos and rattlesnakes and alligators, secessionists, copperheads, and all other noxious reptiles.

We can begin to hear the mosquitoes out on the picket line from Beaufort. We will run a greater risk of coming in contact with them than the rebels. I do not know as the collision would be of as serious a consequence, but it is commonly a great provocation particularly when you want to go to sleep.

I never saw the sea so calm in my life. It looks as smooth and transparent as molten glass. There is not a ripple to be seen, only what the boat makes plowing through it.

The water where we are now is of a greenish hue which is the case when we are on soundings. When off, it is a dark blue. We can see banks of thunderheads laying off to the westward. They are raising above the horizons. If you ever saw a pond in the morning when the surface of the water looked as smooth as a mirror, you can form some idea how the water looks here now, only this differs by being extended as far as the eye can reach, while a pond only covers a very small scope.

Write if the school teacher has been to board with you yet. Write how you get along with the work.

John must work and take all the interest he can in the farm and the stock and not forget what he larnt last winter and be a good boy and he will get some presents before too long. I am going to send to Boston after a microscope for him. It will magnify 500 times and then that fiddle will be a coming and other things that will be worth behaving for.

I suppose that parties will break up till next winter. I suppose that you hear encouraging news from the armies in front of Richmond.

Well, I hope that the news will keep coming, still more encouraging till we hear that the war has ended honorably to the armies of the United States.

S.S. Leavenworth

Beaufort, South Carolina, May 18, 1864

Dear friends,

We have arrived safe and sound at Beaufort at last. The trees are all leaved out and everything looks lively. It is one of the most splendid places that I ever saw. I never saw this place at this time of year before. The fellows that was left here was very glad to see us back, but no more so than we was to get back after leaving New York.

We sailed in Hilton Read Harbor about 8 o'clock, but did not arrive at Beaufort till 2 p.m., on account of delays.

If you could hear the fellows around talking and laughing about the times that they have been having, you would think that a soldier seldom knew care.

If you could only see as warm a day up home as today is, you would be apt to come to the conclusion that ice water and shade trees was a necessity, even if it is the 18th of May. But soldiers commonly do not have the enjoyment of such conveniences.

May 19: This is an extraordinary pleasant morning. The gnats are very troublesome. I have got a piece of work on hand that will keep one in business all day—that is to put my gun in a fit order for inspection.

I suppose that the news from the Potomac is of the most gratifying importance. While I do not care of how much importance it is, as long as it is favorable to our arms.

We had a very scrumptious breakfast. It was composed of a piece of dry bread and a cup of coffee. We eat it in good spirits in hopes that we would have better and more of a variety for dinner. Potatoes and butter and a few commodities would come very acceptable, but as this news from Grant is exceedingly good, we live in hopes of enjoying them in a year's time.

Johnson Dunlap is here in our company. Highland is well represented in Co. B.

Write if John got that money. You must write if you have heard from Hez yet. Write if he gets his bounty. We did not get the bounty in York State. We get it here. As soon as we get it, I will send the money for the purpose that we spoke of.

Sherman S. Leavenworth

The Leavenworth property with stone walls. In the back to the left is the Leavenworth home. Photo: Cynthia Leavenworth Bellinger.

Beaufort, South Carolina, June 2, 1864

Dear Brother John,

I suppose that you are a good boy and take an interest in how the work and affairs goes on at the farm. I presume that is the case.

I will send you a little reward enclosed in this envelope. You will find 10 photographs. Nine different generals of our army and one rebel general. They cost me $2, but I thought in times that amount would be a small sum compared to what your good behavior and maturity, also obedience would be a credit to you and all of us.

Hezy and me is going to make mother a present of an album and you must keep the pictures to put into it. Keep them where thy will keep clean. Write what kind of a girl Anna is.

S.S. Leavenworth

In hopes to end the war within 100 days, there was a push for man power in the summer of 1864, called, *Hundred Days Men*. These volunteers were short-term, lightly trained troops intended to free veteran units to go to the front lines for combat purposes. The 145th Illinois Volunteer Infantry was one of the regiments started with that purpose.

Two of Uncle Justus and Aunt Polly's sons, Benjamin Merwin Hickok and Charles Hickok, lived in Carlisle, Illinois, at the time. They joined the 145th Illinois Regiment, Company B, and mustered in June 9, 1864, at Camp Butler, Illinois. Merwin apparently played the fife, and was listed as musician/fife major. Charles was a private.

The 145th Illinois Regiment was ordered to St. Louis,

"Hauling Cotton to Market." Postcard from a souvenir folder entitled "Sunny South" sent to Aida Austin in 1917 from her nephew Mortimer McKinley Austin. From the collection of Mary Briggs Austin.

Missouri, on June 12, where they served in the garrison in the St. Louis area.

Beaufort, South Carolina, June 21, 1864

Dear Brother John,

You wrote that you was going to school. You must learn all you can. If you go to work and learn a good deal this winter and be a good boy, I will get you a double barreled fowling piece or a rifle.

I will write home to know if you have been a good boy before I fetch it. I will also fetch Hezy and Anna something if they behave, if I live to get home. But I want you to see how much you can learn, for you can learn fast if you are a mind to. Write what you study now. Don't say anything to anyone of what I have wrote you.

I have had a letter from Atwell. He is on Kiawah Island, S.C. He is not far from here. After we come off picket, I will try to get a pass to go and see him. He is well at present. I have had two letters.

S.S. Leavenworth

In July of 1864, a battle took place in Harper's Ferry, Virginia, 600 miles north, and a bit east of Beaufort, South Carolina, where Sherman S. was located. On July 7, during Operations at Harper's Ferry, Edward Higginson, from Illinois, was wounded at nearby Maryland Heights.

Edward was admitted to the U.S. Army Hospital at Frederick, Maryland (a 1,114 bed facility), with gunshot wounds from two Minie balls, one to the left arm and one to the left leg.

Great-Great-Grandpa Edward Higginson was transferred to several hospitals before being taken to Saterlee Hospital, Philadelphia. It was almost a year until Edward was discharged from Philadelphia for disability.

Back in Beaufort, Sherman S. Leavenworth was promoted to Corporal on July 13, 1864.

There was a terrible train accident near Barryville on July 15, 1864. A train carrying 833 Confederate prisoners of war (many of them captured at the battle of Cold Harbor), and 128 Union guards, were on their way to the federal prison at Elmira, New York. The train was on a blind curve just north of Shohola when it collided with an engine

Ann Mary Austin (1827–1864), wife of O.P. Schoonover. Photo: Gary Smith.

pulling 50 loaded coal cars. One account said the train had been mistakenly waved through Lackawaxen by a drunken dispatcher. The accident killed at least 51 Confederate soldiers and 17 Union guards. Five Confederate prisoners escaped in the chaos.

The dead were buried in a mass grave along the tracks. Over 100 injured soldiers were taken to Shohola and Barryville for treatment. Many of them died from their wounds, and two of them, the Johnson brothers, were buried in Barryville.

A cemetery behind the original Congregational Church in Barryville, known at one time as the Union Church, was the resting place for several Confederate soldiers killed on July 15, 1864.
—from several sources including Times Union, Albany, N.Y., June 21, 2009.

Sherman's brother Atwell was again sick in camp in August 1864.

Beaufort, South Carolina, August 3, 1864

Dear Brother John,

In answer to yours of the 24th of July. I am glad to hear that you are all enjoying good health. Hezy and myself is well at present, as I believe the rest of the boys are.

I am glad to hear that you are progressing so well with your work at home. I am glad to see you so industrious and feel certain that you will be rewarded if not in one way you will be in another.

If you take an interest in yourself and employment, rest assured that there will be an interest evinced in your welfare.

If you are an all fired trusty boy you will one of these days, if nothing happens to prevent it, be able to ride your horse which we could not do.

Atwell was on the same island that I was on the fourth of July, but we did not get a chance to see one another which was a great disappointment, as I was making quite a reckoning of seeing him some place during the expedition. I believe it is now three years since I saw him. I would like to get a pass to go up and see him at Folly Island and I think that I shall try to get a pass.

The account of you is very satisfactory and much to your credit and a good account once in a while of your continued good behavior is all that is necessary to assure you of a great many presents one time and another, say for a beginning fiddle pay day.

But if you get a fiddle, you must not spend a minute's time that had aught to be devoted to your more necessary employments.

I do not want you to forget a word that you have learned of your studies, but continue to acquire more learning and if it amounts to but little, when you are employed at your work at home in the summer, you will be ready to commence your studies where you left off or in advance of where you quit in the winter previous.

Rolla, Missouri

Benjamin Merwin Hickok, son of Uncle Justus and Aunt Polly, fought with Company B, Illinois 145 Volunteers, and died in Rolla, Missouri, in the defense of his country on September 7, 1864.

With the outbreak of war, the westward expansion of the Pacific Railroad had stopped at Rolla in 1860, making the town an important site during the Civil War.

The Union forces seized control of Rolla early in the war, and had a big impact upon the town and its operation. Thousands of Union troops and their supplies came to Rolla by train from St. Louis and then were transferred to wagon trails to go to the battles and skirmishes.

The courthouse was used as a hay storage barn and later as a hospital for wounded soldiers. Following the Union defeat at Wilson's Creek, in August 1861, the Union Army fell back to Rolla and built an earthen fort.

Fort Dette, assembled in 1863, was a more detailed fort on what is now the campus of the University of Missouri-Rolla. It was constructed in a cross shape with positions for both 24-pound cannons and ports for individual rifle fire.—www.rollanet.org/areainfo/nwhist.html.

Atwell Leavenworth's sick report on September 7 and 8, 1864. Source: National Archives and Records Administration.

"Plowing with an ox on the old plantation." Postcard from a souvenir folder entitled "Sunny South" sent to Aida Austin in 1917 from her nephew Mortimer McKinley Austin. From the collection of Mary Briggs Austin.

I got the microscope. It was such a miserable article, that I threw it away. I will send you a good one sometime if I ever get an opportunity to select a good one.

I will tell Hezy to write you a letter. He got his letter from you the same time that I got mine. Also, one from Harriet. She was well at the time that she wrote.

I am glad that old Fremont stands a poor sight for the presidency.

You say that G.W.E. [George Eldred] is very valorous. Well it needs valiant men where there are such a few of them and maybe it is best for the safety of Highland that [there are] mighty men of valor as G.W.E.

I hope that Isaac Bradley will not be drafted. Write as soon as you get this.
S.S. Leavenworth

Beaufort, South Carolina, August 1864

Dear Brother John,

I am glad to hear that you prosper so with your work and that you finished haying and harvesting in so short a period. It is almost a wonder to think that you done it alone in so short a time, but on considering it over, it is very easily seen that it can be allotted to nothing else but your industry, and the interest that you take in the work.

Always evince an interest in all that you undertake and you will be sure to prosper in all undertakings. Besides you will have the good esteem and credit of all persons whose estimation is worth having, that is providing that you do not undertake anything that is bad.

I have finished my breakfast. It consisted of a piece of pork about as big as your two fingers, and dry bread and a cup of coffee without milk. Half of the ration of meat was fat. Meat is not very conductive of good health. It is a very unhealthy time of year.

I set up with a man last night that was sick with the brain fever. Last night the doctor hardly thought that he would survive till morning. He was taken first with an attack of the horrors and as he got over them, the brain fever set in. They purty killed him in the first place. If you ever see anyone suffering from an attack of the horrors, you will be sick of liquor.

Whose case has G.W.E. been called upon to plead?

I guess that you will have enough fodder to stand through the winter without buying. I suppose that hay commands a large price, does it not?

It is the fact you done extraordinary well. If you want to make Aunt Sal mad, you must be industrious, and take an interest in the work and it will make her feel awful jealous.

She thought when Atwell went away, that there would not be anyone home that would care about how the work got along, and now that she sees that you work as good as he does, and are likely to get as good a name for working, it makes her feel worse than thunder.

Work good while at home and when you go to school, learn and not have your head excited by amusements and you will accomplish more than it ever lay in the power of one of them to do, and if us boys live, you will get a present for being persevering.
S.S. Leavenworth

Two great-grandchildren of James and Polly Eldred were born in 1864. Charles Egbert Mapes was born to George and Polly V. Eldred Mapes, in Halfway Brook in August; Katie McElroy Gardner was born to Stephen St. John and Louisa McElroy Gardner.

Folly Island, South Carolina, August 13, 1864

Dear Father,
Your letter of the 24th found

me in good health, but reasonably tired, just coming off of three days picket on Cole's Isle.

I was glad to hear that you were all well. I was very glad to hear of Gen. Sherman's success in North Georgia. We hear that Grant has taken Petersburg or cut old Lee's army in two. There is flying reports that the Rebs are in Penn., but no one knows whether to believe them or not. I guess Fremont and his platform will come to nought. It must be his last leap for anything.

I am glad that Congress reduced the drafted men's service from three years to one. When that big draft comes off, let me know who it hits in our town.

I am glad to hear that you had such good hay weather. I would have liked to have been to the pole raising, but I don't know but what I was doing quite as much on that day for the country, that was lying in the rifle pits watching the Rebs. It was warm enough to bake anyone.

My tent mate's name is Jim Holly from Sterling Furnaces, Orange Co., and John (Pawzile) from Sloatsburgh Rockland Co.

There is a man in our company by the name of J. B. Simmons. He is as fine a man as ever I got acquainted with. He lives in Bloomingdale, Tusquehannah Co., Pennsylvania. If I never should come back, make inquiries of him.

It is too bad for Em Myers to have her man go away and leave her when he should be at home.

I got some papers and a letter from Harriet last night. I got a letter from Sherman last night, but cannot answer it on account of not having any postage stamps.

Mother said she wished I could see the garden. I wish I was in it a little while. She would soon wish me out again. I am glad it is so good. I wish I had half a dozen very fine onions out of it.

There is a majority of Germans in our regiment now, but will not be when the old soldiers go home now soon. Some of them are very fine men and others not. There is seven different languages spoken. You know what kind of a friend I always was to foreigners, but now I am a better friend than ever to them.

My leg did not excuse me from duty. There was a rather sore lump raised up and afterwards turned black, but I kept going.

Since I wrote last, I have been to Morris Island and worked on Fort Greg, close to Sumter. While there, I saw a man from the 52nd PA. He said he was from Standing Stone, and knew Uncle John's folks well, and that Oliver Bishop was killed in the battle of the Wilderness and Stephen wounded and had his arm amputated. I think you should write out and find out about it. The 52nd PA belongs to the same brigade that the 56th does.

I am not as fat as I was. In fact, I am quite gaunt, but I don't feel any the worse for it. I can march all the better.

Atwell B. Leavenworth

Uncle John, mentioned in the preceding letter, was probably the husband of Sarah Ingram, sister of Charlotte Leavenworth. Oliver Bishop was about 29 when he died.

In one of Sherman's letters home he mentions to let a family know that Comfort was okay. Comfort's parents were Alexander and Elizabeth Boyd. Comfort A. Boyd was 20, when he enlisted, August 30, 1864, at Goshen, to serve one year. Comfort mustered in as a private in Company L. He mustered out on July 5, 1865, in Charleston, South Carolina.

New York, August, 1864
My Dear Friend, [Cousin Lon],

Excuse me Lonnie for my long delay in writing to you.

I am quite well thank you and hope when you read this, it will find you and your friends in the same state of good health.

How is Mother?

Oh, Lonnie, did Frances send you the song of "Wait for the Wagon?" If not, when you write, let me know whether you have it or not and I will send it to you.

I remain your affectionate friend, Addie

Ann Mary Austin Schoonover, wife of O.P. Schoonover, and daughter of Ralph and Fanny Austin, died August 31, 1864, at the age of 37. Ann Mary was

Atwell Leavenworth's death report, November 14, 1864. Source: National Archives and Records Administration.

not well in Fanny Austin's 1857 letter. Ann Mary wrote in her December 1863 letter, that she had been quite sick. Ann Mary Austin Schoonover was buried in the old Eldred Cemetery. On her headstone is a hand with the index finger pointing up *(see p. 118)*.

In September 1864, Isaac Sergeant, son of Ethel and Letty Gardner Sergeant, reenlisted, this time in Company A, 40th New York Infantry. Isaac had mustered out in October, 1863 because of illness.

Benjamin Merwin Hickok, son of Uncle Justus and Aunt Polly died at Rolla, Missouri (over 100 miles southwest of St. Louis), September 7, 1864. Merwin was with the 145th Illinois Regiment in which forty enlisted men had died of disease. Merwin was buried in the old Eldred Cemetery. His name was included on his parent's stone when they died.

The 145th Illinois Regiment was mustered out of service on September 23, 1864. Their 100 days were up.

Perhaps Merwin's death was a reason his brother, William Hickok, 26, enlisted in September. William enlisted with Company L, of the 56th Regiment Infantry, the same regiment that Sherman S. Leavenworth was in.

Atwell Leavenworth was again sick in camp from September 11 through November, 1864.

John Hancy, husband of Amelia Eldred (Uncle Mulford's daughter), lost an arm as a result of a wound received at the Battle of Winchester in September 1864. John Hancy was discharged from the service on March 27, 1865.

Morris Island, South Carolina, September 21, 1864

Dear Father,

Your letter of the fourth which

Bridge Collapse

Photo of the Barryville-Shohola Bridge with a middle support. Courtesy of Mary Briggs Austin.

One very cold morning, about the first of January 1865, three teams of horses and mules were crossing the Barryville-Shohola bridge with two heavy loads of wood.

The upper cable of the bridge (completed in 1856) parted near the center of the river. The bridge, teams, wood, and six men—Henry Lilly, Oliver Dunlap, William Myers, M. W. Quick, William Loftus, and Charles Deabron were thrown into the river. Three of the mules were drowned. The men were exposed to an hour of very cold water, but lived.

The Barryville and Shohola Suspension Bridge Company refused to rebuild and the bridge was purchased by Mr. Thomas.

He erected a pier, mended the broken cable and used the same material in what he called the new bridge. He established his own schedule of tolls, high indeed, but to which the people cheerfully submitted first, because they wanted the bridge, and second because no power was known higher than Thomas.

It was last erected and completed in 1867, subserved the intended purposes and proved a good source of revenue during the remaining lifetime of Thomas which finally terminated on the fifth day of October 1882.—Johnston, Reminiscences, *pp. 349, 351.*

stated that you were all well and that you had received the check all right. Hezy has been purty sick, but is getting better.

We are on Morris Island. We stand guard and do duty in the front trenches. There is not much danger. The Rebs throw a few Dutch bake ovens once in a while, but generally there is no more serious injury results from them than a waste of powder to the ones that send them.

We have plenty of duty to do being on duty every other night. The duty consists of guard or fatigue work such as mounting guns throwing up entrenchments or loading shells ammunition and sundry other work of the kind.

I have seen Atwell since we have been here. He looks purty lean. The rations in their regiment are very poor. Hezy and myself advised him to keep plenty of money as he looks as if he aught to. The water on this island is very miserable. We could not drink it if it was not for the ice that is supplied by the sanitary commission.

Our fellows at these forts throw a shell in to the rebel fortifications or into Charleston every fifteen minutes. The nearest fort of ours to Charleston is four miles distance. It takes a shell 42 seconds to go from this fort to the city. We are expecting to hear tell of a big fight at Petersburg before long. I guess that if Grant should take Richmond, the Rebels would think that it is best to settle the war.

This island is very sandy. It is composed of nothing but sandhills. The sand drifts like snow sometimes. It rains about every night.

Sherman S. Leavenworth

New York, September 24, 1864

My dear Cousin Emma,

I go to school now and you know with studying lessons and writing compositions it occupies ones time very much, so if my letter is not as long as usual, you must make some allowances for me and besides I have got a most terrible headache, another plea for an excuse.

Mother says that she thinks if your Mother's eye does not get any better she had better come here and have it attended to. She will go to the infirmary with her and she will have the best of care.

I have not been to church at all today, but Nettie and I are going this afternoon and as it is most time for me to prepare, my letter will have to be brief. Your loving Cousin, Tina, My love to all.

*Though others may be dearer
In friendship's brighter glee,
In strong connections nearer,
Emma forget not me.*

"The Times of Lincoln." From an American Missionary Association booklet. Mary Briggs Austin Collection.

Morris Island, South Carolina, October 24, 1864

Dear Brother John,

It is very cold here today. The sand drifts as bad as you ever saw snow yet. We will have to stand it this winter, I suppose.

We boilt a pudding today. Henry Shaw and myself. It was first rate only we did not have very good sauce to eat on it.

The rebel prisoners that were under fire here have been removed. Also, our prisoners have been removed from Charleston to Savanna, so the rumor is, so we will look out for some purty hard times or hot times, but I guess that there will not be much danger. If there is, I will let you know if you want to.

This island is a very desolate place. Plenty of sand and cold and hot weather in turns.

I suppose that you will go to school this winter. If you do, I shall look for a good deal of improvement in your writing,

From an American Missionary Association booklet. Mary Briggs Austin Collection.

spelling, and composing. If you should be in the army a while, you would see the use of learning. So study as diligently this winter as you must have worked this summer and you will get rewarded for it. You can if you will learn more this winter than Harriet knows about books.

We expect pay day all the time. If you are a good boy, if I get home, I will get you a horse besides other presents that you will get before.

As it is purty cold, I will bring my letter to a close. Excuse this writing as it was wrote in a hurry.
S.S. Leavenworth

Morris Island, October 25, 1864

Dear Brother John,

I take this present opportunity to write you a few lines as I have got a good chance to send them home by one of the fellows on furlough. He will be up to our house. His name is Robert McAndrews.

I would like to have a chance for a furlough or have Atwell or Hezy, but maybe the war will end soon and we will get a chance to get home.

I think that after the election, there will be a battle in front of Richmond for I guess that the head men in Washington think that if there is a battle risked and we should loose, that Lincoln would not be as apt to be elected.

It is purty cold here at present. Write how your crops were this year, whether good or bad. Write how many potatoes you have and how much buckwheat and rye you have. How does the sheep get along.

You must not let the fallow next to Bradleys grow up. If we get home safe and sound, we will want it to put horses in.

How does Mr. Sergeant get along with his work and what is he to work at nowadays? Is there any doings going on up home that is in the neighborhood? Do the fish bite in High Pond yet? What boys are there around that you can go with.

I would not wonder but what we will stay in this department this winter and soon as warm weather comes, we will likely go to Virginia as it would be very unhealthy, more so than it is now for to stay here next summer.

The Rebels sow some iron in and about our forts. Our fellows return the compliment in parrot eggs for Charleston.

We hear that Grant is four miles only from Richmond and last night's papers stated that they were moving heavy bodies of troops towards his left, but I guess that he will be wide awake enough for them if the rebels do not have success in the southwest. They will begin to think of coming to terms.

There was a blockade runner

United States Fractional Currency notes were issued by the U.S. Government during and after the U.S. Civil War due to the hoarding and shortage of coins in gold, silver, and copper in denominations of 3, 5, 10, 15, 25 and 50 cents. These notes were in use until 1876 and were redeemable by the U.S. Postal Office at face value in postage stamps. This is an 1874–1876, 10 cent Fractional Currency with an image of William Merideth, Secretary of the Treasury (1849-1850). Collection of Mary Briggs Austin.

sunk trying to get out of Charleston Harbor. I saw them put shots through her. They run her a ground and the crew got off of her.

S.S. Leavenworth

A sad, sad, time for Buckley and Charlotte Leavenworth. Their son, Atwell B. Leavenworth, who had been so ill, died at the age of 20, from diphtheria on November 13, 1864. He was buried the next day on Folly Island, South Carolina, where he had been with Company E, 54th Regiment. Another account says that Atwell died in the Regimental Hospital at Folly Island, South Carolina, and listed improper use of vinegar as the cause of his death. Yet another account said Atwell died of consumption.

Atwell had mentioned to contact J.B. Simmons if he didn't return home. Apparently, someone contacted Mr. Simmons who wrote back the following letter.

Folly Island, South Carolina, December 19, 1864

Dear Sir,

I hasten to answer your communication of November 23rd. In explanation why I have not answered it before, I will state that I have been on picket duty constantly for the last three weeks, and consequently, having no facilities for writing.

In answer to the question "how Atwell felt about dying," I can't say but little, from the fact that I can't find as anyone spoke with him on the subject except myself. Perhaps I ought to state that the nurse's employed in the hospital at the time have all gone to the front at present to take care of the sick and wounded. For you will probably learn before this reaches you that most of the forces in this department have gone to meet Sherman.

Whenever I spoke to Atwell about the probabilities of his not recovering, his answer would be something like this.

"Well, I should like to live to see this rebellion put down, but if it is otherwise ordered, I don't know but what I feel perfectly reconciled. I am not afraid to die. I feel that I am laying down my life in a just cause."

He always conducted himself with strict propriety, and refused peremptorily to join any of his companions in any of the follies of camp life, he was a good soldier, and one that was respected by all who made his acquaintance.

He was buried with military honors, and a large number of the regiment attended his funeral. In regard to the removal of his body, I would think it impractical at present, from the fact there is really no one here that can make the proper arrangements.

If he was taken up at present, a metallic burial case would be needed, and that can't be had here. Perhaps it might be obtained at Hilton Head. His grave is marked by a nice headboard, with his name, letter of his company, and number of his regiment, so that any time for years to come his remains can be removed. They can be removed now, but it would be necessary for someone to come here on purpose and accompany the remains home.

I learned that one of his brothers from the 56th Regiment was here the day before he left for the front—making some inquiries in relation to the removal of his body, if he should return safe, he may make some arrangements to that effect.

I don't know that I can say anything more on this subject in answer to your inquiries. I deeply sympathize with the afflicted parents, and may this deep affliction be sanctified to their

eternal welfare, is the prayer of
J.B. Simmons
Co. E, 54 Regiment N.Y.V.
Folly Island, South Carolina

Remember George W. Eldred, friend of Sherman S. and cousin to the Eldred-Austin families? George had been discharged from service due to illness.

In December of 1864, George W. Eldred married Miss Marietta A. West, daughter of Samuel and Mary West. The ceremony was performed by Felix Kyte at her parents' home in Beaver Brook, New York. The new couple lived at Beaver Brook, and then at the Village where George was a farmer.

New York, December 18, 1864
Dear Cousin Emma,
At last I have seated myself to write to you the long promised letter, although I am almost ashamed to for I have put it off so long.

I have not been to my much loved school for the past week as I am suffering very much with a bad cold in my head.

So our esteemed and most worthy cousin G.E. [George Eldred] has at last stepped into the blissful bonds of matrimony, etc. Congratulate him for me.

Well Emogene, how is that teacher? Have you got any thumps on the nose like the one I received when I was there?

How I wish I had a monstrous piece of pumpkin pie. Do you make it as good as ever?

Is Retta [Henrietta] as fond of feeding the pigs as ever and has Maria gotten stung by any more hornets?

How is Grandmother [Hannah Eldred] and cucumbers getting along? Does she eat as many as ever?

Tell Aunt Mary I am getting very thin for the want of a good dish of string beans and tell Grandmother I have at last learned to like applesauce and apple puddings and if she will only come and see us, I will make her an apple pudding everyday.

But I guess you are getting tired of reading such nonsense and as I have another letter yet to write, I will bring this to a close.

My love to all is the closing sentence of your loving Cousin's letter. Tina

Possibly written in early 1865
Dear Mother [Charlotte],
Since I last wrote, we have went on an expedition to cut the Charleston and Savannah railroad. We have been to three battles and one skirmish. Both times I seen men fall dead and wounded on every side and the bullets and shells and grape and canister flew thick. I tell you Hezy is not along. He was left back on Morris Island on the account that he was not in the enjoyment of the best of health, but he was not doing roughly ill.

The box has come, but I do not see how Hezy is to have any of it, although I wish he could.

It can not be sent there no how and we are not liable to stay here one day. We may make an advance on the railroad and then all that is left of the box will have to be left, that is what we do not carry in our haversacks. I never was so glad to see a box come in my life. Our rations were small and the fatigue that we have to go through gives me an uncommonly good appetite.

I never was more rugged in my life. I am as fat as a hog, and no wonder, we are not a bit backward in confiscating rebel sheep, hots and cattle, and there was plenty of them.

I have got the camp scurvy and that medicine that you sent Hezy I think I shall use as it would get wasted before he will get to the regt. or we go back there. I found out where Atwell was buried and where his things were. He had $10 in money when he died. I did not find out the state of his mind when he died. They were all Germans around him and they can hardly speak a word of English. It was the most brutish regiment that I ever saw.

You must not be uneasy about me. The bullets have flown thick, but it does not scare anyone after he gets engaged.

All the things in the box was alright. Not anything spoilt. Tell Anny and Johnny that I was very glad to get the things that they sent. Tell Johnny that I will send the money as soon as I get paid to get him the gold pen and the other things, as the pen will not be fit for anything unless he gets someone to purchase it for him.

Tell Anna that she must be a good girl and help you. We are at present on the peninsula between the Tilafinna and Coochahatch Rivers. We lay about one mile and three-quarters from the railroad. We attempted to take it one day, but were not successful. The grape and canister flew thick from Rebel batteries.

We however drew the Rebels out of their strong holes and whipped them back again in a hurry.

Coe and our young boys are all well. Also Horton and Comfort.

As I have not got anymore paper, I will have to bring my letter to a close. Write as soon as you get this and let me know if you are all well. You and father must not work very hard.

Sherman S. Leavenworth

Charleston, South Carolina, February 27, 1865
Dear Brother,

We are at Charleston and are in the best of health and spirits. We have just got through a march along the coast destroying and burning. We are about to commence a march west of Charleston. We have done some of the tallest kind of foraging and hope to do some more. This is a very nice place, but not to be compared to New York or Philadelphia.

Last night I seen some of the damage that our shells sent from Morris Island done. Whole blocks of buildings have been destroyed by them. The inhabitants have suffered a great deal of misery here while under the rebel rule. The rebels set the fire when they evacuated it, but the flames were extinguished by our troops when they took possession. They tried to blow up the arsenal and magazines, but the trains were intercepted before they reached the powder stowed for the purpose. We are barracked in a large warehouse with the 107th Ohio.

We hear that Columbia and Wilmington are ours and that Grant has made a successful advance and all so that he has repulsed the enemy in two of their attempts to regain their former position. We are in Charleston, but do not see the last ditch filled with those desperate fighting characters that made their boast that they would die fighting in the last ditch, as we would like to. I think that it must be as humiliating to them to leave this den of rebeldom as it is satisfactory for the detested Yankee to enter it.

Some of the people seem to be rejoiced to see our troops, but a great many by their scowls evince their hatred towards Uncle Sam. All the boys from our vicinity are in the best of health. I would like to write more, but have not time at present however, I will write again soon.

S.S. Leavenworth

Sometime in 1865
Dear Cousin Emma,

You told me not to write to you until I found time to write you a good long letter. I am still going to school; wish you were here to go with me. I expect to graduate soon with the highest honors.

My conduct in school has improved very much since you were here. I had no less than six bad marks last week, but they were well earned. I do not write this because I think I'm smart. No. I am really ashamed of myself.

But Em if you were in school (I mean in my class), I fear you would have a dozen bad marks unless you could control your laughing faculties better than I do.

I never was in a class where the girls loved fun so much as they do in ours. It seems to be the chief thing on which they live. Just as Miss Appleton commences to hear the lessons, some girl will accidentally upset the pitcher of water over the floor, another pretends there was a rat in her desk, gives a yell and jumps most across the room, setting the class in the greatest confusion imaginable while a third is so frightened that she faints away.

By the time order is restored, it is past the lesson hour and ciphering is commenced, thus affording an escape to the girls who did not know their lessons.

Rand is still at Elmira. I wish she was home. It is so lonesome without her. I have to sleep all alone. Can't you persuade your Father to let you come and spend the winter with me? You know you are entirely welcome. I will do all I can to keep you from getting homesick and you won't have to sleep in the little tumble down bedstead, nor in the dark bedroom, for it is packed full of Belle's furniture.

I have the little front bedroom all to myself and we could have nice times if you would only come. If I could have my way, I would have you here in a jiffy. You must try and behave well and not get your Spencer upside down.

We are all well and I am happy to say, behaving well. Write very soon if not sooner and believe me,
Ever your loving Cousin, Tina

New York, March 18, 1865
Dear Aunt Mary,

We have all been sick again (as usual), but I believe we are all convalescent now. I have been playing sick for the last few days but am getting about tired of it. I have been very sick of congestion of the lungs. I have not been out of the house for over a month. I am going out next week if nothing happens.

Cousin George was here to see us about two weeks ago. He looks very well considering the "trying scenes" he has past through lately, don't you think so?

Well how are you all getting along? Mother talks of coming up this summer, but whether it will end in talk or not I can not say.

We were very glad to hear that Uncle Henry was not drafted. How did it happen? I should have thought it would have past been his luck. There has been no battling in our district, nor will there be if the men volunteer fast enough to keep the Provost busy.

Mother finds liberty in employment in worrying about the draft. I don't know what she will do for something to fret about should it pass on without hurting anybody.

How is Grandmother? Give her my love and tell her I have been quite a good girl lately. I have not laughed for sometime for the simple reason that I could not.

How is Aunt Laura's baby? Emogene wrote that it was very sick. I hope she will not lose it. I suppose your boy is quite a young man if he grows at the rate he did when I was there.

I am glad to hear that Billy Myers was so sensible as to not go down with the bridge. (See "Bridge Collapses," p. 121.)

I am getting very tired and will try to bring this to a close before you get quite tired out. Mother sends her best love to you as do all of the rest.

Nettie talks of writing you today. She does not have much time for writing. You must give my love to Uncle Henry, Grandmother, and all my cousins both great and small.

Believe me with love, your affectionate niece,
Addie Austin

On March 27, 1865, William Henry Austin and Mary Ann Eldred Austin had two new arrivals—twin sons. With typical Austin humor, Henry and Mary Ann discussed calling the twins Abe and Jeff after the leaders of the North and South. They settled on Charles Mortimer Austin, for my grandfather, and Edward Augustus Austin, for his twin brother.

I am quite sure I was told that Grandpa Mort Austin was born at the Eldred homestead. I guess that that was in keeping with women going to be with their own mothers for their confinement.
—Melva Austin Barney.

Finally, the horrid and bloody Civil War which took countless lives ended. Lee surrendered to Grant at Appomattox Court House

Methodist Episcopal Church News

Methodist Church Post Card. Courtesy Mary Briggs Austin.

The Pond Eddy Methodist Church was built in 1862. In March 1862, Rev. Henry Litts became the preacher for the Barryville circuit which probably included the churches at Barryville, Pond Eddy, and Eldred— the three churches Rev. H.I. Briggs, my grandfather, would pastor when he arrived in the area around 1935.

In the spring of 1864, Rev. W.C. Hendrickson became the preacher on the Barryville Circuit:

The Congregations were small—the class not well attended—the church records very imperfectly kept in an old book like the counting house blotter.

No marriages or deaths were recorded of the two previous years. The Sabbath Schools were in a very bad condition.
—Barber, Gertrude, Record of the Methodist Episcopal Church.

In 1865, Alexander Wells was the Sunday School Superintendent. Licensed Exhorters included J. Collins, and D. Wells. Trustees were: J. Stage, J. Collins, D. Young, O.P. Schoonover, T. Collins, and Ed Kelso.

Robert Collins, son of James Collins, became the Pastor of the Drew Methodist Church of Port Jervis. Several of Robert's letters to Mort Austin will be in Book Two.

in Virginia. Then, as we all know, a terrible deed happened. President Lincoln was shot. Abraham Lincoln died April 15, 1865, and Andrew Johnson was sworn in as President.

Ten days after President Lincoln died, Hezekiah Bunce Leavenworth, son of Buckley and Charlotte, died. Hezekiah was on the train, traveling home for a sick leave because of dysentery. He died just 14 miles from his parents' home. Hezekiah died of chronic diarrhea, April 25, 1865. Hezzie had been with Company B, 56th Regiment. Hezekiah was the spelling of his name on the tombstone.

This has always been one of the sad family stories to me. So close to home, but his parents, Sherman Buckley and Charlotte Leavenworth did not get to see their son Hezekiah before he died.

If Buckley and Charlotte did plant a tree for each of their boys—to be cut down in their memory, if they died during the war—a second tree was chopped down.

Hezekiah was buried in a large plot in what is now called the old Eldred Cemetery. The plot, which most likely belonged to Buckley and Charlotte Leavenworth, has only a memorial marker to both Hezekiah and Atwell. One side of the monument has information about Atwell and that he was buried at Folly Island. The other side has Hezekiah's information. It is not known if Atwell's body was brought back to Eldred.

Although there are no other gravestones showing in the old Leavenworth plot, Buckley and Charlotte's children who died young—a baby at 2 days, Sarah Jane at age 4, and Amelia Ann at age 2—were probably buried there.

Mt. Pleasant, South Carolina, May 6, 1865

Dear Brother John,

We lay at Mount Pleasant yet. We saw a general order yesterday. It said that we were to be discharged by the first of June. At any rate, the government only issues rations to volunteer troops up to that time.

We may start north by the 20th of this month. It is very warm down here at present, but the warm weather does not come down here till July and August. I am glad that there is prospect of getting north before that time.

I hope that this will find Hezzy improving. Maybe as it is getting warmer weather, he will revive up and get better.

I expect a letter from home or from Harriet today as a boat came in from Hilton Head with mail this morning.

You never write whether you go to school or no. You must not expect us home too confidently for something might turn up that we may have to stay longer than we expect. All the boys from our vicinity are well.

Sherman S. Leavenworth

In 1865, there were 40 tanneries in Sullivan County that produced 8,567,872 pounds of sole leather per year, valued at $2,609,289.

In the spring of 1865, George Mapes, his wife Polly V. Eldred, and son Charles Egbert Mapes, 1, moved to Venango County, Pennsylvania. George had a grocery business there with his brother Thomas. Polly was the daughter of C.C.P. and Effa Eldred.

C.C.P. Eldred had held the position of Lumberland Postmaster from September 1851 to December 9, 1864. In 1865, C.C.P. and Effa lived in the Town of Thompson.

Gordon and Susannah LaBarr still lived in Beaver Brook. Their family included Calvin, 9.

Sherman S. found out that his brother Hezekiah had died in a letter his sister Harriet Palmer wrote. In 1865, Sherman's sister Harriet, 30, and her husband Henry Palmer, 36, lived in the Town of Deerpark, New York. Their daughter Edith was 3-1/2 and their son, Harry was 4-1/2 years old.

A view of the Delaware River from Hawk's Nest Road, Sparrowbush, N.Y. Ten days after President Lincoln died, Hezekiah Bunce Leavenworth, son of Buckley and Charlotte, died. Hezekiah was on the train, traveling home for a sick leave. He died just 14 miles from his parents' home, near Sparrowbush. His parents, Sherman Buckley and Charlotte Leavenworth did not get to see their son Hezekiah before he died. Postcard courtesy of Helen Hensel Oset.

Summerville, South Carolina, June 13, 1865

Dear brother John,
It is very warm down here. I

think that if you could be down here a few days you would observe quite a contrast from the weather here and at home.

We will most probably have to stay until our time is out, but our duty will be easy to what it ever has been before. We are quartered in good barracks.

I will write what our routine of duty includes.
1st roll call and one hour's drill in the morning.
2. roll call at noon.
3. dress parade at five p.m.
4. roll call at 9 o'clock p.m.

Mother must not work too much. I would willingly have her take my money to hire someone to do it for her. If any of you are not well, you must not write that you are. The next time that you write, you must write how Annie's rheumatism is.

When you write, try to put your letters together as good as you can. If you will try to learn, I will do all that I can so that you shall. I received a letter from Harriet stating about poor Hezey's death.

S. S. Leavenworth

Monday, June 26, 1865

Dear Emogene [Emma Austin],

Your letter was received in due time and perused with much pleasure. You say you wish to see me awful bad, but you can not want to see me worse than I do you. But I guess we will have to take it out in wanting, for I shall not be able to get in the country this Summer as much as I want to see you. But what cannot be cured must be endured and so I am trying to be reconciled to my lot.

Mother is busy trying to get away in the Country before the fourth, and the Doctor says we must get Emma [Tina's youngest

"The two trees on the right continued to grow for the two sons that lived—Sherman Stiles and John Ellis Leavenworth."—Alice Willis. Photo: Gary Smith.

sister] off as quickly as possible. She has been very sick with fits and had them so hard and so many of them that we began to fear she would never get over them, but she is getting better now, yet is still very weak.

The Doctor said her mind was too active for her body, that she learned too fast and that we must not let her study or read and said that the country would do her more good than anything else. I wish he would order that prescription for me.

I was very much surprised to hear that you were teaching School. How I should love to be there to see you exercising your authority over the little ones. Are you very severe with them?

I suppose you do not teach them much. Do not misunderstand me, I do not mean to say that I do not think you capable of teaching, for I know

Atwell and Hezekiah Leavenworth Marker in the Eldred Cemetery

Leavenworth cemetery plot in Eldred, New York. Hezekiah and Atwell's grave marker is in the left between two crosses. Photo: Cynthia Leavenworth Bellinger.

Front of Atwell B. and Hezekiah B. Leavenworth's marker. Atwell was buried on Folly Island, originally. I don't know if his body was brought back to Eldred. Photo: Gary Smith.

Hezekiah B. Leavenworth, a soldier in the Union Co. B, 56th Infantry, N.Y.S.V. He died on April 26, 1865 at 18 years old. Photo: Gary Smith.

of no other Cousin of mine who is so well fitted for that position in life as you are. Em, I guess you were just marked out to be a little School teacher for you have an uncommon amount of patience with children, one of the most requisite things which a School Teacher needs.

I am going to try and persuade Mother to let me come up and be one of your pupils during the summer and take lessons of patience from you. Does this proposition meet with your approbation? Write and let me know and tell me more about your school.

Mother sends her love and hopes to see you all soon. Tell your Mother I never eat string beans, but what I think of her and that is pretty often.

You must excuse the blots on the paper as Rand got them for me.

My love to all not forgetting your dear self. I will bring my letter to final hoping to hear from you soon I remain,
Ever your loving Cousin, Tina
    Long may you live
    Happy may you be
    Rest in content
    And often think of me.

In July of 1865, Edward Augustus Austin, son of Henry and Mary Ann Eldred Austin, died at 4 months old. Edward was my grandfather Mort Austin's twin brother.

Edward died in infancy possibly from typhoid.—Robert Austin, son of Edward's twin, Charles Mortimer.

In 1865, Alonzo Eugene Austin Sr. and his wife Belle had two daughters, Olinda, 4, and Henrietta, 2; and a son, baby Mortie.

Corporal Sherman S. Leavenworth

56th Regiment, Virginia Battles
Siege of Yorktown
Lee's Mills
Williamsburg
Turkey Island
Savage Station
Fair Oaks
Seven Days Battle
Bottoms Bridge
White Oak Swamp
Malvern Hill
Carter's Hill
Woods Cross Roads

56th Reg., S. Carolina Battles
Sea Brook Island
Grimball's Landing
Port Wagner
Charleston Harbor
Johns Island
Honey Hill
Coosawatchie
Boyds Point
Deveaus Neck
Mannings Mill
Dingles Mill

56th Regiment, New York
Fall of Charleston and many minor skirmishes.
 Went to front on Nov. 7, 1861, assigned to Gen Casey's Div. Army of Potomac 4th Army Corps until August 1862; transferred to 18th Army Corps at S. Carolina; then to 10 Corps in October 1863. Served there until October 1865 at Charleston, S. Carolina where they were finally discharged on October 17, 1865.

Sherman S. Leavenworth's discharge from the Army document. Courtesy of Linda Leavenworth Bohs.

Several men from the Town of Highland returned home in July. Comfort A. Boyd mustered out, July 5, 1865, as did William Hickok. Since William Hickok mustered out at Charleston, South Carolina, he was able to take Sherman's $100 check (mentioned in Sherman's July 14, 1865 letter) to Buckley Leavenworth when he went home.

James Gardner Sergeant mustered out at the end of July. His brother Isaac had been discharged in May.

It was October before Ira Austin (from the other Austin family in town) and Sherman S. Leavenworth mustered out.

Newbury, South Carolina, July 14, 1865
Dear Brother John,
 We are in Newbury, South Carolina. The port is going to be divided. We do not know where our company is going yet. The

Highland's Civil War Veterans

Ira M. Austin
Jacob Beck
De Witt Brown
George Bunce
Gareth T. Clark
Theo Cotton
George N. Courtright
George Davenport
John Davis
John G. Drake
Johnstone Dunlap
Milo Dunlap
George W. Eldred
Charles Hickok
Merwin Hickok
William Hickok
Charles Jennings
Addison La Forge
Andrew J. Lawrence
Atwell B. Leavenworth
Hezekiah B. Leavenworth
Sherman S. Leavenworth
William Leibla
Dennis S. Middaugh
Adelbert Myers
Charles Myers
Moses Myers
Samuel Myers
William Myers
Gilbert Nelson
Manning S. Nelson
Newton B. Nelson
George W. Parker
Martin Quick
William Schofield
Isaac Sergeant
James Gardner Sergeant
Henry Shaw
William Smalling
William Smith
Harlan P. West
Theo West
Edw. B. Wilson
Horton Wilson
Jas. C. Young
L. Coe Young
Samuel M. Young

Note on the hand written list at the beginning of this chapter (which is repeated here): These names were taken from a record in the possession of Rev. John R. Ralph, pastor of the Barryville M.E. (Methodist Episcopal) Church, who will be glad to receive any names which may have been omitted from this report.

Leavenworth Gravesite. Atwell and Hezekiah marker on the left with a cross on either side. It is likely that Sherman Buckley Leavenworth, his wife Charlotte Ingram, and their daughters that died so young are also buried in this plot. Photo: Cynthia Leavenworth Bellinger.

inhabitants when we first came were very distant towards us, but get more friendly as we get acquainted and the southern girls seem to be on as good terms with the Yanks as they are with Confederate soldiers, if not better. At least we find them very agreeable.

They say that they have more respect for the Yankees now than before the war. We live better now than we did in times of active service. Eggs are 12 cents per dozen, milk 10 cents qt., potatoes $1 a bushel.

There is scarcely a family but what has lost some member and some families two, three and four. Quite a loss to undergo and not accomplish the task they undertook to be compelled to acknowledge the armies of a people triumphant that they always affected to despise.

There is a strip of country about 50 miles wide completely desolated with fire. It is the rout that our army took marching from Georgia north. Columbia is completely destroyed with the exception of the capitol, orphan asylum, and a few other houses.

I sent a check of $100 dollars home with W. Hickock. I wish that father uses it to get things that you most need at home. I suppose Harriet would like to get her pay for the furniture that she got.

If I get out of the service sound, I think that I shall not stay at home long.

Do not forget to learn all you can. If I had a good education, it would be all I would want.

Sherman S. Leavenworth

Finally, on October 17, 1865, Sherman Stiles Leavenworth returned home from the war. He mustered out at Charleston, South Carolina.

Chapter 9
Your Loving Cousin
Eldred-Austin Cousin Letters, 1866–1871

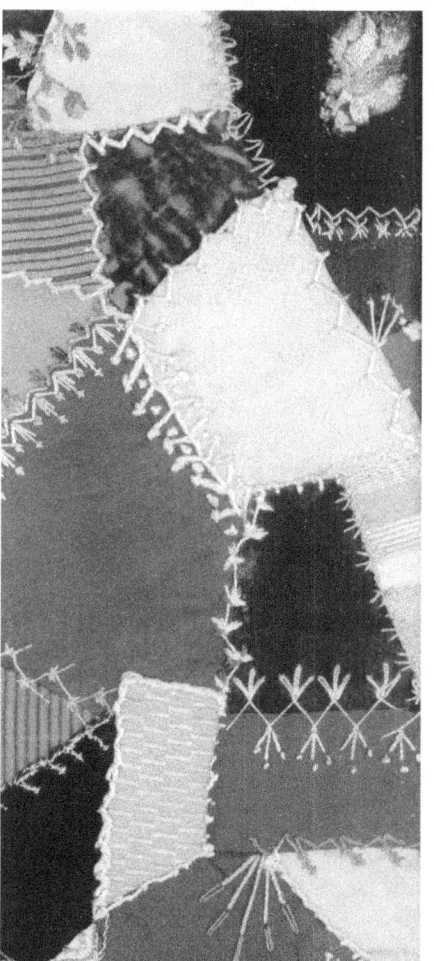

Section of Austin quilt coverlet.

Dear cousin Emma,
I commenced going to school Monday and you must know that it takes the greater part of my time in fulfilling my school duties and so if my letters are not as long as usual, I hope you will make all due allowance for me.

I shall not call this a letter, for it is not deserving of the title, it is only an analogy for one, but I can not help it. I feel unusually out of humor tonight and my ideas are all dull and common place.

Oh Em, you do not know how bad I want to see you. I have got so much to tell you. I cannot write it for it would take too much paper. Sometimes it seems as if I shall never see you again. It seems so long to look forward untill the next summer.

I never make any calculations now, for we do not know what a day may bring forth. Sometimes when we think we shall be the happiest, we have our saddest most sorrowful hours. It is as the minister said at little Mortie's funeral: There is more bitterness in sweet in our cups and that we would have to drain it to the very deep.

Oh Emma, if I did not think I could do a little good in the world, and perhaps make others happy. I would not care how soon death came to me, how soon God saw fit to take me home. The sooner the better. Life has no charm for me now as it once had. It seems as if all happiness had been wrested from me all that I loved has been taken from me.

But I do not wish to make you unhappy. Trouble will come to you soon enough. Would dear Emma that I could shield you from all sorrow and suffering, but we must all have our dark days, and the more trials and temptations we have to endure the better it is for us, for it teaches us not to think too much of worldly things.

I must close for it is getting late. Mother sends her love to your Mother and Grandmother. Write very soon and believe me ever,
Your Loving Cousin, Tina

So ended the January 9, 1866 letter of 17-1/2-year-old Justina Marie Austin, daughter of Uncle Augustus and Aunt Maria, to her 14-year-old cousin, Edith Emogene Austin.

You may recall that the Austin brothers, Augustus and Henry, had married Eldred half sisters, Phebe Maria and Mary Ann. The two families visited each other often—New York City in the winter, and the Village in the summer.

The Eldred-Austin cousins also corresponded by letters. A number

Austin Cousins on Austin property in Eldred, NY. Photo from Mary Ann Eldred Austin's Scrapbook. Melva Austin Barney Collection.

Possibly children of Alonzo Eugene Austin Sr. In the Leavenworth Collection.

of their letters are a part of this story thanks to the collection of Melva Austin Barney.

In 1866, Uncle Augustus and Aunt Maria's children—three sons and eight daughters—were ages 7–29.

Alonzo Eugene Austin, the oldest, was married to Isabelle (Belle) Camp. They had two young daughters, Olinda and Henrietta. Alonzo and Belle's son Mortimer died at age two when he pulled a pail of hot water over himself (Little Mort's death was referred to by Tina in the opening letter).

Uncle Augustus and Aunt Maria had two other sons, Mortimer Bruce, and Edward D., but very little is known about them.

The Austin cousins that wrote many of the cousin letters were Nettie, Addie, Rand, and Tina. The younger daughters were Christina, Clementina, Grace Emma, and Ida Belle. Several of the cousin letters referred to Grandmother, who was Hannah Hickok Eldred.

In 1866, Grandmother Hannah Eldred lived with Henry and Mary Ann Eldred Austin and their seven children: Mary Henrietta, Emma, Maria, Ell (James Eldred), Lon (Albert Alonzo), Aida, and (my grandfather) Charles Mortimer.

February 4, 1866

Dear Emma,

And now Emma you must excuse me if my letters are not as long as usual as I do not feel much like writing and would much rather have you here to talk to, but that is not to be.

We used to have nice times when you were here did we not, even if we did have to sleep in the little bed. And do you remember the night I slept with you, and Grandmother thought it was Maria?

Give Grandmother a bunch of love for me. Tell her that I think of her often and that I like applesauce almost as well as I do myself.

Tell Eldred (Ell) he must have a lot of apples picked for me by the time I come up and I hope he has got over his bashfulness enough to be able to give me a kiss.

But dear Emma, you can not imagine how I long to see you. And I could not wait until next summer if I did not know I had got to.

But I have got a feared headache tonight and as it is Saturday night, I have my lesson to study for Monday.

Emma, you shall know all you want to when I come up next summer.

Give my love to your Mother and Father, and all the rest. Write soon and believe me when I say,
Your loving cousin, Tina

February 28, 1866
My Dear Emma,
I do wish it was summer so I could come up there. I want to see you so much and I long for a change of some description.

Have you seen Aunt Laura lately? When you see her give her my love and tell her I want to see her awful badly and that she must come to New York and see us.

How is Grandmother getting along? Does she keep well and make you laugh as much as ever? How are all the little pigs and big ones. How is Billy Kyte and his pig prospering?

But I must close for I have got to get up early in the morning. So good night and pleasant dreams. Love to all and believe me,
Ever your loving Cousin, Tina

A number of events took place in the Town of Highland in 1866.

You may remember that Martin D. and Jane Ann Myers, parents of Maria Myers (my great-great-grandmother), were country neighbors of Henry and Mary Ann Austin. The Collins family lived between the Austin and Myers families.

Clara Webb, the young granddaughter of Jane Ann, and daughter of Charles and Sarah Shotwell Webb, died in January. Charles C. Webb, son of Jane Ann and her first husband Henry C. Webb, was a half brother to 13-year-old Maria Myers.

Olin Hickock, son of David and Mary Jane Russell Hickok, was born in 1866. Olin, a grandson of Uncle Justus and Aunt Polly, would be a good friend of my grandfather Mort Austin, who was 1-year-old in 1866.

Asa Hickok was a great-grandfather to both Olin Hickok

Eldred and Austin Cousins, 1866

The Cousin Letters refer to the letters of the two Eldred-Austin families—Augustus and Maria Eldred Austin, and Henry and Mary Ann Eldred Austin.

There are other Austin Cousins (descendants of Ralph and Fanny Knapp Austin), and other Eldred Cousins (descendants of James and Polly Eldred Austin). Known cousins are listed here.

Note: The Eldred cousins were half cousins to Henry and Mary Ann Austin's children.

Augustus and Phebe Maria Eldred Austin's family
- Alonzo Eugene Austin Sr., 29; married Isabelle J. Camp.
- Mortimer Bruce Austin (Mort), 27; married Mary L. Millspaugh.
- "Net" (A. Antoinette) Austin 26; married Henry Clinton.
- "Addie" (Adelaide Austin), 25; married Thomas J. Thompson.
- "Rand" (Miranda Adelia) Austin, 21; married Archibald Paton.
- Edward D. Austin, 19; married Evaline.
- "Tina" (Justina Maria) Austin, 18; married Randolph Laing.
- Christina Austin, 15.
- Clementina Austin was about 11.
- Grace Emma Austin was about 10.
- Ida Belle Austin was about 7.

Henry and Mary Ann Eldred Austin's Family
Mary Henrietta Austin, 16.
Edith Emogene (Emma) Austin, 15.
Maria Adelaide Austin, 13.
James Eldred (Ell) Austin, 11.
Albert Alonzo (Lon) Austin, 8.
Aida (Ida) Antoinette Austin, 5.
Charles Mortimer (Mort) Austin, 1.
Henry Ladore, born December, 1866.

Mahlon Irvin and Laura Austin Clark's Family
Ellsworth Clark, 4.
Elbert Clark, baby.

Zophar and Sarah Eldred Carmichael's Family
Harriet Carmichael (Young), 42.
Lewis Carmichael, 41.
John Mulford Carmichael, 37.
Elimina Carmichael (Drake), 34.
Charles Carmichael, 32.
Polly Maria Carmichael (Gregory), 30.
Emeline Carmichael (Lewis), 25.
Sarah Carmichael (Davis), 23.
Decator Carmichael, 21.
Eliza Carmichael (Puff), 18.

Abraham Mulford and Elizabeth Wheeler Eldred's Family
(Abraham died in 1847.)
Amelia Eldred (Hancy), 27.
Benjamin Franklin Eldred, 25.
Augusta Eldred, 22.
Harriet Eldred, 20.
Mary Eliza Eldred, 19.

Charles C.P. and Effa C. Van Tuyl Eldred's Family
George Washington Eldred, 30.
Polly Vanorsdol Eldred (Mapes), 27.
Rebecca Caroline Eldred, 24.
Maria Adeline Eldred (Kendall), 19.
James's Daniel Eldred, 17.
Sarah Jane Eldred, 14.

James K. and Eliza Eldred Gardner's Family
(James K. died in 1860.)
Maria Gardner (Calkins), 33.
Stephen St. John Gardner, 31.
James E. Gardner, 29.
Ann Eliza Gardner, 22.

Postcard of the Barryville Schoolhouse. Courtesy of Mary Briggs Austin.

and Mort Austin. So the boys were both good friends and cousins.

You may also remember that Henry Austin's sister, Ann Mary Austin Schoonover, died during the Civil War. In 1866, Ann Mary's widowed husband, O.P. Schoonover, married Mary A. Murray Parker at the Methodist Church. Mary Murray Parker was a widow with two children, George and Kate Parker.

In the next letter, Cousin Tina mentioned visiting an Uncle Peter. Uncle Peter was most likely O.P. Schoonover's father, Peter Schoonover.

New York, July 29, 1866
Dear Cousin Emma,
So you are going to School in the village? Do you like it as well as you did going here? Mort [Tina's brother] said you came running out of the schoolhouse to meet him and he could not think as to who it was.

Well Emma, I cannot come up this summer and you cannot be more disappointed than I am.

Mother [Aunt Maria] has been very sick but she is better now but her feet trouble her so that she cannot be on them at all. She does not even go out of the house. So you see I have enough to keep me busy and she could not possibly spare me this summer.

I should dearly love to come up if I could for the weather is perfectly intolerable here and I have not been well at all this summer.

Chapel is going to have a picnic on the second of August and I am going to attend. I wish you were here to go with me; but don't you think they ought to wait one more day, for the third of August is my 18th birthday and it would be quite an honor to me for them to celebrate my birthday.

I was to your town to "Uncle Peters." I went the first of July going with the intention of staying over a week, but they urged me to stay much longer than I should like to have stayed, but I thought Mother needed me.

I want you to ask your folks to let you come and make me a good long visit this winter. I should be home all the time and you won't have to sleep in the little old trundle bed either.

Write soon and believe me,
Ever your loving cousin, Tina

There was a horrid train wreck at Narrowsburgh, in August of 1866. A train struck eight tank cars filled with oil. The oil spilled and ignited. The flames engulfed several buildings, including the home of the Charles Williams family.

Mr. Williams carried his young daughters Rosa and Jenevieve to safety, but they were severely burned, and died, as did Mr. Williams. Sarah, his wife jumped to safety from a porch roof. I guess it is no wonder she gave birth to her baby that day.—from Hawker, A., *Town of Tusten History*

Starting in the fall of 1866, Great-Grandpa Henry Austin worked in New York City, where he owned a horse and wagon delivery

Postcard of the Barryville Schoolhouse. Courtesy of Mary Briggs Austin.

business—also called truck farming or carting.

Grandfather Austin went with horse and wagon to the docks in New York City, to get products and delivered them.—Robert Austin, grandson.

James Austin, brother of Henry Austin, had written in 1858, that he (James), and their brother Alonzo (Uncle Augustus), would help teach Henry the ropes of carting. This apparently happened. I am assuming that James and Uncle Augustus still had carting businesses of their own in New York City in 1866.

Henry worked several months at a time in New York City, and possibly stayed with or near his brother Augustus's family who had moved to the City after 1850.

In Tina's September 1866 letter, she mentioned a Carrie Newman. Ralph and Fanny Austin had a daughter Caroline Austin who married a Mr. Newman, but Caroline died in June of 1849. Perhaps Carrie Newman was a daughter of Caroline Austin Newman.

September 17, 1866
Dear Cousin Emma,

This is the second time I have written to you and you have not received it. I directed your letter to Bethel as you told me to and what was to hinder you from receiving it? I cannot imagine.

I was very much surprised when you said in Uncle Henry's letter, "Tell Tina to answer my letter," for I had been looking for one from you for some time. Now I am going to do as the Irishman did who wrote to his friend asking him if he did not get the letter to write and let him know.

Oh dear Emma, how I wish

The Isaac Bradley family, about 1868. Left: Isaac N. on Joanna Brown's lap; Viola in back; Amelia in front; and Mary Frances on Isaac's lap. Photo courtesy of Emily Knecht Hallock.

you could come and stay with me all winter. We would have such a nice time. I am home all the while and we could go out together and enjoy ourselves fine. Can't you coax your folks to let you come?

Have you heard from Carrie Newman lately? I have written to her twice but have received no answer from her and I am afraid she is sick.

I cannot write any more, as I am very weak yet. It is the first I have been up for three days. I came very near having the cholera, so near that there was not much fun in it.

Love to all and write soon. Ever your loving cousin, Tina

In mid-December of 1866, Henry and Mary Ann Austin had another son, Henry Ladore Austin. Ladore, nicknamed Dorrie or Dora, joined his seven siblings ages 21 months to 17 years old.

Judging from what is said in letters, Dorrie had a sad existence.

In 1867, a one-roomed school house was built in Barryville. Behind the school house were falls known at one time as Fish Cabin Falls. Grades one through eight were taught there from 1867 until 1949. My mother, Mary Briggs at the time, attended school there in the mid-1930s. The building is still in use, but not as a school.

In February of 1867, Isaac Newton Bradley was born to Isaac and Joanna Brown Bradley. Baby Isaac had three sisters, Amelia, 6, Viola, 5, and Mary Frances, 3.

Amelia Bradley's future husband, John Ellis Leavenworth, son of Sherman Buckley and Charlotte Leavenworth, turned sixteen in February 1867.

John was a rascal and on the wild side, with a fiery personality and a hot temper. He had tried to enlist in the Civil War, but was too young. When the war was over, he went out west to fight Indians. Anyway, that is the story my dad heard.—Cynthia Leavenworth Bellinger.

A couple years after the Civil War, John was reprimanded for driving the horses too fast. John got mad, left Eldred, and went west at age 16, to serve in the Army in the West.

John was in Custer's calvary, but he grew to a height of 6 feet, 2 inches, which was too tall for the calvary, so he had to switch to the infantry, which guarded the forts. Custer is usually known for the calvary and the battle, but there was also an infantry.—Robert Austin, great nephew.

Apparently in those days, it was expected a son would help out his father until age 21. Sherman Buckley Leavenworth, John's father, wrote as much in his will of 1873. The will was witnessed and signed by Wm. K. Kyte and Isaac M. Bradley.

Whereas my Son John left me at the age of sixteen years or thereabout, and deprived me of all benefit to be derived from his services for a period of five years or thereabout, now therefore, I do hereby release to him, the said John, all claim which I at anytime heretofore may have had or now have to such services and the profits arising therefrom and intend the sum as the only gift or bequest to which he shall be entitled.—excerpt of 1873 will.

John Leavenworth would marry Amelia Bradley, most likely against her father's wishes.

Back in the year 1867, John Henry Clark, son of George Case and Mary (Mercy) Harding Brown Clark, was born in August. John Henry would be the grandfather of Stella Clark, who marries a grandson of Sherman S. Leavenworth.

James Gardner Sergeant, who we read about in Sherman's Civil War letters, married Emma Myers in October of 1867.

Sunday, April 21, 1867
My dear Emma,
Excuse my seeming neglect for we have been very busy cleaning house and have had a great lot of company and my time has been occupied in attending to household duties so that I could hardly find leisure to write to you and now I have commenced I know not what to write about.

I went to church this morning and intended to go to the chapel this afternoon, but was sadly disappointed for no one seemed inclined to do up the dinner work, so I had to remain home and do it myself.

I wish I could be with you and talk for I can not write what I should like to say to you.

I was up to Belle's Thursday and spent the day. Belle and I went out; we had such fun. I enjoyed my visit very much and wish the world had a few more like Belle in it. There would always be happiness and peace if every one were like her. But I am going to write a little note to Belle, so I shall have to close.

With much love to you all, I remain,
Your loving Cousin, Tina

Mount Kisco, Westchester Co., January 1, 1868
My Dear Sister Laura,
You will doubtless be surprised at receiving a letter from me, but James has been talking so long of writing to you, that I came to the conclusion that I would write in his place. It seems as if I knew you for James talks so much about you.

He has been talking of writing you for a long time, but has not made it out yet. I will not wait for him much longer, would you? He thinks he can not spend the time. It does make it bad when a man has such a large family as he has to provide for, but we really do mean to come one of these days.

James has had his picture taken for you. I think it very good, but not quite as good looking as he is. He will send it on as soon as he can get a chance. I have had mine taken, but I guess I will keep it home. I think you will have a better opinion of my looks if I keep it home. I do not pride myself much on my beauty. I am good enough looking to suit my husband and he is all I care to please in that respect.

John Ellis Leavenworth. Cynthia Leavenworth Bellinger Collection.

He is a dear good husband I assure you. Whether he can say as much of me as a wife, I do not know. We have been married four years yesterday. It does not seem so long. James has but one child, that is me.

He does not come home but once a week. The time hangs very heavy on my hands sometimes. I go down to see him quite often though. We live about forty miles from the city on the Harlem Road. We think it very pleasant here and want you to come out and see us. We would love to have you come dearly.

How is Emogene? I would like to see her very much. Give my love to her. I would like very much to visit you. It must be very pleasant where you live. To hear James talk, you would think no other place worth living in, but I do not wonder at it for it was his home. That one word tells the story, for home is the dearest spot on earth and no matter how humble it may be, we would not exchange it for all the wealth the world could offer. But I must close for James wants to add a line.

Hoping to hear from you soon. From your loving sister, Julia

Febuary 1, 1868

Dear Sister Laura,

Julia says I must write a line. I will by one month and a half old already. I think it time to finish this letter and send it a jogging. I did not intend this delay and I would say it is not Julia's fault. I take all the responsibility, but as I only write once in twenty or thirty years, you will excuse me.

I have not forgotten you although I do not come to see you or write. I often think of you and Irvin. I often pray for you. I hope you pray likewise and try to love and serve our Lord Jesus Christ.

Lewis Carmichael and Mary Bunce

Lewis and Mary Bunce Carmichael. Photos courtesy of Marnette Hart Click.

Back in 1848, Mary Bunce wrote a letter to Mary Ann Eldred who was not yet married to Henry Austin.

Mary Bunce married Lewis Carmichael, son of Mary Ann Eldred's half sister, Sarah Eldred Carmichael and her husband Zophar. Therefore Lewis Carmichael was a cousin to the Eldred-Austin families.

In the collection of Melva Austin Barney was a photo labeled Mary Bunce, and one of Lewis and Mary's daughter, Lina Carmichael, born in 1867.

How fun it was to meet Marnette on the internet. She is a descendant of Lina Mae Carmichael Watson. Marnette sent me the above photos as well as some family information on Lewis Carmichael.

Mary Bunce's father and a brother were named Hezekiah Bunce. This gave a very possible connection to the name of Buckley and Charlotte's son, Hezekiah Bunce Leavenworth.

Lewis Carmichael, son of Zophar and Sarah Eldred Carmichael, started working on the railroad at age 15.

Lewis and Mary Bunce Carmichael lived in Iowa by 1854.

In 1865, Lewis was selected by the Union Pacific Railroad to be one of its grading contractors for the construction of the transcontinental railroad.

Lewis and his crew worked in southern Wyoming and Utah's northern canyons until the railroad was completed May 10, 1869.
—www.nebraskahistory.org, Newsletter, September 1999. Special thanks to Marnette Hart Click.

Lina Carmichael born 1867. From Melva Austin Barney.

I hope, if spared, to come and see you sometime.

I send you my good looking face. I will praise it and try and make it out all right although anyone knows it's homely enough.

For want of space I must close, my kind regards to Irvin and all inquiring friends. I should be pleased to get a letter from you.

I will send my photograph by Henry who is coming next Friday.

*Your affectionate brother,
James H. Austin*

In 1868, Alonzo Eugene Jr. was born to Cousin Alonzo Eugene Austin and his wife Belle. Alonzo (Lon) Jr. joined sisters Olinda, 7, and Henrietta, 5. Lon Jr., would be known as Dr. Austin, in later years.

Sad, sad times for the Leavenworth family—Buckley, Charlotte, Sherman S., and Hattie Palmer. Julia Ann, 12, well loved daughter and sister, sometimes called Annie in the letters of Sherman S., died March 15, 1868. Most likely Julia Ann was buried in the old Leavenworth plot in what is now the old Eldred Cemetery.

Sometime in 1868, C.C.P. and Effa Eldred returned to Highland from the Town of Thompson. In June, C.C.P. was again appointed Postmaster.

Monticello, November 9, 1868
Dear Emma,

This is Monday morning. I thought as I had no lesson to learn, I would write to you. The first bell of the Heading has just rung, so I cannot write any more at present, but will try to write some this noon if I have time.

I have just returned from school, so before dinner, the bell is ringing for dinner.

Dear me, what work I have to write. I have just finished eating, so for the third time, I'll try to write. I expect the school bell to ring any moment, but will write till it does ring.

Tell Willie, by the time he gets as far as passing in grammar, I will be home, I think. So I can hear him.

This is the third day I have passed at school. I enjoy it as well as can be expected. I have not got classed much, yet, but think after I get better classed and acquainted, I shall like it first rate. There are 14 boarders here now, all but 3 or 4 are scholars. There are but 2 lodge boarders besides us.

It is nearly 8 o'clock in the evening, so I will again endeavor to write. I have had more fun today than I have before since I have been here. One of the teachers is Mr. John Reardon. I know you don't like the name, but he is just as pretty as he can be. He has black eyes, but I shall not try to describe him anymore.

Oh how I do want to see you. Don't go away untill I come home

From Mary Ann Eldred Austin's Scrapbook. Courtesy of Melva Austin Barney.

so I can see you once more before you go. So good bye from your dear friend Alice. Don't forget me.

Dear Cousin Emmie,

I am of a good mind not to write to you for finding fault with me about writing with a lead pencil. However, as this is the first complaint you have ever made against me, I will have to overlook it, and to be obliging, write you and with a pen.

Aunt Mary cannot get a chance to write as little Ida has been quite sick and she has to tend her a great deal. I guess she got cold coming down or else the change of air does not agree with her.

I have been quite lonesome this last month as Ranny (Randolph Laing, whom Tina marries), and I have had a falling out and consequently not having another beau, I have been compelled to stay in the house and I don't think it agrees with me.

I wish as soon as you come for me, to tell him to write to me and send it by mail or else in with your letter when you answer this.

Afterall Emm, these beaux are more trouble than they are worth, and I am heartily sick and disgusted with both them and myself and have come to the very sensible conclusion never to marry, but live an old maid's peaceful and secluded life.

We have had the greatest lot of snow here, and it has been as cold as Greenland besides and I am tired of winter too.

You see I am in a real discontented mood tonight and you must make some allowances if the tone of this letter seems a little cross. You know I am a real spunky piece of humanity anyway, and sometimes, if I don't give vent to my wrath, I don't know what the consequences might be. Tina

Randolph Laing Austin, the tenth and last child of Henry and Mary Ann Austin, was born December 15, 1868. Perhaps he was named after Cousin Tina Austin's husband, Randolph Laing, whom she married around 1869.

"When Shall We Meet Again", written in Mary Ann Eldred Austin's handwriting.

Before April 2, 1869
Dear Emma,

We have been so busy and have had so much company lately, that it seems as if I should never get a chance to write unless I did it on Sunday and I don't like to write letters on the Sabbath, but will try and not write nonsense though I rarely write anything else.

Black Friday Panic 1869

You may have heard of the money or greenbacks created during the Civil War by the U.S. government, which were backed only by credit.

After the Civil War ended, it was thought that the U.S. Government would buy back the greenbacks with gold.

In 1869, James Fisk and Jay Gould headed a group of speculators who sought to profit by cornering the gold market. They recruited financier Abel Corbin to influence President Grant as Corbin was brother-in-law to the President.

Abel Corbin convinced President Grant to appoint Gen. Daniel Butterfield as Assistant Treasurer of the U.S. Butterfield was to tip the "speculators" off when the government intended to sell gold.

Late summer 1869, Gould began buying large amounts of gold causing prices to rise and stocks to plummet. President Grant realized what was happening and had the federal government sell four million dollars in gold.

Within minutes after the government gold hit the market, the premium plummeted. Investors scrambled to sell their holdings, and many of them, including Corbin, were ruined.

As is the case sometimes, the scoundrels Fisk and Gould, escaped significant financial harm.
—from www.en.wikipedia.org/wiki/Black_Friday_(1869)

Note: The Black Friday Panic of 1869, was one of four contributing factors to the Panic of 1873.

The Panic of 1873 affected the Depression in 1876, the year in which my great-grandfather Henry Austin lost his carting business in New York City.

We will talk about the years 1873 and 1876, and how Great-Grandpa Henry went back to Eldred to farm in Chapters 10 and 11.

But I have no more time to write. Excuse this nonsense and answer as soon as you can.

Mother sends her love to all and says tell Grandmother if she comes up this summer it will be to see her.

Ever yours, Tina

My great-great-grandmother, Hannah Eldred, second wife of James Eldred, died in April of 1869. Hannah, the mother of Mary Ann Eldred Austin, was living with Henry and Mary Ann Austin at the time of her death. She was almost eighty.

Hannah Hickok Eldred's memorial stone says, *We laid her in the hallowed grave with hope in Him who died to save.*

In March a year later is a poem in Mary Ann Austin's handwriting. I wonder if Great-Grandma Mary Ann copied the poem in memory of her mother.

The hymn was reprinted in the "Revivalist" 1868. It is thought that this hymn was composed by three Indians attending Dartmouth College at the time.
—Brown, Butterworth, The Story of Hymns and Tunes.

When Shall we Meet Again
When shall we meet again
When shall we meet again?
Oft shall glowing hope expire
Oft shall wearied love retire
Oft shall death and sorrow reign
Ere we all shall meet again.

Though in distant lands we sigh,
Parch'd beneath the hostile sky.
Though the deep between us rolls
Friendship shall unite our souls;
And in fancy's wide domain
When shall we meet again.

When the dreams of life are fled
When its wasted lamps are dead;
When in cold oblivion's shade
Beauty wealth and fame are laid
Where immortal spirits reign,
There we may meet again.

Mary Ann Eldred Austin loved poetry. She wrote some of her own poetry, but often she copied poems she liked, or cut them out of the newspaper and placed them in a scrapbook. Some of the pictures in Mary Ann's scrapbook are included in this chapter.

The love of poetry was passed along to Mary Ann's children and to my family through her grandson, my father, Art Austin, who often quoted from a number of memorable poems.

Several of the cousin letters indicate that Henry and Mary Ann's daughter, Emma, had some of her writing published. One of Emma's poems is in this chapter. We will read more of both Mary Ann's and Emma's poetry in Chapter Thirteen.

New York, Sunday 24, 1869
Aunt Mary,

This is the first opportunity I have had for writing since I received your letter.

I will send you the pattern of my waist and also a sleeve pattern. I should make it plain waist to button up in front and put the trimming on the waist in the form of a little round cape. Let it run over the shoulder and down quite low in the front and back. They do not make the walking dresses as short as they did at first.

Net has gone up to Paterson and I am advising you the best that I can. You did not tell me whether you were going to trim the skirt or not. They make most of the walking dresses with two skirts. Some of them are made with one skirt trimmed with a bias flounce of the same as the dress.

If Maria is coming to New York, I will fix her skirt for her after she gets here or any thing else I can do for her I will do with pleasure. I am curious myself to know where she is going. I think you might have told me.

Tell her for me that a rich man has not come along yet. I am afraid I shall have to marry a poor man after all, as they seem to be the only kind that are at all "loveable," or else she will have to marry the rich man and take me to live with her.

I am glad that dear little Ida (Aida) was pleased with her doll, but I am afraid that name will take all the curl out of its hair. Tell her I will bring it a new dress for its name when I come.

*With much love,
Your affectionate niece, Addie*

September 20, 1869
Dear Cousin Emma,

I have really been so busy since I came home that I haven't even had a chance to take a peek in any of my interesting books much less find time for writing.

I like housekeeping thus far and I wish you were here to see how admirably I get along. Ranny's mother and sister have been around twice to see me and Em, you would nearly die a laughing to hear Ranny tell them what a splendid cook I am when I haven't hardly cooked anything but beef steak since I commenced to keep house.

He is so afraid I will do too much that he follows me every step I take about the house, to see what I am about.

It has been terrible warm here today and I will be glad now when the warm weather is over for it is having a very bad effect upon me. I am getting to be fearfully lazy.

Have you got a school yet to teach or have you given it up? Em can't you come back with your Father when he goes home?

I wish you would give my love to your mother and remember me to Tommy and his mother. Ranny sends his regards to him and wants him to come and see him when he comes to New York.

Your loving cousin, Tina

Tina's brother, Mortimer Bruce Austin, married Mary Letitia Millspaugh on October 20, 1869. Yet another Mary Austin!

In September, Justina Laing Eldred was born to George W. and Marietta West Eldred, in Halfway Brook. Baby Justina Eldred who was named for her father's cousin, Justina (Tina) Austin Laing, had two brothers, James and Herbert Lincoln Eldred.

Irvin and Laura Austin Clark had a little girl, Eva Clark, who died, sometime before January, 1870.

Before January 1870
Dear Friend and Aunt,

I was very sorry to hear that dear little Eva was dead. I had just been writing to Tina that Eva was very sick, but I little thought so soon to hear of her death.

Your niece, Emma

Little Eva
*Tis true that death's relentless hand,
Tis ne'er with mortal man at rest
He will often come and steal
Away the ones that we love best.*

*Twas when the grass was springing green
Along the hill side in the mead,
That he dear little Eva claimed
And laid her with the silent dead.*

*And she was beautiful divine
As pure as spotless as a saint
A form as lovely and sublime
As skillful lines could so paint.*

*We miss that little one so fair
She's gone no more on earth to be
She dwells in that blest country where
Her Lord and Saviour she can see.*

*Ellsworth, he will miss
That little one so mild
But never more on earth
Will he behold that little child.*

*She was so sweet on earth to stay
Too good for a world like this
So angels thought as they called her away
To that world of heavenly bliss.*

*We would not wish her back again
On this cold earth of misery
From Jesus' arms in that blest place;
Prepared for such as she.
E.E.A. [Edith Emogene Austin].*

Little Eva's brother, Ellsworth Clark. Melva Austin Barney Collection.

The current Pond Eddy bridge built in 1904, replaced the 1870 suspension bridge which had been washed away in a flood in 1903. Photo: Gary Smith.

Side view of the Austin home. Photo in Mary Briggs Austin Collection.

View of the Collins home. Mary Briggs Austin Collection.

The population of New York State in 1870 was 4,370,846. The Town (townhip) of Lumberland had 1,065 townsfolk. Highland township had a population of 958. There were 260 people in Barryville, one of the hamlets in Highland township.

Lumbering was still an occupation in the upper Delaware River region in the 1870s. *Where Timber and Lumber Come From,* a *New York Times* article from Narrowsburg, New York, written May 9, 1872, told the history of lumbering in the Upper Delaware River area.

Circular sawmills, which replaced original slow up and down sawmills, were introduced first in Narrowsburg around 1850. By 1870, the circular sawmills numbered in the hundreds and created ten times the income for the area along the Upper Delaware River. Most circular sawmills continued to use the many streams in the area to provide inexpensive power to run the mills.

In the 1870s, hemlock lumber made up nine-tenths of the timber that was sent to market by river, railroad, and canal. Pine trees, which had been the number one export in the 1820s, were third or fourth in importance, and in danger of disappearing from the market in the Upper Delaware River lands. A small amount of maple, oak, chestnut, and basswood was also included in the almost 200 million board feet shipped from the area.

Even though, the careless stripping of the densely forested land had unfortunately continued, the 1872 *New York Times* article predicted another ten years for "profitable employment of thousands" and "rich returns for the large sums of money invested therein."

Lumbering, though still a source of employment in the early 1870s, was being replaced as a major industry by boarding houses (the subject of Book Two), and the mining of the massive reserves of bluestone in the area. Mills and Cash, and Decker and Kilgore, were two firms that mined the bluestone quarries.

Mr. Decker, a former Town of Lumberland supervisor and a Sullivan County sheriff, supervised the building of the 1870 suspension bridge which was built across the Delaware River at Pond Eddy. The bridge connected the bluestone quarries of Pond Eddy, New York, with those of Pennsylvania on the opposite side. The bridge was called "Decker's Bridge" because Mr. Decker lived so close to the bridge site. Pond Eddy had a store, school, church, mill, and some D&H Company buildings.

Barryville, almost eight miles northwest of Pond Eddy (by way of the Delaware River), had a number of buildings which were shown on the Beers 1870 map. Barryville had stores, a bakery,

1870 Beers Map Town of Highland

1870 Beers map showing A. Mills at top of Hagan Pond, Dr. DeVenoge to the right above Round Pond, and Myers Est. straight south of the "H" in Highland Lake, and the S. Mill (sawmill). Courtesy of Frank V Schwarz.

Martin D. and Jane Ann Myers' home and barn near Hagan Pond Road. Courtesy Stuart and Geraldine Mills Russell.

a drugstore, blacksmith shops, a grist mill, a sawmill, a school, the Union and Baptist Churches, and two hotels—Atkins Hotel and Union Hotel. The D&H Canal had an office. There was also a marble shop.

Halfway Brook Village was called Way Brook on the Beers 1870 Map. The map shows a post office at C.C.P. Eldred's house, a sawmill on Halfway Brook near C.C.P. Eldred's house, two stores, a hotel, a school, and two churches—Congregational and Methodist.

The Beers 1870 Map shows Henry and Mary Ann Austin's property as a large area, possibly 260 acres. In the 1870 Census, William Henry Austin, 46, was listed as a farmer with real estate valued at $4,000. His wife Mary Ann, 43, kept house and was busy with their nine children, ages 1 to 19: Henrietta, Edith (a teacher), Maria, James Eldred (Ell), Alonzo (Lon), Aida, Charles Mortimer (my grandfather), Henry Ladore, and Randolph.

The James Collins family lived on Collins Road near the Austin property. James, 67, was a farmer from Ireland, and had real estate valued at $2,000. His wife, Isabella, 68, was also from Ireland. Their son Thomas R. Collins, 24, worked on the farm.

Their son Robert B. Collins was in New Jersey where he was a minister. Robert had left the Village in the spring of 1862. Robert Collins (R.B. Collins) wrote several letters to my grandfather, Mort Austin, that will be in Book Two.

Martin D. and Jane Ann Myers (my great-great-grandparents) lived close to the Collins family, near the corner where Hagan Pond and Collins Roads met. Their home had been built in the early 1850s. At some point a second home was added.

Martin D. Myers, my great-great-grandfather, was a farmer. Jane Ann kept house. Their son George Washington Taylor Myers was 24, daughter Maria Louisa was 16, son Augustus W. was 13, and daughter Charlotte (Lottie) was 11. The Myers' land was valued at $2,000.

North of the Myers' home and west of Hagan Pond, a small stream flowed out of Hagan Pond's thumb. The Beers 1870 Map denotes a sawmill in that location as "S. Mill." The remains of a sawmill foundation are still there.

The Alexander Mills family had lived on the northeast side of Hagan Pond since 1850. Alexander from Scotland, and his wife Margaret Gillies had seven children, several of whom play a part in this story and in the town of Eldred.

Others in 1870

Alexander Boyd, 78, still farmed in 1870. His property was valued at $2,000. His wife, Elizabeth, 61, kept house. They were parents of Comfort Boyd (mentioned by Sherman S. in his Civil War letters), and James Boyd who married Margaret Mills.

George C. and Mercy Harding Brown Clark lived in Cochecton with six children.

Oliver Calkin, 41, was a farmer. His wife Maria Gardner, 36, kept house and cared for their children: James E., Maria E., and Charles F. Calkin, 1.

Julia Van Tuyl Hallock, wife of Thomas W. Hallock and sister of Daniel Van Tuyl, died at the end of January 1870, at age 78. Her husband, Thomas W. Hallock, had died in December 1865. Thomas and Julia's children included Hosea Ballow Hallock, Daniel Van Tuyl Hallock, William Hallock, and of course, Oliver Blizzard Hallock.

In October of 1870, Oliver Blizzard Hallock married Emma Amelia Schwab. Their son, Samuel Jesse Hallock, born in November 1871, would be Stella Clark's Grandfather.

Another ancestor of Stella Clark Leavenworth, Carrie Etta Bogert, was 5 in 1870. Carrie lived in Little Egypt near Youngsville, N.Y., with her parents, John Bogert from Holland, and Amanda Hogencamp, and siblings. John Bogert had a farm and sold milk in cans with the initials J.B.

Isaac Bradley and Joanna Brown had five children by October of 1870: Anna Amelia, 9, Viola, 8, Mary Frances, 6, Isaac, 3, and baby Lottie.

Robert F. Owen, 39, and his wife Elizabeth Tether, grandparents of my aunt Gladys Myers, had Arthur, William, and twins Frank and Mary.

Edward Tether, 72, and his wife Elizabeth, 71, lived next door, and next to them lived Joseph Tether.

James Gardner Sergeant, who had been in the Civil War had been married to Emma Myers for three

Charles Calkin, son of Oliver and Maria Gardner Calkin. In the collection of Melva Austin Barney.

Julia Van Tuyl Hallock. Photo courtesy of Emily Knecht Hallock.

years. Their son, James W. Sergeant was 1 year old.

Abel Sprague Myers and his wife Hannah Maria Van Schoick, had James L., 11, and Edwin, 7.

Coe Young and his wife, Adaline Adelia Sweezy, had a daughter, Jennie D. Young, who was 1 year old. Coe was the son of Isaac Young and his wife Eliza Gardner, and may have been referred to in Sherman S. Leavenworth's Civil War letters. The Coe Young family lived in Damascus, Pennsylvania.

The Superintendent of the D&H Canal was John Lounberry. His wife, Sarah, kept house.

Joseph and Mary Rixton from Switzerland ran a bakery. Henry and Elizabeth Ennes lived on property valued at $1,200. Henry was a shoemaker.

Edward Wilson, 50, was a farmer with property valued at $2,000. His wife Phebe, 43, kept house and cared for their children: Charles, Anna, William H., and Mary.

In Orange County, Zophar Carmichael, 71, was a farmer with property valued at $9,000. His wife, Sarah Eldred Carmichael, 65, kept house.

Zophar and Sarah's son, Lewis Carmichael, lived in Iowa with his wife Mary E. Bunce and eight children.

Stephen T. Bishop, 30, was a farmer and lived with his mother Sarah Ingram Bishop, 66, who kept house in Standing Stone, Pennsylvania. *Note: C.C.P. Eldred was the Marshall for the 1870 Highland, Sullivan County, New York Census. 182 dwellings/familes, 428 white females, 438 white males, 7 colored female, 1 blind, and 149 people were foreign born.*

Alexander and Margaret Mills' Home on Hagan Pond. Courtesy Stuart and Geraldine Mills Russell.

Martha Mills, 20, would marry George W.T. Myers, son of Martin D. and Jane Ann Myers.

Margaret Mills, 18, would marry James Boyd. Their son Floyd Boyd would have a store in town; and their daughter Isabel would marry Henry Asendorf and play a part in the life of a Myers grandson, as well as run a huge boarding house.

Geraldine Mills Russell, also a descendant of Alexander and Margaret Mills, is a friend of my mother, Mary Briggs Austin. It was exciting to see photos of the Mills and Myers' homes that Geraldine and her husband Stuart contributed for this book and Book Two.

West of the Austin lands lived Mary Ann Austin's brother, Charles C.P. Eldred, a farmer, with real estate valued at $4,000. His wife Effa kept house. Daughter Becca, 27, was a teacher, and daughter Sarah was 18. William Hammond, 19, who worked on the farm, must have boarded with the family.

James E. Gardner, 32, was a merchant with property valued at $1,000. His wife, Rebecca Rider, 31, kept house and cared for their children: Harry, Frank, Charles, Linda, and Susan.

Antoinette Austin Clinton (Net or Cousin Nettie). Melva Austin Barney Collection.

James E. Gardner's brother, Stephen St. John Gardner, 35, and his family lived in Thompson, New York.

Uncle Justus was 78; his wife Polly was 70. Their son Charles, 26, and Charles's wife, Sarah, 24, lived with them. Charles was a farmer.

Henry Austin's sister Laura and her husband, Irvin Clark, lived on the west side of the Village. Irvin was a farmer, and had property valued at $2,000. Irvin and Laura had two sons, Ellsworth, 8, and Elbert, 4.

Irvin Clark's parents, Wilmot Clark and Mary, were both 72. Wilmot was a farmer with property valued at $2,000. Daughter Martha, 22, lived at home. Louisa, 5, and Estella, 1, most likely two granddaughters, also lived there.

Around 1870, Oliver Perry Schoonover, 50, a carpenter, and his second wife Mary, 33, had a daughter Emily. Their first daughter Emily had died at one year old.

Buckley Leavenworth was a farmer with real estate valued at $4,000. Charlotte was keeping house, and their son, Sherman S. Leavenworth, 27, was at home.

Henry and Harriet Leavenworth Palmer lived in Deerpark township in Orange County, New York. Henry was a wood dealer. Harry was 10 and Edith was 9.

George W. and Marietta West Eldred and their three children moved from Halfway Brook Village to New York City in 1870. George W. Eldred worked as a carpenter in the city.

In the following letter, Cousin Addie mentioned her sister Miranda Adelia Austin. Miranda, nicknamed Rand, was married to Archibald Paton.

New York, January 9, 1870
My Dear Cousin Emma,
Uncle Henry tells me that you were disappointed in not getting your school. I am sorry, but if you are successful in getting one in the spring I should not care very much about teaching this winter. I think they treated you very mean though about it. I doubt very much you are dying an old maid.

I am sorry that Aunt Laura has lost her little girl, but she should not grieve too much for the dear little child is much happier than she could ever make her.

Rand has a very nice little baby boy, but I suppose Maria has told you all about it.

I wish I could see you and have a good chat. I think talking is much more satisfactory than writing don't you?

I should think you might have come down with Uncle Henry as you are not going to teach. Nettie sends her love.

Emma is looking anxiously for a letter from Maria. Ida send lots of love to cousin Ida (Aida). Tell Maria I will write to her soon and send her those verses I promised.
Your ever affec cousin, Addie

February 13, 1870
Your Father says he is going home in about three weeks. Don't you dare to let him return without you. I tremble for you both if you do.

Do come back with Uncle Henry won't you? Give my love to your mother and Ranny's. Believe me still Ranny's, (not yours),
Tina M. Laing

I'm not sure when this next letter was written. Aida Austin, was 9 in 1870, perhaps still

Of Sewing Machines, Glen Spey, McKenzie, and Proctor

Since one of the topics of conversation in the Austin cousin letters was sewing (Fanny Knapp Austin was a tailoress), including talking about owning a sewing machine, of interest is the Singer Sewing Machine Company, which just happens to have a connection to the very area talked about in this book.

Singer Corporation, first called I.M. Singer & Co., was established in 1851, by Isaac Merrit Singer with Edward Clark, a New York lawyer.

In 1849, Singer worked at a machinist's shop in Boston where sewing machines were built for industrial purposes, but the machines kept breaking down.

At the owner's request, Singer figured out a solution, then drew up plans for a machine built to his specifications, borrowed funds, and supervised the building of the first prototype. Singer realized the market potential of this machine, and is quoted as saying, "The dimes are what I am interested in."

Singer patented his invention in 1851. His bold advertising campaigns quickly created a market for domestic machines aimed at housewives.
—www.singermemories.com

By 1863, George Ross McKenzie (Singer Sewing Machine Vice President and General Manager at the time), was in the Lumberland area. Mr. McKenzie built a church and a school in the mid-1860s.

From 1882 to 1889, Mr. George McKenzie, then President of Singer Manufacturing Company, established his country estate in South Lebanon. The area reminded Mr. McKenzie of Scotland where he was born, and became known as *Glen Spey*.

Over the years Mr. McKenzie enhanced his 3,000 acre estate to include a school, the Lumberland Town Hall, a church, an orphanage and cemetery.

McKenzie's 3,000-acre estate known as "The Homestead," included Glen Roy and the grounds of the present-day Black Forest Colony.

The grounds outside his castle-like residence were designed and maintained in the highest manner with lakes, ponds, and terraces a common feature.

Soon after the initial development of Glen Spey, McKenzie turned his attention toward the construction of other facilities such as church, schoolhouse and post office. With the addition of carpenter and blacksmith shops, tool houses, granaries, etc., Glen Spey soon became a small village with homes for the tenants and religious and educational privileges for all.
—Lumberland document, www.co.sullivan.ny.us/documentView.asp?docid=647.

William F. Proctor, Treasurer of the Singer Company, also moved to the area, and built large Manor homes for his family in Glen Spey.

Loch Ada, one of Mr. Proctor's homes, was built in 1879. My great uncle Lon Austin, as well as others in the area, worked for the Proctor family in the 1890s. There are letters with the Proctor heading asking for more butter, which we will read in the next book.

young enough to be called "little Ida." Cousin Ida Belle Austin was around 11.

April 4th, 1870?
Dear Aunt Mary,
I received your very welcome letter last week.

You do not know how much I have changed and how homely I have grown. I am afraid you will not like me as well as you used to.

I have quite a delicate letter affair to settle with you, so I will be about it at once and to come to the point at once is to inform you that Phebe Maria, Antoinette Augusta [Net], Adelaide Eliza [Addie], have got it all arranged for you to come down with Uncle Henry when he comes back.

You are to bring little Ida and Mort, and as many more as you can. Should you say one word about not coming, you will be arrested by four policemen hired at your expense and will be brought by force at will. One of the police that will have charge of you looks and acts just like a certain Laing that I wrote to you about before, so you will know what kind of company you will have.

You will all be made to swallow two bottles of machine oil, 1 box of blue pills, 1 paper of pins, 2 of needles, 1 bar of yellow soap, 3 spools of cotton, five yds. of rag carpet. Then for dessert you are to swallow one of Aunt Effie's geese whole. Of course it won't have many feathers, but the little fin feathers and think what a long neck they have, to say nothing of the unmentionable. It will be very hard to do. Well, I guess you will think I have lost what little sense I had.

Ida says tell little Ida that she is cleaning her play house and getting it all ready for you. Addie says and so do I that you need not expect to see our green eyes up there this summer unless you do come.

Tell Emm the men that I have to deal with have no hearts. They have only a gizzard and I can't make any impression, not even a little dent.

Be sure and bring little Ida and Mort. Don't say they have got nothing to wear for that will make no difference. We have got a machine and will make good use of it while you are here.

Don't fail to come.
Much love to you all, Net

In September 1870, Charles-Louis-Napoléon Bonaparte III (the last monarch of France and the first President of the French Republic) was captured in the Franco-Prussian War. The Rouillon and Malinge families lived in France in 1870. Jean Charles Rouillon, 7, son of Lubin Rouillon and Florentine would marry Blanche Olga Malinge, also 7. Jean Charles and Blanche would be the grandparents of Gisele Rouillon, who we meet in the 1940s.

September 30, 1870
Dear Cousin Emma,
Mother and Ida returned home from Middletown last night. And I was very glad to see them. It has been so lonesome without them that I am sorry I did not stay up in the country longer, at least until your Father goes home, and then I could have come back with him.

I have been out house hunting quite a good deal this week, but have not found a place to suit me. The places would do very well, but the rents are enormous and Ranny gets such miserable wages, I don't know how we can keep house and pay rent this winter. And I do dislike to board any longer. I am fairly discouraged. If he only had some prospects of getting something better.

Have you got my book yet and are you going out to the Institute this week and how are you going?

If your school is out, why can't you come to N.Y. when your Father comes.

Well, Emma, I commenced this letter three weeks ago, but having such a fearful headache, I was compelled to give it up. Since then so much has happened that I have hardly had time enough to collect my thoughts sufficiently to write.

I suppose you heard about the death of Rand's dear little baby. We can hardly realize it. It was so sudden and unexpected. She grieves very much about him. He was just 11 months old, just the right age to be so much company to her.

I have been keeping house now a little over a week and that will readily account for my time being so wholly occupied as I had to do all the house hunting and getting things to rights and am not quite settled yet.

I want you to hurry up and come and see me and my two little rooms. Love to all and believe me still,
Your loving Cousin,
Tina M. Laing

Little 9-month-old Justina Laing Eldred, daughter of George W. and Marietta Eldred, died at the end of September 1870, and was buried in the Eldred Cemetery.

Another Eldred cousin family, David and Harriet Carmichael Young, moved from Eldred to Illinois about 1870. You may remember that Harriet was the daughter of Zophar and Sarah Eldred Carmichael. There are some photos of the David Young family in the Appendix, p. 236.

New York, December 1, 1870
Dear Edith,

I arrived home safely on Saturday, found the folks all well but ma. She has quite a bad cold yet, but is much better than she has been.

Maria Calkin came down to Middletown with me on Friday. We stayed at Mrs. Millspaugh's.

Tina was here Sunday. She had the last "Waverly" with a piece of Edith E. Austin's poetry in. I suppose Miss Edith will hardly condescend to write for "Beebe" now. Alas! who will write for "Beebe" now? Have you had the "Waverly?" I am going to get it and will send it to you if you have not got it.

I am real glad you sent a piece to ye editor. I feel almost encouraged to send a piece to the "Clipper" but guess I will wait until I compose it.

I was over to Belle's Tuesday evening. Mort and Mary were there. Net came to repeat "September Leaves" for them. They were delighted with them (the leaves) and told me to tell you to be sure and send them to the "Republican" and give my name if you do not like to give your own.

Give my love to all. Excuse writing. I am going out to night to buy me a pen.

Good bye, Yours, Addie

Sad times again for Henry and Mary Ann Austin. In December 1870, their youngest, Randolph Laing Austin, died at 2 years of age.

I remember Great Aunt Aida talking about the "other baby" dying, as well as Grandpa Mort's twin who was Edward A.
—Melva Austin Barney, great-granddaughter

The following poem is in a booklet of poems and dried flowers that belonged to Mary Ann Eldred Austin. The poem seems to go with the death of her youngest child. Great-Grandmother Mary Ann may have written the poem.

My Flowers, June 1871
*Not all of earth's lightness
Not all of its glee
Its gold or its brightness
Could tempt them from me.*

*For the sweetest and fairest
That bloom in earth's bowers
I would not yield up
The few withered flowers*

*That the hand of a stranger
Hath strewn o'er the bed
Where our baby is sleeping
Our beautiful dead.*

*For though they are faded
Their perfume is gone
No longer they're fair
To look upon.*

*Yet still are they dear
And speak they of love
A stranger hath felt
For our baby above.*

*For the little one resting
Low neath the sod
For the little one living
Above with his God.*

*And though now sweet stranger
Thou art unknown to me
Wherever thou art
I am grateful to thee.*

*I'll remember thy kindness
For thy sake and baby's,
I'll cherish dead flowers
In life's coming hours.*

New York, February 2, 1871
My dear Emma,

I was very much pleased to

Marker in the Eldred Cemetery for Edward Augustus and Randolph Laing Austin that died young. Photo: Gary Smith.

receive another letter from you, but was sad when I read the news it contained. Sorry for you all who have been bereaved lately. But not for the little one who God has so mercifully taken to Himself. What is your loss, is his gain.

Let this comfort you and your Mother. No more care and anxiety for your darling, no thoughts to harass you concerning your child's future, no more prayers to be offered for guidance to bring up your little one in the fear of the Lord. No, God has dealt mercifully in taking your rosebud, that it may open to blossom and bloom forever, a beautiful flower in his paradise. Your little one is safe in the Redeemer's room, guarded and protected 'neath his watchful care. Nurtured by his smile your darling will grow in spiritual grace and beauty.

I do not say as some, do not

Mary Ann's Flower Booklet

Photo: Daniel Smith.

The *Flower Booklet* of my Great-Grandmother Mary Ann Eldred Austin was a few sheets of lined, 8-1/2 × 11-inch paper folded in half with poems written in very nice handwriting.

Along with each poem in the booklet were some fragile dried flowers labeled: Yellow Rose, Columbine, Rosemary, Buttercup, Lemon Balm, and Sweet Pea.

One page with unknown leaves read: *from the Cemetery at Albany, June 1872.* Perhaps they were from Emma's visit to the Albany Cemetery mentioned in her May 19, 1872 letter.

On a separate page was written:
*Sweet fern leaves
And dear as they are beautiful
Are those fern leaves to me.*

Special thanks to Melva Austin Barney for sharing the booklet.

Flowers

God might have bade the earth bring forth
Enough for great and small,
The oak-tree and the cedar-tree
Without a flower at all.

He might have made enough,
Enough for every want of ours
For luxury, medicine and for toil,
And yet have made no flowers.

Our outward life requires them not
Then wherefore have they birth?
To minister delight to man
To beautify the earth;

To comfort man–to whisper hope
Whenever his faith is dim;
For whoso gathereth flowers
Will much more care for Him.
—Mary Howitt, *Birds and Flowers*.

---

mourn for him. To me sorrow for the death of little ones is a holy thing, but while you grieve, forget not the duty you owe to the living and be assured you have my deepest sympathy in this your late bereavement.
Tina M. Laing

New York, February 2, 1871
My dear Emma,
Well Emma, Did you commence your school? You do not know how much I would like to see you.

Have you to teach all summer? I hope not for I shall come up (if nothing happens to prevent) for a couple weeks and I want you home, then. And Emma, if you can, I want you to come and stay a while with me after the closing of your school.

But I must close. Ranny sends much love to you all (me too). Write to me soon dear, and believe me as ever,
Your loving cousin,
Tina M. Laing

New York, June 1, 1871
My Dear Cousin Emma,
Have you read any new books lately? I haven't but I wish I had a real good one just now. Write to me very soon and believe me ever.
Your loving Cousin, Tina

New York, Monday, July 10, 1871
Dear Emma,
I have received your letter and will try and steal time to answer it, although I hardly know how to spare the time.

Why did you not tell me that you wanted the red ribbon—not to gratify my curiosity, but so I would know something about the width. If it is for a sash you want it, you will need more than a yard and be kind enough to tell me what width you want it.

In regard to the overskirt, they seem to be wearing them as much as ever, I think. I do not know whether I can make it for you or not. I have got so much sewing to do now. I am almost crazy. Perhaps after a week or so I may get a chance to do it. If not, I will cut it for you and tell you as much as I can about it.

How do you want it trimmed? I think it would be nice with a narrow racking of the silk like our Aunt Mary's alpaca, only have it narrower, and there put lace below the racking.

If you have it trimmed that way, it will take 6 yards of silk and I cannot get it for less than 12 shillings or 2 dollars per yard and I can get imitation of Guipure lace that will look very pretty for about 50 (?) per yard, while the real lace will be as much as 12 shillings per yard.

So will you please write which I shall get and if you want the skirt lined and if you want the things before you go to the Institute or if you want them for the Institute. There are plenty of ifs in that sentence.

Em, Nett says she wants to come up, but she is very busy and will not be able to get away before the first of August anyway, and I do not know how it will be about my coming. I have a great mind not to try and come now until another summer for I cannot get away until late. I have so much to do. I guess Emma is coming up before long. I want to see you all awful bad and will come if I possibly can.

Give my love to all and believe me with much love,
Your ever affec. Addie

The Great Chicago Fire which killed hundreds and destroyed around four square miles in Chicago, Illinois, started Sunday, October 8, 1871, and burned until early Tuesday, October 10, 1871.

"Field Flowers"

Flowers of the field how much you seem
Man's frailty to portray.
Blooming so fair at morning's beam
Passing at eve away;
Teach this and oh though brief your reign
Sweet flowers ye shall not live in vain.

Go then where wrapt in fear and gloom
Fond hearts and true are sighing
And deck with emblematic bloom
The pillow of the dying
And softly speak, nor speak in vain
Of their long sleep and broken chain.

And say that He who from the dust
Recalls the slumbering flower
Will surely visit those who trust
His mercy and his power
Will mark where sleeps the peaceful clay
And roll ere long the stone away.
—From Mary Ann's Flower Booklet, author unknown.

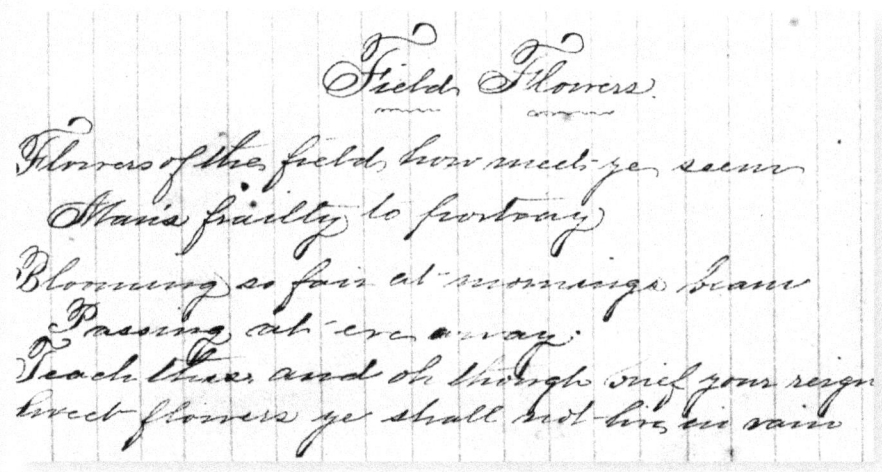

Partial page in the flower booklet, written out by Mary Ann Eldred Austin.

New York, October 15, 1871
Dear Cousin Emma,

By this you will see that me and my bag arrived home in safety and I know you are so anxious to hear from the bag as well as from myself. Well it was of very little trouble to me on my journey home, but I cannot see as its tour to Lumberland has improved its appearance any. In fact, I think it has somewhat detracted from its beauty for it looks pretty scaly and rough.

It does not seem as if a week today I was away up in Sullivan Co., and now am in my own snug little room as Alma says. I can't realize it and Em, bad as I wanted to see Ranny, do you know, still I would love to be in it (house on the hill) today with you all.

Neither have I been to Church. But then I can stand by my basement window and watch the folks coming out which amounts to about the same thing and which does me about as much good.

By the way how is my dear darling Aunt getting along? Give her lots of love.

Emma will you please do me a favor by taking charge of the lock in the trunk and send or

Bluestone

Bluestone, a type of flagstone or flat stone, was quarried along the Hudson River starting in 1820. The blue flagstone was found northeast of Port Jervis in 1830, but it was 1865 before a bluestone quarry was developed in that area.

"There is scarcely a farm on either side of the Delaware River for 100 miles above Port Jervis that has not a stone quarry upon it, and the lofty hills of Pike and Sullivan counties are apparently solid beds of the finest bluestone for miles back in the interior."

In 1868, Waters & Kilgour paid $8,000 for three thousand acres of quarry property in the vicinity of Pond Eddy, which was near the railway and the D&H Canal. Within a year, 100 men were working at the mine.

In the summer of 1869, the Pennsylvania Bluestone Company was founded. John F. Kilgour was made the General Superintendent. Jobs were given to 400 more men.

In 1870, some complicated politics entered the scene. The Erie Railway, headed by James Fisk, a perpetrator of the 1869 Black Friday Panic *(see p. 142)*, and New York City (controlled by William "Boss" Tweed) were combined into the New York and Pennsylvania Bluestone Company with John Kilgour as president.

The Erie Railroad built miles of switches at Pond Eddy and other points to ship the bluestone from the Delaware Valley as "the entire portion of the Delaware Valley on both sides of the River was virtually one vast flagging stone quarry."

The New York and Pennsylvania Bluestone (Fisk-Tweed) Company, intent on monopolizing the bluestone industry in the Delaware Valley, forced individual owners to submit to their control.

The *New York Times* exposed Boss Tweed's schemes. Soon after, Fisk was shot to death by a business associate. The New York and Pennsylvania Bluestone Company collapsed, and "everyone connected with it was ruined."

The Bigelow Bluestone Company of the Hudson River eventually became the owner of the Pond Eddy property.

Some 2,000 men were employed in the Delaware Valley quarries in 1889, when the Delaware Valley bluestone quarries netted $3,000,000.

Source: The New York Times: Fortunes in Bluestone, The Quarries of New York and Pennsylvania: History of the Quarries where Flagstones come from—one of Fisk and Tweed's Monopolies, *March 19, 1889.*

Bluestone is not only found in curbs and sidewalks in New York City. The Empire State building and the base of the Statue of Liberty contain bluestone from Hancock, New York.
—www.upperdelawarescenicbyway.org.

The largest flagstone ever to be quarried was cut at Pond Eddy, N.Y., floated to Philadelphia, Pennsylvania, on a raft, then to New York by boat and placed in front of the City Hall, New York City.—www.minisink.org/hisdoor.html.

New York, Sunday, October 30 [probably before 1872]
Dear Emm,

I received your letter yesterday and was very glad to hear you arrived home safe. I am so sorry you did not stay this week.

Rand came down the day you went home. She was very much disappointed because you did not come to see her. Aunt Julia came down today. She wants to see you very much.

Tina is very much better than when you were here though she hates to own it.

Uncle Henry has decided not to send you things by express. He is coming so soon he says you would not get them much sooner and he will bring them. So you must finish your dress and have it ready for the trimming.

You may think your trimming too dark at first, but they are using trimmings two or three shades darker than the dress. If you do not have enough for a flounce, I would trim it in the form of over skirt and on the front breadth. That Addie of ours knows how.

I hope you will like your hat and all the rest. I haven't spent all your money and hope I have got all you told me to. If not you must write and let me know.

I was glad to hear your sewing machine arrived safe. How do you get along sewing on it?

I was quite surprised to hear that Aunt Mary had found time to sit down and sew on it. I hope she will do so often. Tell her to come home with Addie if she can. I do want to see her so much.

How about "September Leaves?" I am very anxious to see them. Do send them as soon as they make their appearance.

Well Emm, if you will excuse this, I will write a few lines to that neglected sister of mine. Write as

---

give it to Maria Calkins, the first opportunity. It belongs to Dora Johnston and Maria says she wants it. You will oblige me very much by so doing.

Do come and see me and stay a good long time and don't forget my verses. We both send much love to you all.

Write very soon dear and believe me, ever your loving cousin,
Tina Maria

"Maternal Instinct" from Mary Ann Eldred Austin's Scrapbook. Melva Austin Barney.

soon as you receive this.
  Ever so much love to you, from your Net

December 18, 1871
Dear Emma,
  And now Emma please excuse me for not writing sooner as my Dear Ranny has been quite sick and I am not more than half well myself and to tell the honest truth, have not felt like writing.
  I am very sorry to hear that you and Lon have been sick and that little Mortie is ill. I hope he will soon be much better. It seems so dismal and dreary to have sickness in the house.

Mrs. Newcome mentioned in the Austin cousin letters. Melva Austin Barney Collection.

Kate Newcome, mentioned in Addie's 1871 letter. Melva Austin Barney Collection.

Church News

New Members of Lumberland Congregational Church

1866
Jane Ann Myers,
Ida Heyen (Toaspern).
10 new, 376 total.

1868
Emma Austin, Elizabeth T. Kyte, S.B. and Charlotte Leavenworth.
7 new, 387 total.
Note: S.B. Leavenworth was first a member of the M. E. Church in Eldred and in 1868, joined the Congregational Church.

South Lebanon Church
The South Lebanon Church built in the 1860s, was later known as the Glen Spey Hall. It served as a church for the residents of the area until the early 1930s. The hall was used for town meetings, theatricals, and plays.

1866, Mongaup Methodist Episcopal Church
The Mongaup M.E. Church is the oldest on this circuit. The members are general aged and have been connected with the Church for 20 years, owing to a glorious revival about 20 years under the labors of Rev. Mr. Beagle…We have a neat Church edifice.—Barber, Gertrude, Record of the Methodist Episcopal Church.

1866, Pond Eddy Methodist Episcopal Church
The Pond Eddy Methodist church was four years old.

  I was almost worried to death when Ranny was sick for fear I should lose him.
  When do you think you will go to school? I wish you would come and see me and stay a good while. I want to see you so much.

From Mary Ann Austin's Scrapbook.

And now that Ranny is very busy, so that he has to stay down to the store until late at night, we could have many a good cozy chat by ourselves and enjoy ourselves as well as the two friends, old dames who gave a private entertainment in which no one figured but themselves and their cat.

What greater inducements can I offer for you to come unless that I have two or three more new books, which makes quite a pile you haven't read, and which I hope will take you sometime to peruse.

Mrs. Newcome and Carrie called to see me a week ago Saturday. They looked as natural as could be. Mrs. N. is going to send me two or three new books to read and she is just as full of fun and as good company as ever, and I appreciate her very much and her books also or shall when I get them.

Please excuse me for writing with a lead pencil as I am in a hurry and Emma, I am anxious to hear how you are all getting along.

Love to all and believe me,
Yours Truly, J. M. Laing

New York, 1871

Dear Emma,

Mrs. Newcome and Katie called here on Wednesday and brought the material for Ida's cloak. In looking over the patterns we found no small one, only a large cloak pattern and cape. I guess Mrs. Newcome thought Aunt Mary could cut the cloak for Ida from the small cape pattern. Nett is going to try and cut the cloak in the morning before Uncle Henry goes home.

The long sacque pattern and wrapper pattern are for Mrs. Ingram. Mrs. N. said you could use the small cape pattern first and fit to Mrs. Myres, as she (Mrs. N.) had not paper enough for two.

You must shrink the black braid before putting it on the cloak. Mrs. Newcome said she would have written herself, but she has been so very busy since his return home and expects to be for some time to come.

We are all quite well and hope this will find you all "enjoying the same blessings." I suppose our respected aunt and uncle arrived safely. They generally do, I believe.

It is late and I am tired so with much love to yourself and all the rest.

Good night Dear Emma,
Yours ever, Addie

I found the poem, *Put Me in My Own Little Bed*, written out by Great-Grandma Mary Ann Austin. A few unrelated lines were written afterwards.

Put Me In My Little Bed
By Dexter Smith, 1870

1. Oh! Birdie, I am tired now,
I do not care to hear you sing;
You've sung your happy songs all day,
Now put your head beneath your wing;
I'm sleepy too as I can be,
And sister, when my pray'r is said,
I want to lay me down to rest,
So put me in my little bed.

Chorus: Come, sister, come,
Kiss me good night,
For I my evening pray'r have said;
I'm tired now and sleepy too,
Come, put me in my little bed.

2. Oh! Sister, what did mother say,
When she was call'd to Heav'n away?
She told me always to be good,
And never, never go astray;
I can't forget the day she died,
She placed her hand upon my head,
She whisper'd softly, "keep my child,"
And then they told me she was dead.

3. Dear sister, come and hear my pray'r,
Now ere I lay me down to sleep,
Within my Heav'nly Father's care,
While angels bright their vigils keep;
And let me ask of Him above,
To keep my soul in paths of Right,
Oh! Let me thank Him for His love,
Ere I shall say my last 'good night.'

Never give up when trials come
Never
Never sit down.

Chapter 10
Emma Goes To College
1872–1873

Dear Father,
Mr. Bauman directed me to write to the President of the School for any information I might desire. I wrote accordingly and received a reply from Mr. Alden Monday night.

He says the term does not commence until the 3rd Wednesday of February so that I have more time than I thought I had.

My tuition is free, and the books are provided for us. If I am there at the commencement of the term and stay 'til the close, my traveling expenses are paid to me so that there is no expense but that of board and I can hire a furnished room for 1 dollar a week and board myself. He says the majority of the ladies do this. I shall come to New York about the first of February. Your affec. daughter, Edith

In the spring of 1872, Edith Emogene Austin, 22, started Albany Normal, a two-year teacher's college.

Edith Emogene, or Emma as she was often called, her parents, Henry and Mary Ann, as well as the Austin cousins wrote back and forth during Emma's college years. The letters, written snapshots of life at that time, are courtesy of my cousin Melva Austin Barney.

Henry Austin still had his carting business located at 50 Warren St., New York City. Henry stayed in New York City with the City Austin families for what seemed to be several months at a time.

Great-Grandpa Henry also wrote some caring letters home to his son Lonie giving him instructions on how to help take care of the farm while he (Henry) worked in New York City.

The home of Henry and Mary Ann Austin was in Halfway Brook Village, which would soon be called Eldred. Henry and Mary Ann's children, the Austin country cousins—Henrietta, Maria (the quiet one), James Eldred (Ell), Alonzo (Lon), Aida (Ida), Charles Mortimer (my grandfather), and Henry Ladore (Dora, Dorie), ages 7 to 21—often visited their New York City cousins.

Lumberland, January 1872
Dear Father,
I was home a little while yesterday. Mother told me she had received a letter from you. They are all well at home.

Mort is getting better. He insisted about every day on going to the barn. He says he is well enough and doesn't know what the cows must think of his staying away so long. He was out on the stoop a few minutes Sunday. But it has been so cold since, that she has not dared to let him go out.

Julia Kyte died Monday night

Envelope addressed to Edith (Emma) from Lumberland, June 7, 1871.

Henry Austin, 50 Warren Street, NYC

The building at the left is 50 Warren Street. The building is still there and looks pretty much the same.— Melva Austin Barney.

Envelope from Lumberland, January 19, 1872, addressed to W.H. Austin, 50 Warren Street, New York City, New York. Photos from Melva Austin Barney.

and is to be buried Thursday. I hear Mr. Webber is to preach the funeral sermon. It seems dreadful to think of it, it is so sudden. But very few heard of her sickness till the news of her death reached them. She was sick only one day.

Dr. DeVenoge and Dobron were both called, but human aid was powerless to save her from the grasp of the Destroyer. Truly "in the middle of life we are in death" and ought at all times to be prepared for his coming.

I would write more, but I have no room and I fear you will hardly be able to read what I have written, but my excuse for poor writing is as usual, a poor pen and I might also be a poor writer.

Give my love to all my friends there. If you see Tina, tell her I will write as soon as I can, but I am very busy just now and have very little time for writing.

With love to my father and best wishes for his temporal and eternal happiness. I remain as ever his aff. daughter,
Edith E. A.

Julia Kyte mentioned in the above letter died January 15, 1872. She was not yet 20. Julia had been married to William Kyte, son of Felix Kyte, the Congregational Church pastor.

You may remember that Stephen Sergeant, son of Rev. Isaac Sergeant and Mary Richards (who we met in 1799), had been the pastor of the Congregational Church in Lumberland before Felix Kyte.

Stephen Sergeant had died in Wisconsin in 1871. In January 1872, his wife, Anna Penney Sergeant, died, also in Wisconsin. Stephen and Anna Penney Sergeant were buried in Wisconsin.

Rev. Stephen Sergeant was esteemed by some as a saintly man and by others sour and severe.—Quinlan, p. 586.

Stephen and Anna Sergeant's son, Ethel Sergeant and his wife Letty Gardner, had three sons—Alvah, Isaac, and James—who are a part of this story.

Hannah Maria Van Schoick, wife of Abel S. Myers, had died in June 1871, leaving Abel to raise their sons, James and Edwin Van Schoick Myers. (Edwin would be the father of Gladys Myers, the future wife of Charles Raymond Austin).

While Edwin V. Myers was in school one day in February, 1872, his father Abel married Maria Hankins. Edwin learned he had a new mother from his brother James, who had gone to school to tell Edwin the marriage had taken place.

Abel S. and Maria Hankins Myers would have six children, and one would be Archibald Abel Myers, father of Chuck Myers, who has contributed information for this story.

You may remember that George W. Eldred was discharged early from the Civil War due to illness. George had been a teacher and good friend of Sherman Leavenworth, and was also an Eldred-Austin Cousin. George, his wife Marietta West, and their sons James and Herbert lived in New York City in 1872. George was a carpenter.

In mid-February of 1872, George W. Eldred wrote his father, C.C.P. to announce his son's birth. George W. and his wife Marietta initially named the baby Charles, according to the following letter found in Richard Eldred's, *The Eldred Family*, p. 74.

Gravestone markers for Stephen Sergeant and his wife Anna Penney Sergeant.

February 1872
I hardly expected to write so soon again. When I wrote on Thursday, I little thought that events would transpire so soon. But as Jimmie [age 7] says, we have a little Charlie to our house.

I thought you would want to know it. He came (this little Charlie) about 3:30 a.m. Friday morning. Met gave us the usual short notice as I was in bed yet at 2 o'clock. I was unable to get my landlady who lives on the next floor above us, and the doctor in time to give the young gentleman a reception worthy of his appearance. Both child and mother are doing well.

Your son, George W. Eldred

Two weeks later, George W. Eldred accidentally fell from a roof and fractured his skull. George died of his injuries March 2, 1872, and was buried March 6, in the Eldred Cemetery.

Marietta returned to the Village where she and young Charlie (now called George) lived with her parents, according to the 1880 Census. Sons James and Herbert were listed with their grandfather, C.C.P. Eldred.

After his father's death, he [James] stayed with his grandfather, Charles C.P. Eldred, working on the farm and in the mill. He also delivered mail on foot, walking five miles each way.
—Eldred, pp. 74, 105.

Saturday, March 2, 1872
My dear, dear Mother,
I guess I shall be obliged to do as Miss Schoonmaker does and make a sort of diary of my letters for I get so lonesome as it seems to me I must write to you as I can not live without going home.

Yet I like it here very much. But you know it is my disposition to be discontented.

I have had the teethache all day today and this afternoon, I went to the dentist and had one drained.

This morning Mr. Bigelow, a teacher from New York, and a graduate from here, came in for the girls to go up to the legislature. He gave Carrie and I an invitation to go, too. We accepted the invitation and went. I hoped to see Gov. Hoffman, but in this I was disappointed.

I had the pleasure of seeing Senator Madden and hearing him speak. But did not observe anything remarkably brilliant either in his looks or conversation. They spent most of

Timber Rafting the Delaware River in 1872

The Delaware River near Narrowsburg, New York, had originally been so narrow and with such a sharp bend, that there was barely enough room for a raft to pass through its sharp, rocky shoreline. By 1872, the Narrowsburg passage had been made wider and deeper and other places along the Delaware River had been made easier to navigate in the event of a low water freshet.

Even with improvements, timber rafting was still quite challenging in 1872. That didn't stop men who were sixty and as old as eighty from helping raft lumber to market when the Spring freshet came.

Both single and double rafts were guided down the Delaware River to Trenton, New Jersey, where they were towed to markets in Philadelphia, Pennsylvania. A single raft of sawed lumber contained about 75,000 board feet and required two or three men to steer it.

A double raft was 25 feet by 75 feet and contained up to 150,000 board feet. Four men, two at each end, each with an oar, guided and steered the double raft clear of obstacles. The oar was an 8-foot long hemlock blade securely fastened to "a long chestnut or ash handle, made of a sapling, five or six inches in diameter at the blade end, and tapering down to a point."

The most responsible position on the raft was that of the pilot or steersman who gave directions from the left hand side of the rear end of the raft. The steersman shouted out—Jersey, Pennsylvania, or New York—to tell the others which state

The Delaware River Gap was a large break in the Appalachian Mountains. It was one of the very scenic places viewed by timber rafters as they floated their rafts to market on the Delaware River. Aida Austin's postcard in the Mary Briggs Austin Collection.

shoreline to pull the raft to as they navigated down the Delaware.

The Delaware River raft ride in an early Summer freshet flowed through "wooded mountains, extended fertile plains, high, rock-bound shores, gentle slopes, shady groves, tidy farmhouses, and luxuriant farms."

Some of the "grandest scenery, viewed from a raft" could be seen in the vicinity of the Delaware Water Gap—a large break in the Appalachian Mountains, about 40 miles south of Port Jervis, New York, and four miles southwest of E. Stroudsburg, Pennsylvania.

"For miles and miles the river can be seen winding through the valley—on one side mountains rising abruptly from the water's edge, and on the other green fields and receding hills. Far off to the north the lofty summit of the old Poemo Mountain can be seen, over which the busy trains of the Delaware and Lackawanna Railroad toil and steam continually. In a clear, still day the silver threads of smoke from locomotives can be plainly seen rising toward the sky. In every direction hazy hills rise and extend along the scene until lost in the purple, hazy distance."

In 1872, close to 200,000,000 feet of lumber was exported from the Upper Delaware River region by way of rafting down the Delaware River; the Delaware and Hudson Canal; or the Erie, and Delaware and Lackawanna Railroads. There were hundreds of mills which could produce 500,000 to 1,000,000 board feet a year.

Source: The Lumber Trade: History of the business in New York and Pennsylvania; Where Timber and Lumber Come From—Story of a Raft—Location of the Saw-Mills and Statistics of the Trade. *The article was written in Narrowsburg, N.Y., Thursday May 9, 1872, and published May 11, 1872, in* The New York Times.

---

the time in which we were there in disputing the time in which they should meet again and finally decided to adjourn until Tuesday next.

They were rather more dignified and orderly in the Senate than in the House of Representatives. But I did not receive very exalted impressions of either.

We went from the Senate to the State Library and took a look at the books. It is a large and nicely finished building and contains 82,000 volumes of standard literature. We have the privilege of going there to read whenever we please, but are not allowed to take any books from the building.

This afternoon, Roosouth came up for us to go to the Library with him. As we had already been, we went up to the park and had a cold walk, which I for one did not very much enjoy. And I do not think the cold air has been very beneficial to my teeth, as they feel rather sore.

We are going up to the Observatory before long. Dr. Alden thinks it very desirable that we should visit it once during our stay in Albany, but has forbidden us to go more than once as he considers it a very possible place for flirtations and he decidedly objects to anything of the kind among the students of the State Normal.

Mr. Wright tells me that it is the only or at least the principle object of the school to make old maids, and that we sign a contract to remain single when we enter the school, but Dr. Alden says a lady is always entitled to the privilege of changing her mind. So it is not so bad after all.

Wednesday: I wish some of you could write me every Monday so I would know just when to look for a letter from home.

Dr. Alden says we must rest after dinner before we commence studying. I do not usually do so but I feel just indolent enough this afternoon to follow his advice and he says rest is not after all to be rest, but exercise and an entire forgetfulness of our studies. So I am going to spend my rest in the pleasant exercise of writing.

I have not been so tired since I have been here as I am today.

Miss Stoweman gave me the map of Maine to draw on the board and explain to the class. Carrie said I was as pale as could be and my hand trembled so I could hardly draw. I was frightened to death when I commenced, but I got along, at least she said so.

Miss Rutland, my teacher in Arithmetic, said this morning that she was very glad to see that Miss Austin learned her lessons so well. Excuse me for repeating these compliments (they are the first I have had) as if I were proud of them. I am not. They are perfectly worthless to me, except as you may prize them.

I was sorry to hear of George Eldred's death. Poor Mett. It seems hard for her to be left alone with those little children.

Did any of the girls come

Albany Normal School

Albany Normal School, now the University at Albany, was the first Normal School in the State of New York and the third in the United States. It opened December 18, 1844, and offered a two-year teacher preparatory program, modeled on l'Ecole Normale Superieure in France. The goal was to educate and train school teachers in the science of education and the art of teaching for teaching positions in New York as well as the rest of the U.S.

In her letters to her parents from Albany State Normal, Emma Austin mentions Dr. Alden and Professor Husted. Photos of both were in the collection of Melva Austin Barney.

Dr. Alden was the first president of Albany Normal School from 1867–1882. He wrote more than seventy books, including—*Christian Ethics or the Science of Duty*, *The Science of Government*, and *Thoughts on the Religious Life*.

Alden was a firm believer that the study of the English language was just as important as the study of Latin and Greek.

President Alden is perhaps best known for his championing of women faculty who, he believed, should be "paid for the work done and not for the sex of the worker." Alden was also concerned about improving the living conditions of female students.

Albert N. Husted, was appointed a math instructor about 1855, but then resigned his position to join the Union during the Civil War, and mustered into Company E, on September 6, 1862, as a 2nd Lieutenant. Captain Albert N. Husted returned as a Math Professor in November 1864, at a salary of $1,000 per year. Source: www.albany.edu/faculty/aballard/civilwar/normalschool.htm.

Dr. Joseph Alden. Melva Austin Barney Collection.

Albert Husted. Melva Austin Barney Collection.

Henry's 1872 Cartage Book

Henry Austin's Cartage Book. Mary Briggs Austin Collection. (See Appendix, p. 250.)

Henry Austin's 1872 Cartage book is not very large. It lists names and supplies. One of the pages lists hoops in batches of 1,000 and the cost. Sample page:

October 2, 1872
- 1 b Oats 1.30
- Hay 4.50

Nov 6, 1872
- 1 bale of hay 230 lb 4.60
- 1 b oats 1.30
- stabling 2.50

Dec 2, 1872
- 2 b oats 2.80
- 1 b corn 1.55
- 1 b oats 1.50
- 2 b straw .... .14
- stabling 2.50
- freight 3.46

Austin City Cousins in 1872

The Austin city cousins, children of Uncle Augustus and Aunt Maria Eldred Austin:
- Alonzo Eugene Austin, 35, married to Belle Camp. Children: Olinda, 11, Henrietta, 9, Alonzo Jr., 4.
- Mortimer Bruce, 33, married to Mary Millspaugh. Child: Charles Augustus Austin, baby.
- Nettie, 32, married to Henry Clinton. Child: Ida Belle Clinton.
- Addie, 31, married to Thomas Jefferson Thompson.
- Rand, 27, married Archibald Paton.
- Edward, 25, married to Evaline.
- Tina, 24, married to Randoph Laing.
- Christina was 21.
- Clementina was 17.
- Grace Emma was 16.
- Ida Belle was about 13.

home? Give my love to all enquiring friends. And to Father. I suppose he is home.

Write soon to your daughter,
Edith

1872 First Term, Albany, New York
My darling Mother,

I have just received your very welcome letter, and as you wish me to answer so that you can hear from me Friday, I will try and scribble a few lines now, though I have only a few minutes to do it in as it has taken me nearly all the afternoon to work out some questions in Complex Fractions according to a new theory of Professor Husted.

It took me some time to get it so that I could understand it and explain it out. I think I can do so now and this way is much better than any I have ever seen before.

We are nearly through our Physiology and I shall be glad when we are done with skeletons and bones. Miss Stoneman had a skull in class today and took the bones apart, and passed them around the class for the students to look at. I looked, but did not touch any myself. Miss Stoneman was up in our grammar class today.

Allie Van Kleek, one of the graduates, was in the class and she says she is going to make me talk louder. Before I was called on, she complained to Miss McClelland that she could not hear one of the girls and I was so afraid that she would complain of me that I would hardly speak.

I would not have been scared if Miss S. had not been there. Allie said my voice trembled so and my cheeks were so red that she took compassion on me and kept still. The girls wanted to know what made my cheeks so red. I thought my face was burning up and every word choked me and they all laughed about it when I got home.

Tell father I received the money and thank him for me for sending it. I am glad he thinks I have improved in writing.

Tell Ida I am much obliged to her for her letter and will answer soon. With much love,
Ever yours, E.E.A.

Albany, New York, March 1872
My dear Mother,

I have been copying poetry and drawing maps all day and now I am going to write a few lines to my mother as I am tired and I know this will rest me as much as anything.

I am glad we do not have school Saturday. I never should have anytime for writing if they did.

The lessons are not very hard

to learn, but they are hard to recite and it takes me all the time to think what I shall say and how I shall say it when I get up in the class and then I very often forget and say something wrong.

We have been having review in Geography all this week. I asked Mrs. Stoneman yesterday how many failures I had made. She said I had not made any, but my recitation on Tuesday was not very good. She gave me Mr. Parish's to recite from and I could not tell what it was and consequently failed to recite. I was afraid she marked it a failure, but she did not.

I think this school is very good for those who intend to teach. But I think we could learn more in one year at Monticello Academy, than one can here in two.

I am going over now what ought to have been taught me at school just as soon as I commenced studying—grammar, geography, arithmetic, etc. I don't believe a fourth of the teachers in Sullivan County or any other county for that matter, are qualified to teach.

The girls in our class are just as dumb as they can be, which is a great advantage to me. I have this consolation, if I don't pass out of this class, no one of them will.

Since I commenced this, Mrs. Wright has given me a letter from you and one from Mary Darling.

Miss Shoonmaker has not answered my letter yet. Mary seemed quite surprised that I am here and advised me to go to the observatory should I be up for a flirtation and graduate in matrimony, instead of spending my time in the schoolroom. She did not give me anymore information in regard to her getting married from spite. I told her to give me an invitation to the

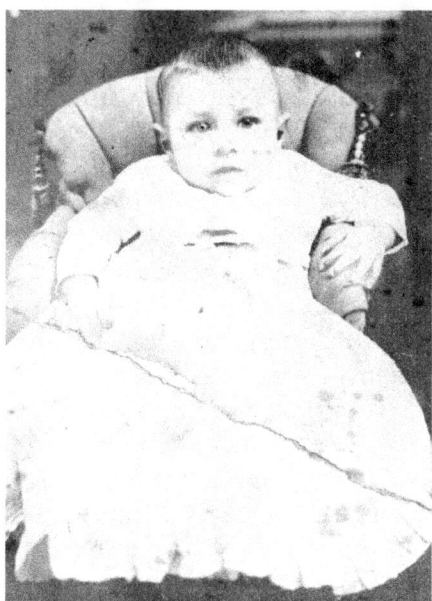
Gussie (Charles Augustus) Austin, son of Mortimer Bruce and Mary Austin. Photo courtesy of Melva Austin Barney.

wedding or save me a piece of the cake.

I was just as lonesome as could be when your letter came. I feel considerably better now. I know you do not have much time for writing. You must not be afraid to send me as many compositions as you are a mind to. I write just as often and will correct them all—sometime, but shall not return them.

I wish Mr. B. had sent a valentine or something so I could have written. It would seem kind of good to hear from him again.

Please burn this letter won't you. I am almost afraid to send this information for fear you will not get it. Emma

The following letter regarding the birth of Charles Augustus Austin, son of Mortimer Bruce and Mary L. Austin, was written by Belle Austin. Belle was the wife of Alonzo E. Austin, Mortimer Bruce's brother. Linnie and Etta mentioned in the letter were daughters of Alonzo and Belle Austin.

Mortimer Bruce Austin, son of Uncle Augustus and Aunt Maria Austin. Photo courtesy of Melva Austin Barney.

Spring of 1872
I suppose you have not heard of the birth of Mort's son. He came to them last Friday and Mary is doing nicely.

Linnie and Etta, are attending school and like it very much. Their school will soon close for the summer and then we expect to go to Massachusetts for awhile.

I suppose your vacation will soon begin. I guess you will not be sorry to see home and friends once more.

Belle Austin

Albany, New York, March 1872
Dear Mother,

Friday once more as I have leisure to write to you and Ida and correct that composition.

I have been very busy this week and it seems so good to be at liberty to talk to you for a few minutes even if I can only talk with pen and ink on a little piece of paper that will not contain one half I want to say.

The composition was very good. I don't think I could have done better myself, as Addie says.

I did not see any fault in the connection of the sentences. I made some changes in the last verse, the last two lines.

"You will think of a Mother's love, And not forget your home."

I changed to, "You'll not forget a mother's love or cease to think of home," because I liked the way it rhymed better.

Since writing this, I have stopped and ironed my clothes. I always iron Friday. Mrs. Wright does my washing and I think she ought to. We pay enough for board though we get ours much cheaper than some of the girls. If I stay another term, I shall board myself. It is much cheaper and I should like it better. I am as careful of my money as I can be and have not lost any yet.

I get along very well in school, at least the teachers tell me my standing is good whenever I ask them.

I have not dared to ask Miss Stoneman yet. She is my teacher in map drawing and penmanship and I am afraid I shall never be able to draw maps correctly anyway. It takes more time than anything else and I do not see any particular use in it.

And then if we do not speak loud enough in our recitation, she marks us the same as for missing. She always tells me to talk louder until I forget what I am going to say, so I suppose my standing in that is not very good though it can not be very low or she would tell me.

Grammar is very easy and I get along quite well in that Miss McClelland gave us sentences to write and analyze the other day. She found quite a good deal of fault with the most of them, and when I got about half way through with mine, she said, "Stop. Miss Austin, that was done beautifully, just the way I wanted it."

I thought it was quite a compliment but did not appreciate it very much at the time for when she spoke out so quick, I thought I had said something wrong and I was so frightened that I did not get over it all day and I would rather she had kept still and marked me 10, without saying anything.

The girls laughed as hard as they could because I jumped so when she spoke. Miss Rutland, our teacher in Arithmetic, gave us an invitation the other day to call on her. Her mother and she live here.

Carrie's giving me lessons in German every night after school. She says I learn it real easily.

We went out last Friday for a walk and went away over to the eastern and northern part of Albany. It was a splendid day and I enjoyed the walk better than any I have taken since I have been here.

How is Mrs. Kyte and family? I dreamed of being there last night and drinking tea with them. I thought perhaps Mr. Kyte was sick as my dream was not very good one and I did not know how to interpret it.

Martin D. Myers grave stone. Courtesy Cynthia Leavenworth Bellinger.

Give my love to her and all the rest of my friends. How is Laura?
Yours with much love, Edith

In March, on the west side of the Village, Atwell L. Bradley, son of Isaac and Joanna Bradley was born. Was he named for Atwell Leavenworth who had died in the Civil War?

Atwell Bradley had four sisters, Amelia, Viola, Mary Frances, Lottie, and a brother Isaac. The Bradley children, including little Nora, not yet born, will play a part in this story in Book Two.

Sad times again for Jane Ann Van Pelt Webb Myers at the end of March. Her husband, Martin David Myers, died March 29, 1872, in Halfway Brook Village. Great-Great-Grandfather Martin Myers was 56. The Myers' children: George, 26, Maria, 18, Augustus (Gus), 15-1/2, and the youngest, Lottie (Charlotte), almost 14.

New York, April 5, 1872

My dear cousin Emma,

I have been past about sick for the last two weeks, so if my letter appears rather sickly you will excuse it, I am sure.

Your father is quite well and says for me to tell you that he will write soon. Enclosed you will find five dollars which he wishes me to send you and says that when he writes, he will send you more, so I guess he means to keep you in 'funds.'

Father [Uncle Augustus] has been quite sick, but is getting almost well again. Mother [Aunt Maria] has a very bad cold, but now the weather is getting pleasant I am in hopes she will soon get rid of it.

Mr. and Mrs. Laing [Tina and Ranny], are going to move the first of May, right on the same block where they are living now,

Entrance to old Eldred Cemetery, fall 2008. Photo: Mary Briggs Austin.

only two doors from the corner of Pitt and Broome.

Are you having pleasant weather in Albany now? It has been delightful here for four days.

I am so glad you are so well pleased with your school. How many classes are there above you?

You asked if any of the girls came home to George Eldred's funeral. Uncle Henry said that Bec [Rebecca, George's sister] came. But that Polly [another sister] was so sick she was unable to leave. I believe Bec intends to remain at home this winter.

Aunt Eliza went home this week Wednesday.

Uncle James I have not seen since last week. He was as well as usual, I believe, but he does look forlorn enough poor fellow! I feel sorry for him.

Net has been over to Belle's serving for her. She (Belle) has been having a new black silk made, a beautiful dress. She expects to wear it to Mary Mott's wedding next Tuesday. Nett is going to wear her Irish Poplin.

Your father had a letter from Aunt Mary Thursday. She wrote that Martin D. Myers was dead. He was buried last Sunday, I believe. I suppose though, you have heard from there since I have.

I received a letter from Aunt Julia last week. I suppose she will be down to see us soon, as she wrote that she was going to start for Bricksburg, the tenth of this month.

I think I should like to visit the State Library. Just read a little for me will you? I think Dr. Alden's views of flirtations very good don't you, but then we would never flirt though, would we if we had ever so good a chance.

Mr. Thompson [Tom, Addie's husband], sends kind regards. We all send much love. Write very soon to your good cousin,
Addie

Albany State Normal School, April 7, 1872

My Dear Mother,

I was very sorry to hear of Mr. Myers death and to hear that Mr. Lindsley had lost his speech. I do not believe he will ever get over the effects of his winter's teaching in HalfWay Brook (which we call Lumberland). That schoolhouse is enough to kill anyone and ought to be burned down.

We came down yesterday for Carrie to go to Bureau of Military Statistics. I did not want to go but I could not help it. Carrie would have me. She says she never enjoys herself unless I am with them.

There was a case filled with Memorials of Lincoln's Assassination among them a pair of gloves worn by one of the delegation at his funeral and several badges of mourning.

In a frame above the case was a piece of poetry commencing:

Weep for the martyr. Weep ye nations.
His cause was yours; and yours his aspiration
Weep freedmen freed from chain and lashes
Weep traitor neath rebellions ashes!

In another were two specimens of Japanese armor and these with the flags and pictures were all I saw that I cared for except a piece of moss from the tree under which Gen. Lee surrendered.

It was after five o'clock and we were half tired to death. I have not taken such a walk since last summer and shall not take "such another."

I received a letter from Addie this morning. I answered father's letter two or three weeks ago, but he has not written yet.

I am writing and Carrie is reading aloud at intervals for my benefit,
Emma

Albany, New York, April 1872

My dear Mother,

Time in his daily round has again brought to me a few leisure moments for communicating with you and gladly do I improve the opportunity he offers.

We are having beautiful weather and I am enjoying myself very much.

We are going to have examinations next week in geography and Arithmetic and

I have been drawing maps and studying rules and explanations all day and if I don't pass out of this geography class, I will not draw any maps anyway.

I might better spend it in writing poetry, do not you think so? By the way, did you like yours and do you think it fit for publication? If so please send me the address of the "Companion" (I think it is Allen and Co., Augusta, Maine), but have nearly forgotten and I will send them to the paper and let them publish them if they will.

Enclosed you will find some written on the death of little Augie Bander. They are not very good and I had forgotten about them till Carrie found them in a book and read them and pronounced them good, so I concluded to send them to you.

[Carrie wanted her to go walking with her and a friend.]

I declined having other and more important work to do. They waited for Miss Lynde a long time and then concluded that she was not coming and went out alone.

They had been gone but a few moments when Belle, who had been detained by company she said, made her appearance. She was very much disappointed and insisted upon my going out with her to find them.

I excused myself as well as I could, and persuaded Mrs. Wright to let Freddie accompany her to the Geological rooms, telling her to come back and wait until they came in if they were not there.

In a few minutes she came in and waited about an hour, when the wanderers returned and they all went out again for another walk.

Carrie has invited us to go with them to Bridgeman's church tomorrow. I do not think very seriously of accepting this invitation though I may conclude to do so.

Carrie gets indignant sometimes because I will not go out every time she happens to feel like it. I believe her brother has advised her not to ask me anymore and she informed me that she had concluded to take his advice. A very wise conclusion and one which will afford me a great deal of pleasure if she only "sticks to it." I went out with her three times in one day and then she wanted me to go again in the evening.

I suppose school will soon commence in the Village. Tell me the teacher's name as soon as you know. I am interested to know if Beck [Becca Eldred] takes it.

Do you ever hear from Mr. Lindseley any more? Where is Maria? Did she finish high school? I hear Mr. Van Auken has sold his place at last. What is W. Ayres doing?

How are Mrs. West's children and ours? Has Dora got over his cold yet? I will close this letter and try and write a few lines to Maria. Tell Ida and Lon if they do not write, they'll wish they had when I write to them again as the letter will be so long they will never be able to read it.

Tell Eldred I think he might favor me with a letter once in a while. He and Lon are home. With best love to all. I remain

Ever your aff. Edith

In Mary Ann Austin's (p. 152) book of poems and dried flowers was a page with unknown leaves from the Cemetery at Albany, June 1872. Perhaps they came from Emma's visit to the cemetery mentioned in this next letter.

Albany, New York, May 19, 1872
My Dear Mother,

Another rainy Sunday! It has been raining all day and I haven't been out of the house since yesterday afternoon when we went up State Street and through the grounds of the Capitol for a walk. The grass is so green, the trees are all leafed out and the flowers in blossom and it is very pleasant here—so much nicer than N.Y.

Only six more weeks and I shall be with you all again. I am so glad I can hardly wait for the 3rd of July. O, mother, I want to see you so much.

Libbie Koffinagle, one of the girls here was taken sick last week. She caught a very heavy cold and I think she is consumptive, though it makes her angry to say so to her. She has been studying very hard and is half tired to death anyway.

The Faculty of the school held a consultation over it Friday and Prof. Husted came yesterday and told her she must go home. She was getting along so well in school it seems almost too bad.

Lord & Taylor, 1872

In 1872, Lord & Taylor moved to a grandiose cast-iron building capped by a tall mansard roof. New York's Lord & Taylor became a destination for not only shopping, but a place that women went for entertainment.

In 1914, the Lord & Taylor store moved to 38th Street and Fifth Avenue in New York City. For many decades, New York City department stores such as Lord and Taylor, promoted everything from Thanksgiving Day parades and patriotic lectures to Art exhibits.

Edith Emogene's Poem for Ida

Ida Belle Austin asked her cousin Emma to sign her autograph book *(see June 11, 1872 letter)*, which Emma took seriously, and wrote this thoughtful poem.

You hand me your album and ask me to write
My name on the snowy white space.
And further you ask that above a few lines
In token of friendship I trace.

I haste to comply with selections
From favorite authors of thine,
And then you assure me that this will not do
That the thought and the words must be mine.

But know you dear Ida the boon that you ask?
Fair words should deck pages so white,
And my heart shrinks from beauty that I shall deface
By the common place lines I must write.

And hopes that perhaps I shall too disappoint
By this poor little gift I bring here
And yet it is Ida the wish of a friend
Simple but loving sincere.

"Tis this since our hearts are the Albums that hold
The names that we cherish most clear,
Life journals where daily we're writing
The record of deeds we do here.

May this album contain only names
Of friends that are true friends and sure
This journal be written in times fairest hand
With sweet words of a life that is pure.

Not of letters of black as these that I trace,
But in characters purest of white,
So fair that in sealing this record of thine
"Well done," the Angel shall write.
Your cousin and friend, Edith E.A.

Ida Belle Austin, daughter of Uncle Augustus and Aunt Maria, and cousin of Emma Austin. Courtesy of Melva Austin Barney.

Miss Daly was in to see her today.

Carrie said she wanted to know where the "little Miss Austin" was. She always calls me little and I'm used to it. There are plenty home smaller than I am and she herself is not much larger.

We met Miss Kirtland on the stairs Friday. Carrie asked her standing and she said it was very good, then turned to me and said, "And Miss Austin's is all right."

Carrie said afterward, "Miss Kirtland meant both of us when she said the standing was alright. She did not mean that yours is better than mine."

I did not suppose that she did. I do not doubt that Carrie's is as good, probably better than mine and I should not have thought anything of her saying so if Carrie had not mentioned it.

Sunday 26th: We were up to the cemetery yesterday and went through the hot houses with Miss Gordon. I never saw so many flowers before. I wish we had some of them home.

[Emma talks about paying $1.50 for a room.]

I wish you could get my money of Mr. Myers unless he has

paid it you, and send it to me. I owe Mrs. Wright some for board room. I paid her 5 dollars of the money Father sent me last. He gave me 4 dollars when I was in N.Y., but I spent some there. I think Mr. Myers ought to pay me now.

I received a letter from Mary Darling last week. She thinks Maria Tassaskmass ought to take the village school and board at Sergeants. I wonder if Joe would not have liked it just as well if she would have kept the Beaver Brook School and boarded there. She says Joe is sick.

I shall have to stop. Please give the enclosed letter to Emma Kelso, and tell Eldred I will write soon to him.

With love to all, and especially my mother,
I am as ever E.E.A.

Albany, New York, Monday, June 11, 1872

My Dear Father,
Your letter was received last Tuesday. You may be sure it was welcome. That afternoon I received one from Mother and Lonny. Mother said she had been sick.

Ida forgot to write the cousins. She had been so busy she did not have time to write. I am quite anxious to hear from Mother again. I hope she is better. I was sorry to hear that Addie was so sick. I hope that she will go up with you.

I wish you were going the third instead of the first. If Dr. Alden will let me, I will not stay for the closing exercises, but will go the first if you will meet me at Newburgh and go home that way. Annie Collins said she always went that way and that it costs less than to go right through from N.Y.

I am very much obliged for the money. I shall owe Mrs. Wright nearly $30 yet when school is out. I have paid her $60 and my washing has cost some. She does the most of it without charging extra. I am sorry it costs so much.

I wish I could teach as soon as I go home. I would just as leave as not if I could only get a school. If Bee would only give up hers for a little time.

I asked Miss Daly my standing this morning and she said it was good in all my classes, and excellent in arithmetic. I know it is good in algebra as Mr. Jones let me see it and I had only one 8, two E's and the rest were 10s. He gives me three 10s in one day some times. We were examined in Physiology Friday and changed it for Physical Geography this morning.

I went with Carrie yesterday morning to hear Bridgeman preach. He is called the Beecher of Albany; the sermon was very good, but I should prefer to hear one from Henry Ward. They raised 26,000 dollars to finish paying for the church. It cost 152,000. And this much had not been paid. Gov. Hoffman as someone called him was there.

I must stop writing and learn my lesson.

Tell Addie I spent yesterday afternoon or a part of it writing verses to Ida (see p. 167). I commenced some to her, but took pity on her and stopped before I finished them. Give my love to her.

Father, if you have not the money to spare now, I guess Mrs. Wright would be willing to wait a little while for it. I am sorry I owe her so much. Please write to me soon and oblige.

Your affec. daughter,
Edith

June 16, 1872

Dear Cousin Emma,
I suppose you heard how sick poor Addie has been. We didn't any of us think she would live and it does not seem to me as if she would live and it does not seem to me as if she would ever get her strength again.

She had another poor spell again last night and Ranny went for the Doctor again for her. She is about the same again today. I think if she could get off in the country, it would do her good. She had to have her hair all cut off, but I don't think she looks bad with it.

I have not been to church today as I have got a sty on my eye large enough to accommodate three little pigs, so I thought I would improve the golden opportunity this afforded by writing to you.

Deer in Eldred's woods. Photo: Cynthia Leavenworth Bellinger.

I hope when you return home, you will do so by the way of N.Y., for I want to see you so much and perhaps I will go home with you and Addie wants to see you too.

Ranny isn't a bit well and has not been for a long time. I feel real worried about him and besides, I guess he is working too hard. I want him to go to the country for I think it will do him good. But my eye pains me so I cannot write any more.

*With much love I remain
Your loving cousin, Tina*

November 3, 1872

My dear Mother,

Your very welcome letter was received the first of October and read with delight as was little Ida's which I received the same time.

I do like my new house ever so much, though I shall be very glad to exchange it for the old one if the time ever comes for me to do so.

I am even afraid that I shall not pass out of elocution, though Mrs. Taylor has once condescended to say that by proper care and training of my voice, I might become a good reader, that my inflections were none of them bad etc., and that she had known persons with weaker voices than mine to become good elocutionists. Encouraging isn't it?

She gave an example of one whom she said she could not hear across the room when she first entered her class and who improved so much that at the close of the course, she read her graduating essay in the clearest purest voice of any one on the stage, as I shall doubtless read mine.

Miss Gaylord one of the girls in our class was kept back last

Child's 1872–1873 Gazeteer

Child's 1872–1873 Gazeteer lists the "yellow pages" in the town of Highland and surrounding area.

Academies
    Callicoon Depot Academy
    Liberty Normal Institute
    Monticello Academy
Architects and builders
Agricultural Implements
Bakers and Confectioners
Ball Bats, Croquet Sets,
Bankers National Union Bank of
    Monticello
Barbers
Bark Mills and Leaches
Barrel Hoop Manufacturers
Blacksmiths
Boarding House
Boat Builders
Books and Stationary
Boots and shoes
Brewers and Maltsters
Brick Manufacturer
Bucksaw Frame Makers
Cancer Doctor
Carding Mills
Carpenters and Builders
Carriage, Wagon and Sleigh
    Manufacturers
Cheese Boxes, Broom Handles
Circulating Library
Clothier
Coal and wood dealers
Confectionery, toys, Etc.
Coopers
Crockery, Glassware, Etc.
Dentists
Dining rooms
Dress and cloak makers
Druggists
Drugs Medicines
Dry goods
Flour Feed and Grain
Fruits, Confectionery, Etc.
Fulton's Champion of the world
Furniture Dealers
General Merchants
Glass and Putty
Groceries and Provisions
Hardware
Harness, Trunks, Etc.
Historian
Hotels
Insurance Agent
Iron Founder and Machinist
Large Beer Brewer
Lawyers
Ladies' Furnishing goods
Leach Manufs.
Leather and Findings
Livery Stables
Lumber Dealers
Marble Works
Millinery
Mowers and Reapers
Music and Musical Instruments
Music Teachers
News Dealers
Painters and Paper Hangers
Paints and Oils
Paper Hangings, Window shades
Papier-Mâché Goods
Photographer
Physician
Pianos and Organs
Pictures and Frames
Printing Offices
Produce Dealers
Public Hall
Railroad Agents
Real Estate Agents
Sash, Blinds and Doors
Saw and Planing Mills
Sewing Machines Agents
Silver and Silver Plated Wares
Stage Proprietors
Stoves Tinware Etc.
Tannery
Tobacco and Cigars
Undertakers
Watches and Jewelry
Wood Dealers
Wood Turning, Scroll Sawing, Etc.
Woolen Mills

Child's 1872–1873 Gazeteer

People and their occupations in the Highland area listed in Child's *Gazetteer and Business Directory of Sullivan County, N.Y.*, for 1872–1873:

Austin, William H., farmer; Lumberland.

Bradley, Isaac M., farmer; Lumberland.

Calkin, Oliver, prop. gristmill, lumberman, commissioner of highways, and with James E. Gardner, farmer; Lumberland.

Clark, George, farmer; Lumberland.

Clark, Mahlon I., farmer; Lumberland.

Clark, Wilmot, farmer; Lumberland.

DeVenoge, Leon allo. physician and surgeon, and farmer; Lumberland.

Eldred, Chas. C.P., lumberman, Post Master and farmer; Lumberland.

Gardner, James E., general merchant and lumber dealer, and with Oliver Calkins, farmer; Barryville.

Hickok, David, farmer; Lumberland.

Hickok, Justice, retired farmer; Barryville.

Hickok, William, stone quarry; Barryville.

Johnston, John W., Sen., lawyer and surveyor; Barrryville.

Kelso, Robert, groceries, dry goods, boots, shoes, etc, and farmer; Barryville.

Kyte, Felix Rev., pastor of Congregational Church and farmer; Lumberland.

Leavenworth, Sherman B., farmer; Lumberland.

Myers, Martin D., manufacture of refrigerators and farmer; Lumberland.

Myers, Moses D., farmer; Lumberland.

Myers, Wm. G., lumberman and farmer; Lumberland.

Owen, Robert F., carpenter and farmer; Barryville.

Owens, John Miller; Barryville.

Palmer, David J., carpenter; Lackawaxen.

Sergeant, Alvah, carpenter and farmer; Lumberland.

Sergeant, Ethel B., shoemaker and farmer; Lumberland.

Shotwell, Caleb G., Justice of the Peace, and farmer; Lumberland.

Shotwell, Stephen C., farmer; Barryville.

Stage, Jacob, farmer; Lumberland.

Webber, Jacob Rev., pastor of M.E. Church; Barryville.

---

term because she spoke so low and Mrs. Taylor told her a little while ago that she had done all she could for her. All I asked her to do for me is to let me pass out of her class and I think she might let me do that to get rid of me if nothing more.

I have written two compositions since I have been here. One a letter to "My dear friend Tina" which has not yet been given back, and one on elocution which I handed to the teacher Friday. I suppose our next one will be an allegory and I dread the very thoughts of it.

By way of changing the subject, Carrie is well and calls on me occasionally. She is quite anxious that I should leave my boarding place and board with her. Her anxiety no doubt arises from motives of purest love and friendship.

Mrs. Bidwell says that Carrie does not get along as well as when I was with her. I think however, that I am just as well off and I would not be with her this term for anything.

I have not yet received that letter of Father's. You did not tell me a word about your visit to N.Y. Net said you came from Poughkeepsie to N.Y. How upon earth did you ever get there? I began to feel a little homesick as soon as I read that.

If I do not pass out of this half of the term, I am coming home, wouldn't you? Our fate will be decided this week. Tell Marie not to commence flirting with Jim as soon as I get away.

Ever your aff. Edith

Albany, New York, November 10, 1872

My dear Father,

Mother wrote me Tuesday that you had written to me sometime ago sending money in your letter. I do not see why I have not received your letter and I am sorry that you sent the money in it as I am afraid I shall not get it.

Do not send me any more money now. I have some yet and there is no use sending it if I do not get it.

But if you can, I would like to have you send me "Woodbury New German Method," in the box with my hat. And if you do not care, I should like to take lessons in elocution of Mrs. Talyson. I do not care to take many perhaps not more than five or six.

If you have not the money to spare, do not get the book as I can get along without. Carrie is anxious to teach me German and as it does not cost me anything, I thought I might as well study it. I was quite surprised to hear that mother had been to New York.

Please write soon to
Edith E. A.

**Albany, New York,
November 24, 1872**
Mr. Wm. H. Austin
Mein Fatur,

I received a letter from you Wednesday and when I came home Friday, I found the box on the table for me. In it I found another letter from you. Also the other things which I was expecting.

I am very much obliged to you for your trouble and for the money. You need not have sent so much. I think ten dollars would have been plenty. I am so sorry about the money you sent in the letter. I went to the PO and inquired for it but could not find out anything about it.

I was very much pleased with the book. I took my first lesson in it Saturday. You must excuse me for commencing to practice writing it in your letter.

Miss Daly says it is not good taste to mix foreign words with our language, but I thought I would write "my father" in German this once, just to see if I could. I like to study it very much; it is a good deal easier than French.

I cannot write anymore. I have been sick all day today and it tires me so to write. I went visiting yesterday and I guess my visit was too much for me. I will write again this week.

Please tell Nettie I liked the hat and obliged to her for getting it.
Your aff. daughter,
Edif E. Auftin

December 8, 1872
Dear Emma,

I was up to Paterson Thanksgiving Day and took dinner with Mort and Mary [Austin]. They had one of the best boys [Charles Augustus Austin] I ever saw. He is no trouble at all. I have made up my mind to go home the 24th and stay until January 2, 1873.
William Henry Austin

December 29th, 1872
My dear Mother,

I wrote to Ida on Christmas and I will write a few lines to you this afternoon.

There is no one here except Miss Sturgis and Miss Turnbell, that is just at present. Charlie and Mrs. Vicks call in every few moments but I do not mind that.

The girls are away somewhere and I wish they would stay. Miss Mc Bain is going home tomorrow and that will be one out of the way. For my part I wish they would all go but Miss Sturgis and I.

Three weeks from Wednesday I hope to be with you all again. I think I shall come right home.

Congregational Church of Eldred, fall 2008. Photo: Mary Briggs Austin.

In the 74 years of its existence, the church has had but 2 pastors, and in the intervals, but very few supplies. Its first 19 years without; then for 8 years it had a shepherd; then for 6 years without; adding then the present pastorate to the former, it gives for the church in the 74 years, 25 without and 49 with.
—James E. Quinlan, *History of Sullivan County*, 1873.

I do not believe I can stay away twenty weeks more. I am so tired; and I cannot rest anywhere except at home. I have concluded to go through Newburgh again. It costs less and will not take me so long.

I suppose father is at home now. If you should receive this before he goes back, tell him that I received his letter, was very very glad to hear from him, and will answer this week.

If I do not write to you again, I wish you would send for me three weeks from Wednesday. That is three weeks from New Year's Day.

Tell the boys I wish they would write.

So Bea has taken the school again. That old building ought to be burned down. It is a perfect shame to have school in such a place.

Halfway Brook Village Becomes Eldred

Halfway Brook had been called "the Village" since before 1831, when the first Post Office was established as Lumberland, and James Eldred was the Postmaster.

On February 12, 1873, the Postmaster, Charles C.P. Eldred, son of James Eldred, changed the name of "the Village" to Eldred. The new name was in honor of his father, James Eldred, or that is what I have been told. The townspeople still referred to Eldred as "the Village" in the 1940s.

In 1873, Dr. Leon DeVenoge was the Supervisor for Highland Township. In the Town of Lumberland, Mr. McKenzie was Commissioner of Highways.

Good by Mother and Happy Happy New Year. Write some if you please and can.
Ever your aff. Emma

In late December, Daniel Rowley Schoonover was born to Oliver Perry Schoonover and Mary Parker who lived on property Perry's father Peter had owned. Rowley, named after his father's friend, had a sister, Emily, and half siblings, George and Kate Parker. Aida Austin wrote about Emily and Rowley Schoonover in her 1940 Diary.

There were weddings for two Eldred cousins in 1872. Maria Adeline Eldred, daughter of C.C.P. and Effa Eldred, married Charles Kendall in January. Ann Eliza Gardner, daughter of James K. and Eliza Eldred Gardner, married Louis Cuddeback in December.

Albany, New York, January 1, 1873
My dear Father,
It is New Years and I have at last an opportunity of answering your letter which was received about two weeks ago and read with pleasure.

We have been so busy this term, especially this last half that I have had very little time for writing.

I have not been sick except to have a cold and sore throat which did not amount to anything more serious than to prevent me from reading in the class once or twice.

The weather has been fearfully cold here. I never saw anything like it. We must be having an unusually cold winter, or else the climate here is much more severe than in Lumberland.

You ask if I am going to New York. I do not think I shall. I have concluded to go home and I think I shall go by Newburgh. It will not cost so much and I will get home quicker and I am anxious to get there.

My paper is getting short and I will bid you good night. Wish you Happy New Year. Please give this to Tina, and write to me whenever you can. As Ever, Edith

February 23, 1873
Dear Lon,
I write to you and let you know that I was well and hope you are well and how is Mort and Dorrie and Eldred and Ida and Aunt Mary getting along?

Is the snow out there now? We have 4 horses and we bought 3 horses—the best of the other horses, and they run away every chance they get. We are going to put in stables this year.

Me and father will have about 2000 bushels of corn this year to husk. I miss you a lot. Good by, from wyk [wyk unknown.]

Albany, New York, Term 3, March 1873
(See March 14th letter also.)
My Dear Father,
I had quite a serious time getting to the depot that morning as I had to change cars several times. I do not know what was the matter with the street cars; they would go a little ways and then stop and go back and would have to change cars. There was a gentleman and lady on the cars going to the same depot and by following them, I managed to get along very well.

When I arrived at Albany, I found the streets so blocked with snow as to prevent the cars from moving further than State Street which was however far enough for me. I got to Mrs. Wrighter about four in the afternoon. The next day I went up to school and after school went in to see Dr. Alden.

At first he seemed to think that I would be unable to make up what I had lost in staying and he was very kind however and said he was perfectly willing that I should try.

As to my voice he said it would not prevent me from graduating, though I had to ask him several times before he answered me. He thought I had better board though and I have concluded to, for a few weeks at least.

A gentleman called last evening to see about that book. He says there are no agents in Albany.

I will write again soon.
Ever your aff. Emma

Albany, New York, March 14, 1873
My Dear Mother,
I must tell you that I arrived here in safety that afternoon about 4 o'clock. When I got here, I found the streets literally blocked

View from hill in Barryville, fall 2008. Photo: Mary Briggs Austin.

with snow. The street cars were only running as far as State Street. This however was just far enough for me. I came at once to Mrs. Wright's where I succeeded in getting board.

I did not go up to see Dr. Alden that evening, but went up to school the next morning. He came to me and wanted to know why I had not come back sooner, if you had received his letter before I came away, etc. etc.

I answered his questions to the best of my ability but evidently not to his satisfaction. He said that I could of course do as I pleased about staying, but that he did not think I could make up what I had lost and that I might better have remained at home this term. He said that you kept me at home simply because you chose to do so and that I must suffer the consequences.

After school I went in to ask him about my voice as I promised to and also to see if he was willing that I should try to make it up, for I thought if he was not, I would not stay. He said that he was perfectly willing for me to try, and very kindly expressed a wish that I might succeed. He even talked as if he would be willing to assist me outside of school some, if he had the time and opportunity to do so.

I would not accept such assistance if I could have it. If I cannot pass out by my own study, I will not pass at all. He tried to avoid giving me any direct answers in regard to my voice, but finally said that it could not make any difference about my graduating.

He was very angry with your letter and I was sorry that you wrote it. I am glad that you did not answer his. He said that I must not care anything about it that he wrote in that way to you because he had not liked what you wrote to him and that he thought I would understand it. He did not say exactly this, but something very near it. I do not care anyway. It all goes ok. The lessons are quite hard and I shall have to study some make up if I could only.

I am quite anxious to hear how you succeeded in getting a house. Please tell me all about it when you write. I shall have to close my letter now.

Tell Lon and Ell to write first for I am awful busy. Did Maria go to New York? Please write soon and tell me everything.

I am ever your aff. Emma

Do you remember Mary E. Bunce who married Lewis Carmichael? Mary Bunce was a friend of Mary Ann Eldred Austin. In March of 1873, Mary Bunce Carmichael died in Iowa where she lived with her family. Lewis and Mary had nine children, including two sets of twins.

In Lumberland in 1872, John and James Kerr purchased land—some from Mary A. Hallock, daughter of Job Rider, and some from Johnston (Forgerson's land in 1835, and then Johnston's mother's property).—*Johnston,* Reminiscences, *p. 269*

I mention this, because my parents were friends with a Kerr family, that I assume was related to John or James Kerr. Around 1964, I met them and remember the property.

Mabel Louise Owen, daughter of Robert Owen and Elizabeth Tether, was born August 25, 1873.

My grandmother, Mabel Louise Owen, was born in Yulan. The Owen family had been in the area since the 1700s. Her father, Robert Owen, lived in Yulan for most of his life and was engaged in several business enterprises in the general area.

Robert Owen was the son of Morgan Owen and Elizabeth Barnes. They are also buried in Eldred Cemetery, so at least in later life made their home there also.—Melva Austin Barney

Mabel Owen would marry Edwin Van Schoick Myers, 10. Edwin would be friends with Mort Austin, my grandfather. Edwin and Mabel would be parents of my aunt Gladys Myers Austin. In June 1873, Edwin Van Schoick Myers's grandfather, Moses Dewitt Myers, died.

James Gardner Sergeant, 36,

1873 Depression

A series of events led up to the Panic of 1873—a severe nationwide economic depression, which lasted until 1879:

- The Black Friday Panic in September, 1869, mentioned in an earlier chapter.
- The October, 1871, Chicago fire and loss of 200 million dollars in property over four-square miles.
- The 1872 *Great Epizoötic* or equine influenza when there were no horses to pull the street cars or to deliver the coal or wood to locomotives. Fires remained unchecked as there was no way to transport water.
- As there were not horses, the U.S. Army Calvary had to fight on foot, and men ended up pulling wagons by hand, and cargo on ships and trains could not be delivered.
- Gold became the standard in the U.S. in February, 1873, and the value of silver fell.
- There were other factors that played a part in what has also been called, "the long depression," but they are outside the scope of this book.

No matter what the cause of the economic woes, my great-grandfather Henry Austin's carting business in New York City would be affected.

There are hints of financial problems in the letters in the next chapter. Henry Austin returned home to Eldred to farm by 1877.—*information from www. en.wikipedia.org: Panic of 1873; Long Depression—Louise Austin Smith.*

The thing that hath been, it is that which shall be; and that which is done is that which shall be done: and there is no new thing under the sun.
—Ecclesiastes 1:9

son of Ethel and Letty Gardner Sergeant and Civil War veteran, died in 1873. James's wife of six years, Emma Myers, was left with three young children.

James Daniel Eldred, son of C.C.P. and Effa Eldred, married Frances J. Payne, August 10, 1873. Frances was the daughter of Charles Henry and Adeline Payne. James D. Eldred wrote some letters to his Austin cousin, Albert Alonzo, which we will soon read.

Grace Emma Austin, daughter and youngest child of Uncle Augustus and Aunt Maria, died May 6, 1873. The cousin letters indicated that Grace Emma was often sick.

November 30, 1873
Dear Lonnie,

I thought I would write and see how you were getting along without Mother. She is not very well.

I am having a good time, but I want to come home and see you all. How is Mort and Dorrie? Tell them I want them to write to me.

Have you any snow? We have not got any, but it is cold enough. How is it up there? I had a very nice time Thanksgiving day. Well, I must stop writing. I send my love to all. Write soon.

Ida A. Austin [Lon's sister]

Ida (Aida) Austin's drawing with her November 30, 1873, letter to her brother Lon.

Life has been difficult for Henry, 49, and Mary Ann Austin, 46. Their twin son Edward died at a few months old, both sets of parents have died, and their youngest son died at the end of 1870.

Mary Ann was often sick or didn't feel well which we find out in later letters. The family was often separated, not seeing each other for possibly months at a time because Henry worked in New York City.

Henry and Mary Ann Austin's children ranged in age from 7 to 23. Emma their oldest was in college. In a few years, the older sons would want to be out on their own.

Life would only be more challenging for Henry and Mary Ann in the rest of the 1870s. So challenging, that eventually Henry and Mary Ann separate.

The following is another poem in Great-Grandma Mary Ann Austin's flower booklet that she copied on August 1, 1873.

In Memoriam by O.G. Warren
Tis not the value of the gift
That friendship's hand may send
Tis not the things intrinsic worth
Though gems of rarest splendor
That makes the hearts best gratitude
Or calls a deep emotion
A simple flower may be the gift
And claim a life's devotion.

These fragrant flowers which thou hast given
I'll ever fondly cherish
What though their brightness fade away
And all their beauty perish.
Yet are they sweet this grateful soul
At time no love can sever
So lives the memory of the gift
It breathes of thee forever.

Chapter 11
Return to Eldred
1874–1877

The fruits are limited to apples, pears, plums, cherries, currants, and a few peaches. Wild berries grow in great abundance. The timber along the Delaware Valley is mostly hemlock, pine, oak and chestnut. On the highlands it is hemlock, beech, birch, maple, ash, and basswood.
—Child, Hamilton, Gazetteer and Business Directory of Sullivan County, N.Y., for 1872–1873.

Building on Austin Farm. Collection of Mary Briggs Austin.

Henry Austin had started his wagon delivery business in New York City in the fall of 1866.

Seven years later, the Panic of 1873 started a depression which affected Henry's business, and by 1877, Great-Grandpa Henry's carting business had collapsed.

Letters indicate that our great-grandpa William Henry had run into serious financial difficulties with his carting business in New York City, in which he had been engaged with his brother.

Henry said his brother could afford to buy into companies they had been doing business with and so rescue himself. William Henry could not.—Melva Austin Barney, great-granddaughter.

Henry went back to Eldred to farm. Years later, daughter Aida would record in her diary about the vegetables, apples, berries, and chestnuts on the Austin Farm.

Henry had purchased 16 acres in 1850, and Mary Ann, his wife acquired seven acres of her own.

It would be interesting to know how and when Henry came to own the Austin land—the large parcel of land that the Beers Maps of 1870 and 1875 show as belonging to W. H. Austin.

Did Henry's father Ralph put up the money for the land originally? Did Henry have half of the property and gain the other half when his brother Augustus Austin and his family moved to New York City after 1850? Did he get some land when his father-in-law James Eldred died in 1857?

This chapter includes several letters Henry (he was 50 years old in 1874) wrote from New York City, to his 17-year-old son Lon in Eldred instructing Lon how to help with the farm.

Henry seemed to be aware business wasn't going well and most likely knew farming was plan B if/when the New York City carting business failed.

Henry's letters home give no hint of the gruffness he was accused of later. In the next few chapters, tempers flare—Henry's as well as Ell's, Lon's, and Mort's.

There were health concerns for both Lon and Emma, as well as Henry's wife Mary Ann, 47, at the start of this chapter.

Emma, who can usually be

Albert Alonzo (Lon) Austin, son of William Henry and Mary Ann Austin. Courtesy of Melva Austin Barney.

counted on to be "together," adds her own concerns for a cousin's baby to the already complicated dynamics at the Austin household.

The Austin country cousins, (ages 7–24) were Henrietta, Emma, Maria, Ell, Lon, Aida (Ida), Mort, and Henry Ladore. They were often in New York City, so it is sometimes confusing whether the letters in this chapter were from Eldred or New York City.

In January 1874, Aida (Ida), in Eldred, wrote Lon who was in New York City. In February, Maria in New York City, wrote Lon who was back in Eldred.

Eldred, January 14, 1874
Dear Brother Lon,

I have not seen Ellsworth yet to give him that 5 cents you sent.

Ell goes with Marry West. He took her to Church last week and Harland went with them and just as they was going down the first hill, Harland stuck out his foot and Ell fell flat and Mary almost fell. Ell was quite mad.

The snow is quite deep. Mort and Henry ride downhill a little and slide on your pond. I do not go out much.

Mother is learning me and I learn the boys. I can not write much as I want to write to Marie and it is time I was studying my lesson, so I will close. Write soon.

My love to all, Ida A. Austin

New York City, Feb. 15, 1874
Dear Brother Lon,

I have been sick since I received your letter. I had the Doctor last Sunday night. Yesterday, I walked to the Bowry for the first I have been out. I have had the toothache for three weeks and hope I will be able to go to the dentist next week and have it out.

Jimmy D. [Eldred] is here so must stop writing and get tea. Do you go to singing school?

Write soon, Maria

New York, February 15, 1874
Dear Son Albert,

I received your very welcome letter with Edith and glad to learn from it that you was well once more.

Business is some better than it was, but is not what it had ought to be.

I think you had better yoke your steers once or twice a week so as to keep them handy. I would not draw everything with them. You must take good care of the small one and have him catch up with the big one and then I think they will beat Eldred's by another year. Be careful when it is slippery and not hurt them.

Get Tommy to make you a yoke for them and I will pay him when I come home. You must not let the cattle run on the fields, nor in around the house. I wish you would write and let me know how the hay holds out.

Has Eldred had much trouble with his steers breaking them?

Hoping to hear from you soon with my best wishes. I will close.

From your loving Father, W.H.A.

New York, March, early 1870s
Dear Son Lonny,

I thought I would write a few lines to you. I wish you would tell Tommy Collins not to get out that frame for the woodhouse, nor draw the wood. If he has not commenced either, tell him that I don't want it done.

I wish you to tell him as soon as you receive this so he won't make any calculation on doing it. I wish you would let it be known that the cattle will be for sale about the first of April. I shall try and come up there about that time so if you see anyone that wants cows, you can tell them, but do not sell any until I come. I haven't heard from Edith since she left here.

Tell Ida I miss her very much. It is quite warm here today, but the streets are in a fearful condition, but I have not much to do, so it doesn't make much difference to me. I wish you would write and let me know how the hay holds out.

With much love to you all, I close, Wm. H. Austin

New York, March 10, 1874?
Dear Cousin Lonnie,

Hope you are getting along nicely with your studies at school and that you will soon be here in a good store making lots of money so when you get to be a man, you will have money enough for your museum and a house on Fifth Avenue.

What kind of weather have you had this last week? It has been so cold as Greenland here and today, it has rained as hard as it could all day.

Father has been home sick since Thursday. Think he is a little better today. He is so weak that he can hardly stand. He has taken a fearful cold and has a good deal of fever, but I hope he will soon be better. The rest of the folks are all well.

Write to me soon Lonnie and tell me all the news with much love to Aunt Mary and all the rest, and a good share for yourself.

I am ever your loving cousin, Net

Eldred, July 29, 1874

My Dear Cousin Tina,

Addie and I arrived at Shohola about 4 o'clock Thursday afternoon and found Robbie waiting for us.

They were eating supper when we got home. We were a little tired, but have been resting ever since and feel much better now than when we were in New York.

I think I shall rest one more week and then I shall go to work again. I do not feel as if I could possibly teach now or should commence Monday. It seems delightful to be at home again.

The country loses none of its charms by a contrasting view of New York City at this season of the year. In winter it is different and New York people seem to have the best of us here.

I should like very much to see you and to have you here with me for a while this summer. The house will be pretty full I suppose and I could not see you much for the next five or six weeks.

Mrs. Newcome is going to wait until fall and I wish you would come then too. It will not be very cold in October and her visit will not interfere with ours. She comes to see mother you know and she is very good company anyway.

Kate is at Aunt Effa's now. Have not seen her yet but she was here just before I came home. We are all well with the exception of mother. She is afflicted like Belle with one of Job's comforters and is almost sick today.

Hope that this will find both you and Ranny better than when I saw you.

With love to you and Ranny. Ever your cousin, E.E. Austin

New York, August 9, 1874

Dear Son Loney,

I will write a few lines according to my promise and I hope you will keep yours and let me know how you have got along since I left you and how you and the steers make it drawing stone. Be careful and don't load them too heavy.

If Tommy has brought the rake home, I hope you will put it away out of the weather.

The times are very dull here at present. I was glad I did not stay away any longer, for both of my stores found fault with my driver. He was too lazy to do what little there was to do. But they seemed pleased to see me back, all of them.

Len Beasley was married the 6th. I have not seen him since I came back. He is on his wedding tour. He will be at the store Monday.

If you can sell the steers, pay Mr. Collins 25 dollars and pay Mr. Kelso the rest. Hoping to hear from you soon with my best wishes to you all from your loving Father.

I will close, W.H. Austin

Lewis Dunlap mentioned in the next letter, was a farmer. He and his wife Emily were in their sixties.

New York, August 26, 1874

Dear Son Loney,

I will answer your very welcome letter which I received on the 21st and should have answered it on Sunday, if I had not had the headache so hard. I did not feel as though I could write and I don't feel much like writing yet.

I was glad to learn that you were getting along so well. I wish I could be with you and help you work, for I am sick and tired of staying here and doing nothing.

My work has not paid for my horsefeed and board since I came back. I don't see any prospect of it getting any better this fall, but if it does not, in the course of two weeks, I will sell it for whatever I can get for it and leave here.

If you haven't sold the steers yet, do not sell them until I come home. I hope you have got the bull home. I wish you would get Lewis Dunlap and have him alter Mort's calve as soon as he thinks best. I will pay him when I come home.

Len Beasley mentioned in Henry's August 9, 1874 letter. From Melva Austin Barney.

How did your shoes fit? I did not get your letter with your measure until the day after Belle went back. I hope you are all well. I was sorry to hear your Mother was sick.

I hope you will see to the buckwheat and not let it get wasted for it stands us in hand to save all we can for if my work doesn't get better, it will be a hard winter for me.

I would like to see you all very much. I hope you will write often and let me know how you all are.

The folks are all well here at present. The weather is quite cold.

I guess Eldred doesn't like his place very well. I told him to quit and go home if he wanted to, but he doesn't appear to care to come home again. He offered to drive for me this winter, but if I can't make pay expenses, I am sure he could not. I guess his boss is a mean man. I would not have stood what he has from no man, but I guess he is better to him now.

I shall try and get him some other job if I can, but it will be hard to find one here now, for there are thousands ready for jobs here and can't get them.

With love to you all, from your loving father, Henry

New York, September 23, 1874

Mr. Albert A. Austin
Eldred, Sullivan Co., New York
Dear Son Lony,

I will write a few lines to let you know that we are all well. I hope these lines will find you all enjoying the same blessing. I have been looking for a letter from you for some time, but have looked in vain, but I suppose you can't find time to write. You must not work too hard.

I believe you said you would like to have some ducks. I will send you a pair by express so you can get them on Saturday. Do not fail to go after them, or they will starve. They are every nice and I hope you will feed them good. They have not got their growth yet. You must shut them up nights so the foxes won't get them. I will pay the freight.

The weather is beautiful here at present, but not much doing. My work is very poor, and I don't see any prospect of its getting any better working in the woods for 12 dollars a month, than I am doing here. If I can, I will come home sometime next month for two or three days. I wish you would write and let me know how you get along. Much love to you all.

From your Father, WH Austin
PS Don't forget to go for the ducks, Saturday, the 26th. I will send them in a light small box. They will be with the Jasinger Train 4:30 p.m.

New York, November 18, 1874

Dear Son Lonzo,

I am here yet, and have been anxiously looking for a letter from you sometime, but looked in vain. I suppose you have so much to do that you don't have much time to write.

Have you got the new plow yet? And how do you like it? And how do the Steers like it? I hope you will take good care of them and keep them good and don't work them harder, then they can stand, but plow what you can until the ground freezes up in that field where I told you.

I looked for Edith last Monday, but was disappointed. Your mother wrote that she was a coming. I am afraid some of you are sick, her not coming. Write and let me know as soon as you can if she is not coming.

Soon I will send you an overcoat by express, if you will let me know. And a fine pair of boots, if you will send the measure of your foot.

Tell Eldred, I don't think that he has kept his promise about writing and if there is anything he wants me to send him, to write and let me know. Tell Mother I would like to hear from her.

I often times have wished my father could be here, for I know there is no place for me that is so dear.

With much love to you all. I will close. From your father, W.H.A.

Dear Brother Lonie,

I thought I would let you know

Snow scene in Eldred. Mary Briggs Austin Collection.

that the bull is all write.

Mortie wants to know when you are coming home. If you stay all winter, will you sell me your chestnuts and tell me how mutch you want for them and I will send you the money in a letter.

I found your pocket book on the table the morning you went to New York and I put it in your box and mailed it up.

Write soon, love to all.
Good By, Ida A. Austin

There were two weddings for Jane Ann Van Pelt Myers to attend in 1874. In September, her son, George Washington Taylor Myers, married Martha Mills, daughter of Alexander and Margaret Gillies Mills, who owned a boarding home on Hagan Pond.

Three months later, her daughter (my great-grandmother) Maria Myers, 21, and my great-grandfather, Sherman Stiles Leavenworth, 31, were married in December. The Collins family, neighbors of the Myers attended the wedding ceremony that was performed by Rev. Felix Kyte.

Eldred, Sunday, December, 20, 1874
Dear Brother Lonnie,

I received your letter the 19th and was glad to hear from you. I do not want you to give me the chestnuts for nothing. Tell me what you want for them and I will pay you.

Mother says tell Nettie or Ranny to be sure to come up with Maria. Be sure and have little Emma to come up with them. Mother says for them to come on Thursday, so they can go to Mr. Burl's donation.

It is snowing quite hard and the ground is covered with snow. The ice on your pond is real thick. We glide on it a good deal. I wish

Sherman Stiles Leavenworth Marries Maria Louisa Myers

Sherman S. Leavenworth many years after his marriage. Cynthia Leavenworth Bellinger Collection.

Maria Myers before she married Sherman S. Leavenworth. Cynthia Leavenworth Bellinger Collection.

From a handwritten account of the Leavenworth wedding, missing a page:

The latest on the program is a wedding that took place at Mrs. M. D. Myers, Wed., Dec. 16th. Mr. S.S. Leavenworth to Maria Myers.

The "Burglars" spoken of in the Republican during the summer are married. We suppose the wedding past off very pleasantly until the "music boys" began. All the boys were—and the music light. Two came out and told the boys if they could not make more noise that they would help. They came out and fired a revolver three or four times. They told the boys if they couldn't make more noise than that they had better go home, then went in the house.

The "music boys" felt highly insulted, then took a desperate start, went, got under the window and in on their muscle. Then making more than Mr. Myers could stand, he rushed out of the house after the boys, which ran out of the yard into the road before they stopped and stood their ground.

One ran and left Mr. M. Then Mr. M. seeing that they ran that far from him, thought that he would race them a little farther. He ran out with coat tail and hair flying, struck at one, ran into him, pushed him down, but before he reached the ground, Mr. M. received a left hander and a kick. (Some said the boys kicked him, others said not), that brought him to the ground with one of the "music boys" on top who choked him.

The first words Mr. Myers was, "I don't want a fuss. Let me up. Don't get my clothes all dirty." Then, "Come out here boys, they have got me down." Then a rush for…page ends here.

Leavenworth pasture land. Photo in the Cynthia Leavenworth Bellinger Collection.

you were here to slide on the pond with us.

Shurman and Maria Myers was married. They had a fight with boys that was making a noise out doors. Tommy, Annie, Mr. and Mrs. Colllins went to the wedding.

Love, to all. Write soon,
Ida [Aida Austin]

There was another wedding in December. Margaret Mills, sister to Martha Mills Myers, married James Boyd. We will hear more of this family in Book Two.

Mid-1870s?
Dear brother Lonnie,

You are an "awful" good boy as Nettie says to stay there and get such a good place.

You do not know how pleased and proud I was. I was quite reconciled to you coming when I left N.Y., and succeeded so well in inspiring mother with this same feeling that I think she was really disappointed when she found you had concluded to stay.

As for the children, they were quite overwhelmed with grief and I think would have "shed tears" could they have left their play long enough.

Mother is so worried about your getting sick and I do hope that you will take care of yourself for her sake at least, if not for your own.

You had better see a doctor Lon if your cough is not any better and do not stay there a day if you think it is injuring your health. You know that this is of the first and highest importance to you and to us.

When we urge you to stay, we do not mean for you to stay if you are unable to do so, but only that we do not want you to get home sick or tired of the city or discouraged in regard to the work and leave on their account.

Do you have any writing to do? I wish you would get a book with Spencer copies and write all the time you have.

When night comes, go to bed and get the rest you need.

Do you go to church anywhere?

Mother may be down in a week or two. I guess she is afraid of the Port Jervis bridge and wants to see the ice safe and out of the river before she attempts a journey to N.Y.

Lon, do not worry about your board rent one bit, and do not try to pay it. Take your money and get your comfortable clothes. I will see that the board is paid this fall. I am now and ever, Your loving sister, Edith (Emma)

New York, May 23, year unknown
Dear Lonnie,

I write you bad news. Father [Augustus Austin] is sick again. He went downtown Monday morning and worked hard all day, came home sick. The Doctor thinks he will not suffer as much pain as he did first, but he is very sick.

Please write when Uncle Henry is coming and tell Aunt Mary to come with him, and as many of the little ones as she can bring.

Addie has been almost crazy with the neuralgia this week. She does not sit up a minute, so we have our hands full.

And write soon, Net

February 21, 1875
Dear Brother Lonnie,

I received your welcome last night and now I set myself to answer it.

You do not think it can be any colder there than it is here. I guess if you had been here a week ago last Tuesday, you would maybe think it was colder here. The snow is awful deep here. It snowed all day yesterday, but the sun is shining bright today.

I suppose you know the M.E. Church has been holding revivals from Eldred, and his wife and George Parker's wife was taken in on probation.

Mother says to tell you to be sure and dress warm and not get cold.

You will have to excuse a short letter as I want to write Marie and a few lines to Emma, so good by.

Your aff. Sister

New York City, Sunday, February 28, 1875
Miss Edith Austin, Lumberland
Dear Cousin Emm,

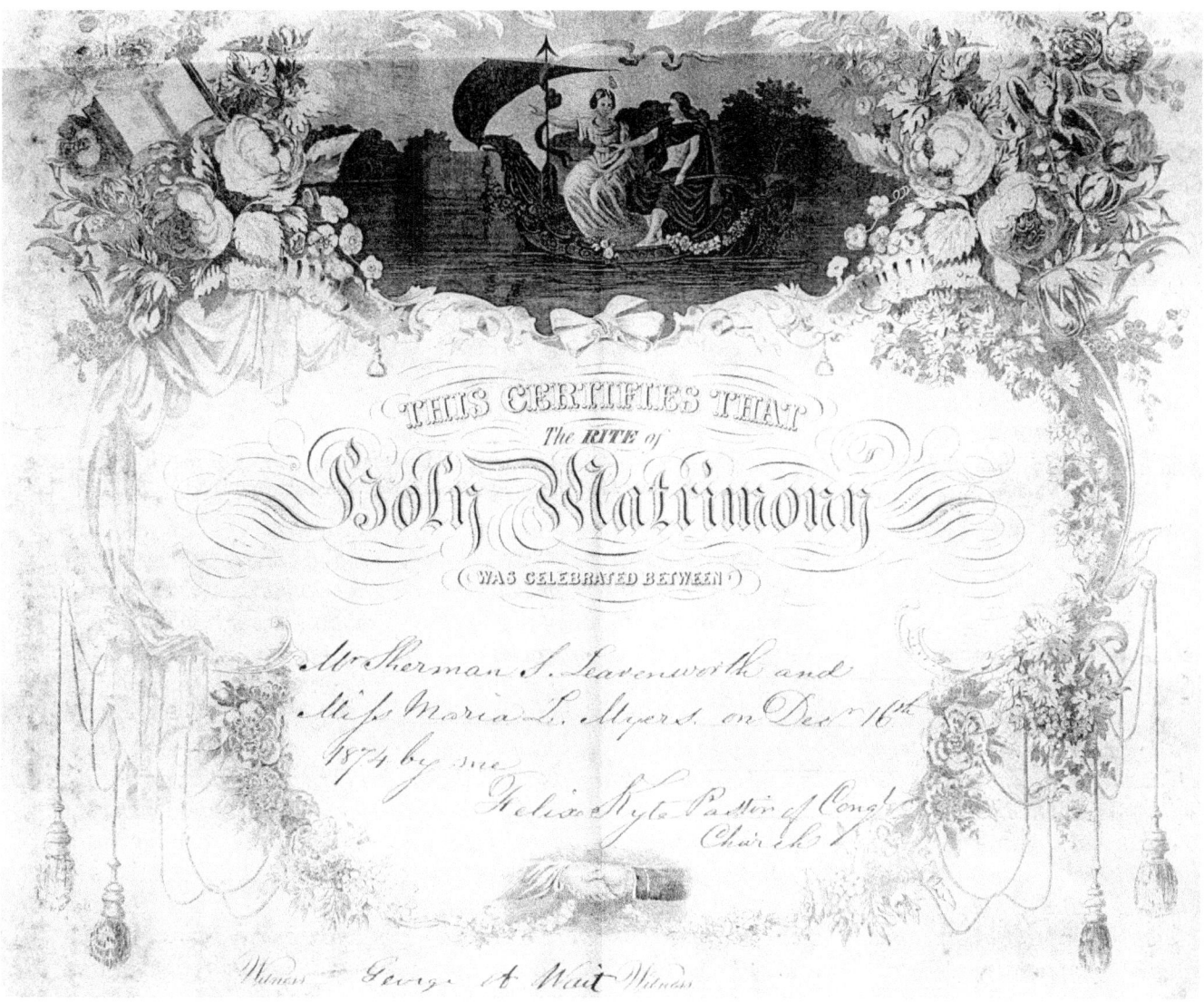

Marriage certificate for Sherman S. Leavenworth and Maria Louisa Myers. Witness: George A. Wait. In collection of Linda Leavenworth Bohs.

I have not been under the parental roof since your return to your native clime, consequently am unable to give you my information respecting the inmates, but presume they are enjoying their usual equanimity as the disturbing element or that which wrought disturbance is now remote.

Ranny and I were to church this morning and listened to an eloquent sermon from our beloved friend and pastor Brother Cheney.

Yet even there my thoughts kept running out to you and I yearned for the exquisite pleasure which your company always affords, but alas, cruel fate has parted us and I must learn to submit patiently to its decrees.

Mr. Cheney inquired kindly about your whereabouts and I kindly gave the required information.

Please remember your promise and burn this letter.
Your true and loving cousin,
Tina Laing

Friday Evening, March 19, 1875
Dear Cousin Emma,
I commenced my letter Thursday afternoon, but was unable to finish it.

I went around to Second St. Church to hear the famous London orator, the Rev. Mr. Barley. The sermon was excellent. I think I never heard a more eloquent or a heart touching one in my life.

Darling, I wish you could have been there. I thought of you so often during the service and wished you were enjoying it with me.

I was around home a little while this afternoon. Nettie was over to Belle's and Rand was going to call on the minister's wife.

Addie and the baby [Gussie Thompson] have both been sick with a cold, but are now better. Mother [Aunt Maria] and Aunt Eliza [Gardner] are coming to spend next Tuesday with me.

Ranny has been home sick two or three days and is looking miserable. I am trying so hard to be a faithful loving wife, a helpmeet instead of a burden.

If God were to take him from me now, how would I bear it.

Do you commence your teaching on the first of April?

Give my love to your Mother and believe me, ever your loving cousin,
Tina Laing

10 Ave. D, New York City, April 8, 1875
Dear Cousin Emma,

I am suffering from a terrible cold; one of my eyes is swollen half shut and from the other a continual stream is pouring and between the two I have a sorrowful time. I have got a cough, a sore throat and am so hoarse I can hardly speak.

I am happy to inform you that my mental condition corresponds well with any personal appearance. I am feeling about as miserable and depressed in spirits as my situation demands.

This the third week that Ranny has been out of work and no prospects of any yet. I am completely disheartened, I do not know what I am going to do. The thought of passing through another such summer as the last is appalling.

And now Emma please grant the favor I am going to ask. Will you write and send me some verses on this subject, "not here shall we be satisfied" or we shall be satisfied in heaven? Do not smile and think I am growing

Haying on the Leavenworth property, in later years. Sherman S. is on the far right. His son Garfield is the tall man in the middle. From Cynthia Leavenworth Bellinger.

sentimental like the Brooklyn scandal folks: but they would be a great comfort to me at present/

April 9th: I commenced a letter to you the third of this month, but my eye has pained me so in writing this that I have had to lay aside my pen and those lines.

Sabbath evening April 11th: I am happy to inform you that my eye has once more unfolded itself to the light. They have assumed a more yellowish and green in color and you know what kind of a character green eyes indicate, look out for me.

April 13th: I have got a most fearful cough and it bothers me so that you will have to excuse the briefness and mistakes of this letter.

Lovingly yours, Tina Laing

The Brooklyn Scandal referred to a court case in which the famous New York City preacher, Henry Ward Beecher, was accused of adultery. Emma Austin liked to hear Henry Ward Beecher preach when she was in New York City.

April 30, 1875
Dear Cousin Tina,

I am exceedingly sorry to hear of your illness, still more to know that you are yet walking in the shadow of your own heart. It is strange how the human soul will cling to its doubts and fears when simply by letting them go, one may claim the precious promises of Christ and clasp in our own the Hand that bringeth peace.

I am sorry to know that you are troubled. Sorrows shared with a friend lose some of its intensity, I know by experience. If you would only share it with him, the one that can help you the most. He will bear your burden if you will let Him, and He can bear it so much better than you can do.

May 7th: I commenced teaching last Monday. I have been very busy. A school always takes up most of my time in one way and another. Even in my dreams I am always busy when teaching.

I am going to attend an anniversary in the church tonight. It is to be a grand affair. All Eldred is in expectation.

Write soon to Emma

Saturday Night, June 5, 1875
Darling Emm,

Ranny is still out of work and it seems as if heaven and earth had combined to render me as

1875 New York State Census: Farms

1875 New York State Census: Farms
The rye crop is much below the usual average yield. The corn and potato crop is above the usual average.

Farmer	IMPROVED LAND	TOTAL UNIMPROVED LAND	WOODS & TIMBER UNIMPROVED
Robert F. Owen	18	75	47
Isaac M. Bradley	45	323	278
Ethel B. Sergeant	20	45	35
Alva Sergeant	10	45	35
S.B. Leavenworth	70	195	125
Rev. Felix Kyte	17	30	13
Robert Kelso	40	600	560
James D. Eldred	—	50	50

Farmer	FARM	BUILDINGS	STOCK	TOOLS	1874
Robert F. Owen	$2,000	$250	$150	$60	$71
Isaac M. Bradley	$4,700	$400	$525	$225	$170
Ethel B. Sergeant	$2,500	$250	$270	$50	$30
Alva Sergeant	$800	$50	$50	$20	—
S.B. Leavenworth	$4,000	$800	$700	$100	$440
Rev. Felix Kyte	$2,000	$100	$350	$300	$100
Robert Kelso	$4,000	$900	$150	$250	$600
James D. Eldred	$150	—	—	$50	—

Tons of hay produced
- Leavenworth 20
- Mahlon Clark 10
- Wilmot Clark 10
- Robert Owen 3
- Isaac Bradley 20
- Ethel Sergeant 12
- Alva Sergeant 6
- Rev. Felix Kyte 5
- Robert Kelso 40
- James Boyd 15
- Charles C.P. Eldred 20
- George W.T. Myers 15
- Henry Austin 16

Apple Trees
- Isaac Bradley 60
- Ethel Sergeant 50
- Alva Sergeant 26
- S. B. Leavenworth 125
- Robert Owen 50
- W. Gallagher 150
- Felix Kyte 25
- Joseph Tether 10

Sherman Leavenworth 1874
14 acres plowed.
31 acres in pasture.
25 acres in meadow.
20 Tons of hay.
1 bushel of grass seed.
5 acres sown in winter rye.
5 acres of oats sown.
150 bu oats harvested.
2 acres sown of buckwheat.
20 bu buckwheat harvested.
2-1/2 acres sown in winter rye.
60 bushels rye harvested.
2 acres planted of potatoes.
300 bushels potatoes harvested.

Sherman Leavenworth 1875
13 acres plowed.
32 acres in pasture.
25 acres in meadow.
1-1/2 acres of oats sown.
5 acres sown of buckwheat.
3 acres planted in Indian corn.
2 acres of potatoes planted.

Sherman Stiles Leavenworth is standing in one of the Leavenworth fields. Cynthia Leavenworth Bellinger Collection.

Halfway Brook. Photo: Cynthia Leavenworth Bellinger.

wretched as possible and they are succeeding admirably. You do not know what a wearisome and painful path my feet are treading.

I wish I could see and talk with you. There is so much that I do not like to write. I used to think we could write better than we could talk, but I have changed my opinion somewhat.

Tina

New York State took a

George Clark, husband of Harriet Covert; brother of Mahlon Irvin Clark. Collection of Cynthia Leavenworth Bellinger.

census in 1875. Sherman Stiles Leavenworth and his bride Maria Myers, lived with Sherman's parents, Buckley and Charlotte. Mary E. Owen, 15, a servant, lived there, too.

John Leavenworth was out west. Harriet Leavenworth Palmer and her husband Henry both 40, lived near Port Jervis, in a brick house. Henry was a wood dealer and their children were Harry, 15, Edith, 14, and James, 6. It is unknown when Harry and James were adopted.

The Leavenworths in Eldred were neighbors of the Bradley family. Isaac Bradley, 38, a farmer, and his wife Joanna Brown had seven children: Amelia, Viola, Mary F., Isaac, Lottie, Atwell, and baby Nora. Benjamin Fletcher, 55, a laborer was listed with the Bradley family.

Ethel and Letty Sergeant were close to 70 years old. Ethel was still a farmer. Daughter Caroline, 32, son Isaac, 40, a carpenter, and grandson James W., 6 (son of James G. who had died in 1873), lived with them. Isaac Sergeant may have thought that he was a confirmed bachelor, but there would be a surprise in store for him in about ten years.

Ethel and Letty's son Alvah Sergeant was a carpenter. Alvah's wife Phebe was at home with children Edgar, 19, Alma, 12, Frank, 14, Morgan, 9, and Thomas, 1. Frank Sergeant would marry Clarissa Clark, daughter of George and Harriet Covert Clark.

It's been a while since we talked about George and Harriet Clark. Harriet's father, William Covert, died in 1875, at the age of 89. Harriet and George Clark had a large family. Their daughter Clarissa was 16.

George Clark was the son of Wilmot, 78, and Mary, 76. Three grandchildren from 6 months to 11 years old, lived with Wilmot and Mary Van Auken Clark.

George's brother, Irvin Clark, also a son of Wilmot and Mary, was 45. Irvin's wife Laura Austin was 42. Their sons were: Ellsworth, 13, Elbert, 9, and Robert around 1.

Uncle Justus Hickok was 84, and his wife Polly was 75. The families of their sons, William, Charles, and David Hickok, also lived in Eldred.

William Hickok was a carpenter. He and his wife Almeda Drake had four children. Charles Hickok, a farmer, was married to Sarah Dehart.

David Hickok was also a farmer. He and his wife Mary had six children ages 4 to 20, including Olin, 9, my grandpa Mort's friend and cousin.

Mary Hickok, a daughter of Uncle Justus and Aunt Mary also lived in Eldred. Mary and her husband William C. Stidd had three children.

The Congregational Minister Rev. Felix Kyte, was 75, and his wife Eliza was 66. Son William, 31, a farmer, and daughter Elizabeth

(Libby), lived with them.

Jacob Stage was 70. Jacob and his wife Martha have played a part in the Methodist Church.

Robert Kelso, 47, from Ireland, was a merchant. He and his wife Amanda had six children (ages 2–19) at home: Emma, Edward, Robert, Ella, Minnie, and Alice. The Kelso family were friends with Henry and Mary Ann's family, at least for a while.

The census lists Great-Grandpa Henry Austin's job as a carman, but had some wrong ages. The Austin household consisted of Henry, Mary Ann, and children Henrietta, Edith or Emma, Mariah, James E. (Ell), Albert (Lon), Ida, Charles M., and Henry Ladore. The oldest sons would soon want to be more independent, and would end up out in Solomon City, Kansas.

Mary Ann's brother, Charley C.P. Eldred was a farmer. He and his wife Effa had a houseful: daughters Rebecca, 32, and Sarah Eldred, 23; grandson James Eldred, 9, son of George W. Eldred who died; and George Harris, 67, a laborer.

C.C.P. and Effa Eldred's son, James D. Eldred, was a farmer and married to Frances Payne.

June was a busy month for C.C.P. and Effa. Their daughter Sarah married William Wait; another daughter, Maria Adeline and her husband Charles Kendall, had a new little one, Nelly Effa Kendall.

James E. Gardner, son of James K. and Eliza Eldred Gardner, was 39, and listed as a gentleman. He had a store in Barryville. James Gardner's wife Rebecca Rider was 35, and their children were listed as Frank, Linda, and Susan.

George W. T. Myers, 29, a farmer, and his new bride Martha

In 1875, Jane Ann Myers and her children lived in one home, George W.T. Myers and his wife Martha Mills, lived in the other. Photo: Courtesy of Stuart and Geraldine Mills Russell.

This photo was taken at the home on the left in the top photo, but at a later time. Jane Ann Myers is the lady by the window sitting down. Cynthia Leavenworth Bellinger Collection.

Mills, 24, lived in the house next to his mother, Jane Ann Myers, 59, and siblings, Lottie, 16, and Augustus, 18.

Summer and fall 1875 was another busy time for Grandma Jane Ann Van Pelt Webb Myers. Charles C. Myers, son of George Washington and Martha Mills Myers was born July 1875. It seems George named their first son after his half brother, Charles C. Webb.

In late October, Anna Mae Leavenworth, daughter of Sherman S. and Maria Myers

Elizabeth (Libby) Kyte, daughter of Felix and Eliza Kyte. Courtesy of Melva Austin Barney.

Others in 1875

John and Marian Wallace were brother and sister from Scotland. John was a farmer.

Anthony Whitney, a farmer, and his wife, Eveline, were from New Jersey.

John Wait, 59, and his wife Charlotte, 49, were from England. John was a farmer. Their son William Wait was 28, and a blacksmith. Son George was 26, and a carpenter.

Mr. Lilly, 82, and his wife 72, had four grandchildren with them.

Sarah Shotwell, 66, had an 11-year-old granddaughter, Gracie Frey living with her.

William Williams, a carpenter, and his wife Charlotte, were from South Wales. They had two daughters and a son.

Eugene and Alvina Dubois were from France. Eugene was a farmer.

Ira M. Austin was a blacksmith. He and his wife Minerva had three children, Nellie, 9, Minnie, 7, and Frank, 2. Ira's father Benjamin C. was 67, and a wagon maker.

John Hickok, 25, was a stone cutter. He and his wife Viola had a 2-year-old daughter.

Alice Amelia Sergeant (daughter of Alvah and Letty Sergeant) and Thomas Alvin Hill Jr. have been married for a year. Alice was the second wife of Thomas Hill Jr. His first wife, Alice's sister, Esther Sergeant, had died in 1873.

Thomas and Amelia Sergeant Hill's son, John Thomas Hill, born in June 1876, would be the father of Alfred Hill. Alfred and his wife Bessie, were friends of my dad and mother, but that is a ways off yet.

Abel S. Myers was 39. His wife of three years was Maria Hankins. Abel's sons from his first marriage, James and Edwin were 16 and 12.

Back of Eldred schoolhouse. The Parker House across the street was built by James Parker in the early 1870s. The year the photo was taken is unknown. Courtesy of Mary Briggs Austin.

Leavenworth, was born—another grandchild for Jane Ann Myers.

Alexander Boyd, 84, died of cancer in May 1875. His wife, Elizabeth Boyd, was 64. Alexander and Elizabeth were the parents of Comfort and James Boyd. James was a farmer and married to Margaret Mills.

Oliver and Mary Parker Schoonover's daughter Emily was about 4-1/2, and their son, Daniel Rowley was 2-1/2.

There were a couple Parker families in town by 1875. James Parker, who built the first Parker House in the early 1870s, would have a daughter and a granddaughter who would play a part in Aida Austin's life (they are mentioned in Aida's 1940 diary), and also in my father, Art Austin's life.

My Grandfather built the original Parker House in the early 1870s. This is a guess from all that I remember hearing. When they opened the first hotel in Eldred, he had the first liquor license in town.—Christena (Teenie) Stevens Myers.

In the year 1875, the records kept by the "Keeper of the Dam" said that 3,140 rafts passed over the Lackawaxen dam by the last of May.

This dam was constructed by the Delaware and Hudson Canal Company, who employed the "Keeper." He guided the rafts from the shore over the dam. If they obeyed his instructions and the raft was broken up, the Canal Company settled with the owner of the raft.

However, if they did not follow his orders, and the raft was damaged, the Canal Company maintained they were not responsible for the loss.—*www.minisink.org/hisdoor.html.*

New York, September 26, 1875

Dear Son Loney,

I will write a few lines to let you know that I am well and I hope they will find you all the same. The weather is very nice here now. It is quite cool here at night. My work is getting better this week and I hope it will last so for sometime. I hope you and Ell get along good and not worry your Mother.

I wish you would ask Edith if

she could pay the interest on the loan mortgage and I will pay her when I see her. I don't like to send it in a letter, and I don't want to come home until the middle of October, if I can help it, for I want to be here while my work is good for I can make more out of it than a driver. The interest is 35 dollars if she can do so. Give it to C.C.P. Eldred and he will get it to the Commissioner if she can't do it. Please let me know as soon as you can. I will pay her as soon as I see her.

How does the buckwheat get along? Have you got it thrashed yet? Is the corn cut, the potatoes cut? It is time.

Did Ell get subscribers enough to get the sowing machine? If he can send the paper to Milford, the first of October, I wish he would. I will pay him when I come home. Tell him to pay the postage on it. I think you had better feed the heifer some meal that we intend to kill—a little everyday and that bull calf too.

I would like to be with you if I could and help do the work. I wish you would write and let me know how you get a long. Has Jim got much wall laid yet?

Tell Mother I would like to have her write if she is well enough. If work keeps good, so I can, I will fetch her a ring when I come.

Hoping to hear from you soon, with much love to you all,

I will close. From your Father,
W.H. Austin

New York, October 3, 1875

Dear Emma,

We arrived home safely and found Tom waiting for us and very glad to see us. Gussie was quite troublesome coming down and for the first two or three days after we got here, he acted perfectly awful, every thing seemed so strange to him. He did not appear to know what to do with himself.

He acts a little better now, but I hardly get a chance to draw a long breath only when he is asleep as he acts worse than ever after me.

I hardly know what I am going to do this winter as Tom seems to have his mind "sot" on staying here. I have used all my eloquence for the past week in trying to persuade him to do as we planned, to no purpose and for this once I give up, but I tell you I do hate to dreadfully for I had my heart set on going with you.

He (Tom) says that he and Mort [Addie's brother] talked the matter over and he told Mort that on Net's account, he would stay this winter if Mort went to housekeeping.

Church News

1874
Methodist Episcopal Church Members in full communion
James E. Austin, Oct. 25, 1874.
Alonzo A. Austin, Sep. 27, 1874.
Olin Hickok, Rebecca E. Ingram,
Andrew J. Ingram,
Perry and Mary Schoonover.

Baptisms at Methodist Episcopal Church, May 31, Rev. S.H. Opdyke, Halfway Brook
Emma Jane Kelso, Adult.
Eden Evert Kelso, Adult.
Robert Sears Kelso, Adult.

Congregational Church New Members
Sarah J. Eldred (Wait).
Lottie Myers (Darling).
Annie Wilson.
Six with the last name of Whitney.
Ella Clark.
Mary Mills (Wait).
Elizabeth Owen (Thompson).
Edward and Sarah Wilson.
Sherman S. Leavenworth baptized and became a member.
18 new, 413 total.

1876
Congregational Church New Members
Margaret Covert,
Margaret MacKenzie.
5 new, 418 total.

1875
Congregational of Highland
Value of church and lot: $2,000.
Seats: 200 people.
Usual number attending: 80.
Number regular members: 70.
Clergy salary: $330.

Methodist of Highland
Value of church and lot: $1,500.
Seats: 150 people.
Usual number attending: 60 Number.
Regular members: 20.
Clergy salary: $100.

Union of Barryville Methodist and Congregational.
Value of church and lot: $2,000.
Seats: 175 people.
Usual number attending: 75.
Number regular members: 25.
Clergy salary: $100.

Barryville and Shohola Baptist
Value of church and lot: $2,000.
Seats: 200 people.
Usual number attending: 30.
Regular members: 15.

1877 Church Fire
The Barryville Union Church (originally Congregational, built in 1835) was destroyed by fire, December 1877. They then worshipped at the Baptist Church (at the invitation of the Baptists), from January 1878, until their new church was built in 1903.

Austin farmland around the 1920s. Collection of Mary Briggs Austin.

The folks are exceedingly kind. Nettie acts more like herself to me than she ever has since I was married. Rand is simply angelic!

Tina is here and is going to stay, I guess. I told her what you said about writing. She did not make much reply. She, and in fact all hands, are quite reserved about speaking about your folks or any one else and of course I am not to be outdone on that score.

You have no idea how much I want to see you all and have a good chat. I am sure Gussie misses you all as much as I do. Tell Aunt Mary that I am quite patient for me with her boy and tell her also to be very careful of her health.

I heard Nett say she was going to write for her to come down soon. Your father said last night that he expected to go home a week from next Saturday. I hope you will come back with him when he comes.

I have not time to write now as Gussie is waking up.
Your ever affec. Cousin, Addie

On October 21, 1875, Robert Kelso and his wife Amanda G. conveyed 100 acres in the Town of Highland, to Sherman B. Leavenworth for $500. The land was bounded on the Northeast by land of John Wait, "on the southeast by land now or formerly owned by Robert Kelso; on the southwest by the lands of George Clark and Gallagher Brothers, or formerly owned by them," and on the northwest by Sherman's own lands.

December 9, 1875
Dear Brother Lonnie,

I will send your book if I can and send my third reader to Harry, for I do not need it (the fourth reader). I have not been to school this week, nor have I been outdoors until today.

Agnes a little girl in school came around on Monday and Tuesday to see when I was coming to school, but has not been around since. I am going around to school this afternoon just to report, not to stay.

Mrs. Sims is in here and I cannot write very well. I hope you are all well. Mother is a little better today. I am glad to hear you are going but wish you was here. I like it here real well and think you would if you were here.

Have you heard anything from Marry West? Are you going to have singing school this winter, or anything else?

Emma says her 5 reader is home in her big trunk. I guess and you can use that untill I can get yours to you.

My love to all. Good bye,
Your aff. sister, Ida Austin

According to a cousin letter, Addie Austin Thompson had been quite ill in 1872. Around 1874, Addie and her husband Tom had a son Augustus, nicknamed Gussie. On January 21, 1876, their son, Tommy Thompson, was born.

It seems that Addie at one point was not caring for baby Tom very well, or that is how Emma felt. One of the letters sounded like Addie was happy to have someone else watch baby Tommy.

In a much later letter, Addie sounds more responsible and thoughtful about little Tom's care.

Perhaps, after baby Tommy was born, Addie was very tired and not feeling well. Whatever the reason, Emma became involved with the care of little Tommy and wanted to claim him as her own.

January 31, 1876
Dear Brother Lon,

I received your very welcome letter last night and was verry glad to hear from you. Harry and I have splendid times riding downhill. My oxen is growing real big. I wish you were home to ride downhill with Harry and I.

Your pond is all covered over with snow. Ell takes Marry to church every once and a while. We are having a revival here in the M.E. Church. I milk a cow and lead my calf to water. Excuse a short letter.

My love to all write soon.
Good by,
Your brother Mortie Austin

February 7, 1876
Dear Brother Lon,

Mother came over on Saturday and stayed all night and I went over and stayed with Addie, and Emma stayed with Addie last night, and I came home. Mother is going back today. Linnie and little Lon [children of Alonzo and Belle Austin] was to Net's on Saturday to see Ida.

I did not go to school this morning because I did not have time to learn my lessons on Saturday as I went over to Addie's early in the morning.

Eldred went to Florida on Thursday. He had to buy a ticket.

When you write, direct your letters to Mother, 11 Picks Street, because we are going to move on Wednesday and I do not know the street or number. Em knows, but she is not here.

I would write you a longer letter, but I have got to write to Maria and I have got to go to Bleaker Dr. and put Mother on the cars. Mortie is going with her and I will be alone until Em comes, so I will close.

Write soon.
My love to all, good by,
Your aff sister, Ida

March 10, 1876, was the first successful telephone transmission of clear speech when Alexander Graham Bell spoke into his device, "Mr. Watson, come here, I want to see you." Watson heard each word distinctly.

Eldred, Wed. May 3, 1876

Dear Sister Emma,

I have been busy and could not answer your letter before school commenced the first of May. I like the teacher real well. She is quite strict and I think she will have a good school after she gets started. She boards to Wilson's. Annie Wilson does not come to school this summer—none of them came but Mary.

Father said he would not pay any of his debts unless Mother signed the deed to him and mother was afraid he would take the money and go away and not pay Mortie.

Father is good enough to her now. I think she will take Henry to New York some day next week. She wants to go.

The two little French boys came to school this summer. How do you spell their name? Tommy Collins spells it Ozer [Oser/Osier] and you spelt it different in your Rollbook last summer.

I can not find out any news to send you, only Bec [cousin Rebecca Eldred], has had a bad cold and has got a sore nose, and Bill Wait is making a picket fence around his yard.

The old school house looks a little better than it did last summer. The wall has been whitewashed and the blackboards has been fixed up. Charlie Wilson painted them. Jim Eldred is making his place look real nice.

Father is going to put a picket fence up the lane and in front of the house. It is splendid here now. Do you think you will come this summer or is Addie coming? Is Addie going to keep house or has she given it up?

Tell Addie I think I would rather have my hat trimmed with bleu.

Write soon, Ida Austin

May 12, 1876

Dear brother Lonnie,

Now you might think this of me as does mother, that I cared for him more than you. You know this could not possibly be so. So with mother, for reasons which we do not know, sometimes for the sake of peace, sometimes from thoughtlessness (you know how absent minded she is) she does things which seem strangely to us. But I know she always does as nearly as she can for the best.

I am glad to know that you did not believe with Maria, Ell and Mortie, that I was entirely to blame. If Maria always entertains as good an opinion of him as she does now, I shall be glad for her sake. What I think of Ell I do not say.

And poor little Mortie is not to blame at all. I never felt so sorry for anyone as him and Ida this winter. If I had known how it was going to be, I should never have let him come. I wish you had been here instead of Ell. You would have known a little, a very little of what I had to contend with.

Ida is the only one that knows all and she does not know how dreadfully angry he made me.

Harry and I went to hear Mr. Beecher last night, but heard Mr. Holliday instead. Harry was nearly as disappointed as myself.

From Mary Ann Eldred Austin's Scrapbook. Melva Austin Barney Collection.

"Evening prayer." From Mary Ann Eldred Austin's Scrapbook. Melva Austin Barney.

I did not care so much for Mr. Moody, but then I only heard him once, and not more than half he said at that. The building was so large and so crowded. I do not see any pleasure in going where there are so many. Or what good it does anyone when you can neither see or hear.

At the opening exercises of the Centennial, the line of people was half a mile in length and a portion of the exercises could not be heard more than 20 feet from the stage. There must have been great satisfaction in it to those at the end of the line.

Has Eldred recovered from the effects of his Florida trip.

Irv has written me to send him the amount due. If I was in your place I would not spend anything for wagons.

Has your school opened up yet? Who is your Methodist minister?

Mother is well, and I believe has written to you. The rest of us are well except Aunt Maria. She is improving slowly.

I was going to write to Ida, but the baby [Tommy Thompson] is waking up and I shall not have time.

Write me again as soon as possible. In haste,
Affectionately, Emma

Maybe 1876
Dear Brother Lonnie,

Your kind letter was very gladly received by me this week and as I have considerable to say and little time to say it in, I proceed to "business" tone.

You tell me not to get you a place until you tell me to do so. Do you know Lonnie that I must get it when I can or else wait if some chance goes by for another. You have missed one or two now and since I wrote you, I could not have found you anything I had wished to buy. Lon will you come when I write for you?

Ida and I went Sunday to hear Mr. Tippley read in Dr. Talmage's church. We don't go out much. Wish I were in Eldred to attend some of those parties. You must have good times. Tell Maria maybe I'll come home if mother comes down about the holidays. I can't get away now. I am dreadful busy.

With love ever yours,
Emma

Around 1876
Dear Brother Lonnie,

I was very glad to hear from you. I am very sorry that I am not to see you this winter, but I am certainly far from being disgusted with you for having plans and wishes of your own even though you follow them sometimes to your own disadvantage. I wish you all happiness and success and only wish that I could see more clearly your way to these.

I am a little selfish, no doubt in my desire to have you here. There are so many places that we could go evenings if you were here to go with us that on this account alone.

How I wished for you at the Centennial. It is wonderful. Lon just to see the buildings alone, that have been erected on the grounds in so short a time and one would think twenty years a little time to have made the immense collections of curiosities exhibited there.

If I could only have spent a week instead of a day, I should have been better satisfied and then I could not have seen the half of what there was to be seen.

Tell mother I hope she will bring Dora. I want to see the little fellow so much that I get homesick just for him, and he can have a nice time here now. Tell him he shall have a great big apple every day just as long as he stays and a pocket knife for his Christmas. When is mother coming? I hope by the middle of December. Ask her if Addie shall send her the money or pay it here after she gets here.

You say that you are growing wild and reckless and sinful. O Lon, you must not say this. I think I would rather die than see you wicked and so unhappy. If you have sinned, you know where to find pardon for the past and strength for the future. Our God is a merciful God and helps in every time of need. And though we turn from Him and grieve him, o'er and o'er, he never turns from us when in true penitence in going to him. You have surely known too much of real happiness to let it slip from you now.

Pray for me and for yourself that God will forgive and help us both. Leave your past with him asking him to make your future as he would have it. And your life shall be as it should be.

Yours ever affectionately,
Emma

New York, October 29, 1876
Dear Brother Lon,

I have got the sweetest teacher ever was. She has gone to the Centennial. I guess she will be back on Monday. I hope so. She went on Friday after school.

Lon, do come down. Write and tell me you will come as soon as Tom gets you a place. Please do. Don't stay there any longer, but come as soon as you can.

Please write soon and tell me all the news.

Good bye, your ever true and loving sister, Ida

January 1, 1877
Dear Brother Lon,

Holidays of all descriptions are dull days with me and this which began so pleasantly this morning, that I thought it was going to prove an exception to holidays in general, is certainly dark and stormy enough to make one feel dull this afternoon.

But it gives me some leisure for writing and wishing you with all love and sincerity, A "Happy New Year," I will proceed with my answer to your letter.

You must not Lon allow yourself to cherish thoughts so injurious to yourself and so ungrateful to your Maker. He of whom you ask is always ready to bestow more ready than we to receive. May He help us both, and Oh, Lon, whatever mistakes you have made or may make never give up your hope in Jesus—He who has bidden us to forgive our enemies "not seven, but seventy times seven," never refuses pardon

Austin barn in collection of Mary Briggs Austin.

which the true penitent seeks.

Mother is very well and apparently enjoying her visit as much as me. O if we were all here. It was a shame not to bring poor little Dora.

I will send a box directed to Father to Shohola Thursday. I suppose it will be there Saturday. Part of the things are for Laura.

I did not have much to give though Santa was pretty good to me. I got seven books, a whole set of Scotts' novels beautifully bound and a history of the Centennial.

Ida got four books, and Addie gave her a work box and a box of perfume and a nice tie. You will think it pretty late for a Christmas box, but better late than never I suppose. I could not get it ready before, there was so much sewing to do.

You must write me soon. Tell me all the news. Where is Annie Wilson? Why don't you go with her? She is worth all the rest of the girls in Sullivan. I wish you had something to do here. How can you be so foolish?

Write me soon. Lon, best wishes from all, from your Emma

PS The box was sent today, Thursday, and will be at Shohola Saturday the 13th I guess. Mr. Collins' soap is in the box.

January 12, 1877
Dear brother Lon,

I will write just a few lines to you today if I can. Tommy is asleep and my work partly done. There is always so much to do lately and I work so slowly that if I stopped to finish all my housework as I should, I should never have time for anything else. If I could spare the money and time (the last is more than the first) I should come home now. I would give $5 for one good night's rest. But there is no rest for the wicked they say and find it very amply exemplified in my case.

I have been sick so much and have been so busy with holiday work and getting the box ready, that I could not think of anything else.

Rand and children, Net, Arch, Mr. Clinton, Uncle Augustus, and Aunt Maria were all here. Rand before Christmas and the rest between Christmas and New Years. I was so sick you can imagine how pleasant it was for me.

Ida is busy with her lessons. What are you all doing home?

How I want to see you.

How are you doing Lon yourself? Better than when I saw you I hope. I did so want a good long talk with you and I had no good chance, but Lon how dreadfully you have changed. You hardly seemed my brother to me.

I thought you did not seem to care and trust me. Have I changed too? I'm afraid so.

I guessed at the collars. Hope they will suit you. If father doesn't like his tie and you can use it, do so. I hope it will suit him. Be good to mother Lon, just as good as you can and to poor Dora.

Write to me soon and may God bless my brother forever.

Ever your sister, Emma

Eldred, January 30, 1877

Mr. Alonzo Austin
Sir:

The pleasure of yourself and company is respectfully solicited to attend a party to take place at the residence of Mr. George Clark on Wednesday evening, January 31, 1877, at 7:30 o'clock p.m.

Compliments of Charles Grinnell Jr.

Louisa McElroy Gardner, wife of Stephen St. John Gardner, died Sept 14, 1877, at the age of 43 years and 8 months. Photo: Cynthia Leavenworth Bellinger.

Dear Sister Maria,

Your welcome letter came.

I am glad the things are coming. I suppose they will be here tonight.

What made you so silly as to send that shirt? I would not have told you what she said if I had thought of such a thing. I am so glad you found the picture.

Change with Laura and send me the other one. If you find Tom's Centennial bell, keep it for me. And that white quail off my hat, tell mother not to lose it.

Aunt Maria and Tina were over day before yesterday. Net is making great preparations for her wedding. She sent Addie considerable stitching to do. Ad wishes you had left the hemmers and tuckers for me to use! Isn't she kind? And didn't I wish you had?

I suppose Will is quite elated by the coming of an heir. Does it resemble pa or ma? or have you not (as Ad says to Guss) seen it yet. She always says to him: "Have you not, did you not, etc." and then tells how properly he speaks.

The two are enough to make a dog sick. I told Tom what you said about little Tom. He seemed very much pleased and is quite proud when Aunt Maria's folks praise him so much. Ad and Gus are as jealous as they can be though she tries to hide it. Tell Tom to come again in your next letter and tell Mort to send some word to him. Tom always asks what Mort says about Tommy when I hear from home. I kissed Tommy and told him Maria sent the kiss. He says, "Why sent kiss" and brings me the letter "from Mary" he says.

He gets a basket and says, "I sell tomatoes, I see nuts," and calls Gus to help him. When Gus gets on the bed or where he can't get, he comes to me and pulls me and "Come, Emma help. Guss bed, I can't." And the other day, he took my sacque out of the chair and when I looked at him, he told me, "I throw sacque down for baby," and ran out and put it around his rag baby. He says almost everything.

How is Annie and Kelso? Aunt E. Eldred wrote to me this week and says she hears nothing from home. I won't try to write anymore, I am most tired to death and it is near supper time.

Write me soon.

Good bye, Emma

Dear Lon,

I received mother's letter this morning. Maria says she will answer that and that I owe you a letter.

Mother is afraid to tell father that I want to bring Tommy and I won't come unless he is willing that I should. I have written to him and wish you would see that he gets the letter. I did not send it to mother for fear she would not give it to him.

Tell her Lon, that there is no use talking of my coming without the baby. I'll never see the place again. I will not go and leave him here. There is no one on earth that loves or needs me as my little innocent darling does, and no one on earth that I love or need as I do him. His sweet, baby love has been as heaven to me in many dreary hours. And I would not leave him when he needs me as much as he ever did and would get much less care.

The very thoughts of it would make my anticipated visit home a penance rather than a pleasure and I am sure that if I left him here, all summer, I should never see him again.

The doctor told us to be very

careful about Tommy having any hard crying spell and if he is sick and I am not where they can call me, he would cry for me until he went into fits and they can not do anything with him.

You can tell mother or show the letter if rather. I cannot write to her, but I cannot go and leave him. Tell her my health is good here and I need not come home on that account.

Ever Yours, Emma

It seems Emma did take Tommy home, because in the October 1877 letter, she had taken him back to the city.

September 14, 1877, Louisa McElroy, 43, wife of Stephen St. John Gardner, died, leaving five children, age 16 and under. There is a large stone marker to her memory in the Eldred Cemetery.

Perhaps Stephen's mother, Eliza Eldred Gardner cared for the children—James K., Katie, Myers, Herbert, and Mary L. Gardner.

Mary (Polly) Wells Hickok, wife of Uncle Justus Hickok, died October 18, 1877, and was buried in the Eldred Cemetery.

Tuesday, July 27, 1877?
Dear Ida (Aida),

I have been about sick for the past three or four days, but Tom is out this evening, so I will pass the time in writing.

It seems real lonely here. Gussie is in Yonkers yet, and insists in saying that he is going to stay there all summer "because Tom is." I do not like to have him there much but they insist on having him stay. They seem to think he will not live if we bring him home, and he is perfectly willing to encourage them in the belief.

Tell little Tom that Papa and Mama miss him and want to see him very much, and that we send lots of love and kisses to our little brown-eyed boy. You must send me a letter from him when you write again.

Do write oftener and tell us some news, even if you have to manufacture some.

How is Aunt Mary and our dear gentle Maria, how is she getting along? Give my love to them both, if they will accept it.

Mrs. Paton and Mrs. Clinton [Addie's sisters], were here two days last week. I am invited to Mrs. Paton's tomorrow. Will go if I am well enough.

Will send you three dollars and will send more when I write again.

I am very tired, so with love to yourself and all, and kisses for my dear little boy, I close. Write soon and often.

Yours, Addie

October 1877
Dear Mother,

I am quite well, but Tommy has been pretty cross since the first day. He did not sleep a bit in the car that day and was considerable trouble about sitting still.

Addie and Ida met us at Jersey. He was very pleased to see them and perfectly delighted with the house. He did not seem to miss any of you until the next afternoon and then he cried to go to "the house" and called you and Maria.

I have to take him out and play with him all the time to keep him still.

He calls Mort and then says he is going to the barn to see Fancy. He gets a paper and reads about Dora, but never calls him. And cries so for that Alice Cary book ("Phebe" he calls it) that we don't know what to do. We have given him every book we can and he looks at them, but throws them down and says he wants Phebe.

Tom makes a great fuss over him now and Tommy is crazy to see him nights. Ida said he was very anxious for us to get home and had a package of grapes for Tommy that night.

Gussie ran as usual and grabbed it. Tom was mad at him and told him just to behave himself. They were for the baby.

Gussie is a little decent before Tom now, but more disagreeable and mean as ever. Tom is telling how good Tommy minds him.

Emma

October 26, 1877
Dear Lon,

The things came all right last night. I am ever so happy for the chestnuts. I wanted them so bad that I bought a pint last week.

Did you measure them? I did but not until Ad and Guss had their share. She must go down and open the barrel. She acted as if they were hers, let Gussie take his hands full, and gave Harry a few and told Gussie to wait until tomorrow for more. She was afraid they'd make him sick.

I put them in a pail and took them out to Ida, picked out some large ones for big Tom and told her to put some in her pocket and said I was afraid you would forget to send them though you promised them to me. She said something about her dealing my chestnuts out very freely. I put the rest in my trunk and she won't get another one unless I am less of a pig than I think.

I will try though very soon and write a little more.

Your sister, Emma

Eldred, December 3, 1877
My Darling Baby Girl,

Great-Grandpa William Henry Austin. Courtesy Melva Austin Barney.

Your Mother is 50 years old today. I feel better today than I have felt in a good many years. How I would love to have all my children home to spend the day with me. I wish you would write to me how Edith is. If she is not able to work, she had better come home. If she won't come home to stay all winter, she had better come and stay until she gets better. Maria might keep house for her.

Your Father thinks you will graduate now as soon as Beals' girls will. What would he say if he knew you did not go to school? I hope you will learn all you can.

Uncle C.P., Aunt E, and Kelso family except the two boys, spent Thanksgiving day with us. Kelso stayed in the evening. Emma K. and the children came up in the evening.

There was a surprise party to Aunt E. in the evening, but Lon and Maria preferred to stay home with their company. Collins and Schoonover went to Rowley's. We invited Collins and Mr. Dubois here next Friday. Anne and Mrs. Dubois were here Wednesday.

We will send the barrel tomorrow, Tuesday 4th, directed to the house if they bring it. Don't pay them for it. Tell them you have a carman to bring it. You can pay them for it. They can leave it or take it back. Or she might offer them 25 cents, but don't pay them more.

I will write to Edith Thursday. I was mistaken about $6 it was $4. Write soon and tell how Edith is. I think she had better come home by all means if she is sick.

*Write soon to
Your loving Mother*

The letters indicate that the Austin family had weathered some storms, or perhaps was in the midst of them. There would be much stormy weather ahead for the family and for Henry and Mary Ann's marriage.

Great-Grandpa Henry, who earlier wrote some endearing letters to Lonnie, was described as being a bit gruff with the family.

William Henry was evidently considered a "grouch." You will find this in at least one letter. William H. did, it seems to me, look after his children's interests quite well, above and beyond what would have been considered necessary in Eldred at that time. He saw his daughters educated as far as they chose to go. He sent Grandpa Mort to Centenary College as far as he chose to go and helped finance his first boarding house venture, etc.
—Melva Austin Barney, great-granddaughter.

There is a lost letter which Henry wrote to his wife Mary Ann explaining that because of his work/money situation, they could not afford to spend the winter in New York City, as she was accustomed to do. This was possibly the splitting point between Henry and Mary Ann.

It is said that when Mary Ann started to sell off property (some may have been hers from her father), for money so she could spend time in New York City in the winter like she was used to, it created a rift between husband and wife. Henry said they could make something of the farm, but Mary Ann had sold off some of the property. Of course, we don't know the whole story.

Ell and Lon (and later Mort), apparently tired of working for their dad Henry, set out to work on their own and end up in Kansas in the next chapter.

My great-grandma, Mary Ann Eldred Austin. Photo from Mary Briggs Austin Collection.

Chapter 12
"In Kansas Bright as Fair"
Solomon City, Kansas, 1878

Ellsworth, Kansas
Dear Sister Maria,
I have been very busy and am five miles from the post office in a ranch. There is four of us boys keeping old bachelor hall.

The other day we went to a Crick on horseback and got into a hole. The water came nearly to the horse's neck and I got a little wet. It was rather a cold bath, so I did not ride after a mile and a half to get home, it did not last long.

I will tell you the name of some of the cricks. Ella Cr., Buffalo Cr. Little Wolf, Black Wolf, Sand, Turkey, Hell Cr., Ash Cr., and lots just such names for other cricks.

Write soon to J. E. Austin

Railroad track. Photo: Gary Smith.

James Eldred Austin, the writer of the letter, was called Ell by his siblings and cousins. Ell seems to be the first of Henry and Mary Ann Austin's children to go west.

Why did the Austin boys go west? One reason could be that it was difficult to make a living in Eldred. Several of the letters suggest that finding work elsewhere was often on the minds of my Austin relatives and their friends.

A family story also indicates that Henry's sons decided they'd rather work on their own than for their father, and headed west.

Both Ell, 23, and Lon, 21, were in Kansas sometime in 1878, maybe before. This left Henry, 54, with two sons, Mort, 15, and Ladore, 13, to help with farming. Aida, 17, seems to be in New York City much of the time, as was Emma, 27, and perhaps Maria, 25. Henrietta at 28, was possibly at home with Mary Ann, 51.

Why Kansas, and why Solomon City, 1,343 miles from Eldred, New York? As a result of the railroads built in Kansas, distribution centers grew up to ship goods, providing new job opportunities to work on railroads, ranches, stores, farms, and any job needed in a new town.

Ellsworth, Kansas, mentioned in Uncle Ell's letter, was 53 miles west of Solomon City, Kansas. Eventually Ell worked for a farmer and then married his daughter. Ell's brother Lon, and later Grandpa Mort (in 1881), worked on that farm for Ell. The letters also indicate that the Austin men worked on ranches, and that Uncle Lon at some point went to California.

At first it seems Ell and Lon worked on the railroad. Uncle Ell was listed in the City of Brookville, township of Spring Creek, Saline County, Kansas, in the June 1880 Census. Uncle Ell

Field in Kansas, about 70 miles from Solomon City. Photo: Joanna Smith.

was listed as single, 23 years old, and a brakeman on the railroad. He lived in a Railroad Hotel with about 40 other railroad workers who were engineers, brakemen, conductors, or workers for the hotel—book keepers, clerks, cooks, and dining room helpers. John Taylor was the landlord of the hotel and his wife's name was Jane Taylor.

I am told there was a letter addressed to Lon at the telegraph on the Railroad, though in the 1880 Census, Lon was a laborer living on Poplar Street, with a friend Charles Evenhoe, whose parents were from Germany.

It had been hoped that Solomon City would become a major shipping center for cattle and produce. But the townsfolk objected when the whole street was taken up by cattle during the cattle drive. The focus was then shifted to Abilene, Kansas, ten miles away, though Abilene never grew very large.

103 Christopher St., New York City, January 16, 1878
Alonzo Austin, Solomon City, KS
Dear Brother Lon,
I watched the old year out and the New Year in at John St. Church. We got home about 10 o'clock. We had quite a nice time. The street was awful crowded and so was the cars. Emma has gone to hear Mr. Beecher.
But I must not write too long a letter to you or I will be too tired to write to the little boys.
My love to all,
Ida [Aida] Austin

James Eldred (Ell) Austin.

Abilene, Kansas, January 31, 1878
A.A. Austin, Solomon City, Kansas
Friend Austin,
I expect to come to Solomon on the train in the morning. Am going out west. Would like to have you meet me there as I will not have time to come up to the house. It gets there 7:40 I think.
Yours Truly, L.L. Craine

James Daniel Eldred, a cousin to Ell and Lon, wrote the following letter. James D., son of Charles C.P. and Effa Eldred, and grandson of James Eldred, was married to Frances Payne. It sounds as if there were some family problems with the in-laws.

Rosedale, Kansas, February 27, 1878
Dear Lon,
Yours of the 23rd received. Mr. Mills has gone to New York to work. Got a job there for two months. Geo. Wait thinks of going along. Whether he is going to work with Mills or not my correspondent did not know. They have been having distracted meetings at Barryville with a good number of inquirers. Some enlisted in the ranks.
Will Skinner has come out to Arkansas and Abe Myers little boy was very sick.
Are you working in town now or are you out on the prairie. You hit the nail on the head when you said some of the Wilsons were the prophets that we would all be back in the spring.
Don't you hear from Gus Osier or have you and he cried quits? He promised Hen Payne work when he made hoops, but they fell out and so Hen has gone to fishing.
When I come out here last fall, my mother-in-law did not

like it because I left Frank where I did. So she has never written to me. Neither has Hen, although I wrote to her. But it is a long lane that has no turn in it and everything is lovely long as the goose lays high. But laying all jokes aside, this will be better here than out there.

They are the ones that are making the most talk about me as near as I can find out. Though I don't trouble myself to inquire about it. Don't say anything about some of this.

Yours truly, J.D. Eldred

Barryville, March 7, 1878
Mr. A.A. Austin, Esq.
Friend Lon,

Your kind invitation received for which please accept thanks. I promised some time ago to go to a donation tonight and suppose I will have to go.

I don't think we can get there at Eldreds as early as you say so. I think you had better not wait for us, but go on over and we will come right to the house.

Hope nothing will happen to prevent our coming for I am sure we would enjoy it very much and hope you will all have a good time any way.

Alfred Skinner

Truman Ellis Leavenworth, second child of Sherman S. and Maria, was born June first. Little Anna Mae, Truman's big sister, was 3. Sherman S. and Maria's children will grow up on the Leavenworth Homestead and have the benefit of their grandparents, Sherman B. and Charlotte, nearby.

The Austin cousins added another to their ranks. John Mortimer, son of Mortimer Bruce and Mary L. Austin, was born in 1878. Mortimer Bruce, you may remember, was the son of Augustus and Maria Eldred Austin, and the grandson of Ralph and Fanny Austin.

In Book Two we will read about a link between George W. Eldred's widow Marietta West Eldred and the future wife of John Mortimer. Baby John Mortimer Austin had a brother, Charles Augustus, 6, and a sister Mary Elizabeth, 4.

Solomon City

Solomon City, Kansas, known as Solomon, Kansas, today, is near the very winding Solomon River.

From Solomon City to:
 Abilene, KS—10 miles.
 Carbondale, KS—108 miles.
 Ellsworth, KS—53 miles.
 Kansas City, KS—157 miles.
 Burlingame, KS—120 miles.
 Rosedale, KS—158 miles.
 Council Grove, KS—70 miles.
 Eldred, NY—1343 miles.

New York, September 23, 1878
Dear Ida,

Tell Lon, Tom inquired about the fare to Kansas at Jersey City and several other places and they told him the fare to Kansas City was $32.75, and took seven days.

Emigrant tickets were only about half as much, but it takes about two weeks to go on an Emigrant train.

I do hope Rob Kelso will go with Lon for he has been around more and is used to "roughing it."

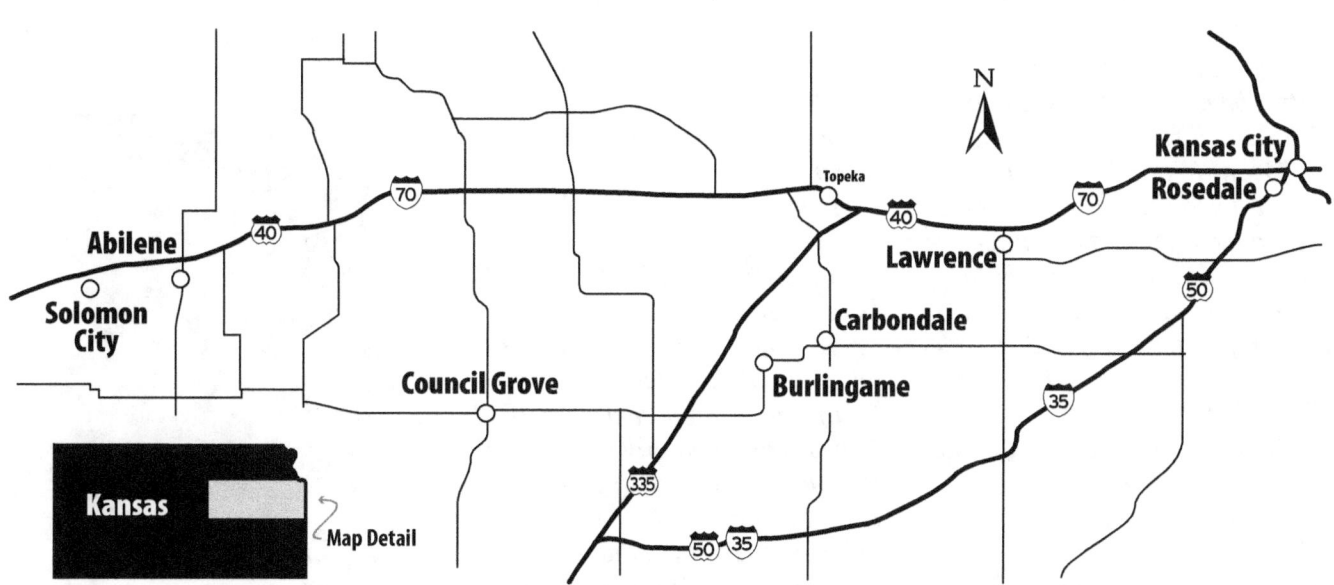

Some of the cities in Kansas mentioned in the letters. Solomon City is on the left.

Photo from Kansas in the Austin Collection of Mary Briggs Austin.

I am looking for Lon down today. Hope he will come and stay this week with us.

The weather was very warm here Friday and Saturday, but is cooler now, looks like rain. I have got the parlor and my bedroom carpet down, have made apple jelly, and am making some tomato catsup today.

Tell Emma I am drying some butter beans for her if she comes, if not, I will send them to her.

I want to get the rest of the carpet down this week if possible. It is so old and needs so much mending, it is really only fit for the ragbag. I shall have a fearful washing and ironing to do beside. Wish you were here to help me, don't you!

How are the little tots getting along? I miss them more than I did at first. Give them lots of love from mama and papa and keep them dressed in their winter dresses if it is as cold there mornings as here, they will need them.

I have forgotten whether I paid Gussie's board up to last Thursday or till this Thursday now coming. Please let me know when you write and also how I paid Emma's. I will write to Em as soon as I can.

If you get to Barryville, I wish you would get my white skirt I left there and my comb I left in "mudders" room. Will send you money to come when I write again.

Love, Addie

Cuba, New York, August 1878

Dear Friend,

Your kind and ever welcome letter was duly received on Saturday last and I was very glad to hear from you and as you said that you would like to come out here, I think it is the best thing you can do to stay where you are although it is none of my business, but it is very hard times. You know that I would like to see you, but as work is scarce and wages low, I do not want to encourage you to leave a good home to go out in the world to seek your fortune as I have done, because it is hard to find it.

If I had news that you wanted to come a month ago, I could a found you a job, but now haying and harvesting is over and jobs are scarce again. Eddie, tell him I want to hear from him soon. Give my regards to Ida and Ria.

Well Lon, it is late I must bring my letter to a close, but by the way are we square on the watch trade? I have forgotten whether we are or not.

Rite soon, if not sooner from your sincere friend, L.L. Myers

Our friend Reverend Felix Kyte, who we met back in 1832, and who performed the wedding ceremonies for both my Austin and Leavenworth great-grandparents, died suddenly Sunday, September 29, 1878, when he was leaving the Congregational Church of Lumberland, where he had preached 46 years. Felix was 72.

Memorial stone to Felix Kyte, in Eldred Cemetery. Felix, born in Lydd, England, Jan. 20, 1800, died in Highland, N.Y., Sept. 29, 1878. Photo: Cynthia Leavenworth Bellinger.

The text taken at his funeral service was Revelation 14:13, "And I heard a voice from heaven saying unto me, Write, Blessed are the dead which die in the Lord from henceforth: Yea, saith the Spirit, that they may rest from their labours; and their works do follow them."—E.J. Kyte.

Eldred, New York, October 16, 1878
Friend Alonzo,

I am well I guess. The girls all went to the city on Monday.

I hope that you are getting along good and will like it out there. I think that I surely will be in that state before six months if nothing happens. Please tell me more particulars the next time and how Eldred your brother is.

Henry Payne and I have dissolved friends. His wife went off and left him about two weeks ago and he had a fight with Mr. Lily and was a going to kill himself, but she came back the second night I guess. There was a dance over to Runselses and she fetched up there. If you write to Jim or anyone else, don't say anything about it or they may find out who told it.

You asked me if anyone said any thing about you and in answer to that, I would say nothing, only that Eddie Kelso asked me if I had heard from you and how you liked it out there, and I saw it in the papers about your going to the west and about Robbie's going. He went one week after you did.

Wells Hickok came home last week and is going back this week again. So good bye from your affectionate friend,
Augustus Osier

Felix Kyte 1805–1878

Felix Kyte, who had first arrived in Lumberland in 1832, resigned as pastor of the Congregational Churches of Highland in 1878. But the church voted to change his position from acting pastor to Senior Pastor during his natural life, July 3, 1878.

Almost three months later, on Sunday, September 29, Felix went with his son, Rev. Joseph Kyte, to Barryville in the morning. He also attended the evening services at Eldred. Felix took part in the services, but his son did the preaching. Felix died after the services.

During the 46 years of his ministry, 244 persons were received to the Eldred church, and 70 at the Barryville church. Mr. Kyte married 253 couples, including both my Austin and my Leavenworth great-grandparents.

Felix preached in "*log houses, lit only by the blazing of pine logs, heaped one on another, until the large fireplace was completely filled with blazing material, sending its rays all over the room and causing those in attendance to defend their faces from the heat by their handkerchiefs and hands.*"

In one instance, Felix started the meeting in darkness when only a single candle was used.

"*In times past, we sometimes preached in barns, and meetings were held in sawmills, and seats of the rudest benches that could be made, or perhaps nothing but slabs laid upon*

Felix Kyte. Courtesy Chuck Myers.

each other. Yet, even in such cases the Word of God was listened to with relish and delight.

"But now we have comfortable, and often ornamental seats—whether we hear with the same relish as formerly, I will not undertake to say."

Felix preached the Word in three adjoining towns mainly on horseback. He estimated he had "*ridden 30,000 miles or more—enough to ride once and a quarter around the world.*"

Mr. Kyte and his wife Eliza Creiger Kyte raised nine children, one of whom became a minister.—*from the Kyte Narrative by Felix Kyte, 1875.*

Eldred, New York, Tuesday, October 1878
My Dear Son,

I received your kind and welcome letter yesterday. Your letter relieved my mind some, yet I can not help but worry for fear you will get sick.

I have many of you to think about; only three of you at home and none of you very healthy or strong, and poor Em sick, fretting and worrying herself to death for something to eat and wear and Aida, my youngest girl, has to be turned off to fend for herself. Not to be able to help them at home seems hard. It makes me more opposed to marrying.

I hope none of my children will ever marry in poverty and have a big family of children to be scattered all over the earth. If I was rich and could have all my children with me and make home pleasant for them, then I would be happy.

I daresay poor Eldred has seen some hard times since he left home. You both had it hard enough at home. I hope you will never have it any harder, but better, for it was hard enough here.

Mort says tell Lon he wishes he was in his place (I can't convince him he is better off here) for it is the same old thing over, just as it was when you was home. Lew Dunlap and Lewis Carmichael worked here yesterday.

Dunlap is here today and your father most days is as cross as ever. He wrote to you two Sundays ago.

I had a letter from Aida saying they reached there safe and all well. Your Father got a letter from you last week.

I thought I would answer it myself if he did not a Sunday. But Collins and Kelso were in here after church and so I did not get time.

Tommy took Em Kelso to the Cars the same day the girls went. She went alone, for the girls went on the early train.

I have left the bad news until the last. The storekeeper Myers' mother, Mrs. Myers [Phebe Hazen Myers], was buried a Saturday. She died Thursday afternoon.

I suppose you have heard of Mr. Kyte's death as he died before Emma wrote you. There was over 400 to the funeral.

Now comes news you will little expect to hear.

The beautiful ornament that adorned our village is in ashes. Mr. Kelso's mansion was burnt Thursday night between 7 and 8 o'clock. The whole village was splendidly illuminated. There were no lights in the church that night.

They worked hard to save the barn, but fortunately the wind blew between that and DeSilvas or they could not have saved it. All the neighbors were there soon. Mr. and Mrs. K. said they never saw men work so hard before. Myers threw off his hat and coat.

I heard Mrs. K. ask Kelso if he found Myers' hat. He said yes.

The fire broke out on the pasture side first. It was not long burning down. They stayed all night.

C.C.P. Eldred went Friday night to Mrs. Wells'. Your Father invited them up, but it rained hard Friday and Saturday forenoon after the funeral. Mr. Collins took them home with him. They stayed there until Monday morning. They stayed last night but went early this morning. The children enjoyed themselves last night.

If they don't get the house ready today, I expect them here tonight again. Mrs. Kelso sends her kind regards to you. She says she finds kind people here as well as you do in the west. She is not a stranger here as you are there. They have not heard from Rob yet and are very much worried about him. I wonder if Aida has heard from him yet. He was here to see her Sunday night before he went on Monday morning for the west.

I don't think your father is any nearer settling than ever he was. No one has come yet to look at the place. I think you write somewhat discouraging if the wind blows any harder there than here. I don't care much to go there unless all my children go there and settle.

I wrote to Eldred three weeks ago and have not heard from him since. I am afraid he will come in contact with the Indians if he is near Ellis City.

My Dear Son, I hope you will be a good man and not get in any bad habits. Seek strength and comfort from your Saviour and all will be well.

I was in hope you and Ell would be near each other and think as much of each other as when you were children.

You are all dear to me. Write soon to your loving Mother

Burlingame, Kansas, October 25, 1878

Aida Austin,
Christopher St., New York
Dear friend,

Having arrived in the wonderful Kansas that we have heard so much about, I thought I would try and write you a few lines and try and give you a little description of the country, but I have not been around hardly any yet. I have been laid up with a bad cold and a stiff neck. I think I caught cold on the cars. I think I will like it here after a while.

This is quite a busy little town and most all the people are eastern folks. Its population is about fifteen hundred. There are three churches and other public buildings.

The country around here is very different to what I expected to find it. I thought it was a level prairie, but I find the country is quite rolling and looks very good. There are some disadvantages here—they have very heavy winds and the water is hard water and has a bad taste.

I have not been up to see your brother yet, but I expect to go before long. They are about 150 miles beyond here. I should have gone before this, not being well, I did not go.

I have a very good job of work here whenever I get well enough to go at it. I will have all I can do all this winter. I suppose you are enjoying the delightful society of New York City. I must say I would rather be there than here. I must own that I feel a little homesick, but I guess I will get over that when I get to work.

I cannot help thinking of the very pleasant evenings we have spent at your house and I hope they are not the last that I will spend there. I have been nearly two weeks and I have not heard one word from home. I had a very pleasant trip out here. I made the acquaintance of two young men going to Texas and we had a very good time.

I suppose this letter will not interest you at all, but you must excuse me this time as I am not well and it is my first.

Aida, I should be very pleased to have one more game of dominoes.

Yours very respectfully,
Robt. S. Kelso

No. 3 Christopher St., New York City, November 1, 1878

My dear brother Lon,

I am getting very anxious to hear from you and to know how you are getting along. Robbie [Kelso] writes to Ida that he has been sick ever since he got there.

I do hope you have been well. Do you think you will take a place by Spring? If you think it better not to do, don't do it on my account. I am in a hurry to come, but I can wait if you are not ready.

I am saving all I can, and will have a letter for you. I guess Aida thinks she will not come unless we promise to send her back if she gets homesick. Have you felt anything of his kind?

You have probably heard of Mr. Kyte's death. Perhaps I told you about it in my last letter. He dropped dead in the churchyard the week before I came back.

Mr. Myers' mother died since and Mr. Kelso's house has been burned. They stayed at Aunt Effa's one night and at Mrs. Wells, Collins, and our house. They have moved into the Piddington House now.

Have you seen Robbie yet? I wish you would write me oftener.

I am keeping the house again but shall not stay longer than I can help. Harry is away. They wished to make a reduction of $2, but finally concluded to pay $13 and a reduction of $1 for coal. Maria is here.

Tell Ell to write and please write yourself as soon as you can to.

Your loving sister, Emma

Eldred, New York, November 10, 1878

Albert Austin,
Solomon City, Kansas
Dear Cousin Lon,

I think that about two weeks more will see me on the road for Kansas City. Will stop there somewhere and look around before going farther and when I stop long enough to write or jot an answer from you will let you know where I am to be found.

We had a red hot time Election day. Three different parties in the field and the Greenbackers made a big fight in our town, as the candidates for county judge and assembly on the Democratic ticket had only one majority a piece in our town, while Beebe for congress had four majority. But we elected a Republican congressman in our district.

Frank Gardner is in Virginia and likes it very well but told me before he went, to look to see him in Kansas in the spring.

Trees near Council Grove, Kansas. Photo: Joanna Smith.

I will leave Frank behind as I can't sell my place and expect to work wherever I can do the best till something turns up, but am coming in about two weeks as that will be as soon as I can get away.

Have you heard from any of the rest of the boys that are out there? I got a letter from Jim Young. He is in Albany working for an Express Co. He says he has got the best job he ever had and wants to know how everybody is and all their folks.

There has been some snow here this last week with pretty cold weather. It caught me with my turnips in the ground, but I dug them out and put them in the cellar yesterday. I heard of a man digging potatoes yesterday, but did not see him. He had damn cold fingers unless he worked with gloves on.

Council Grove Lake, Council Grove, Kansas, about 70 miles from Solomon City. Photo: Joanna Smith.

Hoping to see or hear from you soon, Yours Truly,
Jim D Eldred

Eldred, November 17, 1878
Friend Alonzo,
Have been so busy. I am well and all the rest of the folks around here and hope these few lines will find you the same.

I gave the letter to Jim and he expects to come a week from tomorrow. Today is Sunday. He has moved his wife over to Rundles' to stay there for awhile. I would like to tell you more about it but you can guess more about it. But when Jim comes out there don't say that I ever wrote anything about it.

I suppose you have heard that Mr. Kelso's house burnt down a short time ago and they are living in the Piddington House now.

It was a hard thing for them, but most all the things were saved. I was the first one in the house when it caught on fire and helped take the organ and lots of things and got a gold watch chain from upstairs after the fire had got a good start.

Mrs. Kelso and I went in the back room and got the chain when the fire was falling down in the hall and it is supposed that Emmie's watch was burned up.

It is rather lonesome here now, but we will soon have some fun now as it is time now to have donors and donations. Do they have any dances out there?

I think that if nothing happens, I will come out there at the first of March. Do you see or have many girls to dash around with out there or is there not money out there.

I have got one picked out from here. Maybe I will bring her along with me and if you have got a good one picked out for me I will trade with you if don't get spliced before I get out there.

I saw your father and mother a few days ago and your mother was fretting about you and Eldred since he went to his claim. Tell me how Ell is getting along?

From your true and ever faithful friend, Augustus Osier

The townsfolk that we met at the beginning of this book, were now quite elderly. Felix Kyte's death has been mentioned, but there are four other people who have been a part of this story, that died in 1878—Wilmot and Mary

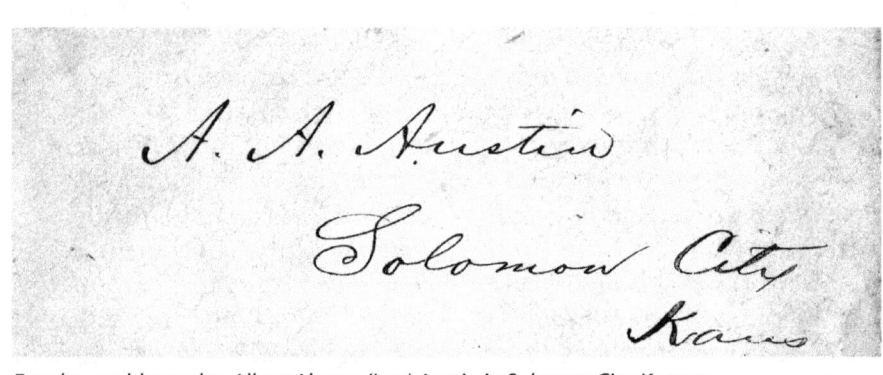
Envelope addressed to Albert Alonzo (Lon) Austin in Solomon City, Kansas.

Clark, Phebe Myers, and Justus Hickok.

Wilmot Clark died in March at the age of 81. Six months later his wife, Mary E. Van Auken, died at the age of 63. At least two of Wilmot and Mary's ten children have been a part of this story—Irvin Clark who married Laura Austin, and George Clark who married Harriet Covert.

George and Harriet Clark would be grandparents to Ella Sergeant, who would be the wife of Garfield Leavenworth, at the turn of the 20th century.

The death of Phebe Hazen Clark Myers in October 1878, was mentioned in two of the letters in this chapter. Moses Myers, Phebe's second husband, had died five years earlier.

Phebe Hazen Clark Myers, mother of half brothers, George Case Clark (the other Clark family) and Abel Sprague Myers, was buried in the Eldred Cemetery. Her Memorial reads, *Blessed are the dead which die in the Lord.*

Uncle Justus Hickok, had not been well at least since 1875. Justus Hickok, brother to Hannah Hickok Eldred, was an uncle to Mary Ann Austin, and a great-uncle to her children. Justus was a great-uncle by marriage to the Austin city cousins.

On November 15, 1878, at the age of 86, Uncle Justus died. His wife, Polly Wells Hickok, had died the year before.

You may remember that Uncle Justus and Aunt Polly's son, Benjamin Merwin (Merwin B. on the gravestone), had died in the Civil War in Rolla, Missouri, and was buried in the old Eldred Cemetery. Merwin's name was also inscribed on the gravestone of his parents, Justus and Mary Wells Hickok.

November 29, 1878
Albert A. Austin,
Solomon City, Kansas
My dear brother Lon,
Kelso has received $1600 insurance on his house. Uncle Justus is dead and Jennie Waite and Miss Kerr have been very sick.
Nettie and Ida were here visiting last week and Aida is returning the visit. We were all at Barnum's Thanksgiving.
Lovingly yours, Em

Eldred, before May of 1879
My Dear Son Lon,
I received a letter from you and Eldred sometime ago and it is not forgetfulness or willful neglect that I have not written before.
I took my box of paper and seated myself to write. Someone came in, so I took off my glasses, laid them in the box, and put it away. Am searching every crevice through and through to find my glasses today. I took down the box to show Em Kelso when lo and behold, there was the long looked for glasses.
I could not answer about Edith's health until I see her. She is much better than what I expected from what they wrote me. So I think she will soon be able to stand the journey well. I suppose she will write particulars.
Your Father wants to sell very much. I don't know if what he will give it away. He is reading Kansas papers which don't make him any more contented to stay here.
Dora is writing to Maria and Mort is upstairs talking Em to death or to sleep. Henrietta and Ella Hickok is to bed.
Write soon to your loving Mother

Memorial stone for Mrs. Phebe Hazen Clark Myers, and her husband, Moses Myers. Photo: Cynthia Leavenworth Bellinger.

Grave marker for Wilmot and Mary Clark. Photo: Cynthia Leavenworth Bellinger.

Gravestone in Eldred Cemetery for Uncle Justus and Aunt Mary Hickok, and son, Merwin, who died in the Civil War. Photo: Cynthia Leavenworth Bellinger.

Mrs. Prindle's Soliloquy

This poem was among the Austin letters of Melva Austin Barney. Pehaps Emma Austin was the author.

It kind-o-seems to me tonight
While darning these stocking by candlelight
That I ain't quite the woman I used to be,
Since I let old Prindle marry me,
Because I was so much afraid
Of living, and dying an old, old maid.

I always used to dress so neat;
My hair was smooth, my temper sweet,
I have learned to be cold, seldom brush my hair,
And don't care a pin about what I wear.
And wonder that ever I was afraid
Of living, or dying an old, old maid.

How loudly that Prindle to snore contrives
Was man ever before so great alive?
It really, sometimes appears to me
He means to be hateful as he can be.
But then, I no longer need be afraid
Of living, or dying an old, old maid.

He smokes and chews and has many a trick
Disgusting enough to make one sick.
And it used to me, and among the rest,
He dotes on onions, which I detest.
But perhaps, that's better than being afraid
Of living or dying an old, old maid.

And then the young one, such graceless imps,
Tom squints, Jack stutters, and Enoch limps.
On two club feet, they fight and swear
Throw dirt, tell lies, and their trousers tear.
Oh no! I shall never more be afraid
Of living, or dying an old, old maid.

Perhaps if I'd married some other man
My life in a different course had ran
But what could I do when my other beaux
All wailed and wailed and didn't propose.
And I was getting so much afraid
Of living and dying and old, old maid.

Sister Sally is forty-five,
And just the happiest soul alive
With no stupid husband to annoy and perplex,
Or quarrelsome children to harass and vex
But Sally was never one bit afraid
Of living, or dying an old, old maid.

How she kids me! But it makes me mad,
For well I remember how grieved and sad
She was when she told me that all my life
I'd repent if I did become Prindle's wife
And I told her I was more afraid
Of living like her, an old, old maid.

Chapter 13
"The Journey's Length"
1879–1880

Dried roses.

Who Keeps dead flowers? Ah who could cast aside
Unheeded and uncared for all the flowers,
Which once have budded, bloomed and died
Along this troubled path or ours?

Though others brighter take their place today
And o'er our path the perfumed radiance cast,
We love them, but we cold not fling away
The dear—the dead flowers of the past.

And which in this eventful life we turn
To friends untried—to senses all new,
Our hearts will oft with eager fondness yearn
For friends beloved, Long-tried, and true.

Who keeps dead flowers? Throughout this life
We all have plucked sweet flowers of joy and light,
It may have been from scenes all thorns and strife,
It may have been from gardens fair and bright,

And these though withered, faded, dead,
Their freshness and their beauty lost,
Their brightness and their life forever fled,
Are loved the best—are cherished most.
—"Who Keeps Dead Flowers"
by Edith E. Austin

Edith Emogene Austin, author of the above poem, was the daughter of Henry and Mary Ann Austin. Emma, as she was often called, loved to read, had been to college, had taught school, and had written poetry, some of which had been published.

Great Aunt Emma, had cared for and become very attached to little Tommy Thompson, the son of her cousin Addie Austin Thompson. In this chapter, Tommy Thompson seems to be back under the care of his mother, but under protest from Emma. The letters indicate that Tommy was sometimes cared for by Aida, and at times stayed with Henry and Mary Ann Austin in Eldred.

In January 1879, Emma, 27, lived in New York City. She had contracted tuberculosis, and was preparing to go to Solomon City, Kansas, to live with her brothers, Ell and Lon Austin. It was hoped that the drier climate in Kansas would provide a cure.

At first, Emma, planned on taking her sister Aida, 18, and

Little girl by bridge, possibly in Barryville. From photos by Aida Austin.

Possibly Edith Emogene "Emma" Austin. Melva Austin Barney Collection.

her brother, Henry Ladore (12 in January 1879), out west with her. Lon was to arrange for a house for them to live in.

New York City, Jan. 7, 1879
Dear Lonnie,
I am still very well, but can not stand it to walk much. I am glad you are doing so well and hope you continue to like it.

Don't take land sooner than you wish to on my account. I am very anxious to be with you, but take all the time you need. I have nearly $30.00 for you. And I am saving that towards a team. Then I shall save my fare and Aida's and spend what I have left for the house and for our clothes. I shall have all the money we need, that is Ida and I.

I will send somethings if you send for what you intended to do.

You must let me know all that you are doing and if you get homesick or not. Do not be afraid of discouraging me. I have more courage and will than you know Lon.

It seems to me sometimes that I could do, Providence willing, almost anything that I wished for you or Aida or my baby boy and it is for him I shall work and save now. I believe he is mine, Lon, more mine then hers, his mothers.

God gave him to me when his own mother turned from him with words and looks of dislike and scorn.

I have burned my hand so badly that it hurts me to write so you will excuse a short letter this time. E.K. [Emma Kelso] is in Poughkeepsie. Their house has been burned lately I believe. I wrote to you about it. Maria is here with Mortie.

You must write me what to send or bring and tell me

everything you can think of—how much you carried, if you can get clothes without trouble, etc. I will bring you six shirts, two white boughten ones, and four calico unless you prefer all white.

Uncle Justus is dead.

The "M. J. Juice" was published and has been creating quite a sensation.

Yours ever, Emma

Before June 1879
Dear Lonnie,

I should have answered your last letter long ago, only I have had so much to do and felt so bad most of the time, that I hated to spend my time writing an epistle that you might never see.

I had hoped to have seen you before this. You can never know how much I would have given many times of late to have been with you—even for an hour. It has seemed to me sometimes that I should never see you and at such times this yearning for you and Dora has been extremely intense and painful.

I am feeling very much better now than for some weeks past and consequently, more hope of seeing you, and I pray, that it will be soon.

Write me soon. I am too tired to write anymore my dear dearest brother.

Yours ever, Emma

Eldred, February 5, 1879
To Solomon City, Kansas
My dear, dear brother Lon,

Thanks for the good long letter which in spite of the floods reached me last evening. We have had no mail until last evening since the bridge was out. Port Jervis went out and then I came through. Mr. Thomas brought it to Barryville from Port.

Do not know when we will get any more and appreciated this accordingly. So appreciate our advantages for mail communication when we see how much worse they might be than they are.

So you like Mr. Varley. I have read his sermons in the "Witness" and must say they come far short of Henry Ward Beecher's in my estimation. I do not mean in earnestness or sentiment, but in eloquence and beauty. Perhaps I would think differently could I hear him for myself. He certainly must possess some power to attract the audiences which he does, and I should like very much to see the man.

Emma

Rosedale, Kansas, February 9, 1879
Dear Friend Lon,

In your last letter you wished me to find out what you could get black tin in Kansas City for.

And as Mr. Millspaugh was going in the day after I received your request he said he would find out, but the only place he could find the material was in a plumber shop and wanted 50 dollars per pound, so he did not get any.

What were you going to do with it? Make a solder? If that is what you wanted of it, you can get that in town for about 12-1/2 to 15 cents per pound.

Do you think of taking up land this spring or not? Will Sam go to farming on his own ranch or will he work for someone else?

What fare can I get out where you are? Have they commenced to work the land out there yet this spring? I have not written to anyone out in Highland, but my own folks since I came out.

Good bye and write soon,
Jim Eldred

Kansas City, Kansas, February 14, 1879
Postcard to Solomon, Kansas
Lon,

I mailed to you today 2 lb. 5 oz. black tin. Had to hunt a good while before finding it. Some half dozen or more places. It was not to be had where it was. Inquired for the first time you wrote about and guess they don't keep much of it in this little village.

Jim D. Eldred

Henry Ward Beecher

Henry Ward Beecher and his sister, Harriet Beecher Stowe. Courtesy of Melva Austin Barney.

In the Austin collection is this newspaper photo of Henry Ward Beecher, the famous preacher that Emma Austin liked.

Henry Ward's sister, Harriet Beecher Stowe, was famous for her novel, *Uncle Tom's Cabin*.

Lilacs. "Spring is here at last." Emma, May 1, 1898. Photo: Cynthia Leavenworth Bellinger.

Rosedale, Kansas, Sunday, February 16, 1879
Dear Lon,

If I had only come right on out there when I first came here it would have been better for me than to have stopped here and try Kansas City. I spent all I brought with me about trying to get something to do and the prospect is that I will get nothing in much less than a month and working for your board is pretty light wages and that is what I am doing.

I would not write back home for money under any circumstances for there is some of the folks out there think that all of us are coming back this spring, but not any on my plate if I work for my board 2 months longer.

If you had any money to spare and could let me have enough to come where you are if Sam goes away, I would put in with you and keep up the ranch like you and him have been running it, if I could get anything to do and that would be better than I am doing now, if I only earned enough to keep me in tobacco above running expenses for the table.

Leo Wait is home. I suppose that your folks keep you pretty well posted as to what is going on. I would like to be back there long enough to give some of them H—L, and that is all I care about. It would not take me long and then good bye forever to that place.

If you can spare a V send it, if there would be any prospect of me getting anything to do so that I could pay you back with interest.

Write soon from a true friend,
J.D. Eldred

Eldred, February 23, 1879
Dear Son Lon,

We are all well here, but myself. I have been quite sick with a bad cold for the last week, but I feel some better tonight. I hope these lines will find you well.

Well I suppose you are a farming out there now, but it looks as though winter had just begun here. It has snowed here for the last week most of the time.

Kelso has got his new store opened and he feels pretty big now. I have done some teaming for him and sold him some corn and buckwheat and he tried to lie me out of five bags. I asked him to settle with me and he refused to deal, so I told him that I should not come there again to settle and then I asked Eddy if he was ready to settle with me, but his father would not let him, so I told them that we would let the law settle it and walked out.

But I did not get far before Eddy came out and called to me. He said his father had not used me right and if I would wait two weeks, he would pay me and I agreed to wait.

What I let them have, I charged to the farm which is E.E. Kelso and Co. I suppose Kelso thought I had charged it all to him. They owe me near $3,00 [possibly $300], and I will wait two weeks and if they don't pay me, then I shall try and get it.

Kelso tells me Rob doesn't like it in Kansas, but I don't know whether it is so or not, for he cares the least for his word of any man that I ever dealt with.

We have been looking for Edith to come home for the last three weeks, but she has not come yet.

Charles Metcalf sent me a postcard for me to send him your address. I will write to him tomorrow. I guess if he thinks that there is any chance in Kansas to do better, he would come out there.

I have been trying hard to sell, but have not succeeded as yet, but I shall keep trying. I am tired a farming here. Henry Lilly is trying hard to sell. He has offered everything for $1300.

I would like to see you very much, but as I cannot, I hope you will write often with my best wishes.

I will close, from your loving Father, Wm. H. Austin
(See p. 251 for two pages of Henry's letter to his son.)

Rosedale, Kansas, March 12, 1879
Dear Cousin,

I have work here this afternoon so will not come out that way at $14 a month and if you would came here, I can get you in on the same place where I am. Please see if there is any letters for me at Solomon. I expect one there this week.

J.D. Eldred

Thursday, March 27, 1879
Dear brother Lon,

I came home last Saturday being unable to stay there any longer. My health was getting miserable and DeVenoge had gone to France without sending my medicine. Mary told Aunt Effa he left it for me and they neglected to send it. I have a little I am taking and my health is better, but I must wait for more medicine.

O Lon if you could know how lonely I am shut up here away from my little one, the only gleam of sunshine my life has seen for the past three years. The little one from whom his own mother (unworthy the name) had turned in hate.

She called me heartless because I shed no tears in parting with them. I found none for the priceless treasure, I was leaving with her. It seemed as if my soul and heart has grown numb with dread agony of this hour and that when the hour came, I felt nothing neither sorrow in leaving forever the sweetest joy of all my life, nor of pleasure in meeting loved ones at home.

I found a heavy covering of snow still upon the ground and it has been stormy and disagreeable ever since I came.

Father is engaged in a law suit with Kelso. I do not know how it will end, but I know that I have been fool enough to lend father money to carry it on and I'm afraid I'll never get it back. I would not have given it to him for anything else, but I hated to see such a rascal cheat an honest man.

If Father sends to you for money, don't send one cent unless I say so Lon. I believe he would take everything from you and pay you by talking about you. I feel sorry for him, but I told mother if he expected us to take care of him, he might better come and live with us than to keep the place for us to support, too. For it won't even pay its taxes.

If you are willing, I will take Dora and teach him until I think he is capable of some situation and get him something to do and if Father can't support Henrietta and mother with Mort's help, it is very strange. What do you think about it?

I will put Dora through as fast as I can and he learns easily. He will not be much trouble or expense to us and Father wants him to go. Maria says she will buy all his clothes.

I wish you would answer right away. I want to go as soon as I am able to get around and find out about the tickets. We are all quite well. Write soon and believe me now and ever,

Your loving sister, Emma

Eldred, New York, 1879
Dear Little Tom,

Emma writes to send you love and kisses.

Mort has two little bossies and his colt yet. Fanny [their horse] took Emma to see Aunt Effa the other day. Mary has six big cats and Henry a big muskrat down cellar. It dams up the spring and eats up the potatoes and bites poor Rover and we can not catch him.

The "Old Min Hammond cat" comes every day and knocks for Mary on the window and when Mary goes to let her in, she turns and cuff away all the cats that have followed her because she knows Mary won't have them and then walks in herself.

Tell Mama Mrs. West will make me one gallon of maple syrup for $1. I will pay her and Addie can give it to Ida for my medicine, or she can send it to her. Shall Mrs. West save the molasses?

Deserted house 70 miles from Solomon, Kansas, 2009. Photo: Joanna Smith.

Tree in Kansas. Photo: Joanna Smith.

Church News

1879 New Members in the Congregational Church
Augustus Ozier.
William and Mary Payne.
Clara Clark (Sergeant).
Margaret Ann Gillespie.
Agnes Gillespie (Wilson).
12 new, 431 total.

Robbie was over to see Emma and says he wants to see Tommy.

So does Emma want to see her dear little birdie. God bless my treasure forever,
Emma

Brooklyn, New York, March 30, 31, 1879
Alonzo Austin,
Solomon City, Kansas
Friend Alonso,

You will doubtless be surprised in the receipt of this note. But since you have started for the "land of the West" I have often thought I would like to have a line from you to know how your projects were and get an idea from one who is in the place as to what mine might be if I were there too.

What chance do you think a carpenter would have in your party? What other way would a man like me have of making a livelihood?

Are the people disposed to be friendly with strangers and is government land easily obtained?

I am heartily sick and tired of dragging along in these parts and if an opportunity to do better seems probable, I think I would like to change.

I have not heard from your father in sometime. His last contained your address which I now take the liberty to use.

I hope this may find you doing well, and in excellent health. I wish your father was going out there now. I think I would try and go with him.

Ever yours,
Charles W. Metcalf

Eldred, New York, Mar./Apr. 26, 1879
My dear Lon,

I received your kind letter and was more than glad to hear from you. I know you can not help but be lonesome if you are not homesick and I think of you so often.

How I would like to see you instead of writing for I can't write all that I want to tell you.

Gus Osier works at Proctors, 12 shillings a day. I wish you had his place. He tells yet of going west.

Henry Lilly is perfectly delighted with his place. He is going to see if he can find a place that we can trade ours for. I have not said anything to him yet about your taking the place, but if he can't sell he will be very glad to get the place. Mort says he talked about getting rid of it at some date.

I had a letter from Aida wanting to come home, but your Father said he would not board Tommy less than 1-1/2 weeks, so I don't know if she will come home or not. She will hate to leave Tommy. I don't suppose Ad will give more than one dollar which I feel sorry for Aida.

I do hope if we can not sell, you will take the place. There is enough work to keep you all busy by subdividing the land that is cleared.

I went to Church forenoon and afternoon yesterday. I like the minister very much.

We had a very hard shower in the afternoon. It blew down some of Uncle C. P. Eldred's door yard fence and one of his apple trees and one of ours. Some were afraid of a cyclone.

We have had very warm weather but it is cold enough now. I think I prefer the warm breezes there to the cold wind here. Things are more forwarded here than I expected.

Your Father has been through some of his own land twice. I am afraid some of the clearings will grow up again if you boys do not come home. I hope you will make enough to get home this fall.

I suppose you will hear through the paper how the place is improving. They are putting a bell on the Congregational Church which is to ring by the fourth of July.

The Methodists are putting in a new roof and a social to raise money for a lamp and carpet. They have dissatisfaction with what has been raised. They say Tom let it all go into Kelso's hands. They raised a hundred dollars, painted the church, but they can not account for all the money, and they think Kelso used it in the store. I tell you, Tom has to take it for standing up for Kelso.

Your loving Mother

Eldred, New York, 1879
Dear Aida,

Your card and letter received Monday. Father happens to be in Monticello attending court this week.

I was so glad of the tomatoes and lemons for I have such a cough and only lemons seem to do me any good. I got well through riding out a short time ago and I began to think my cold was really something pretty serious for a while, but I think I am better. I shall start west next Wednesday. Lon has written two or three times for me.

What made her send such a box? I thought it would be a few tomatoes and radishes and sent Mort over for it. He managed to get the box over though. Thank Addie for me.

I can't write now, but will write all my long letters after I get to Kansas. Tell her I paid Mrs. West that dollar for the molasses.

Henry Austin's Ledger, 1879

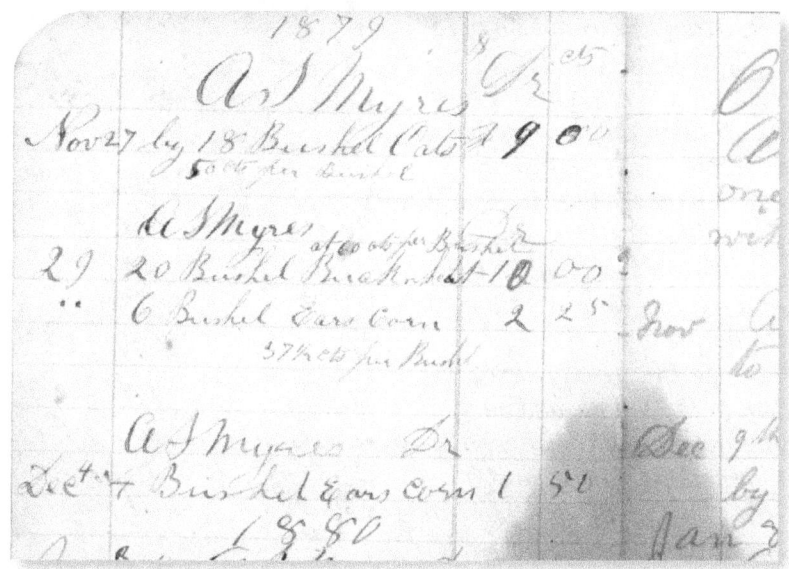

November and December 1879 in Henry Austin's ledger. Courtesy of Mary Briggs Austin.

Henry Austin kept a ledger. The page above shows what Henry sold to Abel Sprague Myers in November and December 1879. What follows are some other entries in Great-Grandfather Henry's ledger.

1878, A.S. Myers
January: 700 hoops, $4.00
June 25: cash, $10.00
Nov. 6: 20 bushel ears corn at 37.5 cents per bushel=7.50

1879, A.S. Myers
Feb. 18: 6 doz. eggs, 1.25
Mar. 29: 11.55 pd. by check
May 26: 12 pounds of rugs
Oct. 13: 30.00, paid by cash
Oct. 23: two dozen eggs, .37
Oct. 24: 25 bushel ears corn, 9.38
Oct. 29: 30 bushel buckwheat, 15.00
Nov. 27: 18 bushel oats, $9.00 (50 cents/bushel)
Nov. 29: 20 bushel buckwheat,10.00 6 bushel ears corn, 2.25 (37.5 cents/bushel)
Dec 4: bushel ears corn, 1.50

So you are coming and little Tom with you. If I had known it when Lon began to build, I should have stayed till fall, but it is better as it is I suppose.

Mrs. Collins is going to spend the day with us and has come already, so I must stop writing.

Write so I can get a letter Tuesday. Tell me what to do with the molasses. Tell Maria to keep her dollar.

Your sister, Emma

Postcard, May 1, 1879
Dear Brother Lon,

I can not start the fifth of May as I wrote you. They have not sent my box from N.Y., and I haven't my medicine yet. I am very sorry. Shall probably start the next Monday, but do not know as you had better write me if it is at all inconvenient. I guess I could find you. Spring is here at last.

Yours ever, Emma

May 10th, 1879

Dear brother Lonnie,

I received your letter a week ago Thursday. I was not sorry to wait a little while as I am getting stronger now every day and I was really afraid of the journey when I came home. I was so miserable.

I hope you are not building just for me. Will it cost you very much and where are you going to build? Do you have work or are times pretty hard?

I am getting strong again. I walked to the Village and back Wednesday. Spent the afternoon with Annie and Mrs. Dubois at Kelso's. Mrs D. told us our fortunes by our hands. She says I have had trouble, but if it is over now, I will never have any more. That the last two thirds of my life is very happy that I will live long, but never regain my strength.

Annie and Tom and E.R. were over to Darlings Tuesday evening. Your humble servant received no invitation. I think Mary is angry at something. I met Mr. Marsh, our new Cong. minister and his wife at Mrs. Kelso's. I was very much pleased with them both.

Polly E. Mapes [daughter of C.C.P. Eldred and wife of George E. Mapes] is coming home next week on account of Jennie's illness.

The weather is very pleasant, but we have not been able to do a thing outdoors until this week. Father is very busy now, ploughing and sowing oats, not a thing done in the garden.

I am ready whenever you are, and Dora is more than ready. The only hurry I am in is that I am spending too much money here. I can not write anymore. Dora is in such a hurry to take the letter.

Write soon Lon do, or I shall go wild. Tell me all you are doing. Your letters are all I care for.

Ever your loving Emma

Old trees and sidewalk near Solomon, Kansas, July 2009. Photo: Joanna Smith.

May 1879

Dear Maria,

Received the box Monday. The things were alright. Bee Gardner has been very kind in this and sends over nearly every day. If it had not been for her, the box would have been there yet.

I can not go yet to Kansas as Lon has had to give up his rooms and go to building. He will send for me as soon as possible, but I do not know when. So it made very little difference to me about the trunk, but I did feel so sorry for Jane. She expected some sweet potatoes and other things and seemed so disappointed every time. I do not know as she could eat the potatoes now.

But Maria can't you get a pint of oysters opened fresh and put them in a small glass can and wrap that in paper and place in an old tin can? I think it would come safe that way. Get a quart of strawberries, a pound or half pound of figs, a quart of tomatoes and two or three peaches if you possibly can and put them in a box and send by express.

If you can not find the peaches, ask Mort to get them at Falton Market, just two or three. She cannot possibly live through this month they think and she longs so for fruit.

I gave mother five oranges, ate one and saved another for us for Jane. Her mouth is parched and dry; she wants something every few minutes and keeps sugar and water by her the whole time.

I gave her the best of the tomatoes. She wanted some and I could not eat them thinking of her. One can hardly keep from crying to see her. She tries so hard to live. Everything she has sent to her she will divide with me.

Emma

May 14, 1879
Dear Lon,

Your card and letter were received in due time. The card was by no means a bad disappointment. I had almost made up my mind to stay and go with Polly anyway. I think she will go about the 25th, though she may go as soon as the 17th. I will send you a card in time for you to meet me.

Dora was so sorry that he almost cried. Father never speaks pleasantly to him and seems angry because he cannot make him do more. Dora has been shamefully neglected. They never try to show him how to work and blame him for every mistake.

It will take a good deal of patience and time to teach him to do things as he ought, but if he only gets so I can trust him in everything, and tries to do right, I shall not mind the trouble. He has very little idea of right and wrong and we must be careful to set good examples before him.

If you are willing, I should like to spend a few minutes of the day either in the morning or evening in reading a chapter of the Bible.

It will give us a knowledge of the scripture that we might not otherwise get and probably do Dora some good. Besides, I want to live so that we may ask God's blessing in our new home and that I may pray him to bless and care for and love the precious treasure I have left here.

I will not try to write the news. I shall see you so soon and I am so tired.

May 15: I have 4 quilts and 2 blankets and have 3 or 4 more quilts nearly ready to join a feather bed bolster and 3 pillows and I guess we will get along pretty well. Have you got smoothing irons?

With best love,
Ever your loving sister, Emma

On May 22, 1879, Sarah Jane Eldred Wait died. Sarah had been married almost four years to William Wait, and was the daughter of C.C.P. and Effa Eldred.

May 25, 1879
Dear Brother Lon,

I will answer your very welcome letter. Let Dora go to a school and learn all he can and I will send him some apples.

How is Mrs. West? Give my love to her. Father is going over to see her. We went out and got a dish of ice cream. Little Net sang all the way home. She goes in Emma's room and looks under the bed and calls her.

Mr. Eldred will tell Emma I am mad at her for taking that school. Please write soon with much love,
I close, Plain Maria

May 30, 1879
To A.A. Austin, Solomon City, Kansas
Dear Brother Lon,

Your letter was very welcome, perfectly satisfactory and has done me a great deal of good. I shall wait until I hear from you again before I start and then write you when to meet me.

Aida will come this fall. I shall be glad to get there. I do dread the journey a little. Have you set out my tomato plants. If not you better get a few and put out yet.

Our gardens are up now and look good. Irvin is real sick. I have been there two days, two weeks. Addie and Polly are home yet. I do not think of any more news. All are well and hope you are the same. Write soon dear Lon and believe me,
Ever loving Em

Sunday, June 11, 1879?
Dear Lon,

I sent word for you to meet me Wednesday, but I wish you would wait until Saturday as I cannot come before then.

We are not ready, but will come Saturday ready or not. We will have two large trunks. I hope you will get this Tuesday. If you do not, I will pay for any expense.

Black-eyed Susan. Photo: Daniel Smith.

1879 Minisink Centennial

On July 22, 1879, there was a Centennial celebration of the Minisink Battle on the actual Battlefield. A Program was created and published by J.W. Johnston and Albert Stage of Barryville, New York.

A monument was built to the memory of the Minisink Battle, and dedicated at the Centennial. The Minisink monument was built with stones gathered from the battlefield. The crown was formed with two flagstones and a boulder from the mouth of the Beaver Brook, contributed by Capt. L.F. Johnston.

The two flagstones were each five inches thick; one 5-1/2 sq. ft. and the other 4 sq. ft. The boulder was of white sandstone and weighed about 1,500 pounds.

In the center of the lower section of the monument was placed a black walnut box, brought from the southern states by Abel S. Myers, Esq., upon his return from the late war, and whose grandfather was a brother of the Daniel Myers who acted such a prominent part in the Minisink battle.

In the box was a paper with the names of those on the committee and others who were interested or helped in the erection of the monument.

The people appointed to committee: J.W. Johnston, A.C. Miller, S. St. J. Gardner, Ira M. Austin, J. Hickok of Barryville; Able S. Myers of Eldred and Horace E. Twichell of Lackawaxen and Albert Stage. Several others were added.

The Minisink Battleground Park was initially established by the Minisink Valley Historical Society in the 1890s in order to head off destruction of the landscape by bluestone quarrying operations. The hillside is still dotted with these quarries, some of them now barely discernable.

Sources: Johnston, J.W. & Stage, Albert, Centennial Celebration of the Minisink Battle on the Actual Battlefield*; www.upperdelawarescenicbyway.org/history/towns/highland/minisinkbattle.php.*

Be sure and meet me Saturday.
In haste, your aff. sister,
Emma

Solomon City, Kansas, July 10, 1879
Dear Sister Maria,

I suppose Ida's letter contains a sufficient account of my journey.

Well then, in the first place I am not sick though I had to lie abed yesterday and today and Dora has been sick ever since he came, but is better today. He was very tired but I think he will soon be all right.

Lon got me some splendid roast beef and is going to buy me a dozen chickens to kill. We have plenty of green peas, beans, cucumbers, cabbages, and green tomatoes, and will soon have green corn. Fruit we have to go buy and it is not so plentiful this year.

My home is getting quite settled and pleasant now and I am happy as I can be without the one little treasure that would make my life rich with perfect joy and it is mine, Maria.

Eldred is working for $1.25 per day. Lon is to stay where he is this year for $500. He will get him a team with what he saves and then he can earn from two to four dollars per day, according to the season of the year.

Ida can get $35 per month for teaching. You can get work for three or four dollars a week, but if you or Ida have a chance, learn all you can of dressmaking if you come here.

Will you come when I've got a great big house? Lon had lots of furniture, more than I wanted, but no churn or chopping knife. He says I shant churn but I tell him I must have mash for my boarders and the knife will come forthwith, no doubt. I will leave my description of the country for Tom's letter.

I shall feel better and will have seen more by next week and will try and write then after I have written to father as I promised, if I have anytime left. Write me soon won't you?
With love, Emma

Eldred, New York, August 3, 1879
Dear Friend Alonzo

You asked me if I had given up the idea of coming out there. Not entirely for I can and am doing as well and perhaps better here than I could there. I have been at work at Proctors for about three months and perhaps will be there 'till winter commences, getting 150 a day every business day.

You wanted to know about the girls around here. There is but a few. We had a wedding out here yesterday. Big Lizzie and Joe Lewis. Several went to it. Tommy Collins, Anna Collins, Emmie Kelso, and my sisters, and several others. Perhaps Tommy and Emmie will be the next.

Please tell me how much you are getting a month out there and how times are there in summer.

Jim Eldred and his woman got back here and Abe Rundle is living with them now all the time.

Minisink Battle Bicentennial

Historically-minded and tourist-conscious residents of Sullivan County will note with interest the plan of the Highway Department to build a County Road connecting the Minisink Battle Ground with State Highway No. 97. Work on this road, Charles J. Geissler (County Superintendent of Highways) states, is expected to be completed during the coming year.

Construction of a Macadam road up a half mile of rugged hillside will grant to nearby inhabitants and a large summer transient population ready access to Sullivan County's only battlefield. Here was fought the last engagement of major importance with hostile Indians in this section of the country.

Up to now, the narrow dirt road, which climbs abruptly to the plateau above, has discouraged all but the heartiest of sightseers. The valiant fight of 90 Goshen militiamen against hopeless odds has, however, not gone entirely unnoticed.

About 46 years after the battle, the bones of the white men, who perished in a vain attempt to punish the Indian raiders, were removed for proper burial. Erection of a monument on the battlefield marked the 100th anniversary. Strenuous efforts were made in 1929 to make the road passable for automobiles. As a result, in July of that year, many a motorist, forcing his car to the limit, struggled up the steep hill to participate in the biggest celebration of all.

With a suitable approach provided, the plateau where Colonel Hawthorn and his men stubbornly defended an acre of ground against a horde of Indian and Tory attackers may well become a major tourist attraction. Unfortunately, in spite of all that engineering skill can accomplish, the last quarter mile of ascent will be formidable.

Tourists who visit the location will, however, be rewarded by a view of a battlefield that has changed very little

The Briggs Family of my mom. From the left: Laura Briggs, Myrtle Crabtree Briggs, Mildred Briggs, Mary Briggs, Minnie Nelson, John Briggs, and Irwin Briggs at the Minisink Monument around 1935.—From the collection of Mary Briggs Austin.

physically since July 22, 1779, when, shortly after sundown, the screaming savages broke through defensive positions and slaughtered a majority of the defenders.

Breastworks of hastily erected rocks are still intact. Hospital rock with its overhanging cliff has not changed since the day it sheltered Dr. Tusten as he gave emergency treatment during the battle to the wounded men. The Doctor, and 17 patients were massacred beneath this cliff when the Indians penetrated the defenses. Initials that are claimed to be those of the celebrated Mohawk chief Thayendanegea are still visible on one of the rocks. Thayendanegea, better known as Colonel Brant, commanded the Indians and Tories who successfully ambushed the pursuing militia.

There is a special reason why some people are looking forward to the bicentennial anniversary. When the monument was erected in 1879, a glass jar containing the names of all those present was placed in the foundation upon which this memorial was located. It was the wish of the witnesses of the original erection that the jar should be dug up and the names read a hundred years later. Many a person will undoubtedly, be present on July 22, 1979, to learn if any of their ancestors were there a hundred years previous.

This new road may arouse in some an interest in the historical aspects of the battle. If so, the History of Sullivan County by J. E. Quinlan gives a wealth of information and supplies reference material that should satisfy the requirements of the most scholarly.
—Arthur L. Austin, written around 1948.
Note: I have been unable to locate the names on the centennial list.

Lessons of Life

Written for the *Sentinel* by Edith E. Austin, Solomon City, Kansas, November 3, 1879

Photo: Cynthia Leavenworth Bellinger.

We need not wait for death
To bring us rest and cheer;
For heaven is found on earth,
Christ Jesus is with us here.
Why dread so much the hours
   of sadness
That's thrown between our days
   of gladness?

We know the flowers grow brighter,
In summer showers of rain,
E'en as our lives grow whiter,
In the shadow of their pain;
By earthward yearnings crucified,
Are heavenly longings satisfied.

'Tis love must satisfy the heart,
And fill the waiting soul,
The love that bids each fear depart,
And binds with sweet control.
The love of Christ, no name beside,
By which the soul is satisfied.

Nor autumn's fairest fruits,
Nor summer's sweetest flowers,
Nor mines of treasured wealth,
Can crown these hearts of ours.
No magic wand doth earth present
To render mortal man content.

Slowly we learn this lesson,
The sweetest on earth to know,
Spurning oft his gift of peace
For doubt which worketh woe;
Grasping the straws on the surging
   tide,
Yet spurning the hands of the
   crucified.

Yet the moment we quit the strife
And hide in him our sin;
The errors of our life
Are as though they ne'er had been.
Our past hath faded, grief hath died,
And we in Christ are satisfied.

From Mary Ann Austin's Scrapbook. Melva Austin Barney Collection.

They live up where Greynells lived, up near the Turnpike road. I have not seen them. I hear that they give Kansas a bad name.

Best regards and hope that you will write before a great while so good bye.

From your friend, A. Osir

Burlingame, Kansas, August 17, 1879
Friend Aida,

As I have heard that you never received my last letter, I thought that I would write to you again hoping that you will receive this and answer.

I wrote to you from Osage City about three weeks before I started to Colorado, but I never received an answer so I concluded that you did not care to write me. I hear that your sister Emma is out here. I was surprised to hear it. I was in hopes that you would have come out with her.

How does she like it out at Solomon? I am well satisfied with the country here since I came back from Colorado and I think that I shall do well here. I liked it in Colorado and should have stayed there, only the climate didn't suit me.

I must tell you about my trip down the Arkansas River when I left Pueblo. I thought that it would be a pleasant trip to go down the river as I bought me a skiff or rowboat and started down the river. It rowed very fine for the first five miles. I could set back in the stern and read.

I had a few choice books such as, "Foul Play," and a "Simpleton" and so I went along alright for about ten miles when I was not watching my boat and it ran into a stump and turned over. I have not seen my boat since nor anything that was in it. It was all I could do to take care of myself. I have had some fine adventures since I have been in the west and I do not think that I should be contented to live in old Sullivan again.

I should like to be there just now and take a run round Hagan Lake. Do you intend to stay long in Eldred? I should be pleased to hear from you as soon as you think proper.

Respectfully, Rob Kelso

New York City, August 17, 1879
Miss Aida Austin, Eldred
Dear Aida,

I am very anxious to hear from you and dear little Buttercup. I received a letter from Emma yesterday saying that she was glad Tommy was in the country, but that she was worried for fear he would get burned as she says they are so careless about having kettles of hot water sitting around, and she has made me feel worried, too, *not that I think they are anymore careless than myself, but they are not used to having children around of late years and therefore are more likely to forget. So my dear, please be very careful of the "dear little tot."*

If you are having such fearful weather there as we are here, you will have hard work to keep him from taking cold. It has rained here steadily for the last three days and from all appearances, it will rain for three more to come.

Does little Tom seem to miss me any? I miss him very much, but still I am glad he is there if he only keeps well, for the children are very troublesome, worse than ever it seems to me.

I do not think Mrs. Braisted will go to the country, as her children remain provokingly healthy!

George was rendered very happy by the receipt of your letter yesterday and Harry correspondingly miserable. He was fairly green with jealousy. I guess however, his wrath had somewhat abated as I see he is writing again tonight.

Mr. Clinton's brother is here and will have the front room for a while, two or three weeks I guess.

Poor Nettie's baby was born two weeks ago today. It only lived five days, died very suddenly on Friday, and was buried one week ago today. Nettie felt dreadfully and no wonder. It was just about the prettiest little boy ever I saw.

Tina went to Rockaway yesterday and Ida to Middletown, I believe.

Em wrote that she has had a touch of chills and fever. Tom has been writing to her today and sending her a remedy. I think it is very fortunate we did not let little Tom go with her as the house she lives in is built right flat on the ground and is very damp besides. I wonder that the boys would think of letting her live in such a place.

Send me word if you need anything for Tom and I will send it. Give him lots of kisses from Mama and Papa and Gussie. Take good care of him. Do not let him get cold nor sick if you can help it, but I know you will not or I would not trust him with you.

If you can get Aunt Laura or Mrs. West to buy a dollars worth of H. Berries for both Nett and myself, I wish you would. Has Mrs. West kept the maple syrup?

Please write soon and tell me all the news. Give my love to all and with love to yourself, believe me affec yours,
Addie E. Thompson

Edith Emogene Austin

Edith Emogene Austin, 28, daughter of Henry and Mary Ann Austin, died from tuberculosis, on the morning of November 13, 1879, at the home of her brothers in Solomon City, Kansas.

At that time, tuberculosis was also called consumption because the disease seemed to consume people from within, with a bloody cough, fever, pallor, and long relentless wasting.

The newspaper obituary commented, *Miss Austin had been in poor health for more than a year past and during the last few months was confined to her bed, and suffered very much.*

The funeral services were conducted by Rev. Mr. Pierson, at the Presbyterian Church, Saturday last. The deceased was greatly esteemed by all who knew her and has left a large circle of mourning friends.

Mary Ann Austin and her

Roses in memory of Edith Emogene Austin. Photo: Gary Smith.

daughter Aida went to Kansas for Emma's funeral. They stayed in Solomon City, Kansas, for a few months after Emma's death.

One hundred years later, Cousin Melva Austin Barney, a grand niece of Emma's, visited Solomon, Kansas.

I went to the graveyard in Solomon, Kansas, several years ago, but I could not identify her grave. There were several tombstones that had the names worn off them. I was told the wind/sand storms were frequent there in 1920s and 30s. There were no burial records in the cemetery office since records were not kept then.

Uncle Ell had purchased a plot there clearly marked Austin and adjoining one which Parmenters had evidently had for a couple of generations. One of the graves with worn stone was very close to this and I assumed that that could be Aunt Emogene.

I have Great-Grandmother Austin's scrapbook which contains the obit and several poems that A. Edith had published in that paper.

One poem she had submitted just a couple of days before her death, was scheduled to be published the same day that her obituary appeared.

There is an article stating that Great-Grandma was there with Aunt Aida and also a couple of poems written by Great-Grandma Mary Ann.

There was no one buried in the Austin plot. All but poor Aunt Edith Emogene finished their days back home in Eldred. All the years later Aunt Aida was still grieving for her.

Great-Grandma Mary Ann Austin's scrapbook was loaned to me by Melva. Several of the poems Melva mentioned are in this chapter and in the Appendix, p. 258.

The Eldred Stage by Halfway Brook. From the Mary Briggs Austin Collection.

Eldred, New York, December 27, 1879
Dear Friend Alonzo

A Merry Christmas. I am pleased to wish you a happy new year if this gets there in time.

I had a good Christmas. I went to South Lebanon to get a Christmas tree on the Eve and on Christmas nite to the village to the tree. I tell you that we had the best tree and the best music and every thing was as good as any tree that ever was around here.

George Mills and I got the tree and we had a hard time of it, but we got as good as, perhaps a better one than they ever had before.

Truly yours,
Guss and Carrie Osier

Great-Grandmother Mary Ann and Aida (and probably Dorrie), left for Eldred in February. One of Mary Ann's poems was printed in March in the Solomon City Newspaper. Mary Ann had some kind words for the people in the area, that were printed in the newspaper.

Solomon City, Kansas Newspaper, February 9, 1880
Mrs. Austin left for her home in New York Monday morning. We are sorry to part with so good a Christian lady as Mrs. Austin.

Mr. Editor: Will you permit me through your valuable paper to thank the people of Solomon for their kindness to my daughter, and am more than grateful to those who have done so much for her; also am very thankful to Miss Jenny for her kind memory of Edith.

M.A.A. (Mary Ann Austin)

Jacksonville Station, Arkansas, February 12, 1880
Friend Lon,

Well old boy, how are you getting along out in that Country?

Was very sorry indeed to hear of your sister's death. It seems very sad and you must miss her very much. You and the rest have my heart felt sympathy in your loss. Is your mother with you yet?

Do not hear from Eldred very often nowadays. But heard there had been a great revival this winter.

I am working here as night operator. Have been here about four months now, but don't like the country much. Get $40 per month. Was working down at south end of this for about a month before the supt. sent me up here.

Have had steady work ever since the first week I came to Arkansas.

I think I would like Kansas better than this state and if I could get a position on some of those roads, would go up there. Can you tell who is Supt. of Telegraph on any of those roads

Edith Emogene Austin, 1851–1879

I Am Tired

Shall I fold my hands and rest from earth?
I am tired of the journey's length,
I have wandered far, I am sick and faint,
I have prayed so long for strength.

I prayed when prayer seemed all unheard;
I have toiled when toil was vain,
I have tried to laugh when the laugh was a cry
From the depths of the soul's wild pain.

I have kept my faith when I could not see
And courage when storms were high,
I had thought to fight the battle through;
Now what can I do but die.

Bear, saith the master, till I come;
Thy work is slow, but wait,
No task I ever set is small,
No burden over great.

I know thou hast toiled when thou couldest not see,
But toiled so long to fail
Never till now when thou bidest hope,
And faith and courage quail.

Thinkest thou because I have given to thee
But pain for thy harvest yet;
If thou art faithful to the end,
That I could once forget?

Bear on, bear on, the harvest sure,
Thou shalt know up there,
That what we thought so strangely here,
Was wisdom, love, and care.

—Edith E. Austin, Solomon City, Kansas, November 11, 1879. Miss Edith Austin, whose death is recorded in another column, was our best contributor and a writer of great merit. "I Am Tired" is her last piece written for "The Sentinel," the day previous to her death.

She is Gone

To the Memory of Edith E. Austin
She is gone, no more we see her,
From earth she has passed away,
The call of the death angel cometh
She would fain—but could not stay.

Not as a flower that is quickly severed
From its stem in the bloom of day,
Without warning sign or footstep,
And is rudely snatched away.

But as once in the summer twilight,
When the sun has sunk to rest:
With the weight of a heavy burden
To the ground is slowly pressed.

We miss her gently presence;
Her place no other form can fill,
While we are left to struggle onward,
And fight the battle still.

Her heart through suffering's crucible,
Attuned to heavenly rhyme,
Breathed forth its parting music
Full of hope of a future time.

—Jennie, "The Haphazard," November 23, 1879

"The Haphazard" was favored last Wednesday with a call from Mrs. Austin, mother of Edith E. Austin, deceased, whose beautiful poems appeared in "The Sentinel." Mrs. Austin was about to return east and wished to say goodbye to Jennie, who it will be remembered, wrote a poem to the memory of her daughter. She presented Jennie with a handsome album, which we understand, will soon be adorned with the portrait of the deceased Edith.

These poems were in Mary Ann Austin's Scrapbook. Melva Austin Barney Collection.

---

near you?

There is a new road from Dallas, Texas, to Wichita, Kansas. Does that come near you and can you give me any information in regard to the supert. of that road?

Please remember me kindly to the rest. Also to your folks at home. I suppose Maria is at home now, is she not? Kind regards to her when you write. Don't think I will ever go back to York State to stay, but may go back for a visit sometime if I live.

Hoping to hear from you soon,
I remain your friend,
Alfred Skinner

March 1880

Dear Mother,
I am getting along all right. I have had the toothache nearly ever since you left here. I had it pulled yesterday. I received your letter the 3rd and was glad to hear from you.

How is Dora? Is he homesick for Kansas yet? I felt a little homesick

Trees and rock wall in Eldred, fall 2008. Photo: Mary Briggs Austin.

this morning when Mr. Follett told me he had sold out. He has sold his bank and residence and will soon move away from Solomon. I am agoing to work for the man that bought him out. Follett says he is a nice man and has got a lot of money. He says he thinks betwixt him and Amos that he can keep me agoing.

I have got 16 more little chickens. I had 18, but the rat caught 3. My corn and peanuts are up and looking fine.

Mable Hill says "tell Aunt Mary if she don't write that I will go back there and go for her."

You say "tell you just what I am doing and how I am getting along." I am getting along alright and am doing as usual: a little of everything.

I do not know of anything now to write and it is getting late so I will bring my scribbling to a close. You did not say anything about where Aida is. Is she home or in New York?

Hoping to hear from you soon, I close with much love to all.

Your aff. Son, Lon

My grandmother, Jennie Louisa Leavenworth, daughter of Sherman S. and Maria Myers Leavenworth, was born in April 1880, at the Leavenworth Homestead. Jennie had an older sister, Anna Mae, 5, and an older brother Truman, 2. Both of Jennie's grandmothers, Charlotte Leavenworth and Jane Ann Myers, were still living in 1880.

November 7, 1880
My dear Son Lon,

Not a day goes by but what I think of you but we have so much to do and lots of company.

Maria is expecting to go to Mary's next week. Aunt Maria and Ida leave for Barryville this afternoon and will go down with Maria. I don't mean to let Aida go back when they do.

Antoinette is up to Mary Jane's place. Says she wants to come home with the girls. Mrs. Wells was gone at what used to be Jane Sergeants.

There's been lots going on here this summer. Kelsos and Perry can't get a long very peaceable.

Perry Schoonover and wife was here yesterday afternoon. They have quite a little trouble having festivals to get money to the Methodist church.

Kelso threatened to shoot Perry, and pointed the gun at him.

"When you was sexton, what became of the money that was taken up? Did you use any of it to get oil with?"

They have got the church fixed up real nice. You would hardly know it. But they are in debt some and are to have another festival here Thursday.

There are quite a number of city boarders. Gillmer, Bradleys, Myers, and Collins are full.

Miss Burnett and Eddie come home before the fourth. They say he is studying for doctor, consequently they call him Doctor Kelso.

Did Aida tell you what good times they are having here? There are two ladies to Mr. Dubois. Aida visited them one afternoon.

I don't think your Father enjoys so much company. He says he will sell at some price. He won't stay here another winter and if the boys would give him $500, he would give them the deed of the place, but that could never get you out of debt with such a big family. I do hope you can come home this winter. There'll be no danger of selling.

Henry Lilly likes it very much in the southern part.

I wish you would send the barrel. Aida will pay the freight. I am afraid the moths will eat the

Edith Emogene Austin's Poetry

To Mother

Cease your weeping, mother dear,
Bury your sorrow with the dying year
And begin afresh this new
With a heart brave and true.

Weep not so for your child—
Check those sobs piercing, wild;
Do not wish her back again,
In this world of care and pain.

We know that you loved her so;
It was hard for you to let her go.
God gave her to you they say,
And it was God that took her away.

She was sent a work to do—
Joy and comfort give to you;
Since she her work hath done,
Has gone to dwell with the Holy One.

The parting it will not be long,
For soon we will all be gone,
Gone to that land of pure delight
Where's no sorrow or darkness of night.

Your daughter will meet you there—
Welcome you to the land so fair;
Then you'll dwell for ever above,
And sing together of undying love.

—Written for the Sentinel by Edith Emogene Austin

Photo: Cynthia Leavenworth Bellinger.

In Memory of Edith E. Austin

We miss our sweet darling today;
What can we do but weep?
They laid her away from our sight—
Laid her away to sleep.

Rest from pain in her father's house;
Finished her work on earth;
He saw she was weary and tired,
And gave her a heavenly birth.

She gathered fair leaves and ferns;
She loved the pure and fair;
She gathered rich pearls for heaven,
And laid up treasures there.

She is missed from our social circle;
Who her place can fill?
Blessed with a mind of living worth
That envyings could not kill.

"I have so much work to do,
I long to tarry yet;"
These are the words she spake to me
The last time we met.

"See! My beautiful flowers are here,
And Autumn leaves to press;
My book is not half finished—
I'll have to leave them all I guess:

For my strength is failing fast;
I pray to God for rest;
And when I look above the earth
I am securely blest."

I know she heard the angels singing
As the earth grew dark,
And saw the sweet, heavenly dove
As she neared the holy ark.

—M.W.M.

The poems on this page were in Mary Ann Austin's Scrapbook. Collection of Melva Austin Barney.

Great-Grandma Mary Ann Eldred Austin. Photo in Mary Briggs Austin Collection.

cloth. Put on the barrel, "handle with care," and make it strong.

I think you boys would do better here in the summer working for Proctor at 12 shillings a day, than you do there. Or have you had your fortune there this summer?

Mother

Lawrence, Kansas, December 12, 1880

Friend Lon,

Your Poetical Epistle received a few days since. Had I known that you had not left Solomon, I should have written a letter to you instead of a card and would have sent it sooner.

We like Lawrence very well by this time, better than we did at first. Lawrence has a great many pretty girls. And you hope that I have found a sweet heart down here do you?

We expect to reach Solomon on the 23rd of December. Our health is good at present. Weather fine.

Yours truly, Wm. G. Sutherland

The following letter, probably from Mary Ann Austin to her son Ell, was written on both the inside and outside of an envelope that had originally been addressed to Aida Austin in Eldred, New York, and dated September 28, 1880.

After September 28, 1880

Dear Son,

I have not wrote half what I want, but it's getting late now. I must write to Maria. She has written to me three times. I have not had but one letter from Aida and don't expect to get another from her until I answer.

Is there any prospect of getting Edith home this winter?

How I do want to see you.

Written on the inside of the envelope:

When he was through talking he gave out other than he sat down and looked them in the face and never closed the meeting. The folks waited awhile and then got up and went out. Ema's [Kelso] face was very red as she tried to make an excuse to Henry, but it did not take with him. Ema is in New York visiting Tom [Collins]. Got a letter in her handwriting yesterday. It takes them a good while to get ready for their wedding.

Mamie West is single yet and home visiting.

They are running oil pipes through by the turnpike. It makes lots of work for teamsters, but it is too hard work for our teams.

The horses around her have had the spozodie [horse influenza]. Fanny [their horse] is not over it yet, but they began to work the team yesterday.

Tell Lon I had a letter from him all right. I am glad the election is over.

Do please write soon to your loving Mother.

Melva Austin Barney's comment on Mary Ann's letter:

I think that the reference to "getting Edith home" would certainly refer to Aunt Edith's body. I seem to remember Aunt Aida being distressed that it was not done, though I don't remember exactly what she said.

I think it partially the memory of this that moved me to go out there all those years later to try and find her grave and feeling quite sad that she alone was buried there, and that her grave was not absolutely identifiable.

At the end of December, a neighbor of the Austins, Thomas K. Collins, 36, of Eldred, a farmer, son of Rev. James Collins, and

Poems

I Locked It In

I took my grief and I locked it in.
And bolted and barred the door,
And told myself it had never been,
And never should be no more.

"For life goes on and must go the same,
For Months," I said, "and for years."
A man and weak, it were scorn and shame,
"Let woman give way to tears."

But lo! In the night I heard a sound.
I woke with a start and cry.
My grief stood there, with its withes unbound,
And looked with its awful eye.
It took my hand, with an icy chill,
And said, with a mock and jeer:
"Your bolts were strong, but I haunt you still.
You thrust me out: I am here."

I seek the crowd; but it follows there—
I cannot drive it away.
The forest wild; it is in the air,
It gnaws at my heart all day.
And at midnight it comes—the ghost!
And it mocks beside my bed.
Oh! Hopeless moan for the loved and lost.
Oh! Hearts that break for your dead.
— George H. Westfield

I'm not sure who wrote out the poem, "I Locked it In," by George H. Westfield. It must be one of the Austins liked the poem, and as they often did, wrote the poem out.

Handwritten copy of "I Locked It In." Courtesy Melva Austin Barney.

An Answer

Can I begin anew and check the tear
With a dirge sounding in my ear
Or a hope lost with the dying year?
Can I bury a pearl without regret?
The form in a coffin can I forget?
Earth may hide them from a brother,
But the grave can never smother
The heart anguish of your mother.

I say not this my dear son to chide;
I wish you to throw all care aside,
And your heart in God confide
I would not with you to brood in grief,
Nor sigh and mourn without relief.
You may be happy in the busy throng,
But be manly, good and strong,
Keep to the right as you pass along.

I thank you for your message kind—
The words are in my heart entwined—
A soothing balm in them I find.
Yes, our darling rests in peace,
Yet my tears will not cease,
Nor will my selfish heart refrain
In my lonely hours, though vain,
Wishing with health her back again.

Your dear sister, but dearer mine—
Her worth to us none can define.
And the loss it is vain to repine
No coming back from eternity,
The past is past, thus let it be.
Though of a golden gem I am bereft,
My thoughts turn to my jewels left,
Seeking help from God for death's theft.

It giveth joy for us to know
That God will meet and look through
All death's stealings here below.
The gold he takes to mansions fair
From death's grasp and jewels rare;
Let us live for God and his love,
Serving him well and faithful prove,
The we will meet our darling above.
—M.A.A.

This poem written by Mary Ann Austin was in her scrapbook. Courtesy of Melva Austin Barney. (See Appendix, p. 258, for two more of Mary Ann Austin's poems.)

brother of Rev. R.B. Collins, married Emma J. Kelso, 25, also of Eldred.

In this next letter, Aida Austin was apparently in New York City with her Austin city cousins. In Book Two, we will learn more about Aida and the Austin city cousins in 1881. Harry will be there (though I don't know his last name) and also the Braisted family.

New York City, December 25 and New Years

How did you spend your Christmas and New Years?

I had a very good time each day and got some nice presents. We had a little Christmas tree for the children and I dressed up as old Santa Clause. My hair which I had for whiskers, caught on fire, but cousin Ida and Addie put it out so quick that it did not do much damage.

The children were greatly pleased and believed faithfully in Santa Clause. We did not receive calls New Years.

Harry and I went to the Park in the evening to skate, but there was no skating, so we came back and stayed at Mrs. Braisteds until 10 o'clock. I have a splendid pair of skates, but cannot skate very good yet.

Aida

Our story started in 1815, when James Eldred entered the Town of Lumberland with his wife Polly (who died ten years later), and their five children. Phebe Maria Eldred was born shortly after their arrival. Two other daughters were born to James and Polly, but died young.

In 1880, four of James and Polly Eldred's children were still living, as was my great-grandmother Mary Ann Eldred, daughter of James Eldred and his second wife, Hannah Hickok.

Zophar and Sarah Eldred Carmichael, 75, in Orange County, New York, had ten children. The families of Elimina Carmichael Drake, Polly Maria Carmichael Gregory Mitchell, Emeline Carmichael Lewis, Decatur Carmichael, and Eliza Carmichael Puff seem to be living in the state of New York.

David and Harriet Carmichael Young and their family had moved to Illinois. The families of Charles Carmichael, Sarah A. Carmichael Davis, and Lewis Carmichael lived in Iowa. Lewis's wife, Mary Bunce

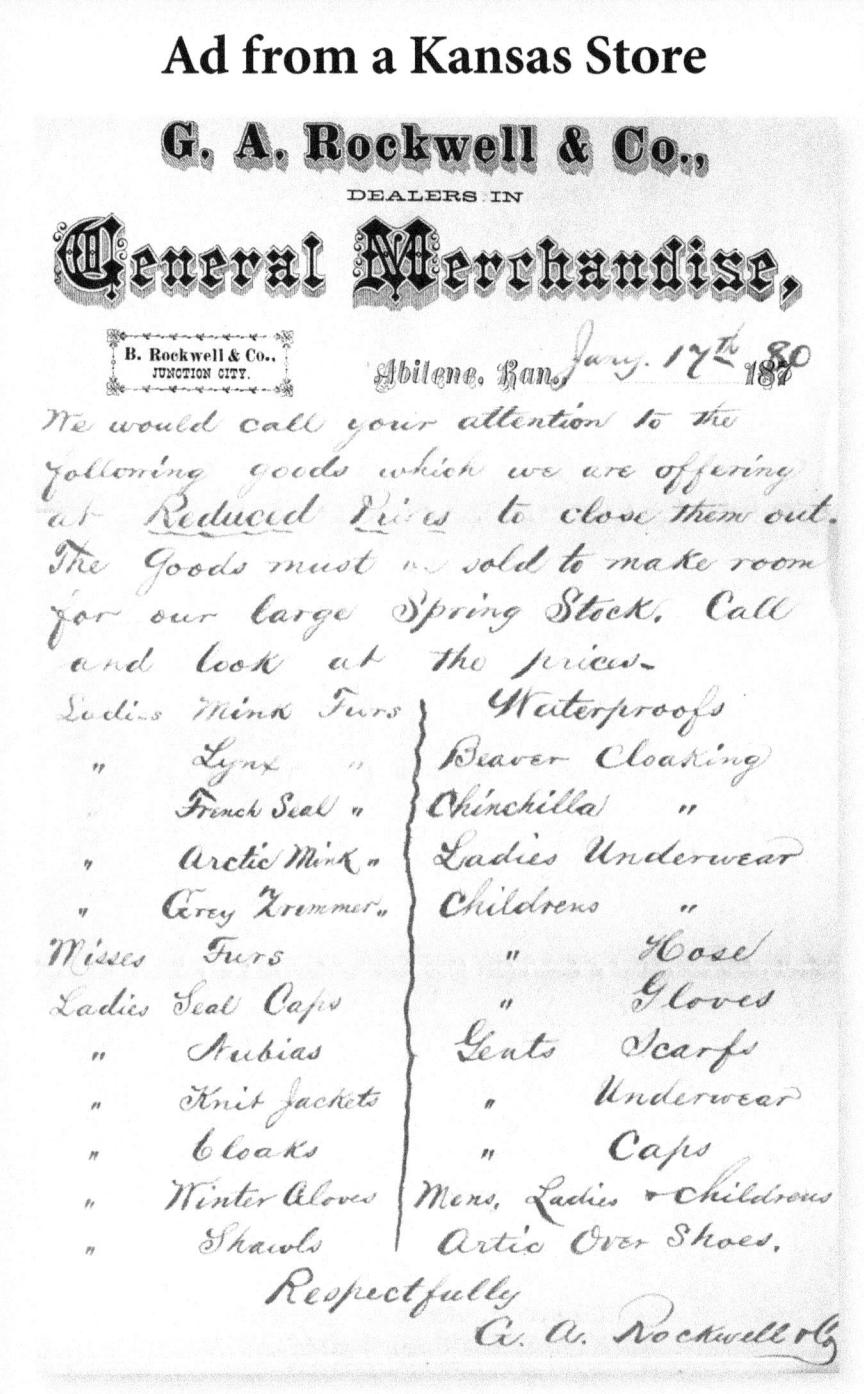

Ad from Abilene, Kansas Store. Melva Austin Barney Collection.

A Reverie or Kansas Romance

Never dreamed of aught so grand
My castle in the air,
Could never build her fancies half
As bright as Kansas fair.

Dear loved ones I left at home,
O, will ye never know;
Kansas beautiful land of song,
Her gentle zephyrs blow.

These who climb the mountain high,
There weary feet would rest,
Your eyes would feast on beauties rare
Where nature does her best.

The moon outvies the eastern sun
In Kansas sunny climes,
The music of the rustling corn
Keeps up a constant chime.

Give me fair Kansas fertile lands,
Where sweet potatoes grow,
No stone to plow, but turn the turf,
Plant plants all in a row.

I love to see the cattle feed
On rich and grassy plains,
We breath the freedom of the air;
In Kansas wide domains.

No jolting over hills and down,
But smooth and level roads,
No falling tree or burning brush,
Or dragging stone boat loads.

Beautiful flowers, that greet us here;
And glowing fields of wheat,
Tells Kansas is the place for me,
With sour grapes to eat.

—Albert

This bittersweet poem was probably written by Lon (Albert Alonzo) Austin, brother of Emma, and son of Henry and Mary Ann Austin. It was published on January 12, 1880.

Abandoned house in Kansas, not far from Solomon City. Photo: Joanna Smith.

Others in 1880

Sarah Shotwell, 66, was listed in the 1880 census, and Grandson Osmer Webb, 9, lived with her. Quite possibly Osmer was the son of Charles and Sarah Shotwell Webb. Charles Webb was the son of Jane Ann Van Pelt Webb Myers.

Stephen C. Shotwell, 49, possibly a son of Sarah Shotwell, was a laborer. His wife was also named Sarah J. Shotwell. They have six children ages 6 to 17, including another Sarah Shotwell, age 2.

Abel S. Myers, 44, was a farmer and merchant. His first wife died, and Abel was married to Maria Hankins, 26, kept house. Abel's son Edwin V. Myers from his first marriage was 17, and a clerk in a store. Abel and Maria Hankins Myers had two children, Jackson, 3, and Sarah, 1. Mary Raub, 22, was a servant.

Coe and Adaline Young lived in Manchester, Pennsylvania, with their daughter, Jennie, 14.

Follett Metzger was a farmer. Living with Follett and his wife were sons Robert and Christian, and his mother, Barbara, 79.

Ira M. Austin, from the other Austin family, was, 38, and a blacksmith. His wife Minerva, 35, kept house. They had six children, and a servant, Kate Sheck.

Ira's father, Benjamin C. Austin, died November 9, 1880, at the age of 72 years, 3 months and 18 days.

Samuel Jesse Hallock, son of Oliver Blizzard Hallock and his wife Emma Scwab, was 9. Samuel's sister Adelia died at 10 and his brother Johney died at 2 days old. Samuel's future wife, Anna May Buchanan in New Jersey, was 4.

John Henry Clark, son of George Case Clark and Mercy Harding Brown, was 13. His future wife Carrie Etta Bogert was 5.

Calvin LaBarr from Beaver Brook married Elizabeth M. Rice in May.

In 1879, J.T. Marsh had been the Congregational pastor. In 1880, Rev. E.W. Fisher became the pastor. Mrs. Fisher wrote Aida Austin some letters that we will read in Book Two.

---

had died in 1873. John Mulford and Mary Schofield Carmichael lived in New York City.

James and Polly Eldred's son, Charles C.P. Eldred, 71, was a farmer and lumberman. His wife Effa, 65, kept house. Their daughter Rebecca (Bec), 37, was at home. Two of C.C.P. and Effa's grandsons lived with them. James Eldred, 14, worked on the farm, and Herbert, 12, went to school. They were sons of George W. Eldred who had died. Joel Crawford, 40, was a laborer, and also lived with them.

C.C.P. and Effa's son, James D. Eldred, whose letters we read, was back in Eldred with his wife Frances J. Payne. James was 31, and a farmer. Abram W. Rundle, also a farmer, boarded with them.

Eliza Eldred Gardner, 69, had been a widow for twenty years. She sometimes visited her sister, Phebe Maria Austin in New York City, but Eliza lived with the family of her son Stephen St. John Gardner, 44, who was lumbering and lived in Barryville.

In November of 1880, Stephen, a widower, had married Margaret Terns. Stephen's son James K. Gardner, 19, was a clerk in a store. Stephen's other children, Katie Gardner, 16, Myers J. Gardner, 14, Herbert D. Gardner, 12, and Mary L. Gardner, 7, were at school. (Several of these children were mentioned in Aida's *1881 Diary*.)

Another son of Eliza Gardner, James E. Gardner, 42, was a carpenter, whose wife Rebecca Rider, 41, kept house. Their son Charles F. Gardner, 18, worked on the canal, and daughters Susan and Anna went to school.

Phebe Maria Eldred Austin, the daughter of James and Polly Eldred, (born in Lumberland, January 1816), lived in New York City with her husband, Augustus Austin. At least five of their ten living children were married in 1880, and had children of their own.

The city Austins still visited their country cousins and vice versa—except for Alonzo Eugene Austin Sr. who lived in Alaska. Alonzo Eugene, his wife Isabelle, and their children, Olinda, Henrietta, and Alonzo Eugene Jr. were Presbyterian missionaries in Alaska's territorial capital, Sitka.

Phebe Maria's half sister, my great-grandmother, Mary Ann Eldred Austin, 52, kept house in Eldred. Great-Grandpa William Henry Austin was 56, and a farmer. Four children were at home in the 1880 Census. Henrietta was 30, and Maria was 25. The boys, my grandfather, Mort, 15, and Henry Ladore, 13-1/2, worked on the farm. Aida, 19, in November, may have been in New York City when the census was taken.

Henry Austin's sister, Ann Mary Schoonover who had died during the Civil War, had not had any children. Her husband O.P. had married Mary Parker, who had two children, George and Kate Parker. In 1880, O.P. and Mary Parker Schoonover's family also included their children, Emily, 9, and Daniel Rowley, 7. Aida Austin considered Emily and Rowley Schoonover cousins even though they were not technically related to her.

The Hickok family descendants in town were related to Aida Austin

Eldred viewed from the east. The bridge on the road, went over Halfway Brook. To the right, the first house was C.C.P. Eldred's. The next is the Parker House. The Methodist Church can be seen in the distance in the middle of the photo. On the far left is the Congregational Church. The buildings mentioned were in Eldred in 1880. Photo in collection of Mary Briggs Austin.

and her siblings. Aida's brother and my grandfather, Charles Mortimer Austin was good friends with his cousin Olin Hickok. In 1880, both Mort, 15, and Olin, 14, became members of the Eldred Methodist Church.

Olin's father David Hickok, was a farmer and his mother Mary kept house, but had a lame back. Olin's siblings were Morris, Elta, and little Justice, most likely named after his grandfather Justus Hickok. George Harris, 72, a servant, lived with the family.

William Hickok, also a son of Justus and Polly Hickok, was a carpenter. William's wife Almeda Hickok kept house. Frances E. Hickok, 25, and Charles Hickok, 13, were at home.

The Bunce brothers, George, 53, and William 44, were both farmers. They lived next to Irvin and Laura Austin Clark, and their family.

Irvin Clark was a farmer, and Laura kept house. Their sons Ellsworth, 18, and Elbert, 14, worked on the farm. Their little brother Robert was about 5. Hannah Raub, 18, was a servant.

Irvin and Laura Clark lived next door to Irvin's brother, George Clark, a farmer.

George's wife, Harriet Covert, kept house. Only three of their six or seven living children were at home. George, 15, and John, 13, were farm laborers. Clarissa Clark, 19, had joined the Congregational Church in 1879.

In eight years, Clarissa would marry Frank Roberts Sergeant, a descendant of Reverend Isaac and Mary Sergeant, who started the Congregational Church in 1799. Frank and Clarissa would be the parents of Ella Phoebe who would marry James Garfield Leavenworth (who would be born in 1882).

Frank Sergeant, 20, was a farm laborer and boarded with his sister, Unita Jane Sergeant and her husband William Livingston. The Livingsons had four children.

Frank Sergeant's father, Alvah, 48, was a farmer and carpenter. Frank's mother Phebe Owen, 46,

Postcard entitled, "The Old Sawmill, Barryville, New York." Photo courtesy of Larry Stern.

The Center of Eldred, date uncertain. Edwin Van Schoick Myers, son of Abel Sprague Myers, stands on the roof waving a flag. Edwin attended school away from home and at a very young age started leaving school in early spring to "go down the river on the logs"—without Abel's permission. Abel said that Edwin could not go back in the fall. Edwin promised to finish out the year, but "had to heed the call of the logs," and headed down at the time of the spring flood. Photo and information courtesy of Melva Austin Barney.

kept house. His brother Morgan, 14, was a farm laborer, and his little brother Alvah was 5.

Frank Sergeant's grandfather Ethel Sergeant, a farmer, was 73. Grandmother Letty Gardner Sergeant was also 73. Their daughter Caroline, 27, was a dressmaker. Their son Isaac, 46, was a carpenter, and still a bachelor. This will change in Book Two.

Ethel and Letty's grandson James W. Sergeant, 11, also lived with them. James W. was the son of James G. Sergeant (who had died in October 1873) and Emma Myers Sergeant. In 1880, Emma Sergeant and her two other children, Claribel Sergeant, 8, and Charles C. Sergeant (7 in August), lived in Brooklyn with her parents Samuel S. and Elizabeth Myers.

The Sergeants lived near my great-great-grandfather, Buckley Leavenworth. Buckley, 72, was a farmer. Buckley's wife Charlotte, 69, kept house. Son Sherman Stiles Leavenworth, a farmer, and his wife Maria Myers and their three children Anna, 4, Truman, 2, and Jennie Louisa, 2 months old, lived on the Leavenworth homestead. Elizabeth Owens, a servant, lived there also.

Buckley and Charlotte's oldest daughter Harriet and her husband Henry Palmer lived in Port Jervis, New York. Henry, 52, ran a wood yard, and Harriet, 45, kept house. Their oldest son Harry, 19, was a clerk in a grocery store. Edith, 18, was a school teacher, like her mother had been. James was 10.

John Leavenworth, the brother of Sherman S., was out west. John would be returning to Eldred soon. One reason possibly being Amelia Bradley (19 years old in 1880), daughter of Isaac, a farmer, and his wife Joanna. (Joanna had become a member of the Eldred Methodist Church in June.)

In Book Two we will read more about Amelia Bradley and her siblings: Viola, Mary, Isaac, Lottie, Atwell, and Nora.

Maria Leavenworth's brother George W.T. Myers, 34, was a farmer, and lived on the east side of Eldred. George's wife, Martha Mills Myers, 29, kept house, and watched their son Charles C. Myers, 3. Maria and George's mother, Jane A. Myers, 64, lived in the house next to George and Martha, and also kept house. Jane Ann's son (brother to Maria and George), Augustus, 23, was a farmer, and also lived there.

Jane Ann's daughter Charlotte (Lottie), 22, was married to Charles S. Darling, 25, who farmed. Lottie and Charles lived about 70 miles north of Binghamton, New York, with their 1-month-old daughter, Ida Darling.

Martha Mills Myers's sister, Margaret Mills, was married to James Boyd and they had three children: Bertha, Isabel (who would marry Henry Asendorf), and James Edward.

Over in France, Jean Charles Rouillon and his future wife, Blanche Olga Malinge, were both 17. It would be a few years before they married and had a son named Cyrus. Cyrus would be the father of Gisele Rouillon, who would one day live in the United States, and marry Jim Leavenworth, whose father Garfield Leavenworth, would be born in 1882.

John Crabtree, the future father of Myrtie Crabtree (my other grandmother), lived in Chicago, Illinois, where he was a shoemaker. In a few years John L. Crabtree would be homesteading in Nebraska, as would his future wife, Ida Emily Higginson, Myrtie's mother.

Ida Higginson was born the year after the Civil War ended to Edward and Mary Higginson. Perhaps you remember that Edward Higginson was wounded in the Civil War. When Ida was seven, her father Edward died of those wounds.

Myrtie Crabtree would marry Irwin Briggs who would be the Methodist preacher in Barryville, starting in the mid-1930s. Irwin's father, Clinton Briggs was in Indiana, in 1880. Clinton's future wife, Marium Indianola Clark, born in Indianola, Texas, was 12.

As this book closes at the end of the year in 1880, the Austin sons, Ell and Lon, were in Kansas. Ell was in Brookville, working for the railroad. Uncle Lon, at one time a telegraph operator for the railroad, was a laborer in Solomon City.

In Book Two, my grandfather Charles Mortimer Austin travels to Kansas to visit and later works with his brothers, who would soon be farming.

It is obvious from a couple of old photos I have seen, that Eldred and the surrounding area had been carelessly deprived of its valuable timber. By 1880, and probably before, the original lumber companies had left the area. A few sawmills continued through the middle of the 20th Century.

Jobs were still available with the D&H Canal (until 1899), the railroad, or bluestone quarries.

The railways had made it possible for New York City folk to easily get away from the city and its summer heat to the natural, restful beauty of the Town of Highland, some 90 miles away. The New York City-ites would travel by train to Shohola, Pennsylvania, where they would be picked up and taken to a nearby boarding home of their choice.

As a result, boarding houses became a source of income for the townsfolk of Highland, including my relatives—the Leavenworths

Halfway Brook, 2009. Photo: Cynthia Leavenworth Bellinger.

with Echo Hill Farm House, and the Austins, a bit later with Mountain Grove—the subject of Book Two.

In Book Two, *Echo Hill and Mountain Grove*, we will renew acquaintances with a number of friends and relatives we have already met. We will read letters written by two grandsons of Sherman S. Leavenworth who will fight during another horrid war.

And the war will again take its toll.

But mainly *Echo Hill and Mountain Grove* will be about the daily lives of the Leavenworths and Austins, their family and friends, and the boarding houses in Highland Township, as told by photos, scrapbooks, postcards, letters, and diaries that have fortunately been preserved by family and friends.

Bibliography

Books

Child, Hamilton, *Gazetteer and Business Directory of Sullivan County, NY, 1872–1873*

Eldred, Richard O., *The Eldred Family: Elisha Eldred of Minisink, New York, and His Descendants*, Baltimore: Gateway Press, Inc., 1988

Johnston, John Willard, *Reminiscences,* Town of Highland Cultural Resources Commission, 1987

Leavenworth, Elias W., *A Genealogy of the Leavenworth Family in the United States,* Syracuse: Hitchock & Co., 1873

Quinlan, James Eldridge, *History of Sullivan County,* Beebe and Morgans, 1873

Other Sources

A Century of Church Life: Centennial of the First Congregational Church of Eldred Celebrated, "The Tri-States Union," Vol. XLIX. No. 33. Port Jervis, N.Y., August 17, 1899

Barber, Gertrude A., *Records of the First Congregational Church in the Town of Lumberland, Sullivan County, New York*

Barber, Gertrude A., *Records of the Barryville Congregational Church, 1836 to 1927,* transcribed by Jane Devlin, http://dunhamwilcox.net/ny/barryville_ny_cong_ch.htm

Congregational Church Centennial (1899) booklet

Kyte, Felix, *The Kyte Narrative,* 1875; Reprinted as a publication of the Shohola Railroad & Historical Society, Shohola, PA, 2000

Methodist Centennial and 150-Year booklets

Werman, Edey, Sullivan County Cemeteries
http://www.usgwarchives.org/ny/sullivan/cemeteries/cemeterytoc.htm

Website Sources of Interest

Barryville:
www.barryvilleny.com/history/history.html

Books (old) on CD:
www.betweenthelakes.com/

Books (old) online:
http://quod.lib.umich.edu/cgi/c/collsize/collsize?summ=all

Conway, John, *Retrospect:*
http://www.sullivanretrospect.com/

Encyclopedia online:
http://en.wikipedia.org/

Minisink Valley Historical Society:
www.minisink.org/hisdoor.html

New York History:
Sullivan, James Dr., *The History of New York State*; Online Ed. by Holice, Deb & Pam: www.usgennet.org/usa/ny/state/his/

Scotchtown, New York:
http://scotchtownhighlander.com/

Town of Bethel:
http://www.townofbethel.com/history/history1.htm

Town of Highland:
www.highlandnewyork.net/

Town of Lumberland:
http://townoflumberland.org/history.htm
www.co.sullivan.ny.us/documentView.asp?docid=647
(Lumberland large file)

Tusten/Narrowsburg:
http://www.tusten-narrowsburg.org/hello.htm

Upper Delaware Scenic Byway:
www.upperdelawarescenicbyway.org/

Appendix

Charles Mortimer Austin Ancestors	232
Jennie Louisa Leavenworth Ancestors	233
Some of the Families Mentioned in the Book	234
Some Rev. Isaac Sergeant Descendants	235
Harriet, Polly Maria, and Clara	236
Other Photos of Interest	237
Maps of Town of Highland and Halfway/Eldred	238
1870/1875 Map of Halfway Brook Village/Eldred	239
Letters of Anthony Austin, Town Clerk	240
Mary Ann Eldred's Letter to Her Parents	241
Phebe Maria Eldred Austin's Letter to Her Sister	242
Fanny Knapp Austin's Letters to Her Children	243
James Austin's Letter to His Mother	247
Mahlon Irvine Clark Marries Laura Austin	248
Fanny Austin's Letter to Her Daughter Laura	249
Henry Austin's Carting Book	250
William Henry Writes Son Lon	251
Eldred Family Information	252
Leavenworth Bible Pages	256
Elizabeth Van Pelt Bible Pages	257
Mary Ann Austin's Poetry	258

Charles Mortimer Austin Ancestors

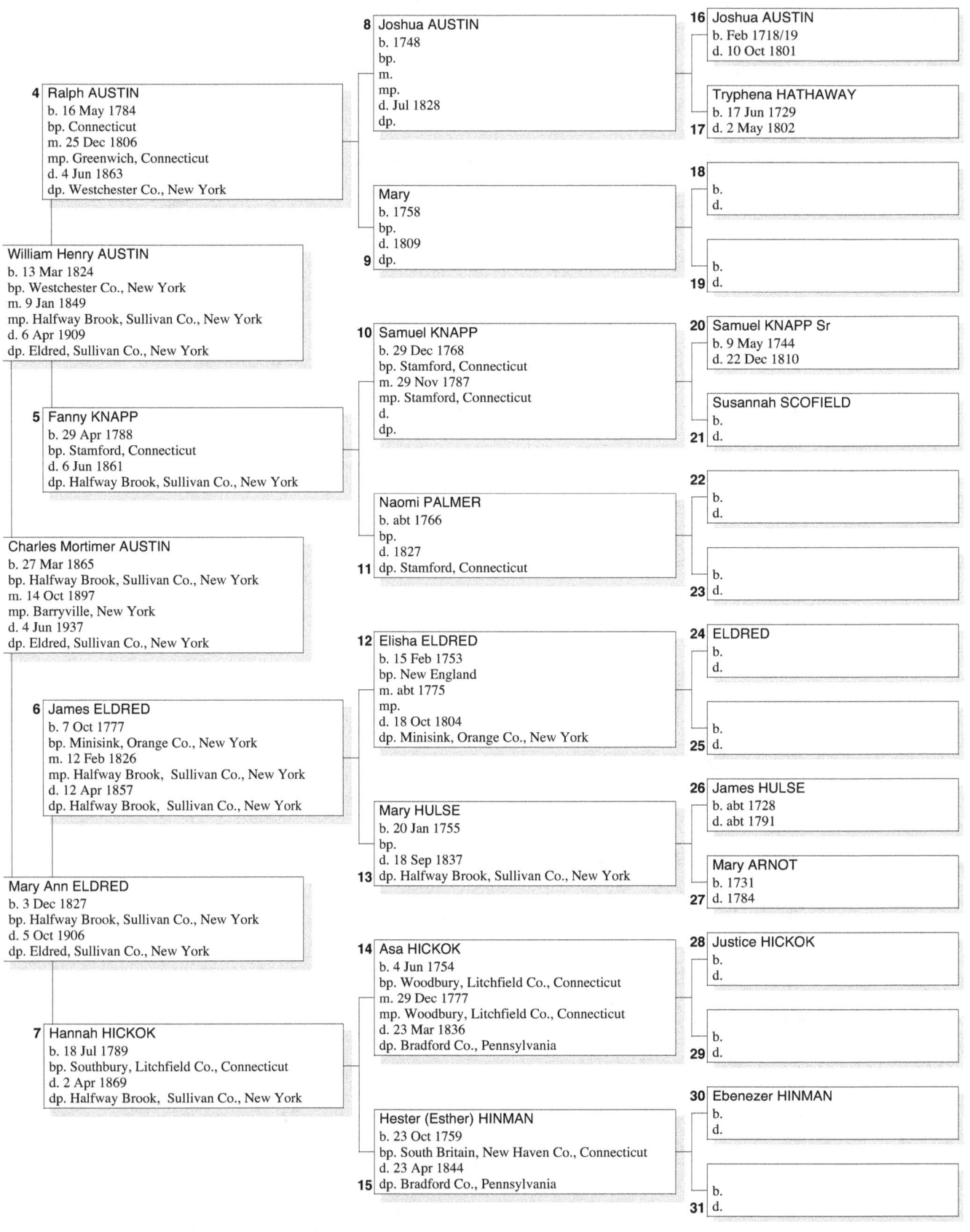

- **4 Ralph AUSTIN**
  b. 16 May 1784
  bp. Connecticut
  m. 25 Dec 1806
  mp. Greenwich, Connecticut
  d. 4 Jun 1863
  dp. Westchester Co., New York

- **William Henry AUSTIN**
  b. 13 Mar 1824
  bp. Westchester Co., New York
  m. 9 Jan 1849
  mp. Halfway Brook, Sullivan Co., New York
  d. 6 Apr 1909
  dp. Eldred, Sullivan Co., New York

- **5 Fanny KNAPP**
  b. 29 Apr 1788
  bp. Stamford, Connecticut
  d. 6 Jun 1861
  dp. Halfway Brook, Sullivan Co., New York

- **Charles Mortimer AUSTIN**
  b. 27 Mar 1865
  bp. Halfway Brook, Sullivan Co., New York
  m. 14 Oct 1897
  mp. Barryville, New York
  d. 4 Jun 1937
  dp. Eldred, Sullivan Co., New York

- **6 James ELDRED**
  b. 7 Oct 1777
  bp. Minisink, Orange Co., New York
  m. 12 Feb 1826
  mp. Halfway Brook, Sullivan Co., New York
  d. 12 Apr 1857
  dp. Halfway Brook, Sullivan Co., New York

- **Mary Ann ELDRED**
  b. 3 Dec 1827
  bp. Halfway Brook, Sullivan Co., New York
  d. 5 Oct 1906
  dp. Eldred, Sullivan Co., New York

- **7 Hannah HICKOK**
  b. 18 Jul 1789
  bp. Southbury, Litchfield Co., Connecticut
  d. 2 Apr 1869
  dp. Halfway Brook, Sullivan Co., New York

- **8 Joshua AUSTIN**
  b. 1748
  bp.
  m.
  mp.
  d. Jul 1828
  dp.

- **9 Mary**
  b. 1758
  bp.
  d. 1809
  dp.

- **10 Samuel KNAPP**
  b. 29 Dec 1768
  bp. Stamford, Connecticut
  m. 29 Nov 1787
  mp. Stamford, Connecticut
  d.
  dp.

- **11 Naomi PALMER**
  b. abt 1766
  bp.
  d. 1827
  dp. Stamford, Connecticut

- **12 Elisha ELDRED**
  b. 15 Feb 1753
  bp. New England
  m. abt 1775
  mp.
  d. 18 Oct 1804
  dp. Minisink, Orange Co., New York

- **13 Mary HULSE**
  b. 20 Jan 1755
  bp.
  d. 18 Sep 1837
  dp. Halfway Brook, Sullivan Co., New York

- **14 Asa HICKOK**
  b. 4 Jun 1754
  bp. Woodbury, Litchfield Co., Connecticut
  m. 29 Dec 1777
  mp. Woodbury, Litchfield Co., Connecticut
  d. 23 Mar 1836
  dp. Bradford Co., Pennsylvania

- **15 Hester (Esther) HINMAN**
  b. 23 Oct 1759
  bp. South Britain, New Haven Co., Connecticut
  d. 23 Apr 1844
  dp. Bradford Co., Pennsylvania

- **16 Joshua AUSTIN**
  b. Feb 1718/19
  d. 10 Oct 1801

- **17 Tryphena HATHAWAY**
  b. 17 Jun 1729
  d. 2 May 1802

- **18** b. d.

- **19** b. d.

- **20 Samuel KNAPP Sr**
  b. 9 May 1744
  d. 22 Dec 1810

- **21 Susannah SCOFIELD**
  b. d.

- **22** b. d.

- **23** b. d.

- **24 ELDRED**
  b. d.

- **25** b. d.

- **26 James HULSE**
  b. abt 1728
  d. abt 1791

- **27 Mary ARNOT**
  b. 1731
  d. 1784

- **28 Justice HICKOK**
  b. d.

- **29** b. d.

- **30 Ebenezer HINMAN**
  b. d.

- **31** b. d.

Jennie Louisa Leavenworth Ancestors

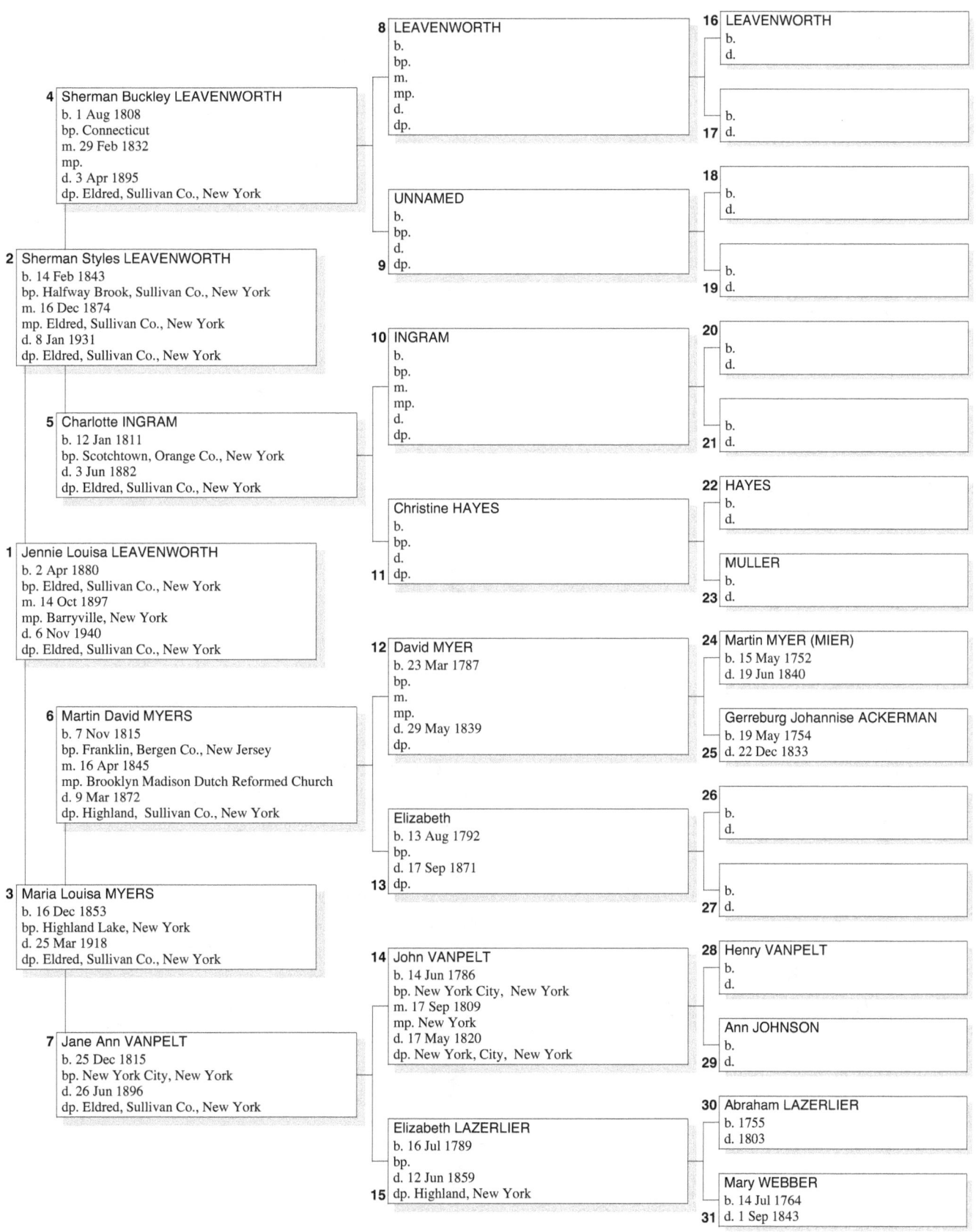

Some of the Families Mentioned in the Book

Joshua and Mary Austin Family
Ralph Austin and Fanny Knapp
Almira (Elmyra) Austin and James Hooker

Ralph and Fanny Knapp Austin Family
Samuel Knapp Austin and Susan Teed
Augustus Alonzo Austin and Phebe Maria Eldred
Clara Austin and Edward Nelson Teed
Emma Eliza Austin
Caroline Austin and Mr. Newman
James H. Austin and Julia
William Henry Austin and Mary Ann Eldred
Ann Mary Austin and O.P. Schoonover
Laura Austin and Mahlon Irvin Clark

James and Polly Mulford Eldred Family
Amelia Eldred and Harvey Wheeler
Sarah Eldred and Zophar Carmichael
Abraham Mulford and Elizabeth Wheeler
Charles Cotesworth P. Eldred and Effa C. Van Tuyl
Eliza Eldred and James Keen Gardner
Phebe Maria Eldred 1
Phebe Maria Eldred 2 and Augustus A. Austin
Harriet Baldwin Eldred
Amelia Ann Eldred

Asa and Esther Hinman Hickok Family
Hannah Hickok (second wife) and James Eldred
Justus Hickok and Mary Wells
Reuben Hickok
Sylvia Hickok
Louisa Hickok
David H. Hickok and Betsey Rice (first wife)

Sears and Mary Keen Gardner Family
Joseph Gardner and Sarah Purvis
Letty Gardner and Ethel B. Sergeant
Mary Gardner and Benjamin C. Austin
Sears Robert Gardner and Mary Ann Creiger
James Keen Gardner and Eliza Eldred
Moses Gardner
Eliza Ann Gardner and Isaac Young

Augustus Alonzo and Maria Eldred Austin Family
Alonzo Eugene Austin and Isabelle Camp
Mortimer Bruce Austin and Mary L. Millspaugh
Augusta Antoinette Austin and Henry Clinton
Adelaide Austin and Thomas J. Thompson
Miranda Adelia Austin and Archibald Paton
Edward D. Austin and Evaline
Justina Austin and Randolph Laing
Joshua M. Austin
Christina Austin
Clementina Austin
Grace Emma Austin
Ida Belle Austin and James Brown

William Henry and Mary Ann Eldred Austin Family
Mary Henrietta Austin
Edith Emogene Austin
Maria Adelaide Austin
James Eldred Austin and Emily Parmenter
Albert Alonzo Austin
Aida Antoinette Austin
Edward Augustus Austin
Charles Mortimer Austin and Jennie L. Leavenworth
Henry Ladore Austin
Randolph Laing Austin

Sherman Buckley and Charlotte Ingram Leavenworth Family
Harriet Elizabeth Leavenworth and Henry Palmer
Sarah Jane Leavenworth
Amelia Ann Leavenworth
Sherman Stiles Leavenworth and Maria L. Myers
Atwell Bishop Leavenworth
Hezekiah Bunce Leavenworth
John Ellis Leavenworth and Amelia Bradley
Julia Ann Leavenworth

Some Rev. Isaac Sergeant Descendants

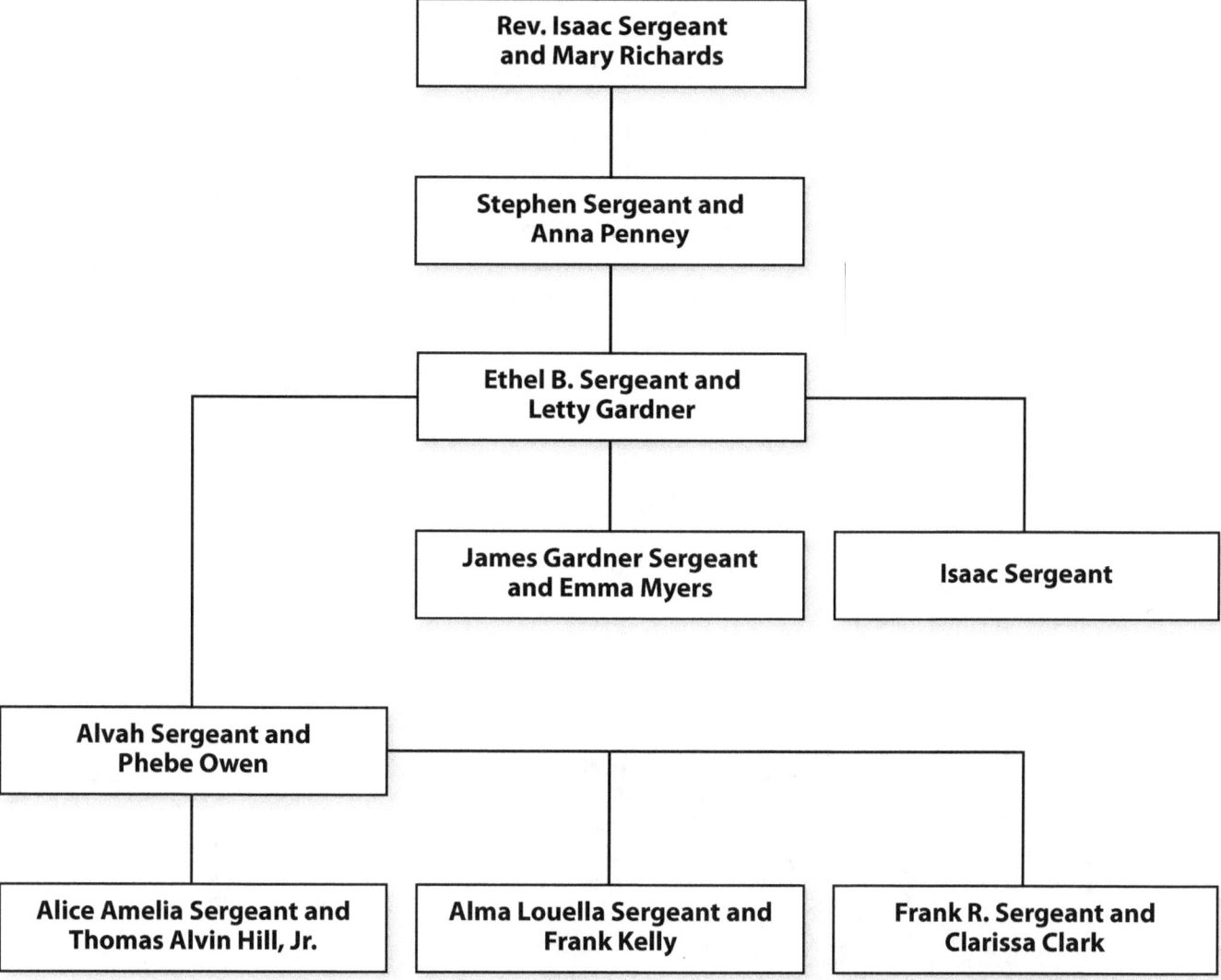

See page 12 for more information about the descendants of Rev. Isaac Sergeant and Mary Richards.

Harriet, Polly Maria, and Clara

Harriet and Polly Maria Carmichael were daughters of Zophar and Sarah Eldred Carmichael, and granddaughters of James Eldred.

These photos were in the collection of Melva Austin Barney.

Harriet Carmichael married David Young and they had nine children.

The family moved from Eldred to Illinois around 1870. I am not sure that they went directly to Illinois from here, but I know they lived there. [See p. 150.]

The two youngest girls, Harriet and Louise, afterward taught in New Rochelle, N.Y. Mother used to speak of those two. Cousin Harriet and her mother were here visiting a number of years ago.—Aida Austin

Polly Maria *(see page 47)* first married Harvey Gregory and second married Robert Mitchell, and lived in Poughkeepsie, New York. Two letters of Clara Gregory to her cousin Lon Austin were in the family letter collection.

Poughkeepsie, New York, January 19
Dear Lonnie,
I was very glad to hear from you as I have been very lonely. I go to school now. The scholars were all very glad to see me. I wished it was so that Ma and I could come back, but I do not think that it would do for ma to come out this winter.

You have not forgotten about our Christmas tree, have you, and our practicing. Does little Dor and Mort speak their pieces yet, or have they forgotten them? Do you remember going to the donation? I never will forget. You must write to me often. From your Clara, if

David and Harriet Carmichael Young.

David and Harriet Carmichael Young's daughter, Libby. (See p. 84.)

Clara Gregory daughter of Polly Maria Carmichael Gregory.

Children of Polly Maria Carmichael Gregory.

Polly Maria Carmichael Gregory Mitchell.

I may, call me so. Ma sends her love to you and to all.

Poughkeepsie, February 18
*Dear Cousin Lonnie,
I received your ever welcome letter. As I am in a hurry to go to school, I will finish it after school tonight.*

*Have you got my valentine yet? I got a very handsome one. You must excuse me for not writing much this time for I must study my lesson for tomorrow. You must write soon and often. From your cousin,
Clara Gregory*

Other Photos of Interest

Aunt Chat on Martin D. Myers side of the family. Linda Leavenworth Bohs Collection.

Aunt Bertha on Martin D. Myers side of the family. Linda Leavenworth Bohs Collection.

Unknown woman. Photo taken in Sing Sing, N.Y. Melva Austin Barney Collection.

Maps of Town of Highland and Halfway/Eldred

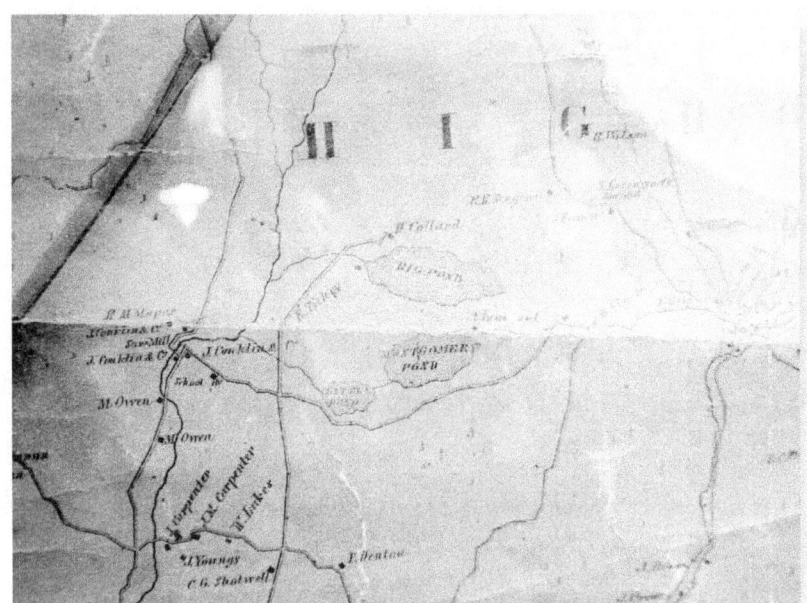

1856 Map of Town of Highland. Courtesy of Kevin Marrinan.

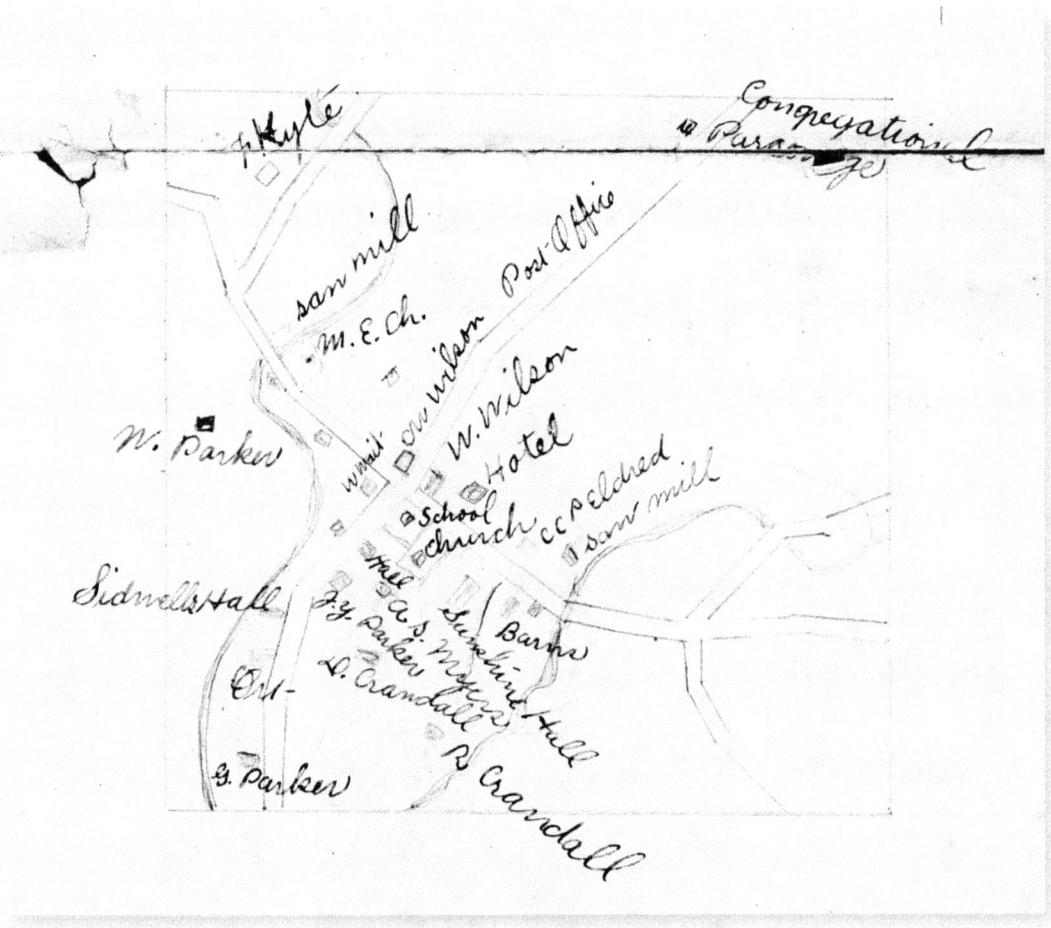

Halfway/Eldred map copied by Aida Austin, possibly from the 1930s. Melva Austin Barney Collection.

1870/1875 Map of Halfway Brook Village/Eldred

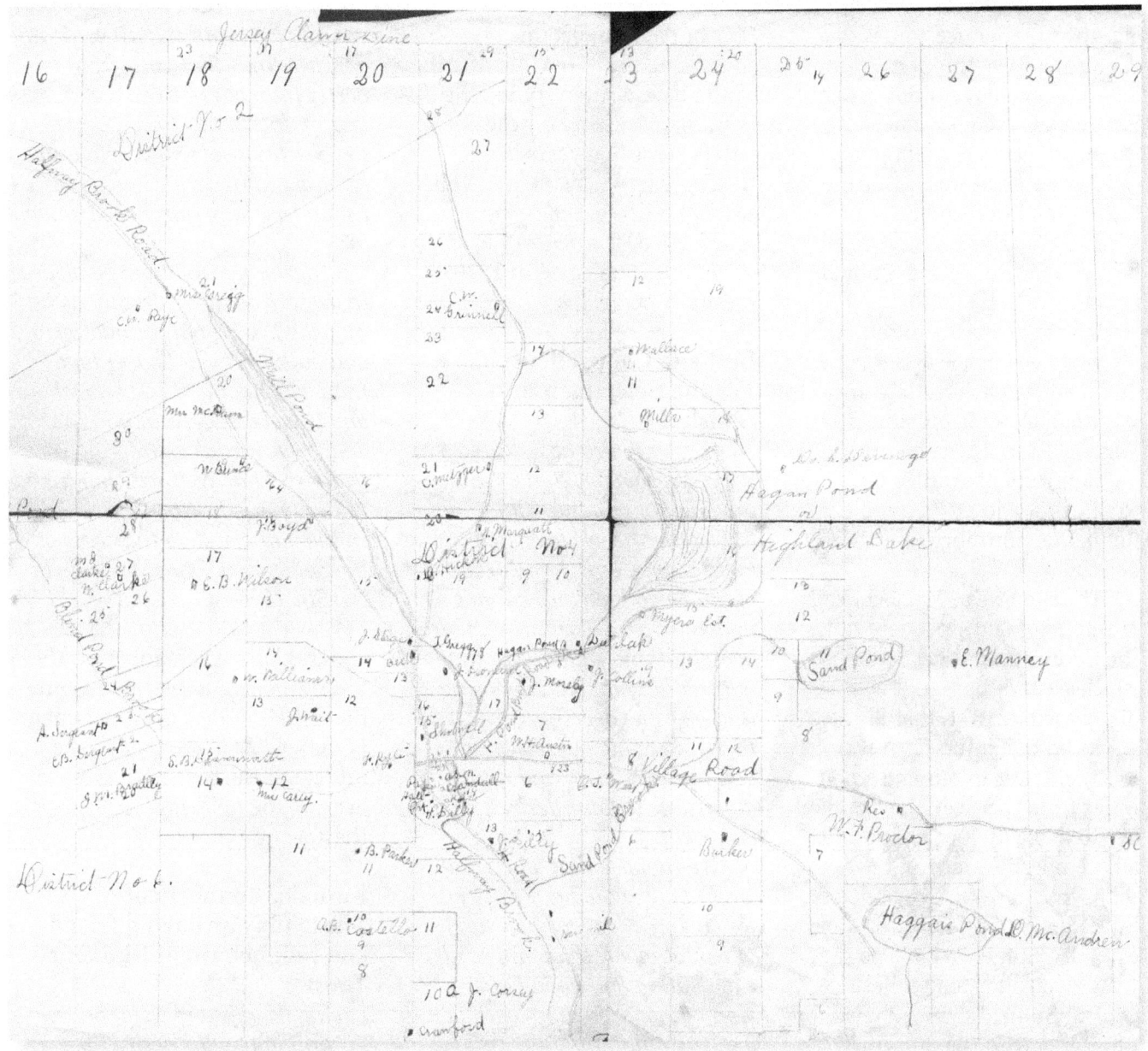

Probably a 1870/1875 Beers Map of the Town of Highland copied in the 1930s by Aida Austin. Melva Austin Barney Collection.

Letters of Anthony Austin, Town Clerk

In the Austin Ancestor sidebar on page 51 of this book, some letters written by Anthony Austin Sr., Town Clerk for Suffield, Connecticut, were mentioned.

The letters were written during the Simsbury Boundary War—a complicated land dispute between Simsbury and Suffield, Connecticut.

Westfield, Massachusetts was also involved in the disagreement. The land Massachusetts granted to Westfield in 1669, did not specify Westfield's southern boundary.

Connecticut granted land to Simsbury, in 1670, but did not define Simsbury's northern border.

The same year, Massachusetts granted Suffield six square miles; the Connecticut River was to be the eastern border. It was discovered in 1671, that Suffield's northern line intersected the Westfield line at four and a half miles from the river, not six miles.

To make up for the one and a half miles in width and two miles in length that belonged to Suffield, the Massachusetts Court, extended Suffield's grant to the west seven and a half miles.

But Suffield's new extension interfered with the Simsbury grant at five miles from the Connecticut River, and involved the title to about 3,000 acres.

The letters from Anthony Austin, the Town Clerk of Suffield, also the school teacher, seem to have been written to try and resolve the boundary ownership problem created between the towns of Simsbury and Suffield.

The diplomacy with which Anthony Austin Sr. wrote these two letters to the citizens of Simsbury, reminded me of something my father, Art Austin, would have written. I thought it quite interesting to read the letters some 300 years later.

These letters written in 1693, are found in Hezekiah Spencer Sheldon's, *Documentary History of Suffield*, published in 1879; Appendix pp. 323, 4.

Suffield, Connecticut
For the Selectmen of Simsbury

"Gentle" and Friends,
We received a few Syners under the hand of one Jno. Slater Sen, but wether he wrote as Select men, Town Clerk, or by order of the Select men, we cannot understand by his writing, there being nothing signified of that nature, therein: but supposing it to be some oversight, we shall therefore apply ourselves to you as select men, and return an answer to your desires, as followeth.

We suppose that when you wrote to us, you did it rather for customs sake, or by way of compliment, than any reall expectation you had of our complying, or joyning with you in any such motion.

Friends, we must tell you that your claims seems to us so unlikely, and also so unreasonable, that we shall be so far from sending men to joyn with yours in running such a lyn; as that on the contrary, if we send any at all, it will be to withstand and oppose you; at least to manifest our dislike of any such motion.

And we would farther, that you should understand that it is our resolve (until it doth evidently appear to us that your right is better than ours), to concerve and maintain our towne bounds to the utmost extent of what our honnoured General Court granted us: and we have purchased an apd for.

Therfore, Friends, pray please to desist from your present motion. For if your foundation you build on be not surer layd than we imagine it is, your labour and travel will certainly in the end prove unsuccessfull and fruitless. Your Well-wishing friend Anthony Austin, Town Clerk
In the name and by the order of the Selectmen. Dated in Suffield the 5th 1693

At the time appointed for the Simsbury perambulators to enter upon their duties, the Selectmen of Suffield sent two men, to be present at the perambulation, bearing the following letter from the Town Clerk:

Suffield, Connecticut
These for our Loving friends and Neighbours of Simsbury Towne

Loving friends and Neighbours, According to your desires, we have sent two of our neighbours, Srg. Joseph Harmon and Serg. David Winchell to meet with your men at the place appoynted, but not to joyn Issue with you in running any such lyne, but on the contrary, to protest against it, it being so unlikely, and also so unreasonable that your bounds should come within a mile and a halfe or two miles at farthest, of the center of our Towne: and besides, friends, we think that we have the Wethergag of you, or the best end of the Staffe in our hands.

For as much as we challenge nothing but what lyes within our province lyne; Your demand is whollily out of yours, but yet, notwithstanding, pray let not us contend, or give one an other hard words, but treat one another lovingly, like Christians, and Let our Authority on both sides Issue the matter: and if it appear to be your right, we shall not desire one foot or inch of it: if not, we desire [we] may enjoy our own peaceably.—Frome, Anthony Austin, Town Cleark. Dated in Suffield Feb 15, 1693

The commissioners appointed by the Massachusetts and Connecticut Colonies to settle the colonial boundary line in 1713, gave the disputed territory to Simsbury.

Mary Ann Eldred's Letter to Her Parents

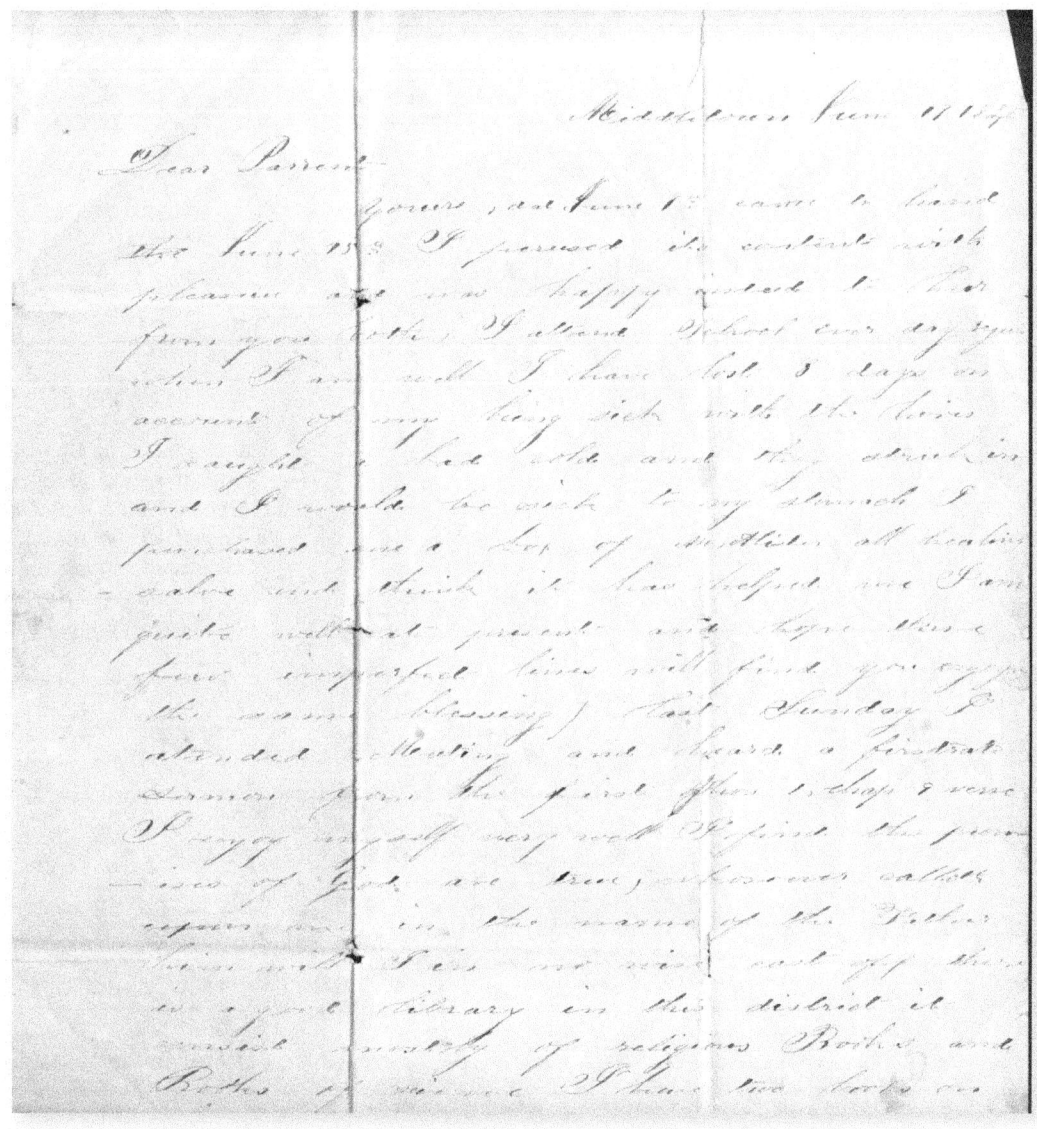

From Mary Ann Eldred, who is with her sister Sarah Eldred Carmichael in Middletown, New York, to her parents James and Hannah Hickcok Eldred, in Halfway Brook, New York, 1845. (See Chapter Six, pp. 54–56.) From the Mary Briggs Austin Collection.

Phebe Maria Eldred Austin's Letter to Her Sister

Letter from Phebe Maria Eldred Austin in Halfway Brook, New York, to her sister Mary Ann Eldred who was with her sister Sarah Carmichael in Middletown, New York, 1846. (See Chapter Six, p. 57.) From the Mary Briggs Austin Collection.

Fanny Knapp Austin's Letters to Her Children

> Halfe way brook January 10th 1854
>
> Dear Children
> You must excuse my not writing sooner I have been waiting for something pleasant to write but sickness and glome over sprads our Neighborho our house had escapd untill yesterday, Henery was brought from Moscow very sick we had the Doctor he pronounced it the Billous feavor but he is better this morning i feal in hopes it is a lite case it is the prevaling eppidemic and the scarlet fevor, the Doctor says he has 40 patients down with them and many that will not recover,
>
> my health is about as it was my cough is better my appitite is good if I do not work to hard a little work goes a good way with me, I have not been able go any ware except when they come after me Mr Stage took me up to his house I was their over a week and would have staid longer but Mrs Stage would wait on me so much I thought that I would come home but it has been so could I was sorry but old Mrs Eldred makes my fire in the morning and washes for me and I knit and work for her, I have not been up to Mr C P Eldreds they have been down for me several times last nite Mr Eldred was hear he said he would send for me i promisd to go and stay all the week they have some Gloves they want Manafacterd I will turn over a knee leaf my hand shakes so bad I cant write much

Letter Fanny Knapp Austin wrote her children, p. 1. (See Chapter Seven, pp. 73–75.) Courtesy of Melva Austin Barney.

Fanny Knapp Austin's Letters to Her Children (cont'd.)

I had a verry plesent New year to Mrs Stges we had good vituels and good company, George was home and Albert they inquire after you and Lacy, George said I must give his Compliments and beast respects to you both Albert said he would rather fetch them him selfe Mrs Stage said you promisd to write to her George and Albert was up to Mr Clarks on new year day he said Mary was greiving a bout your going a way, but Clarry was in good spirits and found it was his birth day and when he started for home she gave him such a snow banling it was a caution, they heard I was their and would have come but it was so slipery they gave it, up you would like to know Mrs Huts donation well they must hav had a very agreable time at evening all the Gentleman except thir sons was Mr Squir Clark and Mr George Elerd he went over to Mrs Mannys and got Catharine and and sister Polly and fetcht them up to Stages after George but was disapointed and had to wait on them both, Isaac Bradly was hear last evening he has been driving team for Mr gohara they tried to get him to take Liza Mariah they offerd him the team and would pay her way, he tolde them when he wante to go he was able to pay his own fary he is sick of the whole of them he talks of coming to Newyork in a few weeks Mr Waterman has mad him a good offer

Letter Fanny Knapp Austin wrote her children, p. 2. Courtesy of Melva Austin Barney.

Wensday Mooning I waited to see how Henery
got along he is better Mr C & Jn Eldred is a
calculating to come to Newyork next week and
and I want you to be shure and come with
him if he does not come soon you must come
the first opportunity the sooner the better
Perry and Ann was up hear and said he would
$1 a week they have got Priscilla Killpatrick
if you come back we will go and stay untill
you are better suited Ann is poorly she thinks
she cannot live untill spring, give my
love to all tell Mortimer to write and I will
tell him all about the wedings Oliver Dunlap
and Caty Devenport was Married on Newyear
their is 3 or 4 more such a coming soon
tell Adeline I will answer her soon
nomore at present I
remain your Mother
with affection

Fanny Austin

I must write to James please to let
him see the last leaf

Letter Fanny Knapp Austin wrote her children, p. 3. Courtesy of Melva Austin Barney.

Fanny Knapp Austin's Letters to Her Children (cont'd.)

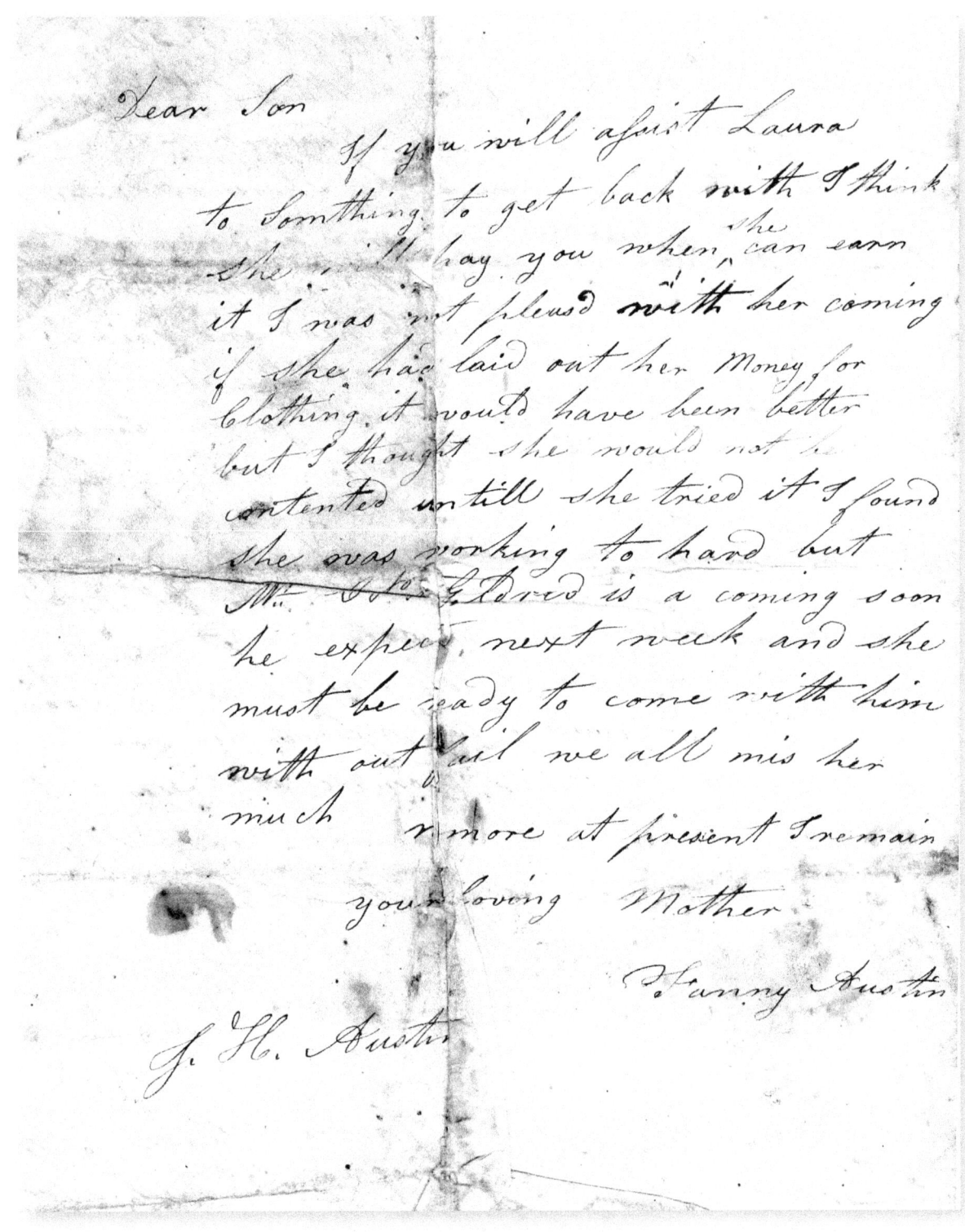

Dear Son
    If you will assist Laura to Something to get back with I think she will pay you when she can earn it I was not pleasd with her coming if she had laid out her Money for Clothing it would have been better but I thought she would not be contented untill she tried it I found she was working to hard but Mr. Eldred is a coming soon he expects next week and she must be ready to come with him with out fail we all mis her much ☙ no more at present I remain your loving Mother

                    Fanny Austin

J. H. Austin

Letter Fanny Knapp Austin wrote her children, p. 4. Courtesy of Melva Austin Barney.

James Austin's Letter to His Mother

> New York Feb 23rd 1858
>
> Dear Mother I again adress you a few lines. I received your letter of the 19th ins yesterday & was glad to hear that you was better but was sorry to hear that you had not received my letter of the 16 inst for I wrote by first Maile after receiving yours by Felix Kyte I think It verry probably that you have received It before this time I hope you did the next Maile I have thought It was misslaid In the Post Office as Is often the case & some times It Happens that letters do not arive at their destination for some time after they are Mailed I again risk Two Dollars by Maile I do not like to Send It this way but you are In want of the Money & So I risk It I should send you a larger Sum If I was Shure you would get It I think before long some person of our acquaintance will be enroute for Lumberland & then I will remitt to you In the mean time get of your friends what things you want to Make you Comfortable & do not pinch yourselves for food or fuel & I will pay the Bill you may rely on it I trust you will not run up a large Bill extravigantly but get all you want to Make you Comfortable keep Laura home with you do not think of trying to live alone It Is my particular wish & request that
>
> read from the third page for the Connection I have made a miss

James Austin wrote to his mother Fanny Austin. (See Chapter Seven, pp. 76–78.) Courtesy of Melva Austin Barney.

Mahlon Irvin Clark Marries Laura Austin

Sullivan County,
Town of Highland } ss:

I do hereby certify, that on the tenth day June instant, at the house of Wm. H. Austin in said town of Highland, Mahlon I. Clark of said town of Highland and Laura L. Austin also of said town of Highland, were, with their mutual consent lawfully joined together in holy matrimony, which was solemnized by me in the presence of James H Austin, Mrs Hannah Eldred, Mary Ann Austin, Ralph Austin and Fanny Austin all of said town of Highland, attesting witnesses. And I do further certify that the said Mahlon I Clark and Laura L Austin are known to me to be the persons described in this certificate; and that I ascertained, the said marriage that the parties were of sufficient age to contract the same; and that there appeared no lawful impediment to such marriage.

Given under my hand this the fifteenth day of June A.D. 1860

George T. B. Stage
Justice of the Peace

This letter, the marriage license of Mahlon Clark and Laura Austin, was found in the collection of my mother, Mary Briggs Austin. *(See Chapter Seven, p. 81.)*

From Mary Ann Austin's Scrapbook. Courtesy of Melva Austin Barney.

Fanny Austin's Letter to Her Daughter Laura

Laura I send Ivins Socks I had no measure to go by Mrs Clarke brought yarn and saide their was enough for 2 Pair I should have made them longer but I thought I would doe as she said but it lacks one knot of being enough and when I get that you shall the other pair, I thought I would send these for he mite want them you must come when you can I had a letter from James he appears to be in good spirits his horse is all write he livs with the same family he did, his Buziness is good and a prospect of its being better than ever it was Augustus his folks all well; I creape along about as well as ever, Mrs Dunlap washd for me yester day my Neighbours calls often to see if I want healpe I have got Wormwood and a going to use it for I think it is dropsy that maks me weak for my appetite is poor I have everything I wish for but do not eat much James told me to get what ever I want and I do,

   my love to you both Adieu

     Fanny Austin

Fanny Austin writes her daughter, Laura Austin Clark. See Chapter Seven, p. 81. Mary Briggs Austin Collection.

Henry Austin's Carting Book

May 1873 page in Henry Austin's 1872 Cartage book. Mary Briggs Austin Collection. See p. 162 for book cover.

Inside cover of Henry Austin's 1872 Cartage book. Mary Briggs Austin Collection. See p. 158 for Building at 50 Warren St.

William Henry Writes his son Lon

Eldred Feb 23rd /79

Dear Son
            I will try and write a few lines to let you know that we are all well here but myself I hev bin quite sick with a bad cold for the last week but I feel some better to night I hope these lines will find you well well I supose you are a farming out their now but it looks as tho winter had just begun here it has snoed here for the last week most of the time Kelso has got his new store opend and he feels

he has sent mee the sunday sun ever since he was here last fall he says the times is dull and I gess if he thinks that their is enny chance in Kansus to due better he would came out their I hev bin trying hard to sell but hev not suceeded as yet but I shal keep trying I am tired a farming here the way I heft to farm Henry Lilly is trying hard to sell he has offerd evry thing for thirteen hundred dollars I would like to see you vary much but as I cannot I hope you will write apton with my best wishes I will close from your loving Father
            W, H, Austin

Letter in the collection of Melva Austin Barney. See letter text on p. 208.

Eldred Family Information

Goshen, N. Y., May 29, 1936.

Dear Miss Austin:—

I received your letter, enclosing copy of letter from W. H. Eldridge; and was greatly pleased with it. Wrote him, telling what we were in search of, and informing him of some things, that I thought would not be included in the copy from the James Eldred Bible. Nor did I tell him about Uncle Jim, and his wife, as I have not the dates of their deaths nor their wedding date, as I remember.

He was pleased with what I sent him, and sent me (it cost him 15 cents postage) quite a package of typewritten notes, carbons of pages he was intending to put in his forthcoming History, when he makes it up. He also enclosed several pages about Elisha Eldred and his family, including quite a number of facts (or rather surmises) based on queries he has made, and in fact, it seemed to me that he really knew more than I did!

However, he himself has not been able to trace Elisha Eldred to his birthplace, altho' he strongly suspects it to be Rhode Island, and his wife a Mary Everett. I agree with him in this, as the first son was named Everett, and he says there was a family named Everett which was very friendly with a family of Eldreds in Rhode Island, and that family of Eldreds did include in it members named Elisha, Susanna, and Mary or Maria, which rather makes it appear that it might be the right one. However, the birth date of no child of which he is sure, coincides with the birthdate of Elisha Eldred of Denton.

If we can ever get to trace Elisha back to Rhode Island (township of North Kingston) it would mean that he was a lineal descendant of a Samuel Eldred who was born about 1620, probably in England. His first appearance of record in this country was at Cambridge, Mass, in 1641, when he joined the Ancient and Honorable Artillery Co. of Boston. He married Elizabeth, but whether before or after his arrival in New England is not known.

Practically all the Eldridges, Eldredges and Eldreds are descended from this man, and it thus appears that we are one of the branches which has carried the family name in its original purity to the present day.

He moved to Rhode Island about 1660, but June 22, 1670 he took the oath of constable at Wickford, under appointment of connecticut. On July 11, 1670, Thomas Eldredge, James Eldredge, Samuel Eldredge, John Cole and 6 others signed as witnesses to the futile efforts of the Constable to call a jury in the case of Walter House (Colonial Records of R. I. 2-344).

Samuel Eldred died soon after 1697 and was buried on the farm. 1/2 acre where he was buried was afterward set off as a family burying ground by his son John. Elizabeth was probably buried there also but there are no headstones for either of them. The births of their first four children are recorded at Cambridge, Mass.
1. Elizabeth Born Oct. 26, 1642. Nothing more known.
2. Samuel.   "   "   "   1644. Married Martha Knowles.
3. Mary.   B. June 15, 1646. D. May 9, 1712. Married Rouse Helme.
4. Thomas. B. 8 Sept.1648. M. Susanna Cole.
5. James. Probably died before 1687.unmarried. In the account of his escape from Bull's Garrison when it was destroyed by Indians in 1675, he is called James Eldredge (Narragansett Historical Register 2-114).
6. John, B. 17 Aug. 1659. M. Margaret Holden.
7. Daniel, Died 18 Aug. 1726.   Vt.
A greatgrandson of Samuel, named John Eldred is buried at Pownal, in the Eldred family lot on the farm of his son Daniel, where his headstone of white marble is very well preserved. (he died May 10, 1784.)

There is a branch of this family, headed by a Gardiner Eldred, which located at Quebec in 1800. Some of the descendants live at Quebec still, some at Vermont, and some elsewhere.

2

That is only a much shortened excerpt of one section of the pages he (Mr. W. H. Eldridge) sent me. If I get to Eldred, I shall bring it to show you. Most of it does not pertain to our branch, but it is very interesting nevertheless.

I had a short note from his only this week, with a little information I asked for. He said that he had not as yet gotten the copy of facts in the Eldred family Bible. I understood you to say that you intended sending them to him. Was I correct?

It is interesting to note that there are several names that run through practically all branches of the family. Samuel, James, Daniel, Thomas, Mary, Susannah, and Sarah. And Elizabeth seems to be the favorite name when marrying a wife. Also they (the men) seem quite fond of marrying Eldred women who were more or less distant relatives. Of course, it was quite the thing in Revolutionary times, for a widower with children to marry his wife's sister--and it worked out pretty well to.

I meant to have answered before, but have been not too well, and had housecleaning to do, also sewing. Finished two dresses this morning, ready to deliver. Want to make up a couple for myself, as I have the material ready. Am all thru housecleaning now except the cellar, and as it is so cold, we have to have a wood fire in the furnace night and morning, about 4 days a week, am sort of putting that off, till there won't be so much dust flying about.

Flowers have been very pretty, but act very queerly this year. I have sorts blooming together, that have been two weeks apart, nearly every year. Even Siberian iris and German iris are together, almost unheard of.

Hope you are in good health. Remember me to Aunt Lizzie Wilson if you see her.

Sincerely yours

Cora H. Carmichael

P. S. I finally found out that Elisha was a member of the Third Orange County Regiment, Land Grant Levy, in a Book known as "New York in the Revolution." There were two or more copies, and it was not in the first, but was in the second. There were other Eldreds even in those days, but mostly they resided in Albany or New York City.

In May of 1926, Aida Austin received information about James Eldred and his ancestors and descendants from Cora Hardcastle Eldred Carmichael.

Both Aida Austin and Cora Carmichael were related to James Eldred. Aida Austin was a granddaughter of James Eldred and his second wife, Hannah Hickok Eldred.

Cora Eldred Carmichael, a great-great-granddaughter of James and Polly Eldred, was related through C.C.P Eldred, and his son George W. Eldred.

Floyd Decatur Carmichael, Cora's husband, was a great-grandson of James Eldred, and related to James and Polly Eldred through Sarah Eldred Carmichael, and her son Decatur.

Four of the six pages of Cora's Letter and Eldred information are printed here. A couple pieces of information in Cora's letter seem to be incorrect. Cora H. Eldred Carmichael mentioned the maiden name of James Eldred's mother, Mary as possibly being Everett. My research, confirmed by the Hulse family, is that Mary Hulse married Elisha Eldred. Mary Hulse Eldred's last name from her second marriage was Forgeson.

James Eldred probably built the Temperance Tavern around 1830, not C.C.P in 1850.

See page 15 for a short biography on the Eldred Family of James Eldred.

Eldred Family Information (cont'd.)

Eldred Genealogy from 1785 to date (1938).

ELISHA ELDRED was born in 1752, probably in Rhode Island (altho we have only indirect evidence to prove this) and died Oct. 18, 1804, aged 52, at Minisink (now Denton, then known locally as The Outlet) in Orange County, New York State. He is buried in the plot known as the Denton Family Graveyard in the field back of the Denton Presbyterian Church at Denton, N. Y. His will (on file in the Orange County Surrogate's Court) was dated the day of his death, and was probated Oct. 25, 1804. He mentioned his wife, Mary; sons Everett, James and Samuel, and refers to other children, but does not name them. The names however, are supplied by the family bible of his son James, and by a descendant of Nathaniel, his youngest son.

The maiden name of his wife Mary is **not** known, but the name Everett, given to their first son, may have some significance. She died at the home of her son James, at Eldred, Sullivan County, N. Y. Sept. 18, 1837, and is buried in the Eldred Cemetery, at Eldred, N.Y. It is rather probable that Elisha and Mary were married in Rhode Island before they migrated to New York State. Their grandson, Gabriel B. Eldred, stated that his father, Ephriam, was born in Rhode Island, but he probably meant his grandfather, as his father was born at Minisink, N. Y. several years after the parents had settled there.

According to records in the Orange County Clerk's Office, Elisha bought land at the Outlet (later known as Denton) in 1785, and later mortgaged, bought and sold several other pieces of land at the same place. He was a member of the Third Company of Orange County Militia under Captain Daniel Denton. Eager's History of Orange County (the oldest locally written) states that a certain farm in Denton "was owned by Elisha Eldred, from New England, who was the first man who kept a store and set up a tavern at the place. This was about the commencement of the Revolution".

Rutterber's History of Orange County, which is accredited with being more detailed and in strict accordance with facts, also states that when the Goshen and Minisink Turnpike was chartered, among the incorporators was James Eldred. This was in 1809. This same history also states that a certain Oliver Young was born at Mt. Hope in 1811, went to Milford, Pa. when about 20 years old, and studied law there under Richard Eldred, and later under Melancthon Dimmock. Elisha's youngest son, Nathaniel, married into the Dimmock family.

According to Rutterber, the town of Minisink was formed March 7, 1788. The first town meeting was held April 1789 at the house of John Van Tyle, and Elisha Eldred was appointed one of the fence viewers. He was also roadmaster over the second District in 1792-3. James Eldred was School Commissioner about 1814. He moved to Sullivan County about 1815, after the death of his father, and most if not all of the family removed at that time, either to Sullivan County, or other places of residence.

Children of Elisha and Mary Eldred.

#	Name	Born
1.	Everett	Born Feb. 1776.
2.	James	" Oct. 7, 1777
3.	Sarah	" 1779
4.	Susanna	" 1780
5.	Mapsah	" 1782
6.	Samuel	" 1784
7.	Richard	" 1787
8.	Mary	" 1789
9.	Ephriam	" 1790
10.	Nathaniel	" Jan. 12, 1793
11.	Amelia	" 1794.

Everett Eldred (Born 1776) married Nov. 10, 1798 Mary Denton, granddaughter of Henry Wisner, one of Orange County's first and foremost settlers. The family was then, and still is quite prominent. Everett died Nov. 18, 1804, just a month after his father, leaving his widow, and a daughter Mary Ann, who was baptized Apr. 4, 1806 at the Presbyterian Church in Goshen. The records of this church show many facts in relation to Elisha's family. The wedding of Everett and Mary and Denton, the baptism of his daughter, the remarriage of his widow to one Robert Boak, Feb. 29, 1812, and the marriage of his daughter Mary Ann to John Wells Aug. 9, 1820 are all there recorded. So it would appear that Everett's widow and daughter remained at the Outlet with her people, who were prominent there, when the Eldred family migrated to Sullivan County or other places.

Page 2.

Skipping James, whom we will take up later on, the next child is Sarah, (born 1779) who married George Bucanna (Buchanan?) on April 25, 1795, according to the Presbyterian Church records. The same records also disclose the marriage of the fourth child Susanna (born 1789) to Jesse Belknap Nov. 3, 1798. From records in the Orange County Clerk's Office, showing partition of same of Elisha's estate, after his death, it would seem that Nathaniel Elmer, and Isaac Little married two of Elisha's daughters, but which of the other three girls not formerly mentioned, viz: Mapsah, born 1782), Mary (born 1789) or Amelia (born 1794) married which man, I have not been able to ascertain.

Samuel (born 1784) died Sept. 1829. Richard (born 1788) was a lawyer at Milford, Pa. He may have lived at Lackawaxon later. Ephriam (born 1790) died March 9, 1823. Nathaniel (born Jan 12, 1793) became a lawyer, and later on migrated to western Pennsylvania. There he came a Circuit Judge, also a member of the State Assembly, so that his career paralleled that bf his brother James in New York State. He married Lucinda J. Dimrick (born 1802, died 1824) and had a son Franklin B. (born 1819, died 1841) and daughter Lucinda J. (born 1823 died?). His wife having died, he married as a second wife, Sarah M. Dimrick, probably a younger sister of his first wife, who born him the following children.

Mary Aseneth (born 1830- died 1868.
Lucinda J.   (born 1832 died 1871)
Sarah E.   (born 1834- died 1851)
Annie E.   (born 1839, died 1863)
Caroline W. (born 1836, died 1917)
Charles F.   (born 1841, died 1897)

Charles F. Eldred married Emma West, and had the following children: Nathaniel B:(born 1867, died 1896); Mary Hamlin (born 1869 --); Arthur G, (born 1877 --); and Nina Otis (born 1879). Arthur G. Eldred married Marie Wheeler, who born him the following children: Alice Elizabeth, Jeannette M., Arthur G.; and John Wheeler.

There is a village named Eldred in Pennsylvania, just as there is one in New York State. It too, is named for its founder, Nathaniel Eldred, who, as stated before, was politically prominent.

JAMES ELDRED: (Elisha)

James was born Oct. 7, 1777, and died Apr. 12, 1857 at Eldred, N. Y. On Oct. 3, 1802, he married Polly Van Arsdale (Osdale) Mulford, who was born May 29, 1787, and died Jan. 24, 1825; On Feb. 12, 1826, James took as second wife, Hannah Hickock, born July 18, 1789, who died Apr. 12, 1869. Polly Van Osdale Mulford's real first name was Mary, as is shown by a deed on record in the Orange County Clerk's Office, signed by James and Mary, his wife.

As James did not remove to Sullivan County until 1815, many of his children were born in Orange County, and probably some of them buried there. After removing to Sullivan County, to a place known as The Village, (now Eldred) he became a member of the Congregational Church there, and was deacon from 1819 to 1857. He was a member of the State Assembly in 1835; and Judge of the Court of Common Pleas for several years. He and his son Charles assisted in organizing the First Congregational Church of Lumberland. At the time he settled in Sullivan, many of the houses were still being built of logs. The present house, known as the old Eldred Homestead, was probably built about 1850 by his son, Charles C. P. Eldred. it was used as a tavern at one time, and known as the Temperance Tavern, the old sign to that effect, having been found in the attic, when the house passed from the possession of the last Eldred to own it.

Children of James and Polly Van Osdale Mulford Eldred:
1. Amelia, born Aug. 7, 1803, died Jan. 10, 1820. Married June 27, 1819, Harvey Wheeler.
2. Sarah, born May 3, 1805, died   . Married Sept. 5, 1822 Zopher Carmichael. son of John and Abigail Carmichael. She is buried in Hillside Cemetery, Middletown, Orange Co. N. Y.

3. Abraham Mulford, born Oct. 18, 1806. Died Sept. 25, 1847. Married Elizabeth Wheeler.
   Children: 1. Amelia, born 1840.
             2. Benjamin Franklin, born 1841.
             3. Josephine.
             4. Augusta Maria, born 1844.
             5. Mary Eliza
             6. Harriet Louise, born 1846.
             7. Elizabeth

Leavenworth Bible Pages

FAMILY
MARRIAGES.

Sherman B. Leavenworth

to

Charlotte Ingram

Feby 29 1832

FAMILY RECORD.
DEATHS.

First child Jany 28. 1833.

Sarah Jane. Sept 22. 1842

Amelia Ann. Oct 3. 1842.

Alvell B. Leavenworth Nov 15th 1864

Hezekiah B. Leavenworth April 26 1865

DEATHS.

Juliaann March 14th 1868

Charlotte wife of S B Leavenworth June 3rd 1882

S. B. Leavenworth April 3rd 1895.

Harriet Elizabeth Palmer

John Ellis Leavenworth March 10. 1916

Maria, wife of Sherman S. Leavenworth March 25, 1918

Sherman S. Leavenworth January 8, 1931

Family records from the Sherman Buckley and Charlotte Ingram Leavenworth Bible. Courtesy of Ric Schroedel. See page 46 for another Leavenworth Bible page.

Elizabeth Van Pelt Bible Pages

FAMILY RECORD.

DEATHS.

John Van Pelt Died 17 of May 1820 Aged 33 years 11 Month and 3 Days

Maria A Van Pelt Died 25 of March 1835 Aged 22 years and 25 Days

Henry Cripps Webb Died 3rd of March 1840 Aged 33 years and 3 Months

John Henry Webb Died 5th of July 1840 Aged 2 years 1 months and 5 Days

David M. Myers Died 21st of March 1830 Aged 1 year 1 Months and 21 Days

Peter L. Van Pelt Died 7th of May 1858 Aged 47 years

Elizabeth Van Pelt Died 12th of June Aged 67 years 10 Month 26 Days 1859

DEATHS.

Martin D. Myers Died 29th of March Aged 56 Years 4 Months & 22 Days 1872

Jane Ann Myers Died 26th of June Aged 60 years 6 Months and one Day 1896

FAMILY RECORD.

MARRIAGES.

John Van Pelt and Elizabeth Lazelier was Married 17 September 1809

Peter L. Van Pelt and Sarah Locker was Married 15 of July 1832

Henry Cripps Webb and Jane Ann Van Pelt was Married 29 of March 1834

Martin L. Myers and Jane Ann Webb was Married 16th of April 1845

Charles C Webb & Sarah Frances Shotwell was Married 18th of June 1851

Family records from the Elizabeth Van Pelt Bible. Courtesy of Cynthia Leavenworth Belinger. See p. 71 for another Van Pelt record.

Mary Ann Austin's Poetry

To My Husband

You, my dear husband I wish to see,
Talk with you about heaven;
Since I left home one has gone there,
Yet there is left us seven.
Now we live for God, blessed thought,
We can pray for each other;
Pray God to watch over our darlings,
Bring us in heaven together.

Far from my home and from thee,
Yet our hearts are united;
God is just, give him praise
Though our hopes are blighted;
The bitterest trial ever I knew,
Edith died from our home,
Thank new friends, yet far from old
The bitter thought will come.

Her release from pain a mixture to me,
Her gain gave me pleasure,
But my loss and depth of my woe
Time can never measure;
Vain her coming to Kansas for health,
Too far gone to bring;
But as mine is much better here
I'll stay longer than spring.

The letters of sympathy I have received
Is sweet comfort to me;
There is welcome waiting of friends
To my dear home and thee.
Time is going and time is coming,
We can scarcely realize
That so many years have passed away,
As thoughts of the past arise.

The prospect of years hath failed us,
We only see the blank page
In our book of which we can fill
Only a leaf at this age;
We must be earnest the time to improve,
Strive for a heavenly theme,
Watch and pray for God to be with us,
For all is blank without him.

Nothing of earth is sure but the grave,
We may never meet in life;
If this be our lot, then my dear husband
Meet in heaven your wife.—*M.A.A., Solomon City, Kansas, March 16, 1880.*

Faith

I received a sweet missive from home,
Bringing good news today;
The Lord is there working mightily,
Pouring down his Spirit's ray.
They feel the warmth his love sheds,
And flee from freezing sin;
Door of their hearts thrown open wide
Lets saving life come in.

And on my stricken houshold band
The Savior's love is shining;
Now I look beyond dark clouds,
For back my faith is coming.
Years and years I prayed for this,
No answer came to me:
My path was tangled and my heart
Was filled with agony.

And dare I say that I was tried
Beyond my strength, ah, no;
The fault was mine, who could I blame,
For God is truth I know.
I am ashamed that I could doubt
My bread on water cast;
Although it floated round for years,
It came again at last.

A servant of God is working here,
Warning night after night
To avoid the thunderbolts of wrath,
Before they fall with might.
He tells us too, of a Savior's love,
His rich and choicest gift;
And if we stray from the loving fold,
In Satan's power we drift.

Come out to church all ye who can,
To hear of living peace;
It will give us strength, renew our lives,
Make angry turmoil cease;
I pray that God in mercy send
A flood of saving grace,
Flashing our souls in his harbor safe,
Cleansing from sin this place.
—*Solomon, Feb 9th, 1880. M.A.A. Written for the* Sentinel.

From Mary Ann Austin's scrapbook. Courtesy of Melva Austin Barney. See p. 223 for another poem by Mary Ann Austin.

Index

54th Regiment, New York, 110
56th Regiment, New York, 94
1832, May Flood, 34
1845 Land Mortgage Sale, 56
1845 and 1848 Letters, 59
1857, Winter, 77
1873 Depression, 174
1875 N.Y. Farm Census, 183

A

A Reverie/Kansas Romance, 225
Albany Normal School, 157, 161
Alden, Dr., 157, 161, 165, 168, 172, 173
An Answer, 223
Antietam, 96
Asendorf, Henry, 148, 228
Aunt
    Bertha, 237
    Chat, 237
    Sal, 109
Austin
    Abigail Holcomb, 51
    Adelaide/Addie, *see Thompson*
    Aida/Ida, 13, 14, 20, 49, 55, 80, 83, 86, 90, 106, 107, 113, 134, 135, 143, 146, 149, 151, 157, 172, 174–180, 185, 186, 188, 189, 193, 195, 196, 199, 200, 201, 205, 210, 211, 213, 216, 217, 218, 220, 222, 224, 226, 234, 236, 238, 239, 273, 253
    Albert Alonzo (Lon), 76, 84, 90, 134, 135, 146, 157, 172, 174, 175–180, 185–197, 199, 201–203, 205, 208, 209, 210–214, 218, 225, 229, 234, 251
    Almira, *see Hooker*
    Alonzo, Eugene, Sr. (Rev.), 46, 47, 50, 55, 57, 67, 84, 90, 130, 134, 135, 140, 162, 163, 189, 226, 234
    Alonzo, Eugene Jr. (Dr.), 37, 67, 140, 162, 226
    Ancestors, 51
    Ann Mary, *see Schoonover*
    Anthony Jr., 51
    Anthony Sr., 51, 240
    Antoinette/Net, *see Clinton*
    Arthur 70, 142, 186, 215, 240
    Augustus Alonzo, 11, 13, 14, 19, 29, 30, 37, 46, 47, 49, 50, 53, 55, 57, 62, 65, 67, 70, 76–78, 80, 81, 84, 90, 103, 112, 113, 133, 134, 135, 137, 162, 164, 174, 175, 180, 191, 197, 226, 234
    Benjamin C., 29, 62, 68, 111, 226, 234
    Caleb, 4, 51, 52
    Caroline, *see Newman*
    Charles Augustus (Gussie), 162, 163, 171, 197
    Charles Mortimer, 4, 14, 45, 50, 104, 127, 130, 134–136, 146, 157, 175, 176, 185, 188, 194, 195, 226, 227, 229, 232, 234
    Charles Raymond, 78, 104, 159
    Christina, 67, 90, 134, 135, 162, 234
    Clara, *see Teed*
    Clementina, 70, 90, 134, 135, 162, 234
    Dawn Lee, *see Sagarra*
    Deborah, 51
    Edith Emogene, 66, 67, 69, 76, 84, 90, 113, 122, 125, 126, 129, 133–138, 140–143, 146, 148–153, 155–158, 161–168, 170–182, 185–196, 198, 201, 203–214, 216–219, 221, 222, 234
    Edward Augustus, 127, 130, 151, 174, 234
    Edward D., 67, 90, 134, 135, 162, 234
    Elijah, 51, 52
    Elizabeth, 51
    Emily Parmenter, 234
    Emma Eliza, 11, 19, 29, 234
    Esther Huggins, 51
    Evaline, 135, 162, 234
    Fanny Knapp, 4, 5, 11, 13, 14, 19, 29, 37, 38, 46, 49, 50, 53, 54, 61, 67, 69, 73, 75, 76, 80, 81, 84, 90, 106, 112, 120, 121, 135, 137, 149, 197, 234, 243, 244-247, 249
    Frank, 186
    Gladys Myers, 37, 47, 72, 78, 80, 83, 104, 147, 159, 173
    Grace Emma, 70, 90, 134, 135, 162, 174, 234
    Gustavus, 52
    Harriet (d/o Benjamin C.), 62
    Henrietta, 130, 134, 140, 162, 226
    Henry Ladore, 135, 137, 146, 154, 157, 166, 176, 185, 190–193, 195, 203, 206, 207, 209, 212–214, 219, 226, 234
    Ida Belle (Belle), *see Brown*
    Ira M., 62, 131, 186, 226
    Isabelle (Belle) Camp, 84, 90, 130, 134, 135, 140, 162, 163, 226, 234
    James Eldred, 70, 76, 84, 90, 134, 135, 146, 157, 175, 176, 185, 187, 194, 195, 196, 205, 218. 222, 229, 234, 247
    James H., 19, 29, 38, 50, 54, 65, 70, 76, 78, 81, 113, 137, 139, 140, 234
    Jennie Louisa Leavenworth, iv, ix, 14, 39, 44, 45, 70, 104, 220, 228, 233, 234
    Joan, *see Geier*
    John Mortimer, 197
    Joshua Jr., 4, 5, 11, 29, 51, 52, 106, 234
    Joshua Sr., 4, 51, 52
    Joshua M., 65, 234
    Julia, 113, 138, 139, 154, 165, 234
    Justina (Tina), *see Laing*
    Laura, *see Clark*
    Margie, *see Maglione*

Maria Adelaide, 67, 69, 76, 84, 90, 134, 135, 146, 157, 173, 176, 179, 185, 189, 190, 192–195, 201, 203, 206, 209, 211–214, 219, 220, 222, 226, 234
Martin Van Buren, 62
Mary (wife of Joshua Jr.), 4, 5, 106, 234
Mary Henrietta, 62, 66, 67, 69, 76, 84, 90, 125, 134, 135, 146, 157, 176, 185, 195, 203, 209, 213, 226, 234
Mary A. (d/o Benjamin C.), 62
Mary Ann Eldred, 14, 25, 30, 33, 35, 38, 45, 46, 51, 54, 55, 57, 58, 59, 60, 61, 62, 64, 65–67, 69, 75, 76, 80, 81, 84, 90, 112, 113, 122, 126, 127, 130, 133–135, 137, 139, 140–142, 146, 148, 150–153, 155–157, 165, 166, 171, 173–175, 185, 189, 190, 194, 195, 200, 203, 205, 216–219, 221–226, 234, 241, 248, 258
Mary Briggs, iv, v, 54, 90, 137, 148, 215, 248
Mary Gardner, 17, 29, 62, 63, 111, 234
Mary Letitia Millspaugh, 135, 143, 162, 163, 171, 197, 234
Melva, *see Barney*
Minerva, 186, 226
Minnie, 186
Miranda (Rand), *see Paton*
Mortimer (Mortie), 130, 133, 134
Mortimer Bruce, 46, 47, 57, 65, 67, 74, 90, 102, 103, 104, 112, 113, 134, 135, 143, 147, 162, 163, 171, 234
Nancy, 60
Nellie, 186
of Schickshinny, 52
Olinda Ann, 90, 130, 134, 140, 162, 163, 226
Phebe Maria Eldred, 13–15, 20, 24, 30, 37, 46, 47, 50, 57, 60, 65, 67, 70, 75, 80, 84, 90, 103, 112, 133–136, 162, 174, 191, 224, 226, 234, 242

Ralph, 4, 5, 11, 13, 14, 18, 19, 29, 37, 38, 46, 49, 50, 52–54, 61, 67, 70, 73, 80, 81, 84, 90, 91, 102–104, 106, 120, 135, 137, 175, 197, 234
Randolph Laing, 141, 151, 234
Robert, 4, 50, 54, 130, 137, 138
Richard, 51
Richard (Asten) Sr., 51
Ruth, 51
Samuel Knapp, 5, 11, 19, 29, 38, 50, 103, 104, 112, 113, 234
Sarah, 62
Sarah Tone, 62
Shadrack, 51, 52
Susan Teed, 38, 50, 104, 112, 113, 234
Tryphena, 51
Tryphena Hathaway, 51, 52
Uncle Ralph, 51, 52
William Henry, 14, 19, 25, 29, 37, 38, 45, 46, 50, 54, 55, 61, 62, 65–67, 69, 70, 73–77, 80, 81, 84, 90, 113, 126, 127, 130, 133, 134, 135–137, 140–142, 146, 148–151, 154, 156–158, 162, 165, 170, 171, 172, 174–178, 180, 183, 185, 187, 189, 194, 195, 205, 208, 211, 217, 226, 234, 250, 251
Ayres
David, 68
W., 166

B

Badger, John, 85
Barker, Jesse and Lucy, 74
Barnes
Almira, *see Eldred*
Cornelius, 14
Elizabeth, 12
Elizabeth, *see Owen*
Family, 9
Henry, 12
Jeremiah, 12, 14
John, 12
John and Elizabeth Holbert, 79
Nathan, 12
Rebecca, 12
Thomas, 12

Barney, Melva Austin, ix, 4, 30, 47, 55, 62, 73, 76, 78, 79, 90, 103, 127, 134, 139, 151, 152, 157, 158, 161, 173, 175, 194, 217, 218, 222, 236
Barry, William T., 30
Barton
Benjamin, 11
John, 20
Beakey, Ellen, 90
Beaks, Stacy, 45
Beasley, Len, 177
Beaver Brook, 26, 214
Beecher, Henry Ward, 182, 189, 196, 207
Bevis, 51
Bishop
Anna, 40
Family, 40, 42
Ichabod, 40, 68
John, 29, 40, 42, 53, 68, 86, 120
Julia, 29, 40
Oliver, 40, 42, 45, 68, 86, 120
Sarah Ingram, 40, 53, 68, 86, 120, 147
Stephen, 40, 42, 45, 68, 86, 147
Stephen, 29
Black Friday Panic, 142, 154, 174
Blind Pond, 39, 40, 42, 44, 83
Blind Pond Brook, 39, 42, 43, 44, 45, 47, 49, 65, 112
Bluestone, 26, 144, 154, 214, 229
Bogert
Amanda Hogencamp, 147
Carrie Etta, *see Clark*
John, 147
Bolton
Ann Eliza Hickok, 54, 59
Lewis, 59
Bowhanan, Sarah Eldred, 5
Boyd
Alexander, 66, 69, 82, 120, 147, 186
Bertha, 228
Comfort, 69, 82, 92, 95, 120, 125, 131, 147, 186
Duncan, 68
Elizabeth, 69, 82, 120, 147, 186
Floyd, 148
Isabel, 148, 228
James, 69, 82, 147, 148, 180, 183, 186, 228

James Edward, 228
Margaret Mills, 147, 148, 180, 186, 228
Bradley
Anna Amelia, 87, 137, 138, 147, 164, 184, 228, 234
Atwell, 164, 184, 228
Charlotte (Lottie), 147, 164, 184, 228
Family, 44, 100, 123, 137, 184, 220
Isaac M., 53, 74, 79, 87, 91, 95–97, 105, 107, 111, 119, 137, 138, 147, 164, 170, 183, 184, 228
Isaac Newton, 137, 147, 164, 184, 228
Joanna Brown, 53, 79, 87, 137, 147, 164, 184, 228
Mary Frances, 137, 147, 164, 184, 228
Nora, 164, 184, 228
Viola, 137, 147, 164, 184, 228
Braisted
Family, 224
Mrs., 217, 224
Brant, Joseph (Thayendanegea), 2, 215
Breen, Ella, *see Gardner*
Briggs
Family, 5, 11, 38, 94
Benjamin and Sarah Jeffries, 11, 74, 84
Catharine Thrush, 74, 84
Clinton and Marium Clark, 84, 229
Irwin, 5, 11, 74, 84, 127, 229
Irwin and Myrtie family, 215
James T., 11, 74, 84
Mary, *see Austin*
Myrtie Crabtree, iv, v, 5, 11, 74, 91, 229, 273
Brown
Ida Belle Austin, 67, 134, 135, 150, 162, 167, 234
James Brown, 135, 234
Joanna Brown, *see Bradley*
Mary (Mercy) Harding, *see Clark*
Silas, 53
Bunce
Elizabeth, 40, 53

Family, 40, 44, 53
George, 40, 53, 70, 82, 92, 110, 112, 114, 132, 226
Hezekiah, 40, 42, 53, 60, 70
Hezekiah Jr., 40, 53
Julia, 40, 53, 66, 70
Julia (daughter), 40, 53
Lucy, 40, 53
Mary Ellen, *see Carmichael*
Thomas, 40, 53
William, 40, 53, 70, 82, 227
Bunk House, 42
Bush, Daniel, 7

C
Calkins, Family, 10
Burton, 10
Charles F., 147
Elias, 10, 61
Moses, 18
Oliver and Hannah Thomas, 10
James E., 147
Maria E. Gardner, 10, 35, 38, 51, 69, 111, 135, 147, 151 154
Marie E., 147
Moses, 18
Oliver, 10, 14, 17
Oliver Jr., 10, 61, 147, 170
Carmichael
Alexander, 10, 14, 18, 19, 24, 29, 32, 53, 55, 62, 72, 86
Charles, 38, 54, 135, 224
Cora Hardcastle Eldred, 253
Decator, 54, 224, 253
Deacon, 12
Floyd Decator, 253
Elimina, *see Drake*
Eliza, *see Puff*
Elizabeth, 62, 65
Emeline, *see Lewis*
Harriet, *see Young*
Ichabod, 12
John Mulford, 38, 54, 135, 226
John and Abigail, 18
Lewis, 30, 38,54, 64, 65, 84, 135, 139, 147, 173, 224
Lina, *see Watson*
Maria, 54
Martha, *see Stage*
Mary Schofield, 226

Mary Ellen Bunce, 40, 56, 60, 64, 65, 84, 139, 147, 173, 224
Phebe, 12
Polly Maria, *see Mitchell*
Sarah, *see Davis*
Sarah Eldred, 12, 13, 15, 18, 20, 24, 30, 38, 47, 54, 56, 57, 64, 75, 135, 139, 147, 150, 224, 234, 236, 241, 242, 253
Stephen, 19
Zophar, 18, 20, 30, 38, 47, 54, 56, 57, 64, 76, 135, 139, 147, 150, 224, 234, 236
Carpenter
Dorcas, 74
James, 14
James and Lucy, 19
James and Mary, 74
John, 14
Joseph, 14, 74
Case
Betsy Johnson, 58
Daniel, 19, 20
Census Sidebars
Some Relatives in 1798, 5
Relatives in 1815, 11
1820 Census, Other Towns, 18
Where They Lived in 1830, 29
Family not in Lumberland 1835, 38
People of Lumberland 1836, 47
Others 1855, 74
Others 1860, 84
Others in 1870, 147
Others in 1875, 186
Others in 1880, 226
Cholera, 32
Church News, 12, 19, 37, 66, 85, 127, 155, 171, 187, 210
Churches
Baptist 61, 85, 146, 187
Congregational Church, 9, 11, 12, 15, 16, 19, 24, 29–31, 36–38, 50, 53, 57, 62, 64, 66, 72, 75, 82, 85, 86, 92, 118, 146, 155, 158, 170, 171, 187, 198, 199, 210, 211, 226–228
Glen Spey (South Lebanon), 155

Methodist Episcopal, 19, 24,
30, 36, 37, 66, 84–86, 127,
136, 146, 155, 185, 187, 190,
211, 220, 227–229
Mongaup, 155
Pond Eddy, 127, 155
Union, 118, 187
Civil War Veterans, Highland, 132
Clark
Carrie Etta Bogert, 147, 226
Carolyn Hallock, 37
Charles, 68
Clarrissa, *see Sergeant*
Clarissa, 68
Edward, 149
Elbert, 135, 148, 184, 227
Ella, 83, 187
Ellsworth, 92, 135, 143, 148,
176, 184, 227
Estella, 148
Eva, 143
George, 10, 18, 29, 53, 62, 68,
80, 83, 96, 170, 184, 188,
192, 203, 227
George (s/o George and
Harriet), 227
George Case, 19, 29, 37, 47, 53,
68, 138, 147, 203, 226
Harriet Covert, 18, 29, 53, 62,
68, 80, 83, 184, 203, 227
John, 227
John Henry, 68, 138, 226,
Laura Austin, 29, 38, 50, 53,
54, 56, 67, 68, 70, 75, 77, 80,
81, 83, 92, 107, 112, 127,
135, 138, 139, 143, 148, 149,
164, 184, 191, 192, 203, 217,
227, 234, 248, 249
Louisa, 148
Mahlon Irvin, 10, 29, 38, 53,
68, 81, 83, 92, 135, 143, 148,
170, 183, 184, 203, 226, 234,
248
Martha, 10, 68, 83, 113, 148
Martin Dominick, 83
Mary (d/o Wilmot), 68, 74
Mary (Mercy) Harding Brown,
53, 68, 138, 147, 226
Mary Jane (d/o George and
Harriet), 83

Mary Van Auken, 9, 18, 29, 53,
62, 68, 73, 83, 148, 184, 202,
203
Moses, 19
Phebe Hazen, *see Myers*
Robert, 184, 227
Samuel, 83
Stella, *see Leavenworth*
Thomas W., 19, 29, 36, 47
Wilmot, 9, 14, 18, 19, 29, 53,
62, 68, 74, 83, 148, 170, 183,
184, 202, 203
Clinton
Antoinette (Net) Austin, 57, 67,
112–114, 122, 127, 134, 135,
148, 149, 162, 171, 177, 179,
234
Henry, 135, 162, 181, 188, 234
Ida Belle, 162
Collins, 84, 135, 144, 146, 179,
194, 200, 201, 220
Annie, 168, 214
Emma, 84
Emma Kelso, 44, 84, 185, 187,
194, 200, 203, 206, 214, 224
Isabella, 84, 146
James, 84, 85, 127, 146, 211,
222
Maria, 84
Mary Jane, 84
Robert, 84, 127, 146, 224
Thomas, 84, 127, 146, 176, 189
200, 214, 222
William, 84
Conkling, John, 44, 45, 114
Connecticut, vii, 3–5, 10, 11, 27,
39, 40, 45, 51, 52, 57, 106
Greenwich, 53
Litchfield County, 15
Middlebury, 5, 29, 41
New Haven County, 29
Simsbury, 240
Stamford, 53
Suffield, 51, 52, 240
Southbury, 18, 41
Waterbury, 5
Watertown, 41
Woodbury, 41
Cooper, Solon 9, 29
Corey,
Betsy, 19
Elnathan, 17, 19, 29

Cornwell Family, 74
Covert
William and Anna Ryder, 11,
29, 62, 184
Harriet, *see Clark*
James, 11
Irene Tompkins, 11
Margaret, 187
Crabb/Crabtree
Amanda Myrtie, *see Briggs*
Arnold and Rachel, 74, 84
Elijah and Priscilla, 84
Family, 5, 38, 91, 94
Ida Emily Higginson, 228
John, 74, 84, 228
Richard and Mary Giggey, 11,
84
Craine, L.L., 196
Crandall, George, 55
Crane,
Abigail, 12
Alfred, 100
Asa, 11,
Calvin, 22
Crawford, 61
Alfred, 100
Joel, 226
Cuddeback
Ann Eliza Gardner, 51, 69, 135,
172
Louis, 172
Abraham, 8
William A., 8

D
Darling
Charles S., 228
Charlotte (Lottie) Myers, 78,
79, 84, 88, 146, 164, 185,
187, 228
Ida, 228
Mary, 163, 168
Davis
Sarah Carmichael, 54, 135, 224
Decker, Mr., 144
Delaware River, 1–11, 14, 16, 17,
21–26, 28–30, 32, 33, 34, 37,
42, 43, 47, 52, 58, 63, 74, 77,
82, 128, 144, 154, 160
Delaware and Hudson Canal, 25,
26, 31, 33, 35, 44, 61, 63,
160, 186

DeVenoge, 83
   Catharine, 86
   Leon, Dr., 83, 86, 145, 158, 170, 172, 208
   Mary, 86
Dodge, 38, 39, 56, 57,
   Benjamin, 8, 35, 44, 45, 114
   Catharine, 66
   Stephen A., 97
Donation, 75
Drake, Elimina Carmichael, 38, 54, 57, 135, 224
Dubois
   Alvina and Eugene, 186
   George, 90
   Mr. and/or Mrs., 194, 212, 220
Duer, John, 4, 8, 56
Dunlap
   Caty Devenport, 75
   Emily, 177
   Johnston, 116, 132
   Lewis, 177, 200
   Oliver, 75, 121
Dunn
   James B., 17
   Thomas, 9, 16
   William, 17

E

Echo Hill Farm House, 42, 44, 45, 82, 229
Eel Weir, 22
Eldred Cemetery, 15, 78, 80, 90, 106, 107, 121, 128, 130, 140, 150, 151, 159, 165, 173, 193, 198, 203
Eldred
   Abraham Mulford, 12, 13, 15, 20, 24, 26, 28, 30, 46, 53, 55-57, 62, 74, 79, 113, 121, 135, 234
   Almira Barnes, 79
   Amelia, *see Wheeler*
   Amelia, *see Hancy*
   Almira Barnes, 79
   Augusta Maria, 53, 62, 135
   Benjamin Franklin, 53, 62, 79, 135
   Charles C. P., 12, 13, 15, 17, 18, 19, 20, 24, 28, 30, 35, 36, 38, 46, 47, 49, 51, 53, 55, 57, 64–66, 69, 73, 74–76, 88, 111, 128, 135, 140, 146–148, 159, 170, 172, 174, 183, 185, 187, 196, 200, 210, 212, 213, 226, 227, 234
   Cora Hardcastle, *see Carmichael*
   Effa Caroline Van Tuyl, 18, 35, 37, 46, 47, 51, 53, 57, 64, 69, 88, 98, 111, 128, 135, 140, 148, 172, 174, 185, 196, 213, 226, 234
   Eliza, *see Gardner*
   Elisha, 5, 9, 15, 76, 252–255
   Elizabeth Wheeler, *see Travis*
   Frances J. Payne, 174, 185, 196, 226
   George, 159
   George Washington, 47, 53, 64, 66, 69, 74, 82, 83, 85, 88, 91, 98, 111, 119, 125, 126, 132, 135, 143, 148, 150, 159, 161, 165, 185, 197, 226, 253
   Hannah Hickok, 11, 15, 16, 19, 23, 24, 25, 30, 33, 38, 46, 51, 54, 61, 70, 73, 75, 76, 81, 84, 114, 125, 134, 142, 203, 224, 234, 241, 253
   Harriet, 62, 135
   Harriet B., 15, 18, 234
   Herbert Lincoln, 143, 159, 226
   James (b. 1777), ix, 2, 5, 8, 10–16, 17, 18–20, 22, 24, 25, 30–32, 35, 36, 38, 49, 51, 54, 55, 58, 61, 62, 64, 69, 75, 76, 142, 172, 224, 234, 241, 253
   James, 143, 159, 185, 226
   James Daniel, 64, 69, 135, 174, 183, 185, 196, 197, 201, 202, 207, 208, 214, 226
   Jane E., 53, 57
   Josephine, 53, 60, 62
   Justina Laing, 143, 150
   Lamont, 53
   Maria Adeline, *see Kendall*
   Marietta West, 84, 85, 125, 143, 148, 150, 159, 161, 169, 197
   Mary Ann, *see Austin*
   Mary (Polly) Mulford, 2, 5, 12, 13, 15, 16, 18–20, 23, 224, 234, 253
   Mary Eliza, 62, 135
   Mary Hulse, *see Forgeson*
   Phebe Maria, *see Austin*
   Polly Vanorsdol, *see Mapes*
   Rebecca, 53, 64, 69, 135, 148, 165, 166, 185, 189, 226
   Sarah, *see Carmichael*
   Sarah, *see Bowhanan*
   Sarah Jane, *see Wait*
Elting, Rev, Cornelius, 34
England, 5, 15, 28, 40, 41, 53, 65, 68, 72, 91, 186
   Bishopstoke, 51
   Hampshire, 51
   Sleaford, 78
   South Hampton, 51
   Tichfield, 51
   Yorkshire, 79
Enlistments in Civil War, 92
Ennes, Henry and Elizabeth, 147
Evenhoe, Charles, 196
Erie Railroad, 43, 61, 77, 81, 154
Ewart
   Albert, 79
   Edith May Palmer, 79, 90, 105, 128, 148, 184, 228
   Pamela Tipling, 79
   William, 79

F

Faith, 258
Field Flowers, 153
Fish, Mr., 59
Fisher, Rev. and Mrs. E. W., 226
Fisk, James, 142, 154
Fletcher, Benjamin, 184
Flowers, 152
Follett, Mr., 220
French and Indian War, 5
Forgerson, Gardner, 27, 29, 33, 61, 173
Forgeson
   John, 15, 253
   Mary Hulse Eldred, 5, 12, 13, 15, 46, 253
Fourth Orange City Regiment, 2
Frey, Gracie, 186
Furman, Mr., 23

G

Gardner
   Albert L., 69
   Ann Eliza, *see Cuddeback*
   Anna (d/o James E)., 226

Anna (d/o Sears R.), 69
Bee, 212
Caroline, 47, 51
Charles, 30, 33, 35, 38, 47
Charles, F., 148, 226
Chauncey, 30, 33
Edna, 88
Eliza Ann, *see Young*
Eliza Eldred, 12, 13, 15, 16, 19, 20, 24, 27, 30, 33, 35, 38, 39, 44, 47, 51 57, 69, 75, 76, 82, 135, 111, 172, 182, 185, 192, 193, 226, 234
Elizabeth, 69, 172
Ella Breen, 88
Felix K., 69
Frank, 148, 185, 201
Harry, 148
Herbert D., 193, 226
Horace, 51
James E., 47, 51, 69, 82, 135, 148, 170, 185, 226
James K. (son of Stephen St. John), 88, 193, 226
James Keen (b. 1805), 17, 19, 24, 25, 27, 30, 35, 38, 39, 44, 45–47, 51, 56, 57, 61, 65, 69, 76, 82, 111, 114, 135, 172, 234
Joseph Lake, 18, 111, 234
Katie, 119, 193, 226
Letty, *see Sergeant*
Linda, 148, 185
Louisa McElroy, 82, 88, 119, 192, 193
Margaret Terns, 226
Maria E., *see Calkins*
Mary, *see Austin*
Mary Ann Creiger, 35, 37, 47, 69, 234
Mary E., 69
Mary Keen, 9, 17, 18, 25, 28, 29, 35, 36, 51, 53, 57, 69, 111, 234
Mary L. 193, 226
Moses, 234
Myers J., 193, 226
Rebecca Jane Rider, 47, 51, 82, 148, 185, 226
Sarah Elizabeth, 47, 51, 69, 76
Sarah Purvis, 18, 234

Sears, 9, 17, 18, 22, 25, 28, 29, 31, 32, 34, 35, 36, 49, 51, 53, 55, 57, 61, 62, 76, 111, 234
Sears E., 69
Sears Robert, 17, 35, 47, 66, 68, 69, 111, 234
Stephen St. John, 27, 38, 51, 61, 69, 76, 82, 88, 111, 119, 135, 148, 193, 214, 226
Susan, 148, 185, 226
William H., 47
Geier, Joan, 47, 49, 79
Gillespie
    Agnes, 210
    Margaret Ann, 210
Grace, Mr., 30
Grassy Swamp, 12
Gray, Elizabeth, 12
Gregory
    Clara, 236, 237
    Polly Maria Carmichael, *see Mitchell*
Griffin, "Uncle Steve", 28
Grinnell, Charles Jr., 192
Gunn,
    Charlotte, 41
    Esther, 41
    Ransom, 41

H

Hagan Pond, *see Highland Lake*
Halfway Brook, ix, 1, 2, 4–6, 8, 9, 11, 12, 13, 14, 16, 17, 20, 26, 27, 28, 30, 32, 33, 34, 35, 44, 47, 49, 55, 57, 62, 64, 65, 146, 184, 227, 229
Hallock
    Anna May Buchanan, 226
    Daniel Van Tuyl, 47, 51, 147
    Douglas, 37
    Emily Knecht, 37, 78
    Emma Amelia Schwab, 147, 226
    Hosea Ballow, 147
    Julia Van Tuyl, 37, 51, 70, 147
    Mary Alice Rider, 47, 51, 173
    Oliver Blizzard, 37, 51, 70, 147, 226
    Samuel Jesse, 147, 226
    Thomas W., 37, 51, 70, 147
    William, 147
Hammond, William H., 148

Hancy
    Amelia Eldred, 47, 53, 62, 79, 113, 121
    John, 79, 113, 121, 135
Hankins, 9, 61
    James, 68
    Maria, *see Myers*
Hardenburgh Patent, 7, 45
Harris, George, 185, 226
Hartwell, 35, 44
Hawks Nest, 12, 82, 128
Hazen, Phebe, *see Myers*
Hemlock trees, 6, 10, 144
Hickok
    Almeda Drake, 70, 82, 184, 227
    Ann Eliza, *see Bolton*
    Asa, 11, 15, 16, 17, 19, 23, 29, 46, 54, 135, 234
    Benjamin Merwin, 54, 59, 70, 82, 117, 121, 132, 203
    Charles, 54, 59, 70, 82, 117, 132, 184
    Charles (s/o William and Almeda), 227
    David H. (s/o Asa), 11, 15, 16, 19, 29, 234
    David Hinman (s/o Uncle Justus), 54, 59, 70, 85, 135, 170, 184, 227
    Elizabeth (Betsy) Rice, 11, 15, 16, 234
    Elta, 227
    Emma F., 70
    Esther Hinman, 11, 15, 16, 17, 19, 23, 29, 54, 234
    Frances E., 227
    Galen, 54
    George W., 70
    Hannah, *see Eldred*
    John and Viola, 186
    Justice (s/o David and Mary), 70, 227
    Justus, Uncle, 11, 16, 18, 29, 32, 36, 54, 59, 68, 70, 121, 170, 184, 193, 203, 214, 234
    Louisa, 11, 15, 16, 19, 234
    Mary, *see Stidd*
    Mary (Aunt Polly) Wells, 16, 18, 19, 29, 54, 59, 70, 121, 184, 193, 203, 234
    Mary Jane Russell, 70, 135, 184, 227

Morris, 227
Olin, 70, 135, 184, 187, 227
Reeves W., 59
Reuben, 11, 14, 15, 16, 19, 234
Robert Land, 54, 59, 70
Sarah Dehart, 184
Sylvia, 11, 15, 234
Wells, 199
William, 54, 70, 82, 121, 131, 132, 170, 184, 226
Higginson
Edward, 84, 91, 94, 117, 228
Ida Emily, *see Crabtree*
Mary Donaldson, 84, 91, 228
Highland Lake, 16, 28, 34, 49, 50, 53, 60, 64, 67, 68, 69, 72, 78, 83, 126, 145, 146, 148, 179
Hill
Alfred, 83, 186
Alice Amelia Sergeant, 83, 186, 235
Bertha, 83
Bessie, 186
Esther Sergeant, 186
Gladys, *see Myers*
John Thomas, 83, 186
Mable, 220
Thomas Alvin, 83, 186, 235
Homan, Benjamin, 7
Homestead Act, 94
Hooker, 21
Joseph, General, 105
Almira Austin, 4, 5, 19, 22, 29, 32, 37, 234
Fannie, 22
James T., 19, 22, 29, 37, 234
R., 14
Howell, Rev., 34
Hudson River, 4, 8, 25, 26, 31, 33, 54, 63, 154
Huguenot, 5, 70
Hulse
David, 45, 114
James, 15
Mary, *see Forgeson*
Mary Arnot, 15
Hurd
Chauncey, 10, 18,
Curtis, 45
Family, 27, 29
Graham, 10, 18
Solomon, 18, 29

Husted, Albert, 161, 162, 165

I
I am Tired, 219
I Locked It In, 223
In Memory of Edith E. Austin, 221
In Memoriam, O.G. Warren, 174
Ingersoll
Abraham, 19, 45, 53, 83, 109, 114
Family, 109
Sarah (Sally), 45, 53, 83, 109, 114
Ingraham, Laurence, 29
Ingram
Andrew and Rebecca, 187
Charlotte, *see Leavenworth*
Christina Hayes, 11, 39
Sarah, *see Bishop*
Tjerck, 37
Unknown, 11

J
Jervis, John B., 26
Johnston
Dora, 154
Jane Crawford, 16, 22
John, 16
John W., 16

K
Kansas
Abilene, 196, 197, 224
Brookville, 195, 229
Burlingame, 197, 200, 216
Carbondale, 197
Council Grove, 197, 201, 202, 218
Ellsworth, 195
Kanasas City, 197, 201, 207, 208
Lawrence, 197, 220, 222
Rosedale, 197, 207, 208, 209
Solomon City, 185, 195, 197, 201 203, 205, 207, 210, 213, 214, 217, 218, 229
Kelly
Alma Louella Sergeant, 184, 235
Frank, 235
Kelso
Alice, 185

Amanda, 44, 185, 188, 200, 202, 212
Edward, 84, 127, 185, 199, 220
Eden Evert, 187
Ella, 185
Emma, *see Collins*
Family, 194
Minnie, 185
Mr. 170, 177, 200, 201–203, 208, 209, 211, 220
Robert Sr., 44, 84, 170, 183, 185, 188
Robert Jr., 84, 185, 197, 201, 215, 216
Kendall
Charles, 172, 185
Maria Adeline Eldred, 64, 69, 135, 172, 185
Nelly Effa, 185
Kilferty, Daniel, 85
Kilgour, John F., 154
Knapp
Clara, 5
Naomi Palmer, 5, 11, 53
Samuel, 5, 53
Knight, Joshua, 11
Kyte
Eliza Creiger, 33, 35, 60, 66, 72, 164, 184, 199
Elizabeth (Libby) Terry, 90, 155, 184, 185
Felix Jr., 33, 58, 85
Felix, Rev., 16, 31, 32, 33, 34, 35, 36, 37, 44, 45, 53, 61, 66, 72, 74, 75, 76, 79, 84, 92, 125, 158, 164, 170, 179, 183, 184, 198, 199, 200, 201, 202
Francis, 35
Joseph, 34, 35, 199
Julia, 157, 158
Thomas, 33
William, 85, 135, 138, 158, 184

L
LaBarr, 29, 47
Calvin, 74, 84, 128, 226
Elizabeth Rice, 226
Gordon Ransom, 18, 29, 47, 74, 128
Jacob, 18, 74
Increase, 74
Mary, 18

Sarah Ammerman, 18, 74
Susannah Fetter, 74, 128
William, 74
Lackawaxen River, 26
Laing
    Justina (Tina) Austin, 60, 65, 67, 90, 122, 125, 126, 129, 130, 133, 134, 135–138, 141–143, 149–152, 154, 156, 158, 162, 164, 169, 170, 172, 177, 181, 182, 184, 188, 192, 217, 234
    Randolph (Ranny), 135, 141, 143, 149, 150, 152, 153, 155, 162, 164, 168, 169, 177, 179, 181, 182, 234
Land, Robert, 28, 29
Lake DeVenoge, 83, 84, 86, 145
Lazerlier
    Abraham Jr., 5
    Abraham Sr., 5, 11, 70,
    Elizabeth, *see Van Pelt*
    Family, 67,
    Jane Ann, 5
    Magdalin, 5
    Mary, 5,
    Mary Webber, *see Taylor*
Leavenworth Family, 41
    Amelia Ann, 39, 42, 53, 128, 234
    Anna Mae, 185, 197, 220
    Atwell Bishop, 42, 45, 46, 53, 68, 82, 87, 90–92, 97, 99, 101, 102, 104–106, 110–112, 114, 117–121, 123–125, 128, 130, 132, 164, 234
    Bible, 46, 256
    Charlotte Gunn, 41
    Charlotte Ingram, 9, 11, 19, 30, 38, 39, 40, 42, 53, 68, 79, 82, 87, 90, 97, 120, 123–125, 127, 128, 132, 137, 140, 148, 155, 184, 197, 220, 227, 228, 234, 256
    Ebenezer, 18, 41
    Elias, 27, 41
    Ella Phoebe Sergeant, 10, 11, 37, 80, 83, 87, 203, 227
    Gideon, 18, 29, 41
    Gisele Rouillon, 112, 150, 228
    Harriet, *see Palmer*
    Hezekiah Bunce, 42, 45, 46, 68, 82, 87, 92, 97, 113–115, 127–130, 132, 139, 234
    James Garfield, iv, 10, 18, 37, 39, 80, 182, 203, 227, 228
    James (Jim) Roberts, 45, 112, 228
    Jennie, *see Austin*
    John, 41
    John Ellis, 42, 46, 53, 68, 82, 87, 97, 99, 114, 125, 137, 138, 184, 195, 228, 234
    Julia Ann (Anna), 42, 46, 68, 82, 87, 94, 95, 101, 105, 117, 125, 129, 140, 234
    Lemira, 41
    Maria Louisa Myers, 44, 45, 65, 67, 68, 71, 72, 78, 79, 84, 87, 95, 135, 146, 164, 179, 181, 184–186, 197, 220, 228, 234
    Sarah Jane, 39, 42, 53, 128, 234
    Sherman, 5, 18, 41
    Sherman Buckley, 9, 10, 11, 19, 27, 29, 30, 38, 39, 40–46, 53, 66, 68, 79, 82, 85, 87, 90, 95, 97, 112, 114, 127, 128–132, 137, 138, 140, 148, 155, 170, 183–186, 188, 228, 234, 356
    Sherman Clinton, 19, 27, 37
    Sherman Stiles, 42, 44–46, 53, 65, 68, 82, 86–107, 109–119, 121–126, 128, 131, 132, 140, 148, 179, 181, 182, 183, 184, 185, 187, 188, 197, 220, 227, 229, 234
    Stella Clark, 19, 37, 51, 68, 69, 138, 147
    Thomas, 41
    Truman Ellis, 197, 220, 227
    Truman Stiles, 27, 29
    William, 18, 41
Lefarge, Samuel, 85
Leibla, William, 92, 132
Lenape, 2, 3, 7, 9
Lessons of Life, 216
Leven River, 41
Lewis
    Emeline Carmichael, 54, 135, 224
    Joe, 214
Lilly
    Family, 62
    Henry, 33, 35, 36, 84, 121, 208, 210, 220
    Jeremiah, 11
    Jonathan, 74, 84
    Lana, 84
    Lydia, 84
    Margaret, 62
    Melissa, 62
    Mr. and wife, 186
Little Eva, 143
Littlefield, Annis Austin, 51
Livingston
    Unita Jane Sergeant, 83, 227
    William, 227
Lord, Samuel, 23
Lord and Taylor, 23, 73, 166
Lounberry, John and Sarah, 147
Loyalists/Torries, 2, 4, 5, 11, 54, 215
Lumbermen, 40

M

MacKenzie, Margaret, 187
Maglione, Margie Austin, 47, 79
Maney, Samuel, 36
Manney, Jacob, 14
Manning, Dick, 23
Many, Robert, 29
Mapes
    Charles Egbert, 119, 128
    George Egbert, 90, 111, 119, 128, 211
    Polly Vanorsdol Eldred, 47, 53, 64, 69, 111, 119, 128, 135, 211
    Theodore, 90
    William and Mary, 66
Maps
    Austin/Eldred Lands, 55
    Austin Property, 50
    Eldred Land, 20
    Eldred Gardner Sawmill, 28
    Halfway Brook Village, 16, 36
    Kansas, 197
    Kyte Family Home, 36
    Leavenworth Property, 44
    Myers Property, 68
    Northeast United States, v, vi
    Round Pond/DeVenoge, 83

Town of Highland, 1879 Beers, 145
Town of Lumberland, viii
Towns on the Upper Delaware River, 3
Marsh, J. T., 226
Mason, Mercy, 12
Mast Hope Turnpike, 8, 77
Maudsley, Louis, 47, 74
McBride, Cornelius, 84
McKenzie
    George Ross, 149
    Mr., 172
Metcalf, Charles W., 208, 210
Metzger
    Barbara, 226
    Christian, 226
    Follett, 226
    Robert, 226
Middaugh, 9, 21
    Asa, 37
    Dennis, 92, 132
    Levi, 9, 22, 23, 29, 30
    William, 11
Mier
    Martin and Gerreberg Johannise Ackerman, 5
Mill Pond, see Stege Pond
Mills
    Alexander, 72, 146, 179
    Archibald
    George, 72
    Geraldine, see Russell
    Ivy, 19
    Margaret, see Boyd
    Margaret Clark, 72
    Margaret Gillies, 72, 146, 179
    Martha, see Myers
Millspaugh
    Mary Letitia, see Austin
    Mr. or Mrs., 150, 207
Minie Ball, 98
Minisink, see New York
    Battle, ix, 2, 214, 215
    Patent, 2, 7, 9, 20, 28, 45, 56
Missouri, 82
    Rolla, 118, 121, 203
    St. Louis, 117
Mitchell
    Polly Maria Carmichael Gregory, 38, 47, 65, 135, 224, 236, 237
    Robert, 236
Mongaup River, 1–3, 26
Moosic Mountains, 25, 26
More, Matthew, 65
Morris, Nicholas family, 22
Mott, Mary, 165
Mrs. Prindle's Soliloquy, 204
Mt. Hope-Lumberland Turnpike, 8
Mulford, Abraham, 5
Murray, Mary A., see Schoonover
My Flowers, 151
Myer, David and Elizabeth, 5, 11, 18, 29, 65
Myers
    Abel Sprague, 29, 37, 47, 51, 53, 72, 79, 84, 104, 147, 159, 186, 196, 203, 211, 214, 226
    Archibald Abel (s/o Abel), 79, 159
    Augustus (Gus) Waterman, 72, 78, 84, 88, 146, 164, 185, 228
    Benjamin, 47, 65, 67, 68
    Charles C. (b. 1875), 185, 228,
    Charles, 90, 107
    Charles Henry (Chuck), 36, 37, 47, 72, 79, 159
    Charlotte (Lottie), see Darling
    Christena Stevens, 186
    David William, 65
    Edwin Van Schoick, 78, 104, 147, 159, 173, 186, 226
    Eliza Jane, 72
    Emeline, 72
    Emma, see Sergeant
    George Washington Taylor, 65, 67, 68, 72, 73, 78, 79, 84, 88, 146, 148, 164, 179, 183, 185, 228
    Gladys Elizabeth, see Austin
    Hannah Maria Van Schoick, 53, 72, 78, 79, 84, 104, 147, 159
    Gladys Hill, 83
    Jackson, 226
    James L., 84, 147, 159, 186
    Jane Ann Van Pelt Webb, 5, 11, 18, 29, 38, 46, 47, 65, 66, 67, 68, 70, 72, 73, 78–80, 84, 86–88, 135, 146, 148, 164, 179, 185, 186, 220, 226, 228
    Letitia Parker, 83, 84, 90, 107
    L.L., 198
    Mabel Louise Owen, 78, 173
    Maria Hankins, 72, 159, 186, 226
    Maria L., see Leavenworth
    Martha Mills, 72, 148, 179, 180, 185, 228
    Martin David, 5, 11, 18, 29, 38, 46, 47, 65, 66, 67, 68, 72, 79, 83, 84, 87, 88, 135, 146, 148, 164, 165, 170, 237
    Mary, 66
    Minnie Sergeant, 79
    Moses, 29, 36, 37, 47, 51, 66, 70, 170, 173, 203
    Phebe Hazen Clark, 19, 29, 36, 37, 47, 51, 53, 70, 200, 203
    Raymond, 83
    Samuel C., 84, 90, 107, 132
    Sarah Griffith, 38, 47, 65
    Sarah, 72
    Sarah, 226
    William, 121, 127, 132
    William G., 170

N

New Jersey, 4, 5, 9, 11, 22, 29, 30, 47, 146, 186, 226
    Bergen County, 65
    Minisink Island, 9
    Trenton, 160
Newcome
    Carrie, 156
    Harriet, 85
    Kate, 155, 156
    Mrs., 155, 156, 177
Newburgh-Cochecton Turnpike, 7, 8, 10, 21
Newkirk, Benjamin B., 8
Newman
    Caroline Austin, 19, 29, 38, 50, 61, 107, 137, 234
    Carrie, 107, 137
    Mr., 50, 137, 234
New York
    Barryville, 1–3, 5–11, 14, 15, 16, 19, 22, 24, 25, 26, 27, 29, 30, 32–37, 57, 58, 61, 74, 78, 81, 82, 85, 88, 90, 101, 111, 117, 118, 121, 127, 136, 137, 144, 170, 173, 185, 187, 196, 198, 199, 206, 207, 214, 220, 226, 227, 229

Beaver Brook (Mills), 3, 12, 14, 18, 28, 29, 30, 33, 35, 38, 39, 47, 57, 58, 84, 125, 128, 168, 226
Bethel, 7, 8, 10, 18, 26, 27, 29, 30, 39, 41, 51, 68, 90, 137
Big Pond, *see Pond Eddy*
Carpenter's Point, see *Port Jervis*
Callicoon, 1, 3, 7, 169
Cochecton/Cushetunk, 1, 3, 5, 7, 8, 9, 11, 12, 26, 147
Denton, 5, 9, 15
Eldred, ix, 2, 14, 15, 23, 25, 27, 28, 30–33, 36, 38, 39, 44, 46, 49, 50, 52, 62, 65, 66, 78, 82–86, 88, 90, 92, 114, 119, 138, 143, 146, 148, 157, 159, 164–166, 172, 174–176, 180, 182, 184, 186, 190, 194, 195, 197, 199, 205, 216, 218, 222, 224, 226, 228, 229, 238, 239
Glen Spey, 7, 11, 18, 29, 34, 49, 149, 155, 218
Goshen, 2, 15, 61, 92, 96, 112, 120, 215
Halfway Brook Village, *see Eldred*
Highland, Town of, ix, 7, 45, 68, 76–78, 80–82, 84, 89, 100, 114, 116, 119, 131, 132, 135, 140, 144, 145, 147, 169, 170, 172, 175, 187, 188, 199, 207, 229, 238, 239
Hurd Settlement, 10, 27, 45
Kingston, 25, 26, 33
Liberty, 7, 169
Lumberland, Town of, vi, ix, 1–23, 25, 26, 27, 28, 29, 30–32, 35–38, 40, 46, 47, 48, 49, 51, 52, 56, 57, 60, 61, 64, 66, 67, 68, 70, 75, 76, 78, 82, 85, 87, 101, 128, 144, 149, 153, 155, 158, 165, 170, 172, 173, 198, 199, 224, 226
Middletown, 8, 9, 54, 57, 90, 94, 101, 150, 151, 217, 241, 242
Minisink, 5, 9, 15
Minisink Ford, 2, 9, 63, 78
Mongaup, 1, 3, 6, 7, 18, 19, 29, 49, 155

Mongaup River, 1–3, 26
Monticello, 9, 13, 27, 31, 32, 35, 41, 51, 56, 163, 169, 211
Narrow Falls, 8, 10, 12, 15, 19, 24, 36
Narrowsburg(h), 1, 3, 5, 7, 8, 58, 59, 61, 62, 77, 78, 92, 136, 144, 160
Orange County, 2, 5, 8, 10, 11, 13, 15, 17, 37, 38, 54, 62, 64, 82, 147, 148, 224
Ossining, 54
Pond Eddy, 1, 2, 6, 7, 8, 9, 16, 17, 22, 26, 28, 29, 30, 47, 49, 111, 127, 144, 154, 155
Port Jervis, 4, 5, 9, 12–4, 22, 25, 26, 28, 37, 43, 44, 61, 79, 82, 83, 127, 154, 160, 180, 184, 207, 228
Ridgebury, 11, 12
River settlement, The, *see Barryville*
Rondout, 25, 32, 33, 67
Scotchtown, 9, 11, 30, 39
Shohola/Shehola, 1–6, 8, 19, 20, 47, 74, 79, 81, 82, 90, 117, 118, 121, 177, 191, 229
South Lebanon, see *Glen Spey*
Sparrowbush, 3, 10, 43, 44, 68, 92, 128
Sullivan County, ix, 2, 8, 18, 25, 27, 37, 38, 39, 45, 56, 68, 69, 87, 107, 128, 144, 147, 163, 170, 215
Ten Mile River settlement, *see Tusten*
Thompson, Town of, 10, 128, 140, 148
Tusten, Town of, 1–4, 7, 8, 9, 16, 29, 32, 33, 53, 57, 61, 68, 72, 78, 100
Wallkill, Town of, 5, 7, 9, 12, 13, 15, 18, 30, 82
Wawayanda, Town of, 9
Westchester County, 4, 11, 13, 18, 19, 29, 38, 50, 51, 53, 90, 106

O

Osborn
   Amanda, 33
   Emily, 60

Osier/Osir, 189
   Augustus (Gus), 196, 199, 202, 210, 214, 215, 218
   Carrie, 218
Owen(s)
   Arthur, 147
   Daniel, 29
   Eliza, 37
   Elizabeth Barnes, 72, 78, 80, 173
   Elizabeth Tether, 72, 78, 80, 147, 173
   Elizabeth Thompson, 187
   Ethalinda, 72
   Frank and Mary, 147
   John Miller, 170
   Mabel Louise, *see Myers*
   Mary Elizabeth (servant) 184, 228
   Morgan, 72, 78, 80, 173
   Phebe, *See Sergeant*
   Robert, 72, 78, 80, 147, 170, 173, 183

P

Palmer
   David J., 170
   Edith, *see Ewart*
   Harriet Leavenworth, 38, 39, 42, 53, 68, 79, 82, 87, 90, 105, 128, 140, 148, 184, 228, 234
   Harry C., 83, 105, 128, 148, 184, 228
   Henry, 62, 68, 79, 82, 83, 87, 90, 105, 128, 148, 184, 228, 234
   James, 184, 228
   Sherman, 83, 87
Parker
   Benjamin and Emaline, 83
   George W., 100, 132
   George and Kate, 136, 172, 226
   James, 186
   Letitia, *see Myers*
   Mary A. Murray, *see Schoonover*
Parmenter, 218
   Emily, *see Austin*
Paton
   Archibald. 135, 148, 162, 191, 234

Miranda (Rand) Austin, 57, 65, 67, 126, 134, 135, 148, 162, 181, 188, 191, 234
Payne
   Adeline, 174
   Charles Henry, 174, 196, 199
   Frances, *see Eldred*
   William and Mary, 210
Pennsylvania, 1, 2, 4, 22, 25, 36, 42, 52, 144, 154
   28th Regiment, 103
   147th Regiment, 103
   Big Eddy, 58
   Bradford County, 29, 68
   Cadis 46, 54
   Chester County, 48
   Damascus, 147
   Delaware Water Gap, 9, 160
   Eldred, 15
   Gettysburg, 107
   Hawley, 78
   Honesdale, 8, 9, 25, 26
   Lackawaxen, 9, 25, 63, 117, 170, 186, 9,
   Luzerne County, 52
   Manchester, 226
   Mast Hope 8, 9
   Milford, 5
   Moscow, 73
   Muhlenburg, 52
   Philadelphia, 5, 6, 154, 160
   Shickshinny, 52
   Shohola, 1–3, 5, 8, 19, 21, 47, 79, 81, 229
   Standing Stone, 42, 68, 86, 147
   Susquehanna River, 52
   Tell, 5, 11, 38
   Water Gap, 9, 160
   Wayne County, 5, 77
   West Damascus, 79
Perkins
   Comelia Dabron, 30
   Dr., 28–30, 67
Persbacher
   Catherine Kreiter, 79
   Elizabeth, 79
   Jacob, 79
Poem for Ida Austin, 167
Poems
   A Reverie or Kansas Romance, 225
   An Answer, 223
   Faith, 258
   Field Flowers, 153
   Flowers, 152
   I am Tired, 219
   I Locked It In, 223
   In Memory of Edith E. Austin, 221
   In Memoriam, O.G. Warren, 174
   Lessons of Life, 216
   Little Eva, 143
   Mrs. Prindle's Soliloquy, 204
   My Flowers, 151
   Poem for Ida Austin, 167
   Put Me in My Little Bed, 156
   She is Gone, 219
   To Mother, 221
   To My Husband, 258
   When Shall We Meet Again, 141, 142
   Who Keeps Dead Flowers, 205
Pool, Daniel, 22
Proctor, William F., 149
Puff, Eliza Carmichael, 135, 224
Put Me in My Little Bed, 156

Q
Quick
   Abraham, 14
   David, 14, 22, 34
   Francis, 14, 22, 23
   Francis and Rachel, 19
   Hugh, 22
   James, 74
   M.W. Quick, 121

R
Reardon, John, 140
Reeves, 14, 19
Revolutionary War, 2–4, 9, 11, 15, 52, 54, 57
Rider
   Augustus, 51
   Fernando, 51
   Job, 47, 51, 82, 173
   Mary Alice, *see Hallock*
   Rebecca, *see Gardner*
   Susan Adeline Van Tuyl, 47, 51
Rixton, Joseph and Mary, 147
Roebling
   Aqueduct, 63, 81
   John A., 63
Roebling-Chauncey Bridge, 81, 121
Ross, Hugh, 85
Rouillon
   Cyrus, 228
   Gisele, 40, 112, 150, 228
   Jean Charles and Blanche Olga Malinge, 111, 112, 150, 228
   Lubin and Florentine, 111, 150
Round Pond, *see Lake DeVenoge*
Rundle, 202
   Abe, 214, 226
Russell
   Geraldine Mills and Stuart, 148

S
Sawmill, 19th Century Up and Down, 48
Schoonover, 14, 194
   Ann Mary Austin, 29, 38, 50, 54, 64, 70, 74, 80, 106, 112, 113, 118, 120, 121, 136, 226, 234
   Daniel Rowley, 172, 186, 226
   Emily, 148, 172, 186, 226
   Mary A. Murray Parker, 136, 148, 172, 186, 187, 226
   Oliver P., 54, 57, 64, 70, 74, 118, 120, 127, 136, 148, 172, 186, 187, 220, 226, 234
   Peter, 64, 136
Segarra, Dawn Lee Austin, 47, 79
Sergeant, 44, 53
   Abigail, 12
   Alice Amelia, *see Hill*
   Alma, *see Kelly*
   Alvah, 29, 36, 53, 68, 80, 83, 85, 87, 111, 159, 170, 183, 184, 186, 187, 227, 235
   Anna Penney, 16, 18, 19, 28, 29, 36, 53, 158, 159, 235
   Caroline, 68, 83, 85, 184, 228
   Charles, 228
   Claribel, 228
   Clarissa Clark, 80, 83, 87, 184, 227, 235
   David R., 16, 19
   Edgar, 83, 184

Ella Phoebe, iv, 10, 11, 18, 37, 80, 83, 87, 203, 227
Emma Myers, 120, 138, 147, 174, 228, 235
Esther, *see Hill*
Ethel B., 16, 18, 19, 28, 29, 36, 47, 53, 66, 68, 83, 85, 88, 111, 121, 159, 170, 173, 183, 184, 228, 234, 235
Frank Roberts, 80, 87, 184, 227, 228, 235
Isaac (son of Ethel B.), 36, 53, 68, 79, 92, 111, 121, 131, 132, 159, 184, 228, 235
Isaac C., 16, 29
Isaac Jr., 12
Isaac, Rev., 11, 12, 15, 16, 79, 83, 158, 226, 235
James Gardner, 36, 47, 53, 68, 85, 88, 90, 91, 92, 95, 97, 100, 105, 111, 130–132, 138, 147, 159, 173, 235
James W., 147, 184, 227
Jane (d/o Ethel), 68
Jane (d/o Alvah), 83, 220
Letitia (Letty) Gardner, 16, 18, 19, 28, 29, 36, 47, 53, 66, 68, 83, 88, 97, 111, 121, 159, 174, 184, 186, 228, 234, 235
Mary (d/o Ethel), 68, 85
Mary Richards, 12, 158, 226, 235
Minnie, *see Myers*
Morgan, 184
Phebe Owen, 36, 68, 80, 83, 85, 87, 184, 227, 235
Stephen B., 16
Stephen, Rev., 11, 12, 15, 16, 18, 19, 24, 28, 29, 31, 36, 53, 55, 56, 83, 158, 159, 235
Thomas (s/o Alvah), 184
Thomas (s/o Rev. Isaac), 12
Thomas L.(s/o Rev. Stephen), 16, 29
Unita Jane, *see Livingston*
She is Gone, 219
Sheck, Katie, 226
Shotwell
Azuba, 84
Caleb, 68, 84
Jane, 84
Sarah, 68, 186, 226
Sarah, *see Webb*
Sarah J., 226
Stephen C., 170, 226
Showers, John, 2
Simmons, J.B., 120, 124
Singer, Isaac Merrit, 149
Skinner
Alfred, 197, 219
Amelia, 19
Daniel (rafter), 5, 7
Daniel, 36, 37, 57, 58
Mary, 57
Oliver, 35
Salome, 37
Will, 196
Smith
Charles M., 69
Samuel, 20
Snow
Barnabus, 11
John, 32
Sparrow, H.L., 3
Sprague
Agath, 84
B.J., 84
Eliza, 84
Josephine, 84
St. John, Stephen, 35, 38, 39, 44, 56, 57, 114
Stage
Albert, 73, 84, 90, 214
Charles, 84
Chauncy, 84
Elizabeth, 84
George, 73, 81, 84, 90
Jacob, 19, 21, 29, 73, 84, 85, 127, 170, 185
Martha Carmichael, 19, 21, 73, 84, 185
Stege's Pond, 49, 50
Stereographs, 103
Stewart, John J. and Sarah, 20
Stidd
Mary Hickok, 54, 59, 70, 184
William, 184
Street, Mr., 30
Sutherland, William G., 222
Swartwout, Peter, 14

T

Talmage, Dr., 190
Taylor
George Washington, 11, 23, 65, 73
John and Jane, 196
Mary Webber Lazerlier, 5, 11, 18, 29, 38, 47, 65, 70, 73
Robert, 11, 73
Teed
Clara, 80, 84
Clara Austin, 11, 19, 38, 50, 61, 80, 112, 234
Edward Nelson, 50, 80, 112, 234
Emma, 80, 84
Harriet, 78
Isaac, 38, 112
Phebe G., 38
Susan, *see Austin*
Susie, 80, 113
Ten Mile River, 1–3
Tether
Edward and Elizabeth, 72, 84, 147
Elizabeth, *see Owen*
Jane, 84
Joseph, 84, 147, 183
Thompson
Adelaide (Addie) Austin, 57, 65, 67, 90, 120, 127, 134, 135, 143, 148, 149, 150, 151, 153, 154, 156, 162, 163, 165, 168, 169, 177, 180, 182, 188, 189–193, 198, 205, 209, 211, 213, 217, 224, 234
Augustus Thompson, 182, 188
Elizabeth Owen, 187
Thomas Jefferson, 135, 162, 165, 188, 234
Tommy, 188, 190, 205
To Mother, 221
To My Husband, 258
Toaspern, Ida Heyen, 155
Travis
Elizabeth Wheeler Eldred, 46, 53, 57, 62, 74, 79, 135, 234
Gilbert, 74, 79
Milton, 74
Tusten
Dr. Benjamin, 2, 3, 215
Tuthill
Ezekiel, 11
Sarah E., 85

V

Van Auken
- Hannah, 9, 11, 68
- Mary, *see Clark*
- Peter, 9, 11, 68

Van Pelt
- Ann Johnson, 5, 70
- Bible, 71, 72, 257
- Catharine, 84, 85
- Elizabeth Lazerlier, 5, 11, 18, 23, 29, 38, 47, 65, 67, 70, 72, 73, 78, 79, 80
- Henry, 5, 70
- Jane Ann, *see Myers*
- John, 5, 11, 18, 70, 72, 73
- John Henry, 38, 47
- Maria, 38, 47
- Maria Anthony, 11, 18, 29, 38, 70, 72
- Peter, 11, 18, 29, 38, 39, 47, 67, 70, 72, 78
- Sarah Looker, 38, 47

Van Schoick
- Hannah Maria, *see Myers*
- Huldah Bross, 53, 72, 78
- William, 53, 72

Van Tuyl
- Daniel, 17, 18, 22, 29, 35, 47, 51, 147
- Charity, 19
- Effa C., *see Eldred,*
- Julia, *see Hallock*
- Family, 21, 22
- Rebecca Writer, 17, 18, 22, 35, 47
- Susan, *see Rider*

Van Wyck, Col., 93–95, 105

W

Wait
- Charlotte, 186
- George, 11, 81, 86, 196
- Jennie, 203
- John, 186, 188
- Leo, 208
- Mary Mills, 187
- Sarah Jane Eldred, 69, 185, 187, 213
- William, 185, 186, 213

Wallace, John and Marian, 186
Wandling, Philip, 70

Watkins,
- Sally, 19
- Samuel, 11, 14

Watson, Lina Carmichael, 139

Webb
- Charles, 2, 9
- Charles Cripps, 38, 47, 65, 67, 68, 73, 84, 88, 135 185, 226
- Clara, 88, 135
- Henry Cripps, 38, 47, 65, 72
- Jane Ann Van Pelt, *see Myers*
- John Henry, 38, 47, 65, 72, 135
- Osmer, 226
- Sarah Shotwell, 68, 73, 84, 88, 135, 226

Webber
- Jacob Rev., 158, 170
- John 5, 73
- Mary, *see Taylor*

Wells
- Anna, 19
- Alexander, 127
- Daniel, 19, 32, 36, 127
- Elizabeth, 74
- Jesse, 14
- John, 19, 28
- Mary (Polly), *see Hickok*
- Samuel, 11, 29, 85
- William, 14, 19, 29, 74

West
- Henry 36
- Margette, 57
- Marietta, *see Eldred*
- Mary, 37, 84, 125
- Richard, 36
- Samuel, 84, 125
- Thomas, 7

Westfield, George H., 223

Wheeler
- Amelia Ann Eldred, 12, 13, 15, 16, 18, 234
- Darius and Frances 16
- Elizabeth, *see Travis*
- Harvey, 16, 18, 19, 234
- John, 29
- Lydia, 58, 59, 61
- Thomas, 19

Whilly, John, 85

When Shall We Meet Again, 141, 142

Whitney, 187
- Anthony and Eveline, 186

Who Keeps Dead Flowers, 205

Wickham, 4, 9
- George D., 8, 16, 27, 56

Williams
- Charles, 136
- Jenevieve, 136
- Rosa, 136
- Sarah, 136
- William and Charlotte, 186

Wilson, 189, 196
- Agnes Gillespie, 210
- Anna, 147, 187, 189, 191
- Charles, 147, 187, 189
- Edward, 66, 74, 85, 132, 147, 187
- Garrett, 19, 20
- Henry and Margaret, 74
- Horton, 132
- Mary, 147
- Phoebe, 74, 85, 147
- Sarah, 187
- W., 18
- William H., 147

Wisner, Rev. J.O., 85
Worth River, 41

Woodward
- Benjamin, 8
- Charles S., 57

Y

Young
- Adaline A. Sweezy, 147, 226
- Coe Finch, 47, 74, 111, 125, 147, 226
- David, 54, 84, 150, 224, 236
- Eliza Ann Gardner, 17, 47, 74, 147, 234
- Harriet Carmichael, 18, 54, 66, 84, 135, 150, 224, 236
- Isaac, 47, 74, 147, 234
- Jennie, 147, 226
- Libby, 84, 236

About the Author

Photo: Gary Smith

Born on the west side of New York State, Louise Elizabeth (Austin) Smith spent most of her growing up years on Peach Street (sans peach trees), south of Detroit, Michigan.

Louise enjoyed reading (biographies were a favorite), sewing, skating, and bike riding.

She wanted to write stories, but gave up writing fiction, when her third grade "Bear Story" was an obvious failure.

Louise's love of music began with several colorful 45 rpm records which included such profound lyrics as "Arf, Arfy the Doggie in the Window." A few years later, favorites were classical orchestral 33-1/3 LP records—supermarket specials.

To reading and listening to classical music, Louise added violin practice when she inherited her grandfather Briggs's violin.

Soon, authors Louisa May Alcott and Jane Austen, whose names had some similarity to *Louise Austin*, became favorite reads for Louise. By eleventh grade, she discovered her all-time favorite book, *Jane Eyre*.

College brought Louise a bachelor's degree in music education from Western Michigan University, and a master's degree in elementary education from Eastern Michigan University.

After eight years of teaching in an elementary school in a small town in Michigan, Louise at last met her husband Gary, and they were married late 1978.

Ten years later, Gary and Louise and their three (now four) children trekked out to Arizona, where most of them still live.

Besides trying to figure out how she got to be sixty years old, Louise finally concluded that nonfiction writing was more her style, and has been writing family stories for over five years.

Family Information Online

http://HalfwayBrook.com
Halfway Brook community blog, on-going projects, resources

Weezy.info
Stories and information about the Crabtree-Higginson,
Austin-Leavenworth,
Smith-Corbridge, and Fallin-Williams families

Other Books by Louise E. Smith

Grandma and Me
Amanda Myrtie Crabtree Briggs was born in 1891 in a sodhouse on her father's Nebraska homestead farm. Over the years she told her children and grandchildren the stories of her growing up as well as those of her parents and her Crabtree and Higginson grandparents—real pioneers of the west. This book is a collection of those stories and includes almost 600 photos and documents.

246 pages
8-1/2 × 11, Softcover

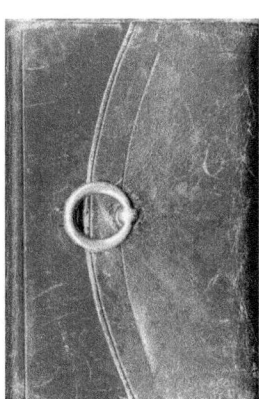

Aida Austin's 1881 Diary
Aida Austin started a diary at the beginning of 1881, the year she turned 20 in November. Aida wrote about her everyday life in both New York City with her Austin cousins, or back at her home in Eldred, New York.

First Edition: 108 pages
6-1/2 × 10-1/4, Softcover